Rule of Prayer, Rule of Faith

Nathan Mitchell
John F. Baldovin, S.J.
Editors

Rule of Prayer, Rule of Faith

Essays in Honor
of Aidan Kavanagh, O.S.B.

Nathan Mitchell
Paul F. Bradshaw
Thomas J. Talley
Robert F. Taft, S.J.
Aelred Cody, O.S.B.
Joanne M. Pierce
Regis Duffy, O.F.M.
John F. Baldovin, S.J.
Peter S. Hawkins
Kenneth Stevenson
Louis Weil
Bryan D. Spinks
Thomas H. Schattauer
David N. Power, O.M.I.
R. Kevin Seasoltz, O.S.B.
James F. White
Jeffrey VanderWilt

A PUEBLO BOOK

The Liturgical Press   Collegeville, Minnesota

A Pueblo Book published by
The Liturgical Press

Design by Frank Kacmarcik, Obl.S.B.

Library of Congress Cataloging-in-Publication Data

Rule of prayer, rule of faith : essays in honor of Aidan Kavanagh,
    O.S.B. / Nathan Mitchell . . . [et at.] ; Nathan Mitchell, John F.
Baldovin, editors.
        p.   cm.
    "A Pueblo book."
    Includes bibliographical references.
    ISBN 0-8146-6158-0
    1. Liturgics. I. Kavanagh, Aidan. II. Mitchell, Nathan.
III. Baldovin, John Francis.
BV170.R85 1996
264—dc20   96-14456
                                                              CIP

Contents

Nathan Mitchell

Preface

In the first chapter of his *On Liturgical Theology*, Aidan Kavanagh warns readers that the author is "about to act as a critic."[1] Four factors, he suggests, have shaped his approach to the theological task. First, *"he is the creature of a deeply sacramental tradition of orthodoxy."*[2] This, Kavanagh argues, is a radical stance, for it means that doctrine derives from doxology, rather than the reverse. "It implies that worship conceived broadly is what gives rise to theological reflection, rather than the other way around."[3] It implies, further, that the world—the created order—is always and inevitably a component in every theological statement. "Christian theology," Kavanagh notes, "cannot talk of God, any more than Einstein could talk of energy, without including the 'mass' of the world squared by the constant of God's eternal will to save in Christ."[4]

The second factor at work in Kavanagh's "author-as-critic" is a preference for "the iconic East" over the "pictorial West."[5] "Pictures," he notes succinctly, "are about *meaning*. Icons are about *being*."[6] The habit of viewing liturgy as an opportunity to display "meanings" has contributed mightily to the Western obsession

[1] *On Liturgical Theology*, (New York: Pueblo, 1984) 3. This book combines and revises two sets of lectures Kavanagh had been invited to present in the early 1980s: the MacKinnon Lectures on Church and World (given at the Atlantic School of Theology in Halifax, Nova Scotia, in 1980) and the Hale Lectures (given at Seabury-Western Theology Seminary in Evanston, Illinois, in 1982).
[2] Ibid.; emphasis added.
[3] Ibid.
[4] Ibid., 4.
[5] Ibid.
[6] Ibid.; emphasis added.

with text-centered logic and linearity. Seated passively in pews, worshippers in the West grip their books (hymnals, missalettes or other "worship aids"), their eyes and minds riveted on the "meaningful" words in front of them. This suggests, of course, that liturgy is a text to be studied rather than a deed to be done. Worse, it promotes the view that worship is most aptly understood as a cerebral endeavor—a positive "learning experience"— rather than an obedient, attentive, awestruck standing in the presence of the living God.

Thirdly, Kavanagh notes that his work "in an interconfessional, university-based school of divinity" has led him to move "back to basics," not as a strategy of reaction, but as a remedial necessity.[7] Students who hope to read Faulkner or write sonnets, he observes, must gain competence in fundamental English syntax and semantics before they enter the complex worlds of fiction or poetry. So too, whoever seeks to grasp (or be grasped by) the liturgy as *theologia prima* must begin with a certain level of ritual and symbolic competence—or must relearn, as Roman Guardini once said, "a forgotten way of doing things." What is needed today, Kavanagh implies, is a kind of remedial primer, a basic grammar of ritual etiquette and assent—a goal provocatively realized in his brief but brilliant *Elements of Rite*.[8]

Fourthly, this author-as-critic takes asceticism seriously, sees it as "native to the Gospel" and "required of all."[9] While it is not necessary to pursue Christian life as a "religious professional" (as monk or nun), it *is* essential, Kavanagh contends, to view the world warily—to love it passionately (as God does), while critiquing what we have made of it. For the real goal of asceticism is not denial or self-discipline, but the "awful truth" about self and world. "Christianity's sustained ascetical stance," he writes, ". . . tells one something about the way any thoughtful person should address self and world, namely, with caution."[10]

These factors have decisively influenced Father Kavanagh's long and distinguished career as educator, writer and lecturer in the

[7] Ibid., 5–6.

[8] Aidan Kavanagh, *Elements of Rite. A Handbook of Liturgical Style* (New York: Pueblo, 1982).

[9] *On Liturgical Theology*, 6.

[10] Ibid., 7.

field of liturgics. By way of introduction to this *Festschrift*, it may be useful to draw attention to the way these convictions have inspired his understanding of (1) the relation between faith and worship; (2) the essential connections between tradition, social structure, cultural cohesion and cultic behavior; (3) ritual as a distinctive species of human and Christian activity; and (4) the kind of *knowledge* that liturgical experience engenders and enacts.

(1) Basic to all of Kavanagh's work is the conviction that liturgy does not merely "express" faith (as clothing, for instance, may be said to "express" a person's fashion sense); it *is* the "church's faith in motion on certain definite and crucial levels."[11] A pivotal passage in the book *On Liturgical Theology* epitomizes this point:

"It cannot be forgotten that the church at worship is not only present to God; far more significantly, the living God is present to the church. This latter presence is not a theological theory; it is a real presence which is there to affect, grace, and change the world. It is an active real presence of God accomplishing his purpose as he will by the gift of himself in his Son through the Holy Spirit. God is not present to the worshipping church by faith but in reality; it is the church which is present by faith to God."[12]

But note well: the question is *not* "whether" or "how" God becomes present in the liturgy—for this leads to largely idle speculation about the mechanics or metaphysics of divine presence. Rather, the question is whether and how *we* can become present to God through the experience of faith transmitted by tradition and enacted ritually. For once again, the point is not that worship "reflects" or "expresses" the Church's repertoire of faith, but that it really and actually "transacts the church's faith in God under the condition of God's real presence in both church and world."[13] For this reason, the liturgy is not merely one more ecclesiastical "work" or one more "theological datum" among many others. "It is simply the church living its bread and butter life of faith under grace, a life in which God in Christ is encountered regularly and dependably as in no other way for the life of the world."[14]

[11] Ibid., 8.
[12] Ibid.
[13] Ibid.
[14] Ibid.

(2) Because it *transacts* faith (rather than "reflects" or "expresses" it), liturgy is inevitably linked to *tradition* in Kavanagh's theology. The authority of tradition, moreover, is inescapably related to cultural cohesion. This theme is powerfully enunciated in an essay published in 1973.[15] "Cultures," Kavanagh noted, "are value-complexes created by real people, in real historical circumstances, for real human purposes, and they emerge through patterns of human activity that are sustained by social structures created by those same people."[16] Because these complexes are highly sensitive to social stress and historical change, they are subject to constant review and renewal. "This process of reviewing and renewing values for the sake of group survival here and now is what gives the group continuity and cohesiveness in space and time, in the real order, in history."[17] This same "process of review and renewal of group values," Kavanagh writes, "is what I understand tradition to be."[18] Moreover, the "agent that discharges this premier responsibility within the social group is what I understand to be the group's authority structure." And finally,

"The functions of conceiving and enacting the values of the group *ad hoc* its particular stress-context are what I understand to be cult. The conceiving aspect I take to be myth, and the enactment aspect I take to be ritual. Both myth and ritual thus appear to me as strictly correlative and inseparable functions: their reciprocal union is what I mean by cult. The outcome of cult, so understood, is what I understand as culture—what Margaret Mead has called '. . . the systematic body of learned behavior which is transmitted from parents to children,' or what I would prefer to call the continuous and cohesive life-style by which a particular group conceives of and enacts what its values mean, thus to survive intact the stresses and threats of existence in the real order of space and time."[19]

[15] Aidan Kavanagh, "The Role of Ritual in Personal Development," in James Shaughnessy, ed., *The Roots of Ritual* (Grand Rapids: Eerdmans, 1973) 145–169; on tradition's relation to ritual and liturgy, see especially, 147–154.
[16] Ibid., 147.
[17] Ibid., 148.
[18] Ibid.
[19] Ibid., 148–149.

In Kavanagh's thought, therefore, culture cannot be imagined apart from cult. If culture is a living "value-complex," cult is the authoritative means by which those values are conceived (as myth), transmitted (as tradition) and enacted (as ritual). Ultimately, then, the review and renewal of values in any culture is a *cultic* (rather than simply a sociopolitical) process.

(3) Ritual is thus a distinctive and essential species of behavior, human and Christian. In his "handbook of liturgical style" entitled *Elements of Rite*, Kavanagh notes that authentic human ritual is inherently "antistructural."[20] This is so because all human structures—however reasonably devised and wisely governed—tend, if left to themselves, to ossify, to oppress, to disintegrate. "Bureaucrats and their bureaucracies implacably become tyrants and tyrannies when they are not regularly undercut, overturned, or reversed. . . . The lesson human wisdom seems to have learned is that although we probably cannot do without bureaucrats and bureaucracies, we certainly can do without tyrants and tyrannies. Ritual and liturgical antistructuralism, therefore, exists not to destroy but to renovate social structures, and it does this not as an end in itself but in service to the general social good."[21] *Archaism*, Kavanagh notes, is one of ritual's common antistructural strategies (though obviously not the only one). "The archaic is not the obsolete; it is to the human story what the unconscious is to the human psyche. Tapping the archaic is to release unrecognized reservoirs of memory, the power of which may well be as overwhelming as it is difficult to control. But it is power still, and nothing less than power of such dangerous magnitude is required when human structures are to be undercut, overturned, and reversed in favor of social survival."[22]

Another strategy liturgical ritual uses to achieve its antistructural ends is rhythm, repetition. For repetition resists another tyranny—that of the compulsive innovator. Kavanagh writes:

". . . [R]hythm, which organizes repetition, makes things memorable, as in music, poetry, rhetoric, architecture, and the plastic arts no less than in liturgical worship. Rhythm constantly

[20] *Elements of Rite*, 40–42.
[21] Ibid., 40–41.
[22] Ibid., 41.

insinuates, as propagandists know. It constantly reasserts, as good teachers know. It constantly forms individuals into units, as demagogues and cheerleaders know. It both shrouds and bares meaning which escapes mere words, as poets know. It fuses people to their values and forges them to common purpose, as orators such as Cato, Churchill, and Martin Luther King knew."[23]

These strategies also shape the relation between ritual (as a species of human activity) and the liturgy of Christians. Kavanagh describes this relation in a memorable paragraph:

"Rite involves creeds and prayers and worship, but it is not any one of these things, nor all of these things together, and it orchestrates more than these things. Rite can be called a whole style of Christian living found in the myriad particularities of worship, of laws called 'canonical,' of ascetical and monastic structures, of evangelical and catechetical endeavors . . . A liturgical act concretizes all these and in doing so makes them accessible to the community assembled in a given time and place before the living God for the life of the world. Rite in this Christian sense is generated and sustained in the regular meeting of faithful people in whose presence and through whose deeds the vertiginous Source of the cosmos itself is pleased to settle down freely and abide as among friends. A liturgy of Christians is thus nothing less than the way a redeemed world is, so to speak, done. The liturgical act of rite and the assembly which does it are coterminous, one thing: the incorporation under grace of Christ dying and rising still, restoring the communion all things and persons have been gifted with in Spirit and in truth. A liturgy is even more than an act of faith, prayer, or worship. It is an act of rite."[24]

Such a position, Kavanagh recognizes, is a "hard sell" today, when ritual is routinely dismissed as "the antithesis of enlightenment and freedom."[25] For rite, he notes, "is sustained by rote and obedience far more than by restless creativity, and obedience is a subordinate part of the larger virtue of justice while creativity is not. In our day it seems to require more courage to obey a rubric

[23] Ibid., 28.
[24] *On Liturgical Theology*, 100–101.
[25] Ibid., 101.

or law than to break it. Creativity of the Spontaneous Me variety condemns rite and symbol to lingering deaths by trivialization, bemusing those who could communicate by rite and symbol to a point where they finally wander away in search of something which appears to be more stable and power-laden."[26]

(4) Ultimately, what is at stake in ritual (for cultures) and in liturgy (for Christians) is a redemptive *knowledge* without which the human project itself cannot continue. Nowhere is this point made more eloquently than in Kavanagh's theology of Christian initiation. The rites of baptism, he notes,

"assert rather than argue, proclaim rather than explain, engage rather than discourse. Their classroom is a river, pool, bath house, or tomb. Their language is asceticism, good works, exorcism, bathing and anointing and dining. Their purpose is gradually to ease one into the love of God for the world through Jesus Christ in his life-giving Spirit, and to do so after the manner in which the Son himself consummated the same divine mystery by death and resurrection. . . . The Christian stands deep in all this, naked, covered with nothing but water and oil as night turns into day and as the fast becomes the Mother of Feasts. This is more than just a saving from sin or a classroom syllabus: it is . . . the divinization of humankind concretely accomplished through the incarnate Son dying and rising still among his faithful ones. It is from within this worldview that doctrinal discourse arises to reenforce and refine the conversional and initiatory experience, thus entering into dialogue with it. The law of worship constitutes the law of belief."[27]

Thus the knowledge baptism brings is not primarily tactical, cognitive or discursive, but redemptive, embodied and visceral. It is a knowledge transmitted not by syllabus or syllogism, but "by the risky images of sexual fertility and . . . the inscrutable terrors of the grave."[28] For the Church "is not a palm potted in academe or a psychoanalyst's office. It is a Tree of Life whose vast branches hold ensnared a living if bloody Lamb; whose taproot sinks deep

[26] Ibid., 102.
[27] Aidan Kavanagh, *The Shape of Baptism: The Rite of Christian Initiation* (New York: Pueblo, 1978) 158–159.
[28] Ibid., 158.

into the rich and murky waters of creation itself. Who would live in Christ must learn to climb with muddy feet, for there is nothing conventional, neat, or altogether logical about a crucifixion or the Church."[29]

For these reasons, Kavanagh critiques Roman Catholicism's almost obsessive fascination with eucharistic questions. "To know Christ sacramentally only in terms of bread and wine," he notes, "is to know him only partially, in the dining room as host and guest. It is a valid enough knowledge, but its ultimate weakness when isolated is that it is perhaps too civil. It lends itself to being conflated by short-term systems of cultural etiquette, thus becoming brittle and soon rendered obsolete when cultural patterns change." Thus, the knowledge specific to Christian baptism is "implacably paschal," a knowledge that confronts and intimidates us with the inherently scandalous improbability of Jesus' dying, rising, and sending of the Spirit.[30] For

". . . however elegant the knowledge of the dining room may be, it begins in the soil, in the barnyard, in the slaughterhouse; amid the quiet violence of the garden, strangled cries, and fat spitting in the pan. Table manners depend on something's having been grabbed by the throat. A knowledge that ignores these dark and murderous human *gestes* is losing its grip on the human condition."[31]

In the final analysis, what is at stake in the liturgical acts of the Christian assembly is nothing less than a world made new. "The paschal mystery of Jesus Christ dying and rising *still* among his faithful ones at Easter in baptism is what give the Church its radical cohesion and mission, putting it at the center of a world made new. That world is a paschal world, and baptism in its fullness is the compound process of act and reflection by which one enters such a world, leaving behind an obsolete world where death is lord. The latter world was made by us all. The former is meant and made by God no less for all."[32]

[29] Ibid., 159.
[30] Ibid., 162.
[31] Ibid., 160.
[32] Ibid., 162–163.

Such is the radiant, inclusive, yet "scandalously improbable" vision that has enlivened Aidan Kavanagh's theology through forty years of lecture and seminar, book and essay. The studies offered him in this *Festschrift* testify to his passionate fidelity to the church's worship, his toughness of intellect, his devotion to teaching, his exquisite style, grace and wit. *Ad multos annos!*

Part I

Historical Essays

Paul F. Bradshaw

1. Redating the *Apostolic Tradition:* Some Preliminary Steps

Ever since the independent researches of Eduard Schwartz and R. H. Connolly early in the twentieth century,[1] the vast majority of scholars have accepted their conclusions that what had formerly been called the *Egyptian Church Order* was to be identified with the *Apostolic Tradition* written by Hippolytus of Rome in the early third century but previously thought to have been lost. Recently, however, in a series of extremely important articles, Marcel Metzger has added his name to the shorter list of scholars who have doubted the attribution to Hippolytus and/or the Roman origin of the document.[2]

If correct—and his arguments are certainly very persuasive—such a conclusion would question not only the authorship and provenance of the church order but also its traditional dating. Its assignment to the early third century was arrived at by earlier scholars principally on the assumption of Hippolytean authorship and not on the grounds of internal evidence or other factors examined dispassionately. Gregory Dix, for example, narrowed the date down to c. 215 more on the basis of the most probable period in the life of Hippolytus for its composition than as a result of the examina-

[1] Eduard Schwartz, *Uber die pseudoapostolischen Kirchenordnungen* (Strasbourg: 1910); R. H. Connolly, *The So-called Egyptian Church Order and Derived Documents* (Cambridge: 1916; reprinted 1967).

[2] "Nouvelles perspectives pour la prétendue Tradition apostolique," *Ecclesia Orans* 5 (1988) 241–259; "Enquêtes autour de la prétendue Tradition apostolique," *Ecclesia Orans* 9 (1992) 7–36; "A propos des règlements écclesiastiques et de la prétendue Tradition apostolique," *Revue des sciences religieuses* 66 (1992) 249–261.

3

tion of its contents.[3] When, therefore, the phantom of Hippolytus is removed from the scene, the dating of the document becomes a much more open question.

It is important to recognize, however, that the effect of Metzger's thesis is not simply to replace Hippolytus as author by another, nameless individual, whether belonging to the same or to a different era. Metzger challenges the whole notion of a single author or redactor being responsible for the composition of the document, and instead regards it as a piece of "living literature" which evolved gradually by constant amplification and revision over a period of time.[4] It would thus be closer in character to the *Didache*, which is also usually thought to have been expanded by different hands,[5] than to the *Didascalia*, which is generally regarded as the work of a single person. Hence, the *Apostolic Tradition*[6] is a multi-layered work, and so may well contain elements that belong to a very early period of the Christian tradition as well as elements from a much later time.

This perception radically affects any attempt to assign a date to the collection of directives, since the dating of certain parts of it is not necessarily an accurate guide to the dating of the whole. Indeed, we cannot really speak of a date of its final recension at all, since it constantly went on being revised, to a greater or lesser extent, by those who copied the manuscript and translated it into the various extant language versions. Even the later church orders which used it as a source—the *Apostolic Constitutions*, the *Canons of Hippolytus*, and the *Testamentum Domini*—are in one sense merely further stages in the process of its growth and change.

All that we may reasonably attempt, therefore, is to establish the likely periods in the life of the early Church in which various parts of the *Apostolic Tradition* may have originated, and from this

[3] Gregory Dix, *The Treatise on the Apostolic Tradition of St. Hippolytus of Rome* (London: SPCK, 1937) xxxv–xxxvii.

[4] On this idea, see further Paul Bradshaw, "Liturgical Texts and 'Living Literature,'" in Paul Bradshaw and Bryan Spinks, eds., *Liturgy in Dialogue: Essays in Memory of Ronald Jasper* (London: SPCK, 1994) 138–153.

[5] For a discussion of some theories of its evolution, see F. E. Vokes, "The Didache still Debated," *Church Quarterly* 3 (1970) 57–62.

[6] For the sake of convenience, I will continue to refer to the document in question by this name, without intending to suggest thereby that this is its correct title.

to postulate the probable date by which it had reached substan-
tially the form known to the compilers of the later church orders.
However, this must of necessity be a cautious exercise. Our
knowledge of the first few centuries of Christian history is extremely limited, and indeed until now the *Apostolic Tradition* had
been thought to provide a substantial part of the reliable evidence
for the liturgical practices of the early third century. In order to
suggest a plausible date for the composition of some part of its
text, we need to employ a comparative method and ask at what
period we hear of similar practices in other sources. While this
may provide a useful guide to the likely time when this part of
the document originated, it is not infallible. It remains possible,
for example, that the practice in question is in reality even older
than the extant witnesses to it, and so this part of the *Apostolic
Tradition* should be assigned to an earlier date. Alternatively, the
practice may have persisted much later than our other evidence
suggests, and so this part of the *Apostolic Tradition* is more recent
than we might suppose.

The *terminus ad quem* for this operation is obviously provided by
the dates of the composition of the church orders that used the
Apostolic Tradition as a source. The *Apostolic Constitutions* is usually
regarded as having been compiled c. 375–380, the *Canons of Hippolytus*
was traditionally dated in the fifth or sixth century but has now
convincingly been shown by René-Georges Coquin to have been
written between 336 and 340,[7] and the *Testamentum Domini* has
tended to be ascribed to the fifth century, but Grant Sperry-White
has recently proposed that it originated in the second half of the
fourth century.[8] On this basis, therefore, there is no reason why
the *Apostolic Tradition* might not have reached the form known to
the redactors of these church orders only at the beginning of the
fourth century—or even as much as a hundred years after the date
usually assigned to it. Is there any internal evidence that would
either support or challenge the hypothesis that the document
evolved by stages and is composed of both more and less ancient
elements? Let us examine some sample passages.

---

[7] *Les Canons d'Hippolyte*, Patrologia Orientalis 31/2 (Paris: 1966).

[8] *The Testamentum Domini: A Text for Students*, Alcuin/GROW Liturgical
Study 19 (Nottingham: Grove Books, 1991) 6.

THE ORDINATION OF A BISHOP (2-3)[9]

I have already argued elsewhere that, in the form in which it was known to the translators and redactors, this section of the *Apostolic Tradition* lacked any mention of the participation of other bishops, and that such references were inserted by these intermediaries.[10] This suggests that the ordination practice which the original text described came from a time after the office of bishop had emerged but prior to the time when it became the custom for other bishops to be involved in the ordination of the bishop of a neighboring church. Our earliest reference to such involvement appears in North Africa in the middle of the third century,[11] but this does not prove that the practice was universal by this date. There is at least some evidence to suggest that in Alexandria the older custom persisted at least until the middle of the third century if not later,[12] and the same may well also have been the case elsewhere. Indeed, the fact that the Council of Nicea (canons 4 and 6) found it necessary to legislate for the participation of other bishops suggests that it was not even universally accepted by the early fourth century.[13] While it is possible, therefore, that this section of the document may have originated as early as the second century, it is also conceivable that it is no older than the beginning of the fourth century.

If we turn our attention to the ordination prayer itself, we need to bear in mind first of all that it may not have been composed at the same time as the "rubrics" of the rite, but may be either earlier

[9] The numbering of the sections of the *Apostolic Tradition* adopted here follows that of the edition by Bernard Botte, *La Tradition apostolique de saint Hippolyte* (Münster: Aschendorff, 1963) and of the English translation by Geoffrey Cuming, *Hippolytus: A Text for Students*, Grove Liturgical Study 8 (Nottingham: Grove Books, 1976), from which all quotations are taken (except for the substitution of "presbyter" for "priest" whenever it occurs, for the sake of clarity).

[10] "Ordination," ed. G. J. Cuming, *Essays on Hippolytus*, Grove Liturgical Study 15 (Nottingham: Grove Books, 1978) 33-38; "The participation of other bishops in the ordination of a bishop in the Apostolic Tradition of Hippolytus," *Studia Patristica* 18.2 (1989) 335-338.

[11] Cyprian, *Epp.* 55.8; 67.5.

[12] See A. Vilela, *La condition collégiale des prêtres au IIIe siècle*, Théologie Historique 14 (Paris: Beauchesne, 1971) 173-179, and the works cited in note 5.

[13] See C. W. Griggs, *Early Egyptian Christianity: From its Origins to 451 C.E.* (Leiden: Brill, 1990) 132-133.

or later. Indeed, the apparent double imposition of hands in those directives—first a corporate act by a group of ministers and then an individual gesture by the one appointed to say the prayer— might be thought to suggest that what we have here is not a single rite which was ever celebrated in this form at all, but rather a conflation of two rites which prescribed different ritual actions. If this is so, it seems likely that the prayer belongs with the second of these, and this may be an indication that it is part of a later layer of tradition, not just because it appears to have been appended to an existing element in the text (since it could have had an independent existence prior to the composition of the first part), but because the practice of silent communal prayer is probably older than a vocalized ordination prayer and the practice of a collegial imposition of hands is probably older than an individual laying on of hands, since all later ordination rites prescribe an individual laying on of hands and not a collegial one.[14]

Secondly, we need to note that the version of the prayer in the *Canons of Hippolytus* lacks all references to the high priestly ministry of the bishop. While it has generally been supposed that these were deleted by the redactor because the early Eastern concept of the episcopate did not include this cultic dimension to the same extent as in the West,[15] yet one cannot entirely rule out the possibility that the redactor may have known an earlier form of the text to which this typology had not yet been added. Eric Segelberg has attempted to discern different strata within the prayer, but he does not take into account the version in the *Canons of Hippolytus* and bases his arguments in part on the presupposition that references to the Old Covenant are a sign of antiquity.[16]

Whatever may be the value of Segelberg's reconstruction,[17] it is certainly the use of sacerdotal language in the prayer which offers the most significant guide to its date. In the text represented by the versions other than the *Canons of Hippolytus* the bishop is described as exercising the high priesthood and as possessing

[14] See Paul F. Bradshaw, *Ordination Rites of the Ancient Churches of East and West* (New York: Pueblo, 1990) 44–45.

[15] Ibid., 47–55.

[16] "The Ordination Prayers in Hippolytus," *Studia Patristica* 13 (1975) 397–408.

[17] See Bradshaw, *Ordination Rites of the Ancient Churches of East and West*, 46.

authority through the high priestly spirit.[18] Tertullian is the first Christian writer to use the term high priest to denote the bishop, and then only once in his writings, in a context which suggests that it may perhaps have been a metaphor occasioned by the particular argument rather than a regular term for the office (*De bapt.* 17.1). Elsewhere he implies that *sacerdos* may have been a commonly used designation for the bishop in the North African church (*De exh. cast.* 11.1–2; *De monog.* 12; *De pud.* 20.10; 21.17); and Cyprian regularly calls the bishop *sacerdos*, reserving *summus sacerdos* for Christ alone (e.g., Ep. 63.14). The *Didascalia*, however, while acknowledging that Christ is the true high priest, does not hesitate to call the bishop "the levitical high priest" (II.26.4), and so provides a third-century parallel to the usage in the *Apostolic Tradition*.

In the light of this evidence, therefore, and since doctrinal developments generally appear in theological discourse well before they find a place in liturgical texts, which are by nature more conservative, it is unlikely that the prayer—at least in the form in which we have it—is older than the middle of the third century.

THE EUCHARISTIC PRAYER (4)

The Eucharistic prayer presents an equally complex situation. On the one hand, it has elements which suggest an early date, as for example references to Jesus as the "child" of God;[19] on the other hand, it displays some features which seem to point instead to the fourth century. There has already been some debate among scholars as to whether the invocation of the Holy Spirit was part of the original prayer, or instead a fourth-century addition to it.[20] But perhaps even more questionable is the narrative of institution. Evi-

---

[18] We must note, however, that the Ethiopic version, quite inexplicably, refers to "priest" rather than "high priest" throughout the prayer.

[19] Except for one occurrence in the *Apostolic Constitutions* (which may be derived from the *Apostolic Tradition* itself), all other instances of this expression in early Christian literature belong to the first two centuries: *Didache,* 1 Clement, *Epistle of Barnabas, Martyrdom of Polycarp.*

[20] See Bernard Botte, "L'épiclèse de l'anaphore d'Hippolyte," *Recherches de théologie ancienne et médiévale* 14 (1947) 241–251 (who defends its authenticity); and also L. Edward Phillips, "The Kiss of Peace and the Opening Greeting of the Pre-anaphoral Dialogue," *Studia Liturgica* 23 (1993) 184–185, who suggests that the dialogue preceding the Eucharistic prayer in the *Apostolic Tradition* may also have undergone revision in the fourth century.

dence from several sources indicates that this unit was only just beginning to make an appearance in other Eucharistic prayers in the middle of the fourth century. The *Sacramentary of Sarapion*, for example, has an unusual bipartite form of the narrative which looks very much like a first attempt to incorporate it into the prayer, and the anaphoras known to both Cyril of Jerusalem and Theodore of Mopsuestia seem as yet not to include the narrative.[21]

In the light of this, it would seem improbable that it was already well-established in the *Apostolic Tradition* early in the third century, and more likely that it was added to an older version of the prayer in the fourth century. It may be noted that E. C. Ratcliff believed that the narrative followed awkwardly upon the reference to the harrowing of the underworld and the resurrection, and so thought it possible that "the want of smoothness and order at this point indicates that the older tradition has here been remodeled and stabilized in accordance with later fashion."[22]

It should also be remembered that the Sahidic and Arabic translations of the *Apostolic Tradition* and the *Canons of Hippolytus* do not include the text of the Eucharistic prayer in their versions of the document, and the Eucharistic prayer contained in the *Apostolic Constitutions* has few points of contact with that of the *Apostolic Tradition*. Although, therefore, these texts do witness to the existence of a Eucharistic prayer of some sort in the version of the *Apostolic Tradition* which lay before them, they cannot confirm that it was identical in form to that lying behind the Latin and Ethiopic translations and the *Testamentum Domini*, which are the only witnesses to its full text. It is quite possible, therefore, that the Eucharistic prayer may not have achieved that form until the middle of the fourth century, or even later if Sperry-White's early dating of the *Testamentum Domini* proves to be too optimistic.

How old, then, might the earlier form of the prayer be? This is a very difficult question to answer because, apart from the forms in Didache 9–10 which have been the subject of much debate, we do

---

[21] See E. J. Cutrone, "Cyril's Mystagogical Catecheses and the Evolution of the Jerusalem Anaphora," *Orientalia Christiana Periodica* 44 (1978) 52–64; Enrico Mazza, "La struttura dell'anafora nelle Catechesi di Teodoro di Mopsuestia," *Ephemerides Liturgicae* 102 (1988) 147–183.

[22] E. C. Ratcliff, "The Sanctus and the Pattern of the Early Anaphora," *Journal of Ecclesiastical History* 1 (1950) 32.

not have any other Eucharistic prayers which we can date with any certainty to the period before the fourth century to provide a solid point of comparison. However, in the light of the parallels which several scholars have traced between elements in the Eucharistic prayer of the *Apostolic Tradition* and passages in early Christian writers such as Irenaeus or Justin Martyr,[23] it is not impossible that it first took shape before the end of the second century.

THE INITIATION MATERIAL (20–21)

In 1968 Jean-Paul Bouhot suggested that this section of the document was in reality a fusion of two distinct rites, the older of which was Roman in origin and the later of which was African and had been interpolated into the former in the second half of the third century.[24] The "African" rite began at the phrase "And at the time fixed for baptizing" in chapter 21 and continued up to and including the bishop's postbaptismal imposition of hands and prayer. Robert Cabié later examined Bouhot's claim and, while judging his precision as to their provenance to be premature, cautiously accepted the idea that there were indeed two sources here,[25] a conclusion with which Victor Saxer also concurred.[26]

The basis for Bouhot's hypothesis was threefold. First, there was a chronological dislocation in the text: having given directions for the immersion itself "at the time when the cock crows," the document then repeated "at the time fixed for baptizing" and introduced a prebaptismal blessing of the oils, renunciation, and exorcism, even though a thorough preparatory exorcism had already taken place on Saturday. Secondly, there was repetition: not only was there this double prebaptismal exorcism, but the postbaptismal ceremonies were also duplicated, with a first anointing

---

[23] See for example R. H. Connolly, "The Eucharistic Prayer of Hippolytus," *Journal of Theological Studies* 39 (1938) 350–369.

[24] *La confirmation, sacrement de la communion ecclesiale* (Lyon: Editions du Chalet, 1968) 38–45.

[25] "L'ordo de l'Initiation chrétienne dans la 'Tradition apostolique' d'Hippolyte de Rome," in *Mens concordet voci, pour Mgr A. G. Martimort* (Paris: Desclée, 1983) 543–558.

[26] *Les rites de l'initiation chrétienne du IIe au VIe siècle* (Spoleto: Centro Italiano di studi sull'alto Medioevo, 1988) 118–119.

10

by a presbyter and an imposition of hands and prayer by the bishop being followed by a second anointing with imposition of hands by the bishop.[27] Thirdly, there were differences of "climate": in the "Roman" rite only one minister—the bishop—was mentioned, while in the "African" rite presbyters and deacons were involved; and the "Roman" rite mentioned elements which appeared to be ancient—cockcrow, "flowing" water (cf. *Didache* 7), and the need for women to loosen their hair—while the "African" rite contained features which appeared more recent—the distinction between the two sorts of oil, the developed profession of faith, the lesser role of the bishop, and the use of "church" to denote the place of assembly.

There is certainly a striking contrast between the material which precedes the point at which the interpolation is alleged to begin and that which follows it. As Cabié has noted,[28] in the earlier part, and indeed throughout the rest of the initiation-related material in chapters 15–19 as well, the process is described very vaguely, and chiefly in impersonal or passive terms (e.g., "let hands be laid on them daily while they are exorcised," and "let prayer be made over the water"). Indeed, apart from two brief references to the activity of the bishop in performing the exorcism of the candidates himself (which may perhaps be later additions, since they are more precise than the surrounding material),[29] no specific ministers are mentioned here in connection with the rites,

[27] Cabie, "L'ordo de l'Initiation chrétienne," 553, disputes the interpretation of the text as referring to a second imposition of hands, which is explicit only in the Coptic version and in the *Testamentum Domini*.

[28] "L'ordo de l'Initiation chrétienne," 552.

[29] "And when the day of their baptism approaches, the bishop shall exorcize each one of them, in order that he may know whether he is pure. . . . at the bishop's decision. They shall all be told to pray and kneel. And he shall lay his hand on them and exorcize all alien spirits, that they may flee out of them and never return into them. And when he has finished exorcizing them, he shall breathe on their faces; and when he has signed their foreheads, ears, and noses, he shall raise them up." It is possible that several other words and phrases in this section of the document are also later additions. The reference to a font (*kolymbethra*) at the beginning of chapter 21, for example, may have been added by a translator, since it seems to reflect later terminology, and both the *Canons of Hippolytus* and the *Testamentum Domini* here speak simply of the water being "pure and flowing." See also the following note for another possible example.

and in chapters 15–19 the only ministers are "teachers" (15, 18), who may be "ecclesiastics"[30] or lay persons (19). In the second part, however, after the bishop has prepared the oils, not only do a presbyter and deacons suddenly come to the fore, but very detailed ritual instructions begin to be given, far more detailed indeed than in any other part of the whole church order: "a deacon takes the oil of exorcism and stands on the presbyter's left; and another deacon takes the oil of thanksgiving and stands on the presbyter's right."

How far, however, does this interpolation extend? Or is it an interpolation at all? Is it not possible that what we have here is actually an older core dealing with the process of initiation which originally ended at this point, and so everything that follows it is later accretion? This would mean that the rite so described was quite similar to that in *Didache* 7. On the other hand, it may be that the section describing the triple credal interrogation and triple immersion was also a part of the original nucleus (or at least a very ancient addition to it), since some such dialogue is certainly implied by the earlier direction that "all those who can speak for themselves shall do so. . . ." Moreover this section too, like the earlier part, appears indeterminate as to the minister of the rite. While its opening words are difficult to establish with certainty because of the very obvious modifications which the various versions have all made to the text at this point in order to make it conform to the rites with which each was familiar,[31] yet it seems likely that the *Testamentum Domini* may have most accurately preserved the original reading here: "As he who is to be baptized is descending into the water, let him who baptizes him say thus [as he lays his hand upon him],[32] 'Do you believe in God the Father omnipotent?'

[30] Although translated by both Botte and Cuming as "cleric," the Greek word here was *ekklesiastikos* and not *kleros* as elsewhere in the *Apostolic Tradition* (e.g., ch. 8). This is otherwise only found in this sense from the fourth century onwards, and so would be very unusual in a third-century source, let alone one which may be older still. Is it possible that the original text was simply that still found in *Apostolic Constitutions* 8, "even if he is a layman," and that this was later expanded?

[31] For further details, see Botte, *La Tradition apostolique*, 46–49.

[32] This bracketed phrase was probably not found in the original text of the *Apostolic Tradition* at this point: all the other versions put it a little further on, in the more natural context of the first immersion itself, except for the *Canons*

And let the one being baptized say, 'I believe.' "[33]

Even the version of the text which lies behind the oriental-language versions appears to acknowledge that the minister of baptism was not specified in the original, since they speak of "the bishop or presbyter" as being the minister here, and none of the versions names the minister again throughout the remaining interrogations and immersions. It is even possible that a few later sentences in the description of the rite also belong to the oldest stratum of the text, as they too share the same general style as the earlier material: "And so each of them shall wipe themselves and put on their clothes, and then they shall enter the church. . . . And then they shall pray together with all the people: they do not pray with the faithful until they have carried out all these things. And when they have prayed, they shall give the kiss of peace."

Although Bouhot maintained that the use of "church" to denote the place of assembly was a sign that the material belonged to a later date, the same usage is found in chapters 18, 35, 39, and 41, most of which seem to be among the earlier portions of the document. Similarly, while he characterized the developed profession of faith as belonging to a later form of the rite, it is consistent in both content and style with the description of baptism given by Justin Martyr in the middle of the second century (*I. Apol.* 61) and with the echoes of credal formulae found scattered throughout his writings.[34] Thus, although one must admit that there is no other explicit evidence for pre-baptismal exorcism or infant baptism until a later date, there does not appear to be anything in this whole stratum which could not have originated from that same period.

If this hypothesis is correct, then all the remaining elements in the text must have been added at some later date. While this could have happened in one single redaction, the apparent duplication of the prebaptismal exorcism and postbaptismal anointing

---

of *Hippolytus*, which has it in both places. It is possible that the manuscript tradition underlying the *Canons of Hippolytus* and the *Testamentum Domini* accidentally copied it twice, and that the redactor of the *Testamentum Domini* then deleted the second occurrence.

[33] Translation taken from Sperry-White, *The Testamentum Domini,* 28.

[34] On the latter, see J.N.D. Kelly, *Early Christian Creeds* (London: Longmans, Green & Co., 1950) 70–76, though Kelly himself would not regard all these as belonging to a baptismal context.

may be a sign that there were at least two distinct stages. If so, then the directives which involve a presbyter and deacons (the blessing of the oils, renunciation, and exorcistic anointing before baptism, and the presbyteral postbaptismal unction) probably constitute a later stratum than the references to actions performed by the bishop alone (that is, the exorcisms before the baptismal day, the postbaptismal prayer, unction, signing, and greeting). Not only does the more detailed character of these instructions suggest that they belong to a later date, but we have no other evidence for the use of oil for pre-baptismal exorcism prior to the middle of the fourth century (Chrysostom, Cyril, and Theodore). This, of course, is not to say that every element in this second layer was a fourth century innovation—Tertullian, for instance, testifies to the existence of prebaptismal renunciation and postbaptismal anointing in his Church at the beginning of the third century—but only that this block of material probably attained its final form and was added to the text at about this period.

Indeed, it appears quite possible that the material in this stratum is drawn from a set of baptismal instructions intended for use when a presbyter presided over the rite in the absence of a bishop: only the phrase "And at the time fixed for baptizing" connects the bishop's consecration of the oils with the occasion of baptism itself, and this may well be a piece of editorial linkage created at the time of the conflation of the two texts. It is true that the bishop is mentioned once again just before the immersion, but we have already suggested above that this too was an editorial addition acknowledging the indeterminacy of the original stratum as to the minister of baptism. However it happened, the whole process would have had to have been completed before the end of the first quarter of the fourth century, since the *Canons of Hippolytus* is clearly familiar with a text which contained all the principal features revealed in the other versions, except perhaps for the second postbaptismal anointing.[35] The resultant composition is thus not a single coherent rite as practiced by a particular local

[35] On this point, see Paul F. Bradshaw, *The Canons of Hippolytus*, Alcuin/GROW Liturgical Study 2 (Nottingham: Grove Books, 1987) 24; J. M. Hanssens, "L'édition critique des Canons d'Hippolyte," *Orientalia Christiana Periodica* 32 (1966) 542–543.

Church but a conflation of different traditions from different periods, and very probably different places.

THE DAILY PRAYER MATERIAL (41)

It has been generally acknowledged by scholars that at one time there were in circulation both longer and shorter versions of the *Apostolic Tradition*, the shorter lacking chapters 39–41, and so having only the brief reference to morning prayer and instruction in chapter 35, which is duplicated and greatly expanded in chapter 41. Although Edward Phillips has tried to present a case for the longer version being the original,[36] his theory involves a number of questionable assumptions: that the original order of the final chapters was significantly different; that part of the text then became lost, giving rise to the shorter version; that a later redactor would have rearranged the material when combining the two versions in order to produce a more thematic order; and that the Sahidic translator would have been creative enough to remove "the clumsy duplication of chapters 42 and 43."

On the other hand, the divergent forms of this part of the text can better be accounted for on the hypothesis of a gradual expansion of the material, with at least four stages: (1) the shorter version; (2) an intermediate version, in which the expanded chapter 41 replaced chapter 35, with chapters 39 and 40 being added immediately before it in the text (the arrangement apparently known to the compilers of the *Canons of Hippolytus* and the *Testamentum Domini*, as Phillips rightly observes); (3) a composite version, in which chapter 35 was retained and chapters 39–41 were instead inserted into the shorter version just before the conclusion (chapters 42–43), thus creating the form underlying the oriental language texts; and (4) the longer version, represented by the Latin translation alone, in which the final portion of the composite version (chapters 39 to the end) was then appended to the conclusion of the shorter version, resulting in a duplication of chapters 42 and 43.

What is more significant in Phillips' article, however, is his argument that the daily prayer material in chapter 41 itself has under-

---

[36] "Daily Prayer in the Apostolic Tradition of Hippolytus," *Journal of Theological Studies* 40 (1989) 389–400.

gone expansion, and that the original pattern here was simply prayer at the third, sixth, and ninth hours of the day, together with midnight: prayer at bedtime and at cockcrow he judges to be later additions to the text. Metzger's analysis of the chapter lends some support to Phillips' hypothesis, since he has pointed out that there are changes in style here.[37] While the material at the beginning taken from chapter 35 is cast in the third person singular ("Let every faithful man and woman . . ."), the additional material shows a preference for the second person singular, usually in the imperative ("pray at the third hour . . ."), apart from the concluding sentence, which uses the second person plural ("And if you act so, all you faithful . . .").[38]

Like the ordination and initiation material, this again suggests that we do not have a single order that was ever followed in its entirety by any one community, but a fusion of different traditions. The redactor who added the hours of daily prayer to the prescription about morning prayer in chapter 35 was not necessarily expecting that readers would do both, but merely recording a variant pattern with which he was familiar, while preserving the original; similarly, the redactor who later added cockcrow to the times of daily prayer was not necessarily expecting both midnight and cockcrow to be observed, but again merely inserting an hour of prayer with which he was familiar while leaving the rest undisturbed. Since North African evidence from the third century (Tertullian, Cyprian) indicates that a fivefold daily horarium was already firmly established there, it seems unlikely that the material advocating a threefold pattern of daily prayer in chapter 41 originated at a later date than that, and it may well have been written much earlier, even if it were not incorporated into the rest of the document until that period.

CONCLUSION

The above observations are no more than the first steps in the necessary task of reevaluating the process of composition of the *Apostolic Tradition*. What is needed—and what I have already

---

[37] "Enquêtes autour de la prétendue Tradition apostolique," 11.

[38] Metzger notes that the directives about prayer at the sixth and ninth hours each include a use of the third person plural, but Phillips has privately expressed the opinion that the verbs here are really meant to be passives.

begun to undertake with a group of younger scholars—is a close scrutiny of the whole document in an attempt to discern the various strata of which it seems to be made up, to identify (as far as the uncertain nature of the text will allow) any distinctive vocabulary and stylistic features which may assist in that delineation, and to pursue further the comparative method outlined here in the hope of establishing the probable date of each layer thus discovered. In the meantime, if it does nothing else, perhaps this initial foray will be enough to discourage those who may still be tempted to cite passages from this church order as though they were the undoubted words of Hippolytus of Rome and constituted a reliable guide to the authentic liturgical practices of that city in the early third century.

Thomas J. Talley

2. Roman Culture and Roman Liturgy

I first entered Rome in 1960, the year before I began graduate study, in the company of the distinguished teacher and scholar whose career this volume celebrates. He was then more scholar than teacher, being himself a student at Liturgisches Institut Trier, but on that trip he taught me much. We had come to the Apostolic City from Trier in a rather early Volkswagen named, appropriately enough, Minerva. In deference to my need to collect my mail as soon as possible, Aidan drove immediately to the offices of American Express, and I first set foot in Rome in the Piazza di Spagna. As I began to walk across the piazza, I was frozen in my steps by the sight of a manhole cover bearing the legend I knew so well from the standards borne by legionnaires in the drawings that adorned my high school Latin books: *SPQR*. Nothing in the happy weeks and months I have spent prowling the fora and cemeteries of the city since that day has spoken to me as powerfully of Rome's awesome continuity with its archaic roots as did that encounter with a very humble twentieth-century artifact declaring its ownership by the Senate and People of Rome.

That continuity, I was assured by the little reading I had done in liturgical history, included much in the liturgical tradition of the city and, eventually, Western Christendom. That seemed to be confirmed by the ever-present dedicatory tablets on Christian monuments assigning them to the initiative of this or that *Pontifex Maximus*, once the title of Rome's chief religious functionary, always the Emperor (Nero and Constantine included) until declined by the Christian Gratian, but used of the Bishop of Rome since the fifth century.[1]

It was especially in relation to certain festivals and fasts, however, that the literature seemed agreed upon foundations in Roman culture for liturgical observances associated peculiarly with Rome. Those suggestions have produced two levels of discussion. At one level, it has been argued whether Christian faith is compatible with the adoption of pagan customs, although the question is seldom posed so baldly. Nonetheless, this concern has led some writers to speak of continuities with pre-Christian custom as Christian acts of adoption and adaptation, while others have spoken of Christian counterobservances, established in opposition to pagan culture. One might say that at this level there is agreement on a process of cultural response, and what is under discussion is its motivation, an issue that perhaps concerns ancient liturgy less than it does the position of a particular writer on the spectrum of views regarding Christ and culture.

In either case, the interpretation of the Christian observance presumes an older Roman observance of compelling similarity as the exclusive stimulus to its Christian form, and those presumptions themselves are frequently open to question. At this second level of discussion the evidence is more complex, and it seems impossible to arrive at only one answer. In some instances no common term can be discerned, contrary to what many liturgical historians have claimed. In other instances, there clearly is such a common term, but there is question of whether the Christian observance is derivative from the pagan. In still other cases, the continuity of a Christian observance with pre-Christian custom seems indisputable, but the precise point of transition from pagan to Christian practice is elusive. Three examples will illustrate these complexities (among others, surely) attending our historical address to the relation of early Roman liturgy to Roman culture.

One of the more characteristic features of Roman liturgy in late antiquity was the appointment of fasts corresponding to the four seasons. Largely forgotten since recent reforms, these week-long observances at the *Quatuor Tempora,* called "Ember Days" in

[1] If we discount Tertullian's sarcastic application of it to Callistus much earlier (*De pudicitia,* 1).

English, were a prominent feature of the liturgical year known to early Roman liturgical books and to Leo the Great, from whom we have a large number of sermons preached on the Sundays before these fasts. Each of those sermons ends with a stereotyped formula urging fasting on Wednesday and Friday and proclaiming a vigil from Saturday to Sunday at Saint Peter's. The Saturdays were fasted as well, and this had been urged for every Saturday in the year by Innocent I in his frequently cited letter to Decentius of Gubbio in 416.[2] That fact throws into sharper relief Tertullian's Montanist complaint that Romans fast on *some* Saturdays other than the Paschal Sabbath, for most of the Church the sole exception to the rule against Sabbath fasting.[3] Normally, one dare not give credence to the testimony of *Liber Pontificalis* for the third century, but this testimony of Tertullian might supply tentative confirmation to a detail in that sixth-century work's account of the pontificate of Callistus, Tertullian's contemporary and *bête noire*.[4] Of Callistus, *Liber Pontificalis* says:

"Hic constituit ieiunium die sabbati ter in anno fieri, frumenti, vini, et olei, secundum prophetiam quarti mensis, septimi et decimi."

In spite of anachronisms (the summer fast, e.g., is never referred to as *quarti mensis* before Gelasius at the end of the fifth century), this testimony has commended itself to some of the more learned commentators on these Roman seasonal fasts. Especially intriguing is the claim that Callistus inaugurated only three Sabbath fasts, since by the time of *Liber Pontificalis* it had long been established that these fasts occurred at each of the four seasons.

It was that and other suggestions that the spring fast in the first week of Lent was a secondary development that led Germain Morin, late in the last century, to argue that these seasonal fasts at Rome represented a Christian adaptation of three *feriae conceptivae*, Roman religious observances distinguished from the state festivals, *feriae stativae*, which fell on dates fixed in the official calendar.[5] As

---

[2] *Ep.*, 25.

[3] *De ieiunio*, 14.3.

[4] L. Duchesne, ed., *Le Liber Pontificalis: Texte, intruduction et commentaire* vol. I, (Paris: 1886) 141.

[5] G. Morin, "L'origine des Quatre-Temps," *Rev. Ben.* 14 (1897) 337–346.

documentation for this distinction, Morin cited the magisterial article on "Feriae" by C. Jullian in the massive *Dictionnaire des antiquités grecques et romains* then recently edited by Daremberg and Saglio, an article that still claims the respect of classicists today.[6] Earlier attempts to establish a pagan origin for the Ember Days, such as that of Nicholas-Sylvestre Bergier who saw them as counterobservances to the Bacchanalia,[7] had failed to find a following. Morin's suggestion fell on more fertile soil, however, and from Paul Lejay's assessment of Morin's hypothesis as *trés séduisante* in 1902[8] to as recently as 1983,[9] the explanation of the Ember Days as Christian adaptations of three Roman agricultural *feriae conceptivae* has been repeated in the literature as one of the secure results of liturgiological inquiry.

Even a casual reading of Morin's sources, however, raises questions that this literature has not addressed. Those questions were raised long ago in my doctoral dissertation, still (and wisely, I am convinced) unpublished. Having had occasion a few years ago to summarize that critique of Morin's explanation of the Ember Days,[10] it may suffice here to observe that of the three *feriae conceptivae* nominated by Morin as pagan ground of the Ember Days of summer, autumn, and winter, only one seems to be known to classical scholarship, *feriae Sementivae*, a local festival of the *pagus* (whence its alternative title, *Paganalia*). This observance in the rural canton has been urged as the basis for the December Embertide by those who repeat Morin's theory, although the *Fasti* of Ovid, cited as authority for *feriae Sementivae* by Morin himself, places the festival between January 24 and 26, a discrepancy noted by neither Morin nor his followers. The other two institutions claimed as basis for the Roman seasonal fasts, *feriae messis* and *feriae vindemiales*, are not found at all among the *feriae conceptivae*

---

[6] C. Jullian, s.v. "Feriae," Daremberg et Saglio, eds., *Dictionnaire des antiquités grecques et romains*, II² (Paris: 1886) 1042–1073.

[7] *Dictionnaire de théologie* III, col. (Lille, 1844) 405.

[8] *Revue d'histoire et de littérature religieuses* 7 (1902) 361–362.

[9] Hansjörg Auf der Maur, *Feiern im Rhythmus der Zeit, I: Herrenfeste in Woche und Jahr.* Handbuch der Liturgiewissenschaft, Teil 5 (Regensburg: Pustet, 1983) 54.

[10] "The Origin of the Ember Days: An Inconclusive Postscript," *Rituels: Mélanges offerts au Père Gy, O.P.*, P. de Clerck and Eric Palazzo, eds. (Paris: Cerf, 1990) 465–472.

recognized by classical authorities. Rather, Jullian, on the basis of some of the same evidence cited by Morin, asserts that these references are not to religious festivals or even to closely defined times, but simply indicate periods in the year when magistrates were justified in taking time away from their duties to look after their own estates during harvest and vintage. In sum, the triad of pagan *feriae* that supposedly constituted the pagan foundation for the Embertides of summer, autumn and winter never existed in Roman culture.

That discovery, forced on me early in my doctoral research, left me much less sanguine regarding claims of classical Roman roots for Roman liturgy. Nonetheless, I recall that at my oral defense Professor Massey Shepherd asked if I recognized *any* instances of Christian observances based on Roman festivals, and I did not hesitate to affirm the foundation of Christmas in the "Birthday of the Invincible Sun," a pagan celebration on the traditional date of the winter solstice, the festival promulgated by Aurelian in A.D. 274. That dependency had been current in the literature since the eighteenth century[11] and had received almost universal acceptance by 1947 when Oscar Cullmann first published the essay that perhaps gives fullest expression to this hypothesis, *Weihnachten in der alten Kirche.*[12] Several years later, at the second *Studientagung* of the Abt Herwegen Institut at Maria Laach, the derivation of Christmas from the Roman solar festival received further explication from Hieronymus Frank.[13] Here, however, that view was countered by a paper of another distinguished Benedictine liturgist, Hieronymus Engberding,[14] who renewed and expanded the suggestion of Louis Duchesne[15] that both the December 25 date and that of January 6 could be understood to be computed from paschal dates, March 25 and April 6, dates associated with the death of the Lord but taken to be as well the date of his concep-

---

[11] L. Fendt, *Theologische Literaturzeitung* 78.1 (January 1953) 1–10, cites Paul Ernst Jablonski and Jean Hardouin.

[12] E. T. by A.J.B. Higgins, "The Origin of Christmas," in O. Cullmann, *The Early Church*, abridged edition (Philadelphia: Westminster, 1966) 17–36.

[13] "Frühgeschichte und Ursprung des römischen Weihnachtsfest im Lichte neurer Forschung," *Archiv für Liturgiewissenschaft* 2 (1952) 1–24.

[14] "Der 25. Dezember als Tag der Feier der Geburt des Herrn," *Ibid.*, 25–43.

[15] L. Duchesne, *Origines du culte chrétien* (Paris, 1889) 250f.

tion. That identification of the paschal date with the conception date would allow the determination of the birth date after an interval of nine months, on December 25 and January 6 respectively. In the following year the entire question received a masterful review by Leonhard Fendt, who concluded that Engberding had at the very least made Duchesne's "computation hypothesis" competitive with the more frequently encountered "History-of-religions hypothesis."[16]

Since then, a number of developments have contributed to the attractiveness of Duchesne's suggestion: Roland Bainton's revelation that the birth date known to Clement of Alexandria was January 6,[17] the deflation of much of the supposed evidence that sought to establish pagan sources for that date,[18] and the explanation of the Montanist April 6 paschal date as 14 Artemisios in the Asian calendar, a solar equivalent to the Jewish Passover date, 14 Nisan. At the same time, several elements of the hypothesis that sought to root Christmas in pre-Christian Roman culture have been reviewed with results that diminish its apparent tidiness. Cullmann's attempt to relate the Christmas/Sol Invictus nexus to Constantine's personal religious history pays no attention either to Constantine's very limited presence in Rome itself or to the absence of any celebration of December 25 as the nativity of Christ in Constantinople during his lifetime.[19] Also, many of the cited evidences of the identification of Christ with the Sun, a common association based on Malachi 4:2, in fact antedate the establishment of the festival of Sol Invictus by Aurelian in A.D. 274. This has led one French scholar, Anselme Davril, to suggest that the setting of

[16] See note 11 above.

[17] R. Bainton, "The Origins of Epiphany," Early and Medieval Christianity. The Collected Papers in Church History, I (Boston: 1962) 22–38. However, the research reported here was developed during Bainton's doctoral research and first published in his article, "Basilidian Chronology and New Testament Interpretation," Journal of Biblical Literature 42 (1923) 81–134.

[18] I was both humiliated and gratified to discover how wrong had been my dependency on the attempt of Eduard Norden in 1924 (in Die Geburt des Kindes: Geschichte eine religiösen Idee) to establish an Egyptian winter solstice festival on January 6 in the twentieth century before Christ on the basis of the Julian calendar. Details in Studia Liturgica 14:2–4 (1982) 41–42.

[19] I presented the evidence in "Constantine and Christmas," Studia Liturgica 17 (1987) 191–197.

the nativity on December 25 was already established when Aurelian promulgated his festival, and was a decisive element in his taking that step. The connection between the two festivals can be affirmed, he believes, but the dependency is the reverse of what has been supposed.[20] The tidiness of the view expressed by Cullmann would be further disturbed by the suspicion, still inchoate, that the nativity was first identified with December 25 in North Africa, and not at Rome at all.[21]

Whatever might come of such suspicions, there is no reason to doubt that December 25 was seen at Rome as an important turning point from which the days became longer and the lengthening hours of darkness began to give way to an increase of the light. That in itself was a cultural rather than an astronomical phenomenon. The winter solstice actually fell some days earlier, on December 20 in the third century and December 19 in the fourth, if we can project from Ginzel's table for the Julian dates of the spring equinox.[22] The tradition that set the solstices and equinoxes eight days before the kalends of April, July, October and January seems to be astronomically correct for the late fourth century B.C., about the time of the founding of Alexandria. It is possible that this dating for the quarter-tense days had an established authority in Alexandrian tradition and was passed to Rome by Sosigenes, the Alexandrian astronomer who devised the calendar reform of Julius Caesar. These assignments, in any case, appear in the later *Fasti*, although such astronomers as Ptolemy († c. A.D. 170) were aware of the true dates. It was probably this traditional assignment of the winter solstice to December 25 that informed Aurelian's dedication of that day to the birth of the Sun, *dies natalis solis invicti*, as that would lead later to the assignment of the same date to the birth of Mithras, addressed in many dedications as *Sol Invictus Mithras*.

[20] Anselme Davril, O.S.B., "L'origine de la fête de Noël," *Renaissance de Fleury* 160 (Noël: 1991) 9–14.

[21] See L. Fendt, *op. cit.* (note 11 above); also M. H. Shepherd, "The Liturgical Reform of Damasus I," *Kyriakon. Festschrift Johannes Quasten*, II (Münster: Westfalen, 1970) 854.

[22] F. K. Ginzel, *Handbuch der mathematischen und technischen Chronologie*, I (Leipzig: 1906) 101. In both instances, of course, there are fractions of days as well.

If, by contrast, it was historical considerations that led to the identification of March 25 as 14 Nisan in the year of our Lord's death, the year of the consulship of the two Gemini,[23] that date for the crucifixion would nonetheless coincide with the traditional Roman date for the spring equinox. And if that date was taken to be also that of the Lord's conception, his birth nine months later would also coincide with the traditional Roman date for the winter solstice. It is unlikely that a Christian festival on that date would long resist relation to the prevailing cultural climate, and the preaching of Leo is concerned to distinguish the two.[24] Such "inculturation" is nonetheless different from choosing a relatively new pagan festival as determination of the date of the nativity, a festival that would soon mark the beginning of the Christian year, as Christmas does in the martyrs' list in the Chronograph of 354 (a list most commonly dated to 336 on analogy to the parallel list of bishops' *depositiones*).

One final ambiguity should be added: the March 25 date for the death of Christ was arrived at when and where the liturgical observance of Pascha was firmly keyed to the structure of the week rather than a fixed date, and it seems clear that the same day was identified as the date of the conception of Christ long before there was a liturgical festival of the Annunciation. Similar nonliturgical chronological determinations can be found in Eastern sources, predicated on the Montanist paschal date of April 6. We should not, then, assume that reflection on the date of the nativity had a liturgical observance in view from the outset. The effect of that consideration on the continuing dispute regarding the origin of the December 25 date, however, is probably neutral. Beyond that, there seems little reason to doubt that the appearance of the commemoration in the martyrs' list in the Chronograph of 354 indicates a liturgical observance. It would be difficult otherwise to account for its position as the beginning of the year.

[23] The paschal table carved into the right side of the chair of Hippolytus' statue in the Vatican Library lists (in the left-hand column) the dates on which the fourteenth day of the lunar cycle in March will fall in various years. The last in the list indicates March 25 as the date of the passion of Christ. This is confirmed in a work attributed to Tertullian, *Adversus Iudaeos* VIII.18, where the consulship of the Gemini is specified.

[24] *Sermo* XXVII, e.g.

The concern of Leo to protect the celebration of the nativity from contamination by the concerns of the old religion points to the pervasiveness of Romans' gratitude for the return of the light. Whether this manifested itself in a public pagan festival in Leo's day, however, is more doubtful. Still, another observance of pre-Christian Rome seems to have survived the withering of paganism to take on at some point a Christian dress. This was a procession and sacrifice to seek protection of the grain from the mold known as "wheat-rust." That agricultural disease was personalized as *Robigus*, or (in Ovid[25]) *Robigo*, less a distinct deity than a personified aspect of the rustic Mars, according to Mommsen.[26] It was Numa, the first king after Romulus, we are told, who instituted the festival of the god. While the historicity of that attribution is perhaps less than secure, it does show that Roman historians regarded the *Robigalia* as belonging to the very early foundations of Roman culture, and it does not seem to have been observed anywhere else. The festival fell on April 25, and began with a procession to the *lucus Robigi*, at the fifth milestone on the Via Claudia, where the *flamen Quirinalis*, minister of the Sabine Mars, sacrificed two victims, a ewe and a dog. The procession evidently followed the Via Flaminia as far as Ponte Milvio, that being the only route to the junction with Via Claudia.

While it is easy to understand how agricultural concerns might have kept this observance alive after the passing of paganism, J.-A. Hild observes that the pagan observance itself continued long after the grain fields had disappeared from the region.[27] In such a case, we can only suppose that it was the great antiquity ascribed to the *Robigalia* that secured the continuation of the observance, eventually under Christian auspices. At what point the *Robigalia* became *Litania maior* is unknown, and seems likely to remain so. What is clear is that the observance was firmly rooted in Roman liturgical tradition well before April 25 became also the Feast of St. Mark the Evangelist.

The first notice we have of the Christian observance comes from the time of Gregory the Great. The register of his letters includes

[25] *Fasti*, IV, 905ff.

[26] *C.I.L.*, I, 391.

[27] S.v. "Robigus, Robigalia," in Daremberg et Saglio, ed., *Dictionnaire des antiquités grecques et romains*, V, 874f.

his announcement of the procession at St. Mary Major, evidently read on the Sunday before the observance in 592. He calls the faithful to gather on the following Friday at San Lorenzo in Lucina for the procession to St. Peter's.[28] Further details are supplied by the Gregorian Sacramentary. After the gathering (with a prayer) at St. Lawrence in Lucina, the procession moved along Via Lata through Porta Flaminia and out of the city to St. Valentinus where there was a station. This, like the stations to follow, is provided with a prayer. Proceding out Via Flaminia, the procession moved to the second station at Ponte Milvio. Then, abandoning the old route out Via Claudia, the procession turned back toward the city along the opposite bank of the Tiber. A third station was made at a cross erected outside the walls. A final station was made in the atrium of St. Peter's, and the Mass followed in the basilica.[29] There can be no doubt that this function is in recognizable continuity with the old *Robigalia*, following as it does much of the same route for a procession on the same day. Neither Gregory's announcement nor the prayers preserved in the Sacramentary make any specific agricultural reference. The concern of the procession is rather to obtain deliverance from the many troubles that our offenses have incurred, *variis continuisque calamitatibus pro nostris culpis atque offensionibus affligamur*, as Gregory says. Given Hild's suggestion that the observance continued after its original agricultural concern ceased to be relevant, there is no clear reason to suppose that the Christian procession had an end very different from that of its pagan precursor.

It has been noted that there is no reason to suppose that this Christian disposition of an established and very ancient urban custom was an initiative of Gregory.[30] Nonetheless, it is not surprising that he would appear as one solicitous for its observance, having served as Prefect of Rome prior to his monastic profession. The absence of any reference to this day in the Old Gelasian may be significant, especially in the light of its appearance in the

[28] For the text, see M. Andrieu, *Les Ordines Romani du haut moyen âge*, III (Louvain, 1961) 239, n. 5.

[29] Jean Deshusses, ed., *Le Sacramentaire Grégorien*, Tome I. Spicilegium Friburgense 16 (Fribourg: Suisse, 1971) 211–213.

[30] Andrieu, *op. cit.*, 239, says, "Rien n'indique qu'elle fût alors d'institution récente."

Frankish Gelasian Sacramentaries of the eighth century. There the prayers of the Gregorian are provided, and a bit later in the century *Ordo* XXI adapted the observance, shorn of any reference to the topology of Rome, for the use of any bishop in his see city.[31] Given those later developments, the silences of Leo's preaching and the old Roman core of the Gelasian could well encourage one to doubt that the Christian expression of this urban observance immediately replaced the pagan *Robigalia*. Paganism, of course, showed considerable tenacity in Rome. Franz Cumont cites an eyewitness to the Isis processions in Rome as late as 394,[32] well after Gratian's highly symbolic removal of the statue of Victory from the Senate. Even so, it seems unlikely that dogs were sacrificed at the *lucus Robigi* in the days of Leo the Great. If it is also unlikely that Gregory the Great or one of his predecessors would institute *de novo* a pagan procession that had fallen into total desuetude, then we should probably imagine a continuation of the procession that was no longer identified with paganism, but perhaps not yet a formal liturgical function presided over by the bishop. It would be a mistake to conceive this as a "secular" hiatus, because we today are almost certain to overstate the meaning of that term. It is not so unlikely, however, that a civic function that could claim roots almost as ancient as the city itself could continue to enlist significant participation by the populace, even as the religious commitment of the populace shifted.

However the old custom came under Christian direction, the continuity of *Litania maior* with *Robigalia* was eventually reduced to little more than a common date. It was noted above that in the late eighth century *Ordo* XXI presented a form of the procession adapted to Gallican use and with no reference to Roman topography. Obviously, the similarity to the path followed by the *Robigalia* procession (before the turn back to St. Peter's) was specific to Rome. A somewhat diffuse note on the Roman observance in *Ordo* L (incorporated into the Romano-Germanic Pontifical of the tenth century) suggests that the old processional route out Via Flaminia to Ponte Milvio had been abandoned, and the pontiff set

---

[31] *Ibid.*, 247–249.
[32] Franz Cumont, *Oriental Religions in Roman Paganism* (New York: Dover, 1956) 85.

out on this day from the Lateran. In the Roman recastings of the Romano-Germanic Pontifical in the twelfth and thirteenth centuries there is no mention of *Litania Maior,* but the form that meets us in the *Ordinarium* of Innocent III[33] suggests the Frankish Ordo XXI much more than the old pagan procession. Starting from the Lateran, stations are made at San Clemente, Santa Maria Nova, San Marco, San Lorenzo in Damaso, Hadrian's bridge, St. Maria de virgariis, and into St. Peter's, where *Te Deum* and Mass are sung. If the final goal remains the same as in the Gregorian arrangement, both the starting point and the route are radically different, and, apart from the date, it would be difficult to find anything in the observance that suggests continuity with *Robigalia.* By that time, of course, the date marked also the feast of St. Mark. Nonetheless, it is clearly the litany that is the primary liturgical responsibility of the pope. According to the Paris ms. of the *ordinarium,*[34] it is only after he has heard the Mass of the feast celebrated by a bishop or cardinal presbyter at the Lateran that the pontiff assumes his Lenten vestments for the procession to follow, and it is he, the pope, who celebrates the Mass that concludes the litany at St. Peter's. However diminished the sense of continuity with its pagan predecessor, *Litania Maior* remained in the thirteenth century a major observance of the Christian community of a Rome deeply cognizant of its own distinctive traditions.

From all these considerations, what can we conclude about the relationship between Roman culture and Roman liturgy? In the first instance, the supposed foundation of the old Roman seasonal fasts on three pre-Christian *Feriae conceptivae,* we must, in some embarrassment, admit that liturgical historians seem to have grasped for an explanation out of a hunger that could not find the patience requisite for inquiry into matters where a body of disciplined scholarship already exists. This, however, is not to say that the seasonal fasts at Rome did not reflect their culture. While hardly unique to Rome, sensitivity to the turning of the seasons is characteristic of all cultures in temperate zones. That the Roman Church observed this division of the year liturgically is surely a re-

[33] Stephen J.P. van Dijk and Joan Hazelden Walker, "The Ordinal of the Papal Court from Innocent III to Boniface VIII and Related Documents," Spicilegium Friburgense 22 (Fribourg: 1975) 386–393.

[34] Paris, BN, lat. 4162A.

sponse to surrounding culture, even if there is no reason why
other churches in temperate zones might not have done the same.
These seasonal observances manifest the sensitivity of local liturgy
to local culture, even if they are not derived from identifiable
pagan observances of the same sort. And the same is true, at the
very least, of the celebration of the nativity of the Lord on December 25, a time in which the cultural environment was suffused
with gratitude for the lengthening hours of daylight. The oldest of
the Christmas Masses at Rome, that *in die*, seems to have had
from its earliest documentary evidences a gospel reading, the
prologue of John, that declares, "the light shines in the darkness,
and the darkness has not overcome it." The continuing dispute
over whether that date was assigned to the nativity on the basis of
an existing Roman festival or was arrived at on the basis of a
historical inquiry into the date of the passion, a date that came to
be taken also as that of the Annunciation to Mary, is not a dispute
over whether the early Roman Church was sensitive and respon-
sive to its cultural context. It was, even if we should find one of
these days that the nativity was first identified with December 25
elsewhere than at Rome. That same sense of cultural involvement
would inform the clearest instance of Roman liturgical continuation of pre-Christian urban tradition. We perhaps cannot know
how closely that rogation procession was still identified with its
pagan precursor when the bishops of Rome began to preside over
it. What seems more clear is that it was identified with the cultural life of Rome, and as historical developments assigned to the
bishop of the city a growing responsibility for its security and
integrity, that Roman tradition became liturgical.

The inculturation of the liturgy is an inescapable function of
such simple responsibility. It does not ask of us that we invent
clever ritual puns on the life patterns of those to whom we are to
bring the gospel. It asks only that we be ever mindful that we are
sent to preach the gospel to all, whoever and wherever they may
be, because Christ is all, in all, and for all. The early Church in
Rome was open to Roman culture, not as a ploy to lure the reluc-
tant to baptism, but simply because those who came to faith and
those who received them were Romans. Already in the second
century, Justin Martyr, having castigated "the myths which the
poets have made" as the deceptions of wicked demons, explains

to Antoninus Pius how those just baptized join in common prayer, "for ourselves and for the baptized person, and for all others in every place, that we may be counted worthy, now that we have learned the truth, by our works also to be found good citizens. . . ."[35]

---

[35] *First Apology, 65.*

Robert F. Taft, s.j.

3. Understanding the Byzantine Anaphoral Oblation

Antiochene-type anaphoras, of which the Byzantine anaphoras of Chrysostom (CHR)[1] and Basil (BAS) are typical examples, have a structure in the postsanctus comprising, in the following order:

1. the narrative of salvation, including
2. the words of institution and,
3. in some anaphoras though not in CHR, the command to repeat ("Do this in memory of me") reported in 1 Corinthians 11:24, Luke 22:19

---

[1] Abbreviations:

BAS = The Liturgy of St. Basil (Byzantine redaction unless otherwise specified).

CHR = The Byzantine Liturgy of St. John Chrysostom.

CPG = *Clavis Patrum Graecorum* I–V, ed. M. Geerard, F. Glorie (Corpus Christianorum, Turnhout: 1983–1987).

CSEL = Corpus Scriptorum Ecclesiasticorum Latinorum.

Hanssens = J.-M. Hanssens, *Institutiones* = Idem, *Institutiones liturgicae de ritibus orientalibus* II–III (Rome: 1930, 1932).

LEW = F. E. Brightman, *Liturgies Eastern and Western* (Oxford: 1896).

PE = A. Hänggi, I. Pahl, *Prex Eucharistica* (Spicilegium Friburgense 12, Fribourg: 1968).

PTS = Patristische Texte und Studien.

SC = Sources chrétiennes.

SC 320, 329, 336 = *Les Constitutions apostoliques*, ed. M. Metzger, tome 1: livres I–II (SC 320, Paris: 1985); tome 2: livres III–VI (SC 329, Paris: 1986); tome 3: livres V–VIII (SC 336, Paris: 1987).

Stevenson, *Eucharist* = K. Stevenson, *Eucharist and Offering* (New York: 1986).

4. the anamnesis
5. the oblation
6. the epiclesis
7. the commemorations/intercessions.

In this paper I shall discuss some problems that arise in interpreting the oblation [5], especially in the light of the preceding institution narrative [2] and the following consecratory Spirit epiclesis [6]. However, the history of the later theological dispute between Greeks and Latins concerning the "form" and "moment" of Eucharistic consecration is beyond the scope of this study:[2] what interests us here is the meaning of the CHR/BAS texts, regardless of whose theology it may confirm or challenge.

I. THE BYZANTINE OBLATION

The texts of CHR/BAS—with the oblation in question [5] italicized[3]—read as follows:[4]

CHR	BAS
3. [missing]	Do this in memory of me. For as often as you eat this bread and drink this cup, you proclaim my death, you confess my resurrection.
4. Remembering, therefore, this saving command and all that was done for our salvation: the cross, the tomb, the third-day resurrection, the ascension and sitting at the right hand, the	Therefore we too, O Master, remembering his saving passion, the life-giving cross, the three-day burial, the resurrection from the dead, the ascension into heaven, the sitting at

---

[2] It has already been handled magisterially and irenically in J. H. McKenna, *Eucharist and Holy Spirit. The Eucharistic Epiclesis in 20th Century Theology* (Alcuin Club Collections No. 57, Great Wakering, Essex: 1975).

[3] As to why the finale of the priest's *ekphonesis*, κατὰ πάντα καὶ διὰ πάντα, is translated as it is ("always and in every way") instead of the more customary personalized version, "in all and for all," see A. Raes, "*KATA ΠΑΝΤΑ ΚΑΙ ΔΙΑ ΠΑΝΤΑ*. En tout et pour tout," *Oriens Christianus* 48 (1964) 216–220.

[4] CHR: LEW 385–386 = PE 226–228; BAS: LEW 405–468 = PE 234–238. I omit the diaconal "Amens" as irrelevant for our purposes.

CHR

second and glorious coming again,

5. *offering you your own from what is yours,*

always and in every way

[People:] we hymn you, we praise you, we thank you, O Lord, and we pray you, O our God!

6. *Again we offer you this reasonable and unbloody worship, (τὴν λογικὴν ταύτην καὶ ἀναίμακτον λατρείαν)* and we invoke and pray and beseech you, send down your Holy Spirit upon us, and upon these offered gifts, and make *this bread* the precious body of your Christ, and *that which is in this chalice* the precious blood of your Christ, changing them by your Holy Spirit, so that for those who receive [them] they might be for sobriety of soul, for forgiveness of sins, for communion in your Holy Spirit, for fullness of the kingdom, for filial confidence before you, not unto judgement or damnation.

BAS

your right hand, God and Father, and his glorious and awesome second coming,

offering you your own from what is yours,

always and in every way

[People:] we hymn you, we praise you, we thank you, O Lord, and we pray you, O our God!

Wherefore, all-holy Master, we too, your sinful and unworthy servants, deemed worthy to serve at your holy altar . . . because of your mercies and compassions which you have so abundantly showered upon us, dare to approach your holy altar and, offering you the *figures (τὰ ἀντίτυπα)* of the holy body and blood of your Christ, we pray you and beseech you, O holy of holies, that, by the favor of your goodness, your Holy Spirit may come upon us, and upon these offered gifts, and bless them, and hallow them, and *show (ἀναδεῖξαι)* this *bread* [to be] indeed the precious body of our Lord and God and Savior Jesus Christ, and this *cup* [to be] indeed the precious blood of our Lord and God and Savior Jesus Christ shed for the life of the world, so that all of us who partake of this one *bread and chalice* may be united with one another in the communion of the one Holy Spirit, and that the partaking of the holy body and blood of your Christ may be for none of us unto judgement or condemnation, but that we might find mercy and grace together with all the saints [there follows the commemoration of the saints and of the dead].

7.1 *Again we offer you this reasonable worship (τὴν λογικὴν ταύτην λατρείαν) for our forefathers in the faith who have gone to their rest . . . [there follows the commemoration of the saints and of the dead].*

Again we pray you, remember, Lord . . . [the intercessions in several sections, each beginning with the "Remember, Lord . . ." incipit].

7.2 Again we beseech you, be mindful, Lord, of the whole Orthodox episcopate . . .

7.3 *Again we offer you this reasonable worship (τὴν λογικὴν ταύτην λατρείαν) for the whole world . . .*

Just what does this oblation [5] offer? And is it the same oblation or a different one than the thrice-repeated CHR epiclesis/intercession incipit [6–7.1/3], which has no parallel in BAS?

II. PRAENOTANDA

One must be extremely cautious in asking ancient texts to furnish univocal answers to such questions. As both Gregory Dix and Kenneth Stevenson have pointed out, the sequence of ideas connecting anaphoral oblationary expressions with the rest of the Eucharistic action vary greatly.[5] In all Eucharists, offerings of

---

[5] G. Dix, *The Shape of the Liturgy* (London: 1945) 225–230. K. Stevenson, " 'Anaphoral Offering': Some Observations on Eastern Eucharistic Prayers," *Ephemerides Liturgicae* 94 (1980) 209–228, esp. 227–228.

bread and wine are put on the altar, prayer is said over them, and they are consumed. Regarding that prayer over them, the anaphora, the basic hermeneutic principle has been enunciated by Dix: "the 'second half' of the prayer"—i.e., following the institution narrative—"looks back to the offertory and expresses in words the meaning of that. It looks forward to Communion and prays for the effects of that."[6] Different church traditions do this in greatly different ways. One of those differences is in just where the expressions of "offering" occur: accompanying the ritual act of depositing the gifts on the altar—a clear sign of "offering" in any nontendentious view of the Eucharist; and/or at one or several points of the oblation prayer ("anaphora," after all, means "offering") that explains its meaning.

Stevenson has recently reviewed again the development of this part of the Eucharistic anaphora, and I am in basic agreement with his conclusions. Until the Protestant Reformation, no Christian doubted that the Eucharist was a sacrifice. But *how* was it a sacrifice? Who offers what to whom? These are questions that have not always received the same answer. Jesus offered himself on the cross. The true sacrifice of Christians is their offering of self in imitation of that self-giving. The Eucharist somehow represents both these offerings. But how the self-offering of Christians is related to that of Christ, and how they join and are expressed sacramentally in the Eucharist, are problems that have received various solutions—or better, are widely accepted realities that have reached diverse expression in more than one "model" of the Eucharistic service. For "sacrifice" is a metaphor, and metaphors do not originate in, nor are they designed for, the kind of microscopic laboratory analysis, the self-conscious reflection, which theological controversy provokes.

Methodologically, then, this must be our first caveat: unless provoked into being otherwise, liturgical language is symbolic, typological, metaphorical, more redolent of Church and bible than of school and thesis, more patristic than scholastic, more evocative than probative. It is what the theologians call *"theologia prima,"* first level theology, the faith expressed in the life of the Church antecedent to speculative questioning of its implications, prior to

---

[6] *Shape* 226-227. Cf. Stevenson, "Anaphoral Offering," *loc. cit.*

its systematization in dogmatic propositions resulting from *"theologia secunda,"* systematic reflection on the lived mystery in the Church. *Theologia prima* is to *theologia secunda,* what cooking and eating are to a history of cuisine.

In the heat of dogmatic controversy, teaching will acquire theological refinements, but such refinements cannot be read back into texts composed before the problems arose which led to those precisions in the first place. Thus, to pounce upon expressions describing the offered gifts that occur before or after some later-determined or supposed "moment of consecration," and then to exploit these expressions as arguments for or against the identification of that moment, is an anachronistic procedure devoid of any legitimacy except in the case of texts written with that problem in mind. As Stevenson has pointed out, when unaffected by controversy liturgies evolve organically, not self-consciously. In the process of organic development, theological "emphases are sharpened as the tradition develops." Furthermore, the understanding of a text can change even when its language—and "liturgical language is inherently conservative"—remains the same.[7]

III. OBLATION IN THE EUCHARIST

With these caveats in mind, let us seek to discover just what the Church is said to be offering the Father in the Eucharist. Any sacrifice can be understood in three ways:

1. the sacrificial rite itself
2. the sacrificial victim offered in that rite
3. the inner oblation of the offerer which 1–2 are meant to represent.[8]

Number 3 is always included implicitly, and is undoubtedly so in our case too. But the text itself gives no explicit clue for choosing between 1–2—i.e., for affirming that what we offer is not simply the "service *(λειτουργία)*" in general, for which God is thanked in the presanctus of CHR, but rather the gifts or oblation offered in that service. And if the latter, then which offerings, bread and wine or body and blood? Our offering, or Jesus' offering made ours through the rite?

---

[7] Stevenson, *Eucharist* 1–3.
[8] Stevenson, *Eucharist* 3–4.

Throughout its history the anaphora "expands and develops, contracts and abbreviates, reforms and deletes, renews and reintroduces certain themes and ideas" concerning offering, sacrifice, gift, in three aspects: story, gift, response.[9] The story is the narration of the economy of salvation in Jesus, the basis for the whole business. Gift refers to how the prayers speak of the bread and wine. The response describes what the Eucharist is supposed to do to/for its participants—or, to put it another way, what we, the Church, are supposed to be and do in response to the story the Eucharist tells.

And what the texts show is that oblationary expressions can occur repeatedly, scattered throughout the anaphora, as in CHR/BAS (texts above, CHR nn. 5, 6, 7.1, 7.3; BAS nn. 5, 6) or Maronite *Sharar*.[10] Let us see these oblationary expressions at work in some early sources.

IV. OBLATION IN SOME EARLY ANAPHORAS AND COMMENTATORS

1. *The* Apostolic Tradition *(ca. 215)*

The way this story-response dynamic flows, and, within it, how the gifts are spoken of, is relatively consistent in anaphoras of the Antiochene type, in spite of later developments. The earliest such text, the *Apostolic Tradition* 4, reads as follows:

1. "We render thanks to you, O God, through your beloved child Jesus Christ, whom in the last times you sent to us as a savior and redeemer and angel of your will; who is your inseparable Word, through whom you made all things, and in whom you were well pleased. 2. You sent him from heaven into a virgin's womb; and conceived in the womb, he was made flesh and was manifested as your Son, being born of the Holy Spirit and the Virgin. Fulfilling your will and gaining for you a holy people, he stretched out his hands when he should suffer, that he might release from suffering those who have believed in you.

[9] Stevenson, *Eucharist* 4.

[10] This ancient anaphora has multiple oblations in the preanaphora, in the postsanctus, after the institution narrative, and at the beginning of the intercessions: J.-M. Sauget (ed.), *Anaphorae Syriacae* (Rome: 1973) II.3:301.4, 303.12, 19–20, 305.10.

3. "And when he was betrayed to voluntary suffering that he might destroy death, and break the bonds of the devil, and tread down hell, and shine upon the righteous, and fix a term, and manifest the resurrection, 4. he took bread and gave thanks to you, saying, 'Take, eat; this is my body, which shall be broken for you.' Likewise also the cup, saying, 'This is my blood, which is shed for you; 5. when you do this, you make my remembrance.'

6. "Remembering therefore his death and resurrection, 7. we offer to you the bread and the cup, giving you thanks because you have held us worthy to stand before you and minister to you.

8. "And we ask that you would send your Holy Spirit upon the offering of your holy Church; 9. that, gathering her into one, you would grant to all who receive the holy things (to receive) for the fullness of the Holy Spirit for the strengthening of faith in truth; 10. that we may praise and glorify you through your child Jesus Christ, through whom be glory and honor to you, with the Holy Spirit, in your holy Church, both now and to the ages of ages. Amen."[11]

The structure is clear:

1. We thank God for salvation in Christ Jesus (1), recounting the *story* which motivates our thanks (2-4).

2. Recalling this story (6), we offer *gifts* of bread and wine (7) as Jesus did and as we believe he wished us to do in memory of him (5).

3. And we ask that the Spirit be sent to sanctify this *oblation of the Church* (8).

4. So that it may be for us unto salvation, forgiveness, unity, holiness of life, and eschatological fulfillment: *response* (9).

Stevenson understands "we offer" (7) as referring to the gifts of bread and wine, and the "oblation of the Church" (8) to comprise the entire Eucharist as celebration, Eucharistic Communion, eccle-

---

[11] Trans. R.C.D. Jasper and G. J. Cuming, *Prayers of the Eucharist: Early and Reformed*. Texts translated and edited with commentary (3rd ed. New York: 1987) 35 (numbers added).

sial communion in the life of faith it symbolizes.[12] The later, dependent text of the *Testamentum Domini* I, 23, furnishes a similar couplet: in the anamnesis it has the same "we offer you the bread and cup." Then, after thanking God for making us worthy to minister unto him, resumes: "We offer you this thanksgiving (qūbaltāybūtā)."[13] But I am skeptical of seeing such nuances or distinctions in these ancient texts.

2. *Theodore of Mospuestia (c. 388–392)*

The ambiguities of just where to locate the oblation, and what it means, in the description of the Eucharist in Theodore of Mopsuestia, *Hom.* 15–16, seem truer to the ancient, less precise ways of eucharistic discourse. Theodore speaks of the bread and wine on the altar as the "oblation (qūrbānā),"[14] while in the same breath he affirms unequivocally that it is only in the anaphora that the bishop begins the "offering of the oblation," which Theodore has just defined as meaning "to immolate the oblation,"[15] the memorial of the sacrifice already accomplished on the cross. Here in the liturgy we accomplish its memorial.[16] All this, mind you, occurs in Theodore's description of the anaphora preceding the epiclesis.[17] And if he makes no mention of the oblation there, it is doubtless because the whole service is "offering," "anaphora," the very essence of our "service (liturgy)." I believe it is as erroneously anachronistic to seek the "moment" of the oblation as it is to seek the "moment" of consecration.

3. *The Papyrus Strasbourg 254 (Fourth–Fifth Century)*

Other ancient anaphoras are equally imprecise. The fourth-fifth century papyrus *Strasbourg* Gr. 254 has: ". . . giving thanks to you, we offer the spiritual sacrifice, this unbloody service."[18]

---

[12] Stevenson, *Eucharist* 21.

[13] *Testamentum Domini nostri Jesu Christi*, ed. I. E. Rahmani (Mainz: 1899) 42–43 = PE 221.

[14] *Hom.* 15, 44, ed. R. Tonneau & R. Devreesse, *Les homélies catéchétiques de Théodore de Mopsueste* (Studi e Testi 145, Vatican: 1949) 528–529.

[15] *Hom* 15, 44 & *Hom.* 16, intro. and 1–2, 5, ibid. 528–531, 533–537, 540–541.

[16] *Hom.* 16, 9–10, ibid. 546–551.

[17] *Hom.* 16, 12, ibid. 552–553.

[18] PE 116.

40

4. The Liturgy of Addai and Mari

The Anaphora of Addai and Mari, the *Urform* of which probably dates to the beginning of the third century,[19] speaks more boldly: "the commemoration of the body and and blood of thy Christ, which we offer to thee upon the pure and holy altar, as thou hast taught us."[20] But even this, like the other texts adduced above, tells us nothing more than the obvious: we offer bread and wine, we offer the liturgy, without much theological precision beyond such inclusive assertions. Do they mean that we offer Jesus' sacrifice, his body and blood? That would be an inference, one to be found, indeed, as early as Cyprian (d. c. 258).[21] But it would not be an exegesis of the texts.

---

[19] A. Gelston, *The Eucharistic Prayer of Addai and Mari* (Oxford: 1992) 28.

[20] Ibid., 51–52, segment E nn. 39–40; W. F. Macomber, "The Oldest Known Text of the Anaphora of the Apostles Addai and Mari," *Orientalia Christiana Periodica* 32 (1966) 335–371, here 364; cf. id., "The Ancient Form of the Anaphora of the Apostles," in N. G. Garsoïan, T. F. Mathews, R. W. Thomson (eds.), *East of Byzantium: Syria and Armenia in the Formative Period* (Washington: 1982) 73–88, here 77, 86.

[21] In *Ep. 63*, 14, Cyprian says:

"For if Jesus Christ our Lord and God is himself the high priest of God the Father, and first offered himself as a sacrifice to the Father and ordered that this be done in remembrance of him, then of course that priest truly acts in the place of Christ who imitates what Christ did and offers now, in the Church, the true and complete sacrifice to the Father, if he so begins to offer in accord with what he sees that Christ himself offered." CSEL 3.2:713.

R.P.C. Hanson, *Eucharistic Offering in the Early Church* (Grove Liturgical Study 19, Bramcote Notts: 1979) 19, has argued that Cyprian opens the way to later, unambiguous statements that in the Eucharist the Church offers Christ to the Father. But since what Christ offered was his own body and blood in the bread and wine, that, for Cyprian, is what the Church offers too:

"For who is more a priest of the high God than our Lord Jesus Christ, who offered a sacrifice to God the Father, and offered this same thing that Melchisedek offered, that is, bread and wine, in other words his own body and blood." *Ep. 63*, 3, CSEL 3.2:703.

For my part, I do not really see how what Cyprian affirms is not contained implicitly in what Origen (see note 54 below) and others say. Nor do I see how a witness as ancient as Cyprian can be viewed as a problem to be accepted or rejected in the light of our theology, rather than vice-versa. On the point in question see J. D. Laurance, *'Priest' as Type of Christ. The Leader of the Eucharist in Salvation History according to Cyprian of Carthage* (American University Studies, Series 7, vol. 5, New York: 1984); id., "Le président de

5. Early Sahidic Basil (Seventh Century)

And at least one text would seem to exclude that interpretation explicitly. In the earliest witness to the Liturgy of St. Basil, the *Louvain Fragment* of the Sahidic redaction of Egyptian BAS in four parchment folia from the first half of the seventh century,[22] the anamnesis places the offering in the past: *"Nos autem memores . . . proposuimus [προεθήκαμεν] tibi et coram te tua de tuis donis, quae sunt hunc panem et calicem.''*[23] Raes called this *"le fameux aoriste . . . προεθήκαμεν crux interpretum,''*[24] and judged it (rightly) to be the intrusion of an Egyptianism. This is clear from parallel expressions in the Coptic Anaphora of St. Cyril,[25] and Sarapion 13:12–14, where προσηνέγκαμεν is repeated five times.[26] Do these Egyptian texts wish to insist that the offering is of bread and wine, and that it has been accomplished earlier? Lietzmann, who as usual makes more of this than the freight will bear, associates this offering with the deposition of the gifts on the altar.[27]

But here, too, I would tread lightly. It is hardly sustainable that the Egyptian aorist wishes to say that the bread and wine placed on the altar constitute the entire Eucharistic oblation, and that it is over and done with before the anaphora has even begun!

importance of the anaphora

6. Conclusion

From these texts, one conclusion seems ineluctable: in the oblationary expression following the institution and anamnesis we offer the memorial of Jesus' sacrifice, and, integral to this memorial, we offer bread and wine which are sanctified by the

l'eucharistie selon Cyprien de Carthage: un nouvel examen,'' *La Maison-Dieu* 154 (1983) 151–165.

[22] On the ms and dating, see J. Doresse, E. Lanne, *Un témoin archaïque de la liturgie copte de S. Basile* (Bibliothèque du Muséon 47, Louvain: 1960) 1–5.

[23] Ibid., 18; the Greek is from the retroversion, 21.

[24] A. Raes, ''Un nouveau document de la Liturgie de S. Basile,'' *Orientalia Christiana Periodica* 26 (1960) 403–404.

[25] Hanssens III, 349 no. 1195 and LEW 178:15 = PE 138.3.

[26] F. X. Funk, *Didascalia et Constitutiones apostolorum*, 2 vols. (Paderborn: 1905) II, 174 = PE 130 lines 7–8, 9, 14, 19–20, 23. Cf. Hanssens III, 365 nos. 1211, 1213; B. Capelle, ''L'anaphore de Sérapion,'' *Le Muséon* 59 (1946) 425–443, esp. 429–435.

[27] H. Lietzmann, *Mass and Lord's Supper*, with intro. and further inquiry by R. D. Richardson (Leiden: 1979) 158–160. See also Stevenson, ''Anaphoral Offering'' (note 5 above) 223–226.

power of the Holy Spirit and returned to us as our spiritual food and drink—God's gift to us, not ours to him.

As in Dix's adage, the prayer looks backwards and forwards, and its beginning and end, the deposition of the gifts on the altar and the Communion, are clear. But the ordering of the elements in between is not always the same, and how to interpret these elements is by no means clear.

V. OBLATION IN IRENAEUS OF LYONS (c. 185)

This theology is substantiated by Irenaeus, the first church Father to discuss the matter at any length, in his *Adversus haereses* IV, 17–18:

IV, 17:5. "Again, giving directions to his disciples to offer to God the first-fruits of his own created things—not as if he stood in need of them, but that they might be themselves neither unfruitful nor ungrateful—he took that created thing, bread, and gave thanks, and said, 'This is my body.' And the cup likewise, which is part of that creation to which we belong, he confessed to be his blood, and taught the new oblation of the new covenant; which the Church, receiving from the apostles, offers to God throughout the whole world, to him who gives us as the means of subsistence the first-fruits of his own gifts in the New Testament, concerning which Malachi . . . thus spoke beforehand: 'I have no pleasure in you, says the Lord almighty, and I will not accept sacrifice at your hands. For from the rising of the sun unto its setting, my name is glorified among the gentiles, and in every place incense is offered to my name, and a pure sacrifice. . . .' [Mal 1:10-11], indicating in the plainest manner, by these words, that the former people shall indeed cease to make offerings to God, but that in every place, sacrifice shall be offered to him, and that a pure one; and his name is glorified among the gentiles. . . . 6 . . . Since, therefore, the name of the Son belongs to the Father, and since in the omnipotent God the Church makes offerings through Jesus Christ, he says well on both these grounds, 'And in every place incense is offered to my name, and a pure sacrifice.' Now John, in the Apocalypse, declares that 'incense' is 'the prayers of the saints' [Rev 5:8].

IV, 18:1. "The oblation of the Church, therefore, which the Lord gave instructions to be offered throughout all the world, is ac-

43

counted with God a pure sacrifice, and is acceptable to him; not that he stands in need of a sacrifice from us, but that he who offers is himself glorified in what he offers, if his gift be accepted. . . . We are bound, therefore, to offer God the first-fruits of his creation . . . so that man, being accounted as grateful by those things in which he has shown his gratitude, may receive that honor which flows from him [God]. 2. So the genus 'oblations' has not been set aside. For there were oblations there [among the Jews] as well as here [among Christians]; sacrifices there were among the [chosen] people, sacrifices there are, too, in the Church: only the species has been changed, inasmuch as the offering is now made, not by slaves, but by freemen. . . . 3. For at the beginning, God respected the gifts of Abel because he offered with single-mindedness and righteousness. But he had no regard for the offering of Cain, because his heart was divided with envy and malice, which he cherished against his brother, as God says reproving his hidden [thoughts], 'Though you offer rightly, still, if you do not divide rightly, have you not sinned? Be at rest' [LXX Gen 4:7], for God is not appeased by sacrifice. For if anyone shall endeavor to offer a sacrifice merely in outward appearance, though properly, in due order, as is laid down; while in his soul he does not give to his neighbor that fellowship with him which is right and proper, nor is under the fear of God; he who thus cherishes secret sin does not deceive God by that sacrifice which is offered correctly as to outward appearance, nor will such an oblation profit him anything, but only the giving up of that evil which has been conceived within him, so that sin may not the more, by means of the hypocritical action, make him the destroyer of himself. . . . Sacrifices, therefore, do not profit a man, for God stands in no need of sacrifice; but it is the conscience of the offerer that sanctifies the sacrifice when it is pure, and thus moves God to accept [the offering] as from a friend. . . .

Conscience as sanctifying

4. "Inasmuch, then, as the Church offers with single-mindedness, her gift is justly reckoned a pure sacrifice with God. . . . For it behoves us to make an oblation to God, and in all things to be found grateful to God our maker, in a pure mind, and in faith without hypocrisy, in well-grounded hope, in fervent love, offering the first-fruits of his own created things. And the Church

44

alone offers this pure oblation to the creator, offering him, with thanksgiving, [things] of his creation. But the Jews do not offer thus: . . . for they have not received the Word, through whom it is offered to God. . . .

5. . . . "But our opinion is in accordance with the eucharist, and the eucharist in turn establishes our opinion. For we offer to him his own, announcing consistently the fellowship and union of the flesh and Spirit. For as the bread, which is produced from the earth, when it receives the invocation of God, is no longer common bread, but the eucharist, consisting of two realities, earthly and heavenly; so also our bodies, when they receive the eucharist, are no longer corruptible, having the hope of the resurrection to eternity.

6. "Now we make offering to him not as though he stood in need of it, but rendering thanks for his gift, and thus sanctifying what has been created. For even as God does not need our possessions, so do we need to offer something to God. . . . For God, who stands in need of nothing, takes our good works to himself for this purpose, that he may grant us a recompense of his own good things. . . ."[28]

These two aspects of the Eucharist, the sacramental offering as act of worship and the sanctification of this offering through its acceptance by God, are *both* the image and repetition of what Jesus himself did, *both* part of his sacramentalization of his self-offering at the Last Supper and in the liturgy, and not to be explained as if the *Church* offers bread and wine, whereas *Jesus* offers his body and blood; or as if the Church *first* offers bread and wine, and *then* offers the Eucharist. The whole business is part of one and the same movement. What the Church offers is what the New Testament has Jesus order us to offer: the memorial of his own self-offering. *That* is the sacrifice of the Church. What none of the earliest liturgical texts of this "shape" of the liturgy

[28] Irenée de Lyon, *Contre les hérésies*, Livre IV, tomes 1–2, eds., A. Rousseau avec B. Hemmerdinger, L. Doutreleau, Ch. Mercier (SC 100, Paris: 1965) 590–612 = *Sancti Irenaei episcopi Lugdunensis Libros quinque adversus Haereses*, ed. W. W. Harvey, 2 vols. (Cambridge: 1857) II, 197–210; trans. adapted from *The Ante-Nicene Fathers*, eds., A. Roberts and J. Donaldson (Grand Rapids: 1969–) V.1:430–33.

states explicitly, however, is that the Church offers in the Eucharist the sacrifice of Christ, or his body and blood, even if such affirmations are found as early as Cyprian (d. c. 258),[29] and later theological reflection will justify such claims by affirming the identity, sacramentally, of that sacrifice with its memorial, not two sacrifices but one, differing in mode but not in number.[30]

De Jong has analyzed this Irenaean theology in several stages, which I resume here in de Jong's own theses:[31]

1. Bread and wine are the Church's offerings, which render visible its interior spirit of sacrifice (*Adv. haer.* IV, 17:5).

2. There is no offering of the Church apart from the offering of Christ. He is the head of the Church, and makes the Church's offering, the sign of its self-giving, his offering to the Father by making it his body and blood, and by offering it to the Father with and for the Church (IV, 17:6; 18:5).

3. The offering of Christ is his earthly humanity united to ours, and as such it is able to include in itself the whole of creation and of redeemed humanity (III, 18:2).

4. The sacramental offering as cultic action *(Kultakt)* in the offering of bread and wine becomes sanctification *(Heiligungsakt)* inasmuch as the earthly offerings, which the whole Christ, head and members, offers to the Father, are elevated through God's word to become the gifts of his Son, his body and blood, and are returned to us in communion for our heavenly nourishment (IV, 17:6–18:1).

5. The epiclesis is for Irenaeus the sacramental proclamation, and hence the cause of this reality (IV 18:5; cf. V, 2:3), though we cannot here press the sense of 'epiclesis' to fit our modern meaning, and would do better to interpret it simply as what is

---

[29] See note 21 above.

[30] See the good summary of the Greek patristic tradition on this point in A. Gerken, *Theologie der Eucharistie* (Munich: 1973) 70ff, contrasted with the more problematic Western medieval Eucharistic theology (97ff, 157ff).

[31] J. P. de Jong, "Der ursprüngliche Sinn von Epiklese und Mischungsritus nach der Eucharistielehre des hl. Irenäus," *Archiv für Liturgiewissenschaft* 9.1 (1965) 28–47, esp. 31–40.

said over the gifts in order to express to the congregation the meaning of the rite.

VI. INTERPRETING THE BYZANTINE OBLATION

I believe that the Byzantine anaphoras CHR and BAS continue this primitive Eucharistic theology, especially if we prescind from the later interpolations into the oblation, and the later theological precisions added to make the epiclesis explicitly consecratory. By that I do not mean to imply that these developments in any way contradict the earlier theology. But they do explicitate it in a way that is simply not expressed earlier.

To return, then, to our original question: what is the Church offering the Father in the expressions, "offering you your own from what is yours (τὰ σὰ ἐκ τῶν σῶν σοι προσφέροντες = [5] of CHR/BAS), the thrice repeated "again we offer [you] (ἔτι προσφέρομέν [σοι])" of CHR [6, 7.1,3], and, in BAS [6], "offering you [the Father] the figures (ἀντίτυπα) of the body and blood of your Christ"? The texts are admittedly "vague and obscure," as Hanssens observed,[32] but a "close reading" of them within the context of the theology of the fourth century, when they were doubtless composed, may shed some light.

1. The Common Oblation Ekphonesis

In [5], the oblation *ekphonesis* common to CHR/BAS, we offer God his own gifts to us. But since that, unless specified further, encompasses the whole of creation, such an affirmation hardly advances the argument. Considered in the context of the anaphora, however, its meaning is clear. In Antiochene-type anaphoras, the oblation flows logically from the institution narrative and command to repeat: having been ordered to offer in remembrance of Jesus' passover, recalling it we offer. *The Apostolic Constitutions* VIII, 12:38 makes it explicit: "We offer you, king and God, according to his command (διάταξιν)."[33] What we are offering, then, is what we were commanded to offer: the Eucharist. That does not, however, of itself, imply anything concerning the ontological state of the gifts of bread and wine at that moment, questions that no

[32] Hanssens III, 451 no. 1320.
[33] SC 336:198.

one was trying to answer via the interpolation into the anaphora of the oblationary exclamation.[34]

2. The Repeated Oblationary Incipit in CHR

The "spiritual and bloodless worship" we offer in the immediately following segment of CHR [6], is an obvious enough reference to the Eucharist, although the exact sense of it is not clear. And what of the repetition of the incipit in [7.1,3]? At least one can say that its repetition before and after the consecratory Spirit epiclesis excludes any possibility of interpreting it, in function of that epiclesis, as offering something different from the common oblation ekphonesis [5].

3. The Offering of "Antitypes" in BAS

The BAS epiclesis gives "the figures (ἀντίτυπα) of the body and blood of your Christ" [6] as direct object of the offering preceding the epicletic blessing of the gifts. What does BAS wish to imply by calling the bread and cup "figures" or "antitypes" of Jesus' Eucharistic body and blood after the institution narrative but before the invocation of the Spirit to hallow the gifts?[35] Later Orthodox teaching has attempted to exploit this as proof that the gifts are not yet consecrated at this point of the liturgy, between the words of institution and the epicletic blessing.[36] But the argument is anachronistic and baseless. "Antitype" can mean the earthly form

---

[34] I discuss why I believe it to be an interpolation in: R. Taft, "The Oblation and Hymn of the Chrysostom Anaphora. Its Text and Antecedents," *Bolletino della Badia Greca di Grottaferrata*, n.s. 46 (1992) 319–345; and "Structural Problems in the Syriac Anaphora of the Twelve Apostles (I)," at press in *ARAM Periodical* (Oxford), special number in honor of Prof. Sebastian Brock.

[35] A weaker term, "gifts" (δῶρα), is used instead of "antitypes" at this point in Egyptian BAS and Sahidic UrBAS: Doresse-Lanne 21; PE 236, 352. But the term "gifts," especially when modified by the epithet "holy" (τὰ ἅγια δῶρα), can also refer to the consecrated species, as in LEW 338.13, 344.21. John Chrysostom's Constantinopolitan (398–404) sermon *In Heb hom.* 17, 3, PG 63:131 (= CPG 4440) uses "antitypes" only for the Jewish sacrifices. They are only types, he says, and have not the force (ἰσχύν) of Christ's offering (PG 63:131).

[36] See, for instance, the interpretation of BAS in John Damascene (ca. 675–753/4), *Expositio fidei* 86:163–166: "Moreover, although some may have called the bread and wine antitypes of the body and blood of the Lord, as did the inspired Basil, they did not say this as referring to after the consecration (τὸ ἁγιασθῆναι), but to before the consecration, and it was thus that they called the [unconsecrated] offertory bread (προσφοράν) itself." B. Kotter (ed.), *Die*

corresponding to a heavenly reality, i.e. the perceptible realization of its τύπος or prefiguration, and thus, in the Eucharistic context, the exact equivalent of the English expression "the Eucharistic species" understood as the consecrated gifts received in Communion in the form of bread and wine. This is perfectly clear in Greek sources earlier than or contemporary with BAS.[37] Cyril/John II of Jerusalem (post 380), *Cat.* 5, 20, commenting on the communion responsory, Ps. 34:9, "Taste and see how good the Lord is!" says: "We are bidden to taste not bread and wine, but the antitype *(ἀντίτυπον)* of the body and blood of Christ."[38] And *Cat.* 4, 3, uses

---

Schriften des Iohannes von Damaskos II (PTS 12, Berlin: 1973) 197 = *De fide orthodoxa* IV, 13, PG 94:1152C–53B; trans. Saint John of Damascus, *Writings*, trans. by F. H. Chase, Jr. (The Fathers of the Church 37, Washington: 1981) 360–361. The glosses are mine; "prosphora (offering)" is the ordinary Byzantine Greek term for the unconsecrated eucharistic loaves used at the liturgy. As we saw above in section VI.3, John Damascene's interpretation of BAS is simply false, though it is resumed in the iconodule Council of Nicea II in 787 which condemned the iconoclast Council of 754. This definition was the fruit of the iconoclastic troubles, and not directly concerned with the later formula of consecration dispute between East and West in the fourteenth century. See the debate at Nicea II, Session 6 (Mansi 13:261E-268A), where the relevant texts of the Council of 754 are preserved because they were read into the Acts of Nicea II and condemned. A complete English translation of these texts, with the sections from the Acta of 754 set off in italics, is conveniently provided in D. J. Sahas, *Icon and Logos: Sources in Eighth-Century Iconoclasm* (Toronto/ Buffalo/New York, 1986) 92–96. For the debate on the use of "antitype" for the Eucharistic species, see Mansi 13:256C = Sahas 95.

[37] Cf. the *Apostolic Tradition* 21 (c. 215), B. Botte (ed.), *La Tradition apostolique de S. Hippolyte. Essai de reconstitution* (LQF 39, Münster: 1963) 54; the *Apostolic Constitutions* (c. 380), V, 14:7, VI, 30:2 (SC 329:250, 390), VII, 25:4 (SC 336:54); Gregory Nazianzen (d. c. 390), *Or.* 8, 18, PG 35:809–811 (= CPG 3010). G.W.H. Lampe, *A Patristic Greek Lexicon* (Oxford: 1961) 159, citing LEW 329:24, wrongly interprets "antitypes" in BAS in the other sense, as meaning the offered but not yet consecrated gifts, though the term becomes restricted to this sense only later. Further texts in the following notes.

[38] Cyrille de Jérusalem, *Catéchèses mystagogiques*, introduction, texte critique et notes de A. Piédangel, trad. de P. Paris (SC 126bis, Paris: 1988) 170. The date of this witness to the intercessions/commemorations in the hagiopolite Eucharistic anaphora depends on the much controverted question of authorship between Cyril during his turbulent episcopacy (348–357, 362–367, 378–386) and his successor John II (386–417). Piédagnel has reviewed the dossier, and the weight of opinion seems to be leaning toward the following conclusions: the catecheses are from the end of the century, most likely after 380 (Cyril

"τύπος" in the same sense: "For in the figure *(ἐν τύπῳ)* of bread is given to you the body, and in the figure of wine is given to you the blood. . . ."[39] Similar language is found in the fourth century *Spiritual Homilies* of Ps.-Macarius of Egypt/Symeon of Mesopotamia. *Homily 27, 17,* says:

"In the church are offered bread and wine, antitype *(ἀντίτυπον)* of his flesh and blood. And those receiving of this seeming bread, spiritually eat the flesh of the Lord."[40]

By the fifth century, however, the use of "antitype" for the Eucharistic species begins to be impugned as equivocal,[41] and from at least the sixth century Byzantine Orthodox authors, especially during the iconoclastic troubles (725–843), will explicitly reject this usage, restricting "antitype" to the unconsecrated elements, undoubtedly in order to affirm beyond all possible doubt the reality of the real presence.[42] But once again, one cannot use such later shifts to interpret the language of earlier texts, as the 1987 New Skete version of BAS does at this point:

----

died in 387); *in their present form* they are attributable to John as their final redactor; but they probably go back to texts of Cyril that were used year after year, undergoing redactional emendations in the process; they still retain elements derived directly from Cyril (ibid., *Introduction*, 21–28 and *Appendice* I: *L'auteur des Catéchèses mystagogiques* 177–187, esp. 185–187).

[39] Ibid., 136.

[40] H. Dörries, E. Klostermann, M. Kroeger, eds., *Die 50 geistlichen Homilien des Makarios* (PTS 4, Berlin: 1964) 227 line 25 = PG 34:705B (= CPG 2411); on the author, see J. Quasten, *Patrology*, 3 vols. (Utrecht/Antwerp: 1975) III, 162–168.

[41] M. Jugie, "L'épiclèse et le mot antitype de la Messe de Saint Basile," *Echos d'Orient* 9 (1906) 193–198.

[42] *Apophthegmata patrum* (fourth century and later), Daniel 7, PG 65:157 (= CPG 5560); Eutychius, Patriarch of Constantinople (552–565, 577–582), *Sermo de paschate et de ss. eucharistia* 2, PG 86.2:2393B (= CPG 6939); Anastasius of Sinai (d. after 700), *Viae dux (Ὁδηγός)* 23.1, K.-H. Uthemann (ed.) (Corpus Christianorum series Graeca 8, Brepols: 1981) 307–308 (= CPG 7745); Ps. Sophronius, *Commentarius liturgicus* 3 (twelfth c.), PG 87.3:3984 (= CPG 7677); and esp. John Damascene (c. 675–753/4), *Expositio fidei* (= CPG 8043) 86:114–115, 163–166, ed. B. Kotter, *Die Schriften des Iohannes von Damaskos* II (PTS 12, Berlin: 1973) 195, 197 = *De fide orthodoxa* IV, 13, PG 94:1152C–53B. For the relevant texts of Nicea II (787) see note 36 above.

"Now that we have set forth *this bread and wine which are to be the body and blood of your Christ*, we pray and beseech you, O holy of holies, that . . . your Holy Spirit may come upon us and upon these gifts. . . ."[43]

This constitutes an interpretative paraphrase of the text determined by present Orthodox theories of the consecration, rather than a translation of what the Greek actually says.

4. *The Eucharist as "Figura"*

The early Latin tradition also employed such symbolic language for the Eucharist. Saxer has shown how the term *"figura,"* the Latin equivalent of "antitype," is used for the Eucharist from c. 150 A.D. in the sense of the visible sign or sacramental symbol of the consecrated bread and wine. Saxer rightly identifies it as belonging to the *"fonds commun des prières eucharistiques en usage de l'an 200 à 400"* in both Greek and Latin, and later in Syriac.[44] Its equivalent is found in the *Apostolic Tradition* 21,[45] the *Testamentum Domini* II, 10,[46] Ambrose, *De sacramentis* IV, 5.21, citing the *Canon missae* as he knew it in Milan.[47]

5. *The Epiclesis as Theophany or Transfiguration*

This hallowed expression conforms nicely to the epiclesis prayer of BAS [6], with its petition that the Father send his Spirit on the gifts to bless and hallow and *show (ἀναδεῖξαι)* the bread and wine to be the body and blood of Christ.[48] This expression in no way weakens the consecratory sense of the epiclesis,[49] any more than 1 Tim 3:16, when it says that Jesus "was manifested *(ἐφανερώθη)* in

---

[43] *The Divine Liturgy* (New Skete: 1987) 167.

[44] V. Saxer, "Figura corporis et sanguinis Domini," *Rivista di archeologia cristiana* 47 (1971) 65–89 (citation is from p. 88).

[45] Ed. Botte (note 37 above) 54.

[46] Ed. Rahmani, (note 13 above) 130.

[47] CSEL 73:55.

[48] LEW 329–330.

[49] See the debate on the liturgical use of this verb in E. Peterson, "Die Bedeutung von ἀναδείχνυμι in den griechischen Liturgien," in *Festgabe Für Adolf Deißmann zum 60. Gerburtstag 7. November 1926* (Tübingen: 1927) 320–326; O. Casel, *Jahrbuch für Liturgiewissenschaft* (1927) 273–274; A. Baumstark, ibid. 357. Cf. also J. A. Jungmann, *Pastoral Liturgy* (New York: 1962) 277–282.

the flesh," intends that the incarnation was only apparent![50] To ask God to *show a figure to be what it represents* is obviously to ask that it actually be that transfigured reality.[51] This is basically the same sense in which the Latin texts adduced by Saxer use the term *transfigurare*—for instance, Ambrose, *De fide* IV, 10:124: "For we, as often as we receive the sacrament, which is *transfigured* into the flesh and blood by the mystery of the sacred prayer, 'we proclaim the death of the Lord.'"[52]

Note again that this issue does not in any way prejudice *later* theological views on the form(ula)/moment of consecration. My point remains the same: such later precisions cannot be read back into, or derived from, an earlier text composed without such concerns in mind. The illegitimacy of such a hermeneutic should be perfectly obvious from the fact that BAS continues to refer to the gifts indifferently as both "bread and cup" or "body and blood" even after the epiclesis, when they have already been consecrated according to anyone's theology:

"so that all of us who partake of this one *bread and cup* may be united with one another in the communion of the one Holy Spirit, and that the partaking of the holy body and blood of your Christ may be for none of us unto judgement or condemnation. . . ."[53]

---

[50] In this context one recalls inevitably the famous dictum of Adolf von Harnack concerning the difference between the symbolic theology of the patristic period and the later rationalism: "Wir verstehen heute unter Symbole eine Sache, die das nicht ist, was sie bedeutet; damals verstand man unter Symbol eine Sache, die das in irgend welchem Sinne wirkliche ist, was sie bedeutet. . . ." *Lehrbuch der Dogmengeschichte* (4th ed. Tübingen: 1909) I, 476.

[51] See in this regard the *Apostolic Constitutions*, VII 12:44, SC 336:202.

[52] "Nos autem quotiescumque sacramenta sumimus, quae per sacrae orationis mysterium in carnem transfigurantur et sanguinem, 'mortem domini annuntiamus.'" CSEL 78:201; cf. id., *De incarnationis dominicae sacramento*, CSEL 79:234; cf. Saxer (note 44 above) 79–84, referring to A. Wilmart, "Transfigurare," *Bulletin d'ancienne littérature et d'archéologie chrétiennes* 1 (1911) 282–292. A few years ago, the watchdogs got nervous when some began to speak of the eucharistic consecration in terms of "transignification." The above texts provide, perhaps, a traditional and unimpeachably orthodox context for further reflection on such terms.

[53] LEW 330:13-20 = PE 238.

VII. CONCLUSION

On the basis of related texts and the early theological expression of the Eucharist in Irenaeus, I think it legitimate to say that in CHR/BAS:

1. The Eucharistic memorial in its entirety is considered a sacrifice offered in memory of Jesus, and in obedience to his command, as recounted in the story told in the prayer.

2. In the course of this ritual memorial, again following Jesus' command, the Church offers bread and wine, the antitypes (BAS: τὰ ἀντίτυπα) of Christ's body and blood.

3. The Church then prays that the Father's acceptance of these gifts be confirmed by the coming of the Holy Spirit on them, so that they be sanctified for our salvation.

4. When the prayer is over, the Church believes in faith that this has been accomplished.

At any rate it is perfectly obvious that the oblationary incipit of the epiclesis [6], "Again we offer you this reasonable and unbloody worship *(ἔτι προσφέρομέν σοι τὴν λογικὴν καὶ ἀναίμακτον λατρείαν),"* practically a topos for the Eucharist *tout court,* is patient of no other interpretation. I believe the same must be said for the offering of the "antitypes of the body and blood of your Christ" in BAS [6], *pace* the later interpretations tendentiously and/or anachronistically imposed on the text. Nothing in CHR/BAS nor in the theology contemporary with those two texts permits us to affirm that what is offered in the oblation "offering you yours from your own" before the epiclesis [5], and in the "again we offer" that both opens the epiclesis [6] and follows it twice [7.1.3], are not one and the same offering.

There is one single offering of the Church within which several things happen. These things are expressed in various ways and moments according to the several preformation traditions of East and West, all of which agree on the basic ritual elements in the anaphoras of their traditions. These classical anaphoras express that the Eucharist is a sacrifice, the sacramental memorial of Christ's own sacrifice of the cross, in which the Church, repeating what Jesus did at the Last Supper, invokes God's blessing on bread and wine so that it might become Jesus' body and blood, our spiritual food and drink.

Origen, *Contra Celsum* 8.33, sums it up when he says:

"We give thanks to the creator of the universe and eat the loaves that are presented with thanksgiving and prayer over the gifts, so that by the prayer they become a certain holy body which sanctifies those who partake of it with a pure intention."[54]

All attempts to squeeze more out of the words of the prayer, to assert that the "bread and wine" in no. 2, elevated by the deacon in a sign of offering as the priest chants the oblation *ekphonesis* [5], is or is not at that moment "consecrated," is an inference that can be made only by imposing on the text the results of later theological reflection and/or polemics. To argue that expressions like "This is my body, this is my blood," "antitypes," "bread and cup," mean that the gifts are already, or are not yet, "consecrated," or to determine a "moment" or "form(ula) of consecration," and then interpret all preceding and following descriptions of the gifts in function of that dividing line, are, in my view, as anachronistic as they are fatuous. BAS calls the consecrated gifts we receive in Communion, "bread and cup." Would anyone wish to argue that this text implies the gifts are not consecrated even then?

So the most one can say is that the "offering" expressions that fall between institution and epiclesis in BAS and CHR neither confirm nor exclude any particular theological thesis of when or by what particular part of the anaphoral prayer the consecration is effected, or just *what*, beyond the Eucharistic service in its most general sense of the Church's offering of the memorial Jesus is believed to have commanded the Church to repeat, is offered: bread and wine, body and blood, the "reasonable and unbloody sacrifice" of the Church, the sacrifice of Christ represented in its sacrament.

My own view is that later precisions, in the sense in which they are sometimes posed today as the result of confessional disputes, are sterile and pointless. Since they were in no one's mind in the fourth century, I would prefer to assume that the earlier liturgical

---

[54] Origène, *Contre Celse*, Tome IV (Livres VII–VIII), ed., M. Borret (SC 150, Paris: 1969) 246; trans. Origen, *Contra Celsum*, trans. H. Chadwick (Cambridge: 1965) 476.

language, which is metaphorical and evocative, not philosophical and ontological, includes *all these "offerings,"* if implicitly and not self-consciously. In short, in the Church's liturgical oblation, whatever Jesus and the Church meant to be offered was, in fact, being offered. Only later doctrinal problems will lead to the sorting out of what, exactly, that meant in the more dogmatically precise terms of *theologia secunda.* I am of course aware that these remarks do not make further ecumenical discussion of such later precisions superfluous. But that is the topic of another paper.[55]

[55] For some recent discussions of these issues in an ecumenical spirit, see R. Meßner, "Prex Eucharistica. Zur Frügeschichte der Basileios-Anaphora. Beogachtungen und Hypothesen," in E. Renhart & A. Schnider (eds.), *Sursum Corda. Variationen zu einem liturgischen Motiv. Für Philipp Harnancourt zum 60. Geburtstag* (Graz: 1991) 121–129; H.-J. Schulz, "Hochgebet und Darbringung. Das wiedererschlossene Zeugnis der Liturgie in seiner ökumenischen Bedeutsamkeit," ibid. 140–146; and, somewhat earlier, G. Kretschmar, "Opfer Christi und Opfer der Christen in den eucharistischen Texten der Russischen Orthodoxen Kirche," in *Das Opfer Christi und das Opfer der Christen* (Ökumenische Rundschau, Beiheft 34, Frankfurt: 1979) 56–75.

Aelred Cody, O.S.B.

4. An Instruction of Philoxenus of Mabbug on Gestures and Prayer When One Receives Communion in the Hand, with a History of the Manner of Receiving the Eucharistic Bread in the West Syrian Church

When people receive Communion in the Roman rite today, they are often encouraged to receive the consecrated Eucharistic bread on their hands rather than on their tongues. While some people enthusiastically support this practice, others strongly oppose it. Those opposing it sometimes claim that the Church has never admitted it, or that it would scandalize Eastern Christians.

As far as the Western Church is concerned, the truth is that Western Christians once did receive the consecrated bread in their hands and that they continued to do so at least through the eighth century.[1] The practice was abandoned partly out of fear that persons receiving the sacred species in their hands might carry it off for some frivolous purpose, or even for some darkly sacrilegious purpose, and partly because of the increasingly widespread idea that respect for the holy precludes our touching holy things with unconsecrated hands.[2] A peculiarly Western contribu-

---

[1] Joseph A. Jungmann, *The Mass of the Roman Rite (Missarum Sollemnia)*, trans. Francis A. Brunner, 2 vols. (New York: Benziger Brothers, 1955) 2:379 n. 33.

[2] Ibid., 2:381–382. Jungmann suggests that in Western Europe the change was facilitated by the contemporaneous adoption of unleavened wafers which adhere easily to the moist tongue of the communicant.

tion to the idea that only priestly hands should touch the consecrated bread may have been made when the Frankish Church began consecrating the hands of priestly ordinands.[3]

In most Eastern churches today, lay people do not receive the Eucharistic bread in their hands, but in earlier times lay people in the Christian East received the body of the Lord in their hands just as Westerners did, and in one of the Churches rooted in ancient Syrian Christianity they continue to do so now. Did Christians in churches whose ecclesiastical culture is expressed in Syriac manage better than those in other parts of Christendom to continue integrating the awe and reverence they felt for the Eucharistic elements as *mysterium tremendum* with their sense of the fundamental holiness of a Christian belonging to the Church with both body and soul? In this contribution to the collection of essays honoring my confrere Father Aidan Kavanagh, I should like first to publish an old West Syrian text indicating gestures and sentiments apt for the very moment in which the Lord's body is held in one's hand. Then, I should like to trace the history of the practice of giving the Eucharistic body of the Lord to lay people on the eastern frontier of classical Christianity, starting with the time when Christians in Syria and Persia were still undivided, then following the trace in the West Syrian Church after the ecclesiastical divisions of Syrian Christendom.

I. PRAYER AND GESTURES WHEN THE
BODY OF CHRIST IS RECEIVED IN ONE'S HANDS

The text published here for the first time consists mainly of a prayer. The prayer itself exists in a longer form, preserved in British Library Add. 14,529, fols. 16v–17r (paleographically datable to the seventh or eighth century),[4] in which it is preceded by brief

[3] Pierre-Marie Gy, "Quand et pourquoi la communion dans la bouche a-t-elle remplacé la communion dans la main dans l'église latine?" in *Gestes et paroles dans les diverses familles liturgiques* (Conférences Saint-Serge: 1977), Bibliotheca "Ephemerides liturgicae," Subsidia, 14 (Rome: Centro Liturgico Vincenziano, 1978) 117–121.

[4] W. Wright, *Catalogue of Syriac Manuscripts in the British Museum Acquired since the Year 1838*, 3 vols. (London: The Trustees of the British Museum, 1870–1872) 2:917–921 (Wright's no. dccclvi). Wright does not specifically mention our text (see n. 7 below).

instructions on gestures, and in a shorter form, included in British Library Add. 17,125 (paleographically datable to the ninth or tenth century).[5] The text of the longer form is easy to read and to photograph. The text of the shorter form is so faded that photographs are of little use, even when the British Library's technicians have used infrared photography to produce them. I have been able to transcribe almost all details of the shorter text directly from the manuscript, however, because the ink, badly faded, and in many places completely gone, has had a chemical effect on the vellum page, making it distinctly more translucent where the ink once was. When the page is held against a light, the form of the faded Syriac letters can still be seen as translucent lines on the vellum. These translucent lines are especially clear on the other side of the page, where they can be read backward.

The longer form of the prayer is given in the literary form of an instruction for people receiving Communion, and the codex in which the instruction is preserved is a collection of texts useful in combatting diverse heresies. The assortment of heresies combatted makes it easy to identify the codex as one compiled in a specifically West Syrian monophysite environment. The instruction with which we are concerned is placed at the end of a series of extracts from the works of Philoxenus included in a *catena* of "select judgments of the holy fathers against the heresy of Julian of Halicarnassus." Our instruction's inclusion at the end of the Philoxenian texts in the *catena* as it is given in this manuscript is curious.[6] There is certainly nothing overtly polemic about it, although the phrases emphasizing the physical manifestation of the hidden God in the incarnation and in its Eucharistic analogy could conceivably be meant to counteract the aphthartodocetism ascribed to Julian. Wright, in his detailed description of the contents of the manu-

---

[5] Ibid., 1:123–125 (Wright's no. clxxv). Our prayer is item 3b on p. 124.

[6] The antijulianist *catena*, with varying components, is found in several manuscripts (see R. Draguet, *Julien d'Halicarnasse et sa controverse avec Sévère d'Antioche sur l'incorruptibilité du Christ*, Universitas Catholica Lovaniensis, Dissertationes ad gradum magistri in Facultate Theologica consequendum conscriptae, series 2, vol. 12 [Louvain: P. Smeesters, 1924] 83–85). Its shortest form is the one in British Library Add. 14,529 to which the instruction containing our prayer has been appended.

script in his great catalogue, has overlooked our text entirely,[7] and it would have escaped my attention if André de Halleux had not mentioned it in his analytic survey of published and unpublished texts of Philoxenus, giving as his considered opinion that it is indeed an authentic text of Philoxenus.[8]

The manuscript in which the shorter form of the prayer is found is a codex containing the Psalter and the biblical canticles needed for the West Syrian morning office, followed by various other texts, including five occasional prayers. The inclusion of prayers attributed to Severus of Antioch and Philoxenus of Mabbug, leaders of the monophysite party in the late fifth and early sixth centuries, as well as the characteristically West Syrian liturgical division of the Psalter into *marmyātā* subdivided into *šūbḥē*, leave no doubt that the codex was produced in the West Syrian Church. Of the five occasional prayers, the last two are explicitly designated for use by monks. The first three are communion prayers, and of these three Mar Philoxenus is indicated as the author of the second one, to be said before Communion, and of the third one, to be said at the moment of Communion while someone holds the living body on his hands before conveying it to his mouth. This third occasional prayer is the shorter form of our prayer.

The fact that the prayer in its longer form is preceded by a brief, equally interesting exhortation to perform certain acts of devotion at the moment of receiving the consecrated bread in one's hand shows that the prayer was composed as part of an instruction. Given the prayer's length, its presentation in the form of instruction, and the theoretical nature of the collection in which it is preserved, we are probably justified in taking it as a prayer composed not for actual use but as a model in which Philoxenus has

[7] As Wright, *Catalogue*, 2:918–19, lists the pieces constituting the antijulianist *catena*, he passes directly from the last of the Philoxenian texts which he does mention, the extract of a letter of Philoxenus to a certain Uran (?) beginning on fol. 16r, to an extract from a work of Severian of Gabala beginning on fol. 17r. Our overlooked Philoxenian instruction is placed between these two texts.

[8] André de Halleux, *Philoxène de Mabbog: Sa vie, ses écrits, sa théologie,* Universitas Catholica Lovaniensis: Dissertationes ad gradum magistri in Facultate Theologica vel in Facultate Iuris Canonici consequendum conscriptae, series 3, vol. 8 (Louvain: Imprimerie Orientaliste, 1963) 296. He suggests that this component of Add. 14,529 is part of a lost Philoxenian *mēmrā.*

suggested thoughts appropriate for the ritual moment.[9] The entire text is valuable as a witness to gestures and thoughts which Philoxenus considered fitting when someone received Communion in the West Syrian rite of his day. The shorter form of the prayer, however, is found in a practical collection, and the prayer is short enough to be memorized easily. These facts suggest that the phrases of the shorter form were extracted from the longer text by someone who wanted to produce a Philoxenian prayer for actual devotional use. Its value thus lies in the evidence it provides for the practice of receiving Communion in the hand at a fairly late date.

The complete text of the instruction in Add. 14,529 is published here with a translation. The sections of the prayer extracted in the shorter text of Add. 17,125 are underlined in both the text and the translation. The variant readings of the shorter form are given in the notes, where "S" is the shorter form in Add. 17,125 and "L" is the longer form in Add. 14,529. The successive order of the extracted passages remains the same in the shorter form, so the reader can reconstruct the complete short text in Add. 17,125 by reading first its heading in note 10, then the underlined sections in the order of their occurrence, noting S's variants and concluding doxology in the notes. Diacritical points in Add. 14,529 are reproduced just as they are. The fine Syriac font used here was designed by Fr. Harry Hagan of St. Meinrad Archabbey.

First, the text in London, British Library, Add. 14,529, fols. 16v–17r (L), with the extracts (underlined) and the variants in Add. 17,125, fol. 78r (S).

---

[9] A model prayer to be said while communicants are holding the consecrated bread on their hands, before bringing it to their mouths, is given in the *Testament of Our Lord Jesus Christ* 1.23, ed. Ignatius Ephraem II Rahmani, *Testamentum Domini nostri Jesu Christi* (Mainz: F. Kirchheim, 1899) 46–47. This prayer is, in English:

"Holy, holy, holy! Ineffable Trinity, let me receive this body unto life, not unto condemnation, and let me produce fruits that please you, so that by being found pleasing to you I may live in you, following your precepts, and may boldly call you 'father,' calling to myself your kingdom and your will. Hallowed be your name in me, Lord. For you are strong and glorious, and to you be glory forever. Amen."

 (fol. 16v, col. 2)
 (fol. 17r, col. 1)
---

[10] The heading in S:

[11] *Sic,* for

[12] S:

[13] S:

[14] was originally written here. The correction was made by a second hand, to judge from the different styles of the dot over .

[15] S adds a final , faintly visible in ink, and clearly visible when the page is held against the light and inspected from its other side, in the translucence caused by the action of the ink on the vellum. The result is a combination of two pronominal object suffixes, the first person singular followed by the first person plural. The context requires the first person singular, as in L.

[16] *Sic* the superscript point in L, absent in S.

[Syriac text, 8 lines, including "(fol. 17r, col. 2)" and footnote markers 17–24]

And now, a translation of the text:

Another Text of St. Philoxenus[25]

"When you have extended your hands and taken the body, bow, and put your hands before your face, and worship the living Body whom you hold. Then speak with him in a low voice, and with

[17] S omits the ܘ
[18] S: ܬܩܠܝܢ
[19] S: ܘܐܝܕ̈ܝܟ,
[20] Illegible in S except for the ܘ
[21] S: ܬܘܟܚܢ
[22] S: ܘܣܓܘܕ ܗ̇ܝ, instead of ܐܠܘܗ ܗܘܝܬܐܡ, ܕܝܗܘ,
[23] S adds ܚܝ
[24] S adds ܩܪܝܒ and a concluding doxology:
ܘܠܟ ܫܘܒܚܐ ܘܬܘܕܝܬܐ ܘܠܐܒܘܟ ܢܫܘܚ ܐܠܟܘܢ ܠܥܠܡ ܐܡܝܢ..

[25] S has the heading "Another [prayer], of the same [Philoxenus], when someone has received the living body on his hands."

your gaze resting upon him say to him: 'I carry you, living God who is incarnate in the bread, and I embrace you in my palms, Lord of the worlds whom no world has contained. You have circumscribed yourself in a fiery coal[26] within a fleshly palm—you Lord, who with your palm measured out the dust of the earth. You are holy, God incarnate in my hands in a fiery coal which is a body.[27] See, I hold you, although there is nothing that contains you;[28] a bodily hand embraces you, Lord of natures whom a fleshly womb embraced. Within a womb you became a circumscribed body, and now within a hand you appear to me as a small morsel.

"As you have made me worthy to approach you and receive you —and see, my hands embrace you confidently—make me worthy, Lord, to eat you in a holy manner and to taste the food of your body[29] as a taste of your life. Instead of the stomach, the body's member, may the womb of my intellect and the hand of my mind receive you. May you be conceived in me as [you were] in the womb of the Virgin. There you appeared as an infant, and your hidden self was revealed to the world as corporeal fruit; may you also appear in me here and be revealed from me in fruits that are spiritual works and just labors pleasing to your will.

"And by your food may my desires be killed,[30] and by the drinking of your cup may my passions be quenched. And instead of the members of my body,[31] may my thoughts receive strength[32] from the nourishment of your body.[33] Like the manifest members of my body, may my hidden thoughts be engaged in exercise and in running and in works according to your living commands and

---

[26] The Syrians, mindful of the live coal brought from the altar which blotted out the prophet's sins when it was touched to his lips (Is 6.6-7), call a particle of the consecrated Eucharistic bread a "fiery coal" (gᵉmûrtā).

[27] Literally, "a [burning] coal of body," an epexegetical genitive.

[28] "Hold" and "contain" represent the same Syriac verb.

[29] Meaning "the food which is your body," another epexegetical genitive.

[30] Instead of "be killed," S has a verb with the three consonants of the stem arranged in a different order (qṭl in L, ṭlq in S), "be dispersed," which may be the original reading.

[31] S: "And [together] with my body."

[32] S: "vital strength."

[33] S: "holy body," followed by a concluding doxology, "And to you, Christ God, be glory and thanksgiving and worship forever. Amen."

your spiritual laws. From the food of your body and the drinking of your blood may I wax strong inwardly, and excel outwardly, and run diligently, and attain to the full stature of an interior human being. May I become a perfect man, mature in the intelligence [residing in] all [my] spiritual members, my head being crowned with the crown of perfection of all of [my] behavior. May I be a royal diadem in your hands, as you promised me,[34] O hidden God whose manifestness I embrace in the perfection of your body."

II. COMMUNION IN THE HAND UNTIL AFTER
THE CONFESSIONAL DIVISIONS

How do this instruction, written around A.D. 500, and the abbreviated prayer extracted from it and found in a monastic codex written for practical use some four hundred years later, fit into the history of the way in which the consecrated bread is received in the West Syrian Church which rightly claims Philoxenus as one of its early fathers?[35]

In the early Christian centuries, references to the practice of receiving the consecrated bread in one's hands show that it was taken for granted, both in solidly Syriac inland Syria and in the largely hellenized cities like Antioch and Jerusalem. The custom of touching the Lord's body to one's eyes, alluded to by Aphraat the Persian Sage, writing in Syriac on the Persian side of the imperial

[34] An allusion to Is 62.3.

[35] For what follows, it may be helpful to recall that the ecclesiastical divisions of Christendom in Syria and Persia in the fifth and sixth century resulted in a christologically Chalcedonian Melkite Church, turned toward the Greek world, and two churches closely identified with the regions in which they thrived and strongly disposed to use Syriac almost exclusively as their literary language. Of these two churches, one, the East Syrian Church, was committed to the christological stance associated with the name of Nestorius. It was the major church on the Persian side of the *limes* dividing the Roman and Persian empires, and in our own time it is called the ("Assyrian") Church of the East. The other, the West Syrian Church, was committed to the christology of Cyril of Alexandria and specifically to the monophysite position of Severus of Antioch. Its historical centers lay mainly within the East Roman Empire, but it had, and still has, its extension on the Persian side of the old imperial frontier, in what is today Iraq. The West Syrian Church, once commonly called Jacobite, is now officially designated the Syrian Orthodox Church.

frontier shortly before A.D. 345, presupposes the communicants'
holding the body in their hands.[36] A little later, Ephrem, writing
on the Roman side of the frontier, in the region where the future
independent West Syrian Church's origins lay, tells his hearers to
gather into the palms of their hands the treasure of life (the Lord),
hidden in his bread.[37] Addressing the pearl who is Christ, he says
that the apostles "laid you in the palms of human beings as medicine of life,[38] and elsewhere he laments the fact the destruction of
Nicomedia in 358 has made it impossible for the inhabitants to go
to the Lord's temple to carry away his words in their ears, "holiness" in their hands, and the medicine of life on their lips.[39] Still
more clearly, he declares in a Eucharistic context that "we have
God in our hands."[40] Less clear, as far as our present interest is
concerned, but significant, nevertheless, is his poetic image of fire

[36] Aphraat *Demonstrations* 7.21, 20.8, ed. Jean Parisot, Patrologia syriaca, 1
(Paris: Firmin-Didot, 1894) 349, 905 (Syriac) 350, 906 (Latin translation).
Parisot's translations *ante oculos* in 7.21 *(sibi ante oculos propositum)* and *coram
oculis* in 20.8 *(quando Corpus eius tollunt ponuntque coram oculis suis)* miss the
point, as Franz Joseph Dölger, *Antike und Christentum*, vol. 3 (Münster:
Aschendorff, 1932) 235, well advised by Anton Rücker, pointed out. The Syriac
sāymîn leh 'al 'aynayhōn (7.21) and pagreh dᵉšāqlîn wᵉsāymîn 'al 'aynayhōn (20.8)
might more accurately be translated, respectively, as *id ponentes super oculos
suos* and *(id est,) Corpus eius quod tollunt et ponunt super oculos suos;* cf. the
French translations of Marie-Joseph Pierre, *Aphraate le Sage persan, Les exposés*,
2 vols., Sources chrétiennes, 349, 359 (Paris: Editions du Cerf, 1988–1989) 1:433,
2:795: "le mettent sur leurs yeux" (7.21) and "qui prennent son corps et le
portent à leurs yeux" (20.8).

[37] Ephrem *Hymni de ecclesia* 13.20, ed. and trans. Edmund Beck, *Des heiligen
Ephraem des Syrers Hymnen de Ecclesia*, Corpus Scriptorum Christianorum
Orientalium (henceforth: CSCO) 198–199 = Scriptores syri, 84–85 (Louvain:
Secrétariat du CSCO, 1960) 198:33 (Syriac), 199:36 (German translation).

[38] Ephrem *Hymni de fide* 85.8 (= *De margarita* 5.8) ed. and trans. Edmund
Beck, *Des heiligen Ephraem des Syrers Hymnen de Fide*, CSCO, 154–155 = Scriptores syri, 73–74 (Louvain: L. Durbecq, 1955) 154:261 (Syriac) 155:222 (German
translation).

[39] Mēmrē *on Nicomedia* 8.664–66, extant only in Armenian, ed. Charles
Renoux, *Ephrem de Nisibe, Mēmrē sur Nicomédie*, Patrologia orientalis, 37/2–3
(Turnhout: Brepols, 1975) 152–153.

[40] In one of Ephrem's hymns which have survived only in Armenian translation: Hymn 47, line 29, in *Hymnes de saint Ephrem conservées en version
arménienne*, ed. Louis Mariès and C. Mercier, Patrologia orientalis, 30/1 (Paris:
Firmin-Didot, 1963) 220–221.

and spirit poured into the hands of the Lord's disciples,[41] not to speak of his petition—made in poetic identification with every Christian—that he be allowed to take hold of the Lord in the bread.[42]

Of the Eastern Mediterranean authors writing in Greek as the fourth century closed, Cyril (or John) of Jerusalem has left us his famous instruction on approaching Communion with hands extended and fingers closed, the left hand serving as a throne for the superimposed right hand whose palm is to receive "the king," the body of Christ.[43] John Crysostom provides evidence that people received the consecrated bread in the right hand in Antioch, too, in the late fourth century,[44] and Theodore of Mopsuestia does the same for the neighboring coastal region of Cilicia around the same time.[45]

---

[41] *Hymni de fide* 10.14, ed. Beck, *Hymnen de Fide*, 154:51 (Syriac) 155:35 (German translation).

[42] Ephrem *Hymni de virginitate* 32.2, ed. and trans. Edmund Beck, *Des heiligen Ephraem des Syrers Hymnen de Virginitate*, CSCO, 223–224 = Scriptores syri, 94–95 (Louvain: Secrétariat du CSCO, 1962) 223:117 (Syriac) 224:101 (German translation). In Beck's German translation, the parenthetical "(in my hand)" translates nothing in the Syriac text, but it may perhaps be justified on grounds that the Syriac verb *šᵉqal* used here (represented by the translation's "dass ich . . . nehme") means more than simply to receive something, that it often conveys the idea of taking hold of something or carrying something. It happens to be the verb used in the heading of our Philoxenian prayer in Add. 17.125, "when one *has taken*."

[43] Cyril of Jerusalem *Catecheses mystagogicae* 5.21, ed. Auguste Piédagnel, trans. Pierre Paris, *Catéchèses mystagogiques*, Sources chrétiennes, 126 (Paris: Editions du Cerf, 1966) 170–171. Franz Joseph Dölger, *IXΘYC, 2: Der heilige Fisch in den antiken Religionen und im Christentum* (Münster in Westf.: Aschendorff, 1922) 513–514, sees behind these prescriptions a reverence for the body of Christ, but also the ancient idea that crumbs falling from the table belong to potentially malicious spirits.

[44] See John Chrysostom *Ad illuminandos catecheses* 2.2, PG, 49:233; *In Epistolam 1 ad Corinthios 27* 5, PG, 61:231; also the comments of Frans van de Paverd, *Zur Geschichte der Messliturgie in Antiocheia und Konstantinopel gegen Ende des vierten Jahrhunderts*, Orientalia christiana analecta, 187 (Rome: Pontifical Oriental Institute, 1970) 387–389. In his homily *In Matthaeum 50* 2, PG, 58:507, John Chrysostom speaks of touching Christ when we receive Communion, but he does not explicitly say that we do so with our hands.

[45] See Theodore of Mopsuestia *Homiliae catecheticae* 16, the ritual introduction and §28, ed. and trans. Raymond Tonneau, *Les Homélies catéchétiques de Théo-*

As the monophysite movement gained intensity, Communion in a lay person's hand remained normal in Antioch itself during the reign of the great monophysite patriarch Severus (512–518), whom Philoxenus actively supported.[46] Philoxenus' instruction for the moment of receiving the Lord's body on one's hand is itself clear evidence that Communion in the hand was taken for granted in the late fifth and early sixth centuries, but for what place or region does it serve as evidence of this?

Unlike Severus, who was a man thoroughly Greek in culture and, thus, a prelate who fitted well in cosmopolitan Antioch, Philoxenus used Syriac both in his family and at school and learned Greek as a secondary language. Born in the Persian Empire, beyond the Tigris in the province of Bet Garmay, he had gone to school in the Syriac heartland on the Roman side of the imperial *limes* at Edessa in Osrhoene, and indeed in the renowned "School of the Persians," where the theological authorities were Theodore of Mopsuestia and other Antiochenes, and the ecclesiastical ideology was Nestorian. Hence, the ritual customs which Philoxenus learned in his formative years were those of Persia and then of Edessa. When he was a student in Edessa, the rector of the School of the Persians may still have been Narsai.[47] Thanks to Narsai himself, we know that in the contemporary rite of Edessa

---

dore de Mopsueste, Studi e testi, 145 (Vatican City: Biblioteca Apostolica Vaticana, 1949) 535, 579.

[46] See Severus of Antioch Homiliae cathedrales 122, ed. and trans. Maurice Brière, Les Homiliae cathedrales de Sévère d'Antioche, Patrologia orientalis, 29/1 (Paris: Firmin-Didot, 1960) 116–117.

[47] The frequently repeated claim that Narsai transferred the school from Edessa to Nisibis, just across the border in Persian territory, in 457, when Philoxenus was probably not old enough to have finished his studies, are based on a false interpretation of a passage in the Chronicle of Arbela. The school was not closed in Edessa until 489, and Philoxenus, by then a convinced Cyrillian and a bishop, surely favored its closing: see de Halleux, Philoxène, 49 with the sources cited in his n. 77. Narsai's own move to the ecclesiastical and political safety of Nisibis took place before the move of the school itself, however. Arthur Vööbus, The Statutes of the School of Nisibis, Papers of the Estonian Theological Society in Exile, 12 (Stockholm: Estonian Theological Theology in Exile, n.d. [1961]), 15–19, concludes that his departure from Edessa took place sometime after 471.

the people received Communion in their palms,[48] and that they did so with the right hand over the left to form a cross.[49] Did Philoxenus have the rite of Edessa in mind when he composed his prayer for the moment of Communion in the hand?

In Philoxenus' case the alternative: Edessa or Antioch may be unnecessary. The fact of his prayer's conservation in a Jacobite codex suggests, however, that it was written after he had become a zealous Cyrillian, a convert to the monophysite cause, and had left Edessa for Antioch. In the ecclesiastical politics of the time, his Cyrillian credentials led to his appointment as metropolitan of Mabbug in 485, where he remained until his strongly monophysite stand led to his exile in 519.[50] Mabbug (which the Greeks called Hierapolis), capital of the *provincia euphratensis* in the Roman civil diocese of the Orient, lay about halfway between Edessa and Antioch on the road from Mesopotamia to the Mediterranean.[51] Its liturgical practices were presumably similar to those of the patriarchal city of Antioch, but since most people in Mabbug spoke Syriac, and many of them were of the Nestorian party when Philoxenus arrived, close contact must have existed between Mabbug and Edessa. Philoxenus' prayer, taken together with the contemporary remarks of Severus and of Narsai, allow us to conclude confidently that, as the fifth century turned into the sixth and the confessional divisions were taking shape, Communion was being given in the hand both in urban Antioch and in the cities of the Syriac speaking interior like Edessa and Mabbug.

III. THE PRACTICE IN THE WEST SYRIAN CHURCH AFTER THE CONFESSIONAL DIVISIONS

Already in the late seventh century there were signs of change in the manner of lay persons' receiving the consecrated bread in

[48] Narsai *Homilies* 26, trans. R. H. Connolly, *The Liturgical Homilies of Narsai, Translated into English with an Introduction*, Texts and Studies, 8/1 (Cambridge: University Press, 1909) 60.

[49] *Homilies* 17, trans. Connolly, *Liturgical Homilies of Narsai*, 28.

[50] On all stages of the talented and controversial Philoxenus' often dramatic life, see de Halleux, *Philoxène*, 3–101.

[51] See René Dussaud, *Topographie historique de la Syrie antique et médiévale*, Bibliothèque archéologique et historique, 4 (Paris: Paul Geuthner, 1927), map 14 between pp. 472 and 473; de Halleux, *Philoxène*, the map on (unnumbered) p. 563.

the independent Syriac-speaking church organized by leading promotors of the monophysite cause. In the canonical responses, preserved afterward in the West Syrian *Synodicon*, written by the learned but somewhat intransigent James of Edessa, bishop of Edessa from 684 to 688 and again briefly in 699, one sees a new discomfort with the idea of persons taking the consecrated bread in their own hands if they are not ordained deacons or priests. In James's series of responses to the presbyter Addai, he states in no. 23 that it is right for a man who is a secular (strictly speaking, a man who is not a monk, but in this context probably one who is not a bishop, priest, or deacon) or for a woman to take the consecrated bread *(qurbānā)* from the bowl *(kᵉpāptā)*,[52] *"when no priest is near"* (emphasis mine), since "those who have done this have done nothing proper to the priesthood."[53] In response no. 41 of the same series, he lays down the rule that a deaconess may never touch the holy table (the altar) or take the mysteries (the consecrated species) from it, but that in monasteries of nuns a deaconess may take the mysteries from the chest (or cupboard, or shrine, *parda[y]sqā* in Syriac, obviously the place where the mysteries were reserved),[54] and give them to the sisters or to small children, *if there is no presbyter or deacon near* (again, emphasis mine).[55]

---

[52] I translate *kᵉpāptā* as "bowl" to avoid giving the impression too readily that James is talking about the paten used in the actual celebration of the Eucharist. In no. 31 of the same set of responses to the presbyter Addai, he uses another word, *kāsā*, to designate the vessel which, as he explicitly says, is one of the vessels of the altar. A *kᵉpāptā* is any hollow vessel (the bowl of a censer, for example). Was this word the one used in James' time to designate a vessel in which the consecrated bread was reserved for Communion outside the Eucharistic liturgy?

[53] Arthur Vööbus, *The Synodicon in the West Syrian Tradition*, CSCO, 367–368, 375–376 = Scriptores syri, 161–162, 163–164 (Louvain, Secrétariat du CSCO, 1975–1976) 367:261–262 (Syriac) 368:239 (English translation).

[54] In a *kᵉpāptā* (see n. 52 above) kept inside the *pardaysqā?*

[55] Vööbus, *Synodicon*, 367:266 (Syriac) 368:242 (translation). The provision for Communion given by a deaconess in a monastery of nuns if no priest or deacon is available is found already in no. 9 of the "Chapters Written from the East" (ibid. 367:165 [Syriac], 368:159 [translation]), a work probably written c. 532–534 by monophysite Syrian bishops exiled in Egypt (see Arthur Vööbus, *Syrische Kanonessammlungen: Ein Beitrag zur Quellenkunde*, vol. 1, *Westsyrische Originalurkunden*, 1/A, CSCO, 307 = Subsidia, 35; 1/B, CSCO, 317 = Subsidia, 38 [Louvain: Secrétariat du CSCO, 1970], 1A:172–175). For members of the

In no. 3 of James's canonical responses to John the Stylite, the learned bishop holds that it is all right for a man who is a secular, or for a woman, to carry a pearl to the sick;[56] he believes it proper for them to carry it wrapped in a clean piece of linen, or in a piece of writing material to be burned afterward, or in a cabbage leaf or piece of soft unconsecrated bread to be eaten afterward, but if the case is urgent and the nonordained person simply brings the bread in his or her own hand and puts it into the sick person's mouth, James finds this tolerable on grounds that to do so "does not seem" to be doing something proper to priesthood.[57] As for the sick persons themselves, he writes that it does not matter, ultimately, whether they take the pearl directly into their mouth or take it into their hand and then convey it to their mouth. His way of wording this opinion suggests 1) that communicants' receiving the particle of consecrated bread directly into their mouths without first taking it in their hands is a relatively new custom, one which "now is" but has not always been, and 2) that there are now people in his milieu who feel that taking the consecrated bread in the hand shows contempt for the Eucharist.[58]

James knows the custom by which people who are not priests receive the consecrated bread in their hands. In his decisions, his main concern is not with receiving in the hand but with taking in

---

monophysite party, those were troubled years, when an acceptable priest or deacon (the sixth-century work says a "pure" priest or deacon) might indeed be hard to find in the neighborhood. To that earlier provision of the "Chapters Written from the East" James of Edessa has added his insistence that deaconesses in general may not touch the altar or take the mysteries from it, that their work is to sweep the altar (without touching it), to light the church lamps, and to anoint women in the baptismal rite.

[56] A "pearl" is one of the pieces broken off from the consecrated loaf and received in the rite of Communion. See n. 68 below.

[57] Vööbus, *Synodicon*, 367:247 (Syriac) 368:226–227 (translation).

[58] Ibid. The syntax in this part of the response is complex. Vööbus has in several respects deformed the text's meaning in his translation (368:227, lines 1–7). I propose instead the following translation of these lines:

"If he [the sick person] takes the pearl in his mouth rather than in his hands, as is now the custom of many, he does not give great[er] honor to the Eucharist [the *qūrbānā*] in this way, and if he takes the pearl in his hand and puts it into his mouth, he does not show contempt for it in this way. As for the one who brings it: if the situation is urgent and he takes it in his hand and puts it into the mouth of the sick person. . . ."

the hand to give to someone else. The decisions that he hands down with this concern in mind are based on the principle that persons not ordained should not take the consecrated bread in their own hands to give it to others when a priest is available. He writes nothing about the precise matter of receiving into one's own hand the body of the Lord given by the hand of a priest in the Eucharistic celebration itself. The main significance of his decisions for the historical question with which we are dealing lies in his comments on reception of Communion by sick persons to whom it is brought. These comments reveal 1) that a lay person's reception of the body of the Lord directly in the mouth, without receiving it in the hand to convey it to the mouth, was already the custom of many people in James's environment, and 2) that a corresponding negative attitude toward Communion in the hand had risen.[59] In dealing with these issues James may have represented views more rigorous than those of many of his West Syrian contemporaries.[60] Nevertheless, he did not accept the negative atti-

[59] It was just at this time that the Chalcedonians, assembled in the Quinisext or Trullan Council (A.D. 692), rejected the practice by which the faithful received Communion not by presenting their hands in the form of a cross (the manner which the council still considered correct) but by bringing vessels made of gold or some other material in which, evidently, they would receive the consecrated bread and put it in their mouths by tilting the vessel, or would even use the vessel to convey the consecrated bread to someone else; see J. D. Mansi, *Sacrorum conciliorum nova et amplissima collectio* (reprint, Graz: Akademische Druck- und Verlagsanstalt, 1960) 11:985–988 (the council's canon 101). Was this being done by Jacobites in northern Syria also, and if so, did they call the vessel a *k*ʰ*pāptā* in Syriac (see n. 52 above)? The fathers of the Quinisext Council explicitly denounced an idea which, they suspected, lay behind the use of the vessel in preference to the presentation of crossed hands, namely, that to receive Communion in one's hand shows insufficient reverence for the Eucharistic body of the Lord. This in itself is evidence of the presence of such ideas in the Christian East in the late seventh century, and of their effect on liturgical practice.

[60] His insistence on law and order as he saw them and his penchant for combating established ways of which he did not approve got him into trouble with his clergy in Edessa. The twelfth-century Jacobite patriarch Michael reports that on one occasion James of Edessa demonstrated his attitude in Antioch itself by burning a book of canons (compiled by himself?) in front of the patriarchal residence, in protest against what he saw as the general failure of the clergy and the people to observe the canons in the book: see J.-B.

tude toward a lay person's Communion in the hand as an attitude worth raising to a canonical principle.

Be that as it may, the ancient practice of receiving the mysteries in the right hand supported by the left hand lost ground in the West Syrian Church. It was still a familiar practice in the eighth century, at least in the Jacobite East (the maphrianate, comprising the West Syrian dioceses in the former Persian Empire), for George, bishop of the Arabs in Mesopotamia from 686 until his death in 724,[61] mentions it in his liturgical commentary.[62]

On the other side (the western side) of the old imperial frontier, John, bishop of Dara, in his ninth-century commentary on the Eucharistic liturgy, carefully states who should communicate whom, but he says nothing at all about the way lay persons receive the sacred species.[63] Is this because there was no longer a single way of receiving them, or is it because Communion in the hand was already going out of fashion in the Jacobite West (as it was in the neighboring Chalcedonian Churches) but was still the regular practice in dioceses of the Jacobite East like the diocese of George of the Arabs (and among the Nestorians of the same region)? John of Dara mentions something new and significant: the presence of a spoon on the altar.[64] There is no need of a spoon if the consecrated bread is still being put on the communicant's hand. In this same century, the ninth, Yaḥya ibn Jarir tells us for the first time that there were three different ways of receiving Communion in the West Syrian Church: with a spoon, on the hand, and in the

---

Chabot, ed., *Chronique de Michel le syrien, patriarche jacobite d'Antioche (1166–1199)* 4 vols. (Paris: E. Leroux, 1899–1910) 2:474 (French translation) 4:445–446 (Syriac).

[61] George's residence was probably at Kufa, according to Jean Maurice Fiey, "Les diocèses du 'maphrianat' syrien, 629–1860," *Parole de l'Orient* 5 (1974) 369. Kufa was in south-central Mesopotamia, well to the south of modern Baghdad.

[62] George of the Arabs *Exposition of the Mysteries of the Church*, ed. and trans. R. H. Connolly and H. W. Codrington, *Two Commentaries on the Jacobite Liturgy* (London/Oxford: Williams and Norgate, 1913) 11 in Syriac letter-numerals (text), 20 in arabic numerals (translation).

[63] See Jean Sader, *Le lieu de culte et la messe syro-occidentale selon le "De oblatione" de Jean de Dara: Etude d'archéologie et de liturgie*, Orientalia christiana analecta, 223 (Rome: Pontifical Oriental Institute, 1983) 125–128, with the references he gives there.

[64] Ibid., 66, 128.

mouth.[65] Communion in the hand is still known, but practice at Communion is clearly no longer uniform in the West Syrian Church as a whole, and in the Jacobite West the liturgical spoon has arrived at Dara.

In the Jacobite East at the end of the ninth century, Moses bar Kepha, bishop of Bet Raman (Ba Rimma) and Bet Kiyonaye (Bawazij) in the middle Tigris region from 863 until 903, included in his own liturgical commentary the substance of what George of the Arabs had written on the subject around two hundred years earlier.[66] Bar Kepha, more interested in the religious values expressed by the ritual of his church than he was in ritual details for their own sake, tended to draw upon George of the Arabs for material expressing those values; hence, it is not impossible that he incorporated George's brief remarks on the position of the hands for receiving Communion not because Communion in the hand was still normal in Bar Kepha's own time but because of what George had so finely written, at that precise point in his own earlier commentary, of the union of ourselves with God the Word effected by our reception of the mysteries, and of the position of our hands as a "sign" expressing the "magnificence of the gift that is given, which is a pledge of immortal life."

Nevertheless, we may tentatively accept Bar Kepha's inclusion of this passage from George's commentary as evidence that around A.D. 900 Communion in the hand was still admitted, at least as an option, in the West Syrian Church, and specifically in its maphrianate of the East, where Moses Bar Kepha, like George of the Arabs, was a bishop. Ritual practice in the Jacobite East did come to differ in some respects from that of the Jacobite West, although for the ninth century that is hard to document.[67] The presence of

[65] See Paul Hindo's French translation of this passage from Ibn Jarir's unpublished *Al-Muršid* in *Disciplina antiochena antica, Syri*, vol. 3, *Textes concernant les sacrements*, Sacra Congregazione per la Chiesa Orientale, Fonti, 2/27 (Vatican City: Tipografia Poliglotta Vaticana, 1941) 193 n. 1.

[66] Connolly and Codrington, *Two Commentaries*, Syriac letter-numerals 84 (text), arabic numerals 88 (translation). A reference to the passage in the commentary by George of the Arabs is in n. 62 above.

[67] In the last years of Bar Kepha's long life he was also administrator of the most important dioceses of the West Syrian Church's eastern zone, in what had been the Persian Empire: Mosul to the north of his own diocese, and Tagrit to the south: see Fiey, "Les diocèses du 'maphrianat,'" 348–351. This

the shorter form of our prayer by Philoxenus in Add. 17,125, a codex compiled for practical use in some West Syrian monastic community (in the Jacobite East?), shows that in that monastery, unfortunately not identified in the manuscript, Communion in the hand was still a living reality around the same time, if Wright's paleographic dating of the manuscript to the ninth or tenth century is correct.

After that, there is silence. In the allegorical commentary on the West Syrian Eucharistic liturgy written by Dionysius bar Salibi, bishop of Marash (1154–1166) and, simultaneously, of Mabbug (1155–1166), then of Amida (1166–1171)—dioceses in the Jacobite West—nothing at all is said of the manner in which the clergy and the faithful receive Communion.

IV. THE LATE THIRTEENTH CENTURY: BAR HEBRAEUS

We do know that in the latter part of the thirteenth century there was still variety in the way of giving Communion, because Barhebraeus (Grigurius Abu l-Faraj ibn al-'Ibri), who died in 1286 as maphrian of Tagrit and Mosul and catholicos of all the East, that is, as the head of the West Syrian Church in what had in earlier centuries been the Persian Empire, knew and described these three ways of communicating the faithful: 1) the priest gives the precious body, and the deacon presents the chalice for the communicant to drink from it; 2) the priest dips the body into the chalice held on his right by the deacon and then communicates the person receiving, "as we do it in the West"; 3) the priest moistens the pearls of the Eucharistic bread (the small sections marked off by incisions on the Eucharistic bread) with the consecrated wine in the chalice before he breaks them off at the fraction,[68] then at Communion he communicates the faithful by giving

---

marks him as a responsible exponent of any eastern usages of his Jacobite Church diverging from those of his patriarchate in the West.

[68] The round, flat loaf of leavened Eucharistic bread used in the West Syrian Church is divided into small sections by lines incised before the bread is baked. The resulting segments are called pearls. At the time of Eucharistic fraction before Communion, they are detached from one another, and each person receiving Communion receives one of them. The use of the word "pearl" in this sense is based on Ephrem's metaphor of Christ as pearl (see Ephrem De margarita, referred to in n. 38 above.

to each person one of the pearls thus mingled with the consecrated wine, as "the Easterners do it."[69]

If Communion in the hand was still practiced in Barhebraeus' day, it had to fit the first of these three ways of communicating which he describes. In this first way, the pearl is given separately from the sacred blood, and the priest can either put the pearl directly into the communicant's mouth or put it on his or her hand. Unfortunately, Barhebraeus specifies neither. For that matter, his first way, in which the priest places the Eucharistic particle either in the communicant's hand or directly on his or her tongue, may have been obsolescent, if not already obsolete, in the West Syrian Church when he wrote. His description of it differs from that of the other two ways: he seems to feel the need to justify the first way by declaring it "right and legitimate," and he does not say that it is the way of communicating actually practiced in any particular region, as he does for the second and third ways. When he described his first way, was he thinking of practice in the East Syrian Church rather than in his own?

---

[69] Barhebraeus *Nomocanon* 4.5, ed. Paulus Bedjan, *Nomocanon Gregorii Barhebraei* (Paris/Leipzig: Otto Harrassowitz, 1898) 45–46. Joseph Aloysius Assemani's Latin translation of the passage can be found in *Disciplina antiochena antica*, *Siri*, 3:193–194. In the *Nomocanon*, especially in the first seven chapters, which are devoted entirely to ecclesiastical administration, to rites, and to the sacraments, Barhebraeus cites many precedents from earlier times. I have not depended upon these precedents *apud* Barhebraeus, because he cites them freely enough to subordinate them to his own opinions (see the examples of this given by Vööbus, *Syrische Kanonessammlungen*, 1/1/B:528–535), and one even wonders whether he drew his precedents from an official, solidly traditional collection like the *Synodicon* or from the works of individual authors which he happened to have on hand (see Walter Selb, *Orientalisches Kirchenrecht*, vol. 2, *Die Geschichte des Kirchenrechts der Westsyrer (von den Anfängen bis zur Mongolenzeit)*, Österreichische Akademie der Wissenschaften, philosophisch-historische Klasse, Sitzungsberichte, 543 = Veröffentlichungen der Kommission für antike Rechtsgeschichte, 6 [Vienna: Österreichische Akademie der Wissenschaften, 1989] 155).

Some precedents of interest to us here do turn up in earlier sources, and a comparison of them there with their form in the *Nomocanon* of Barhebraeus confirms what Vööbus and Selb have written about the learned maphrian's approach to earlier texts. Barhebraeus is an excellent witness to the practices of his own time, but for earlier times I have used only sources less derivative and less systematically subjected to editorial change.

Barhebraeus' second and third ways do not serve well as descriptions of Communion in the hand. The liturgical spoon could be used in both of these ways of giving Communion, but he says nothing about the spoon in this context.[70] The second way, he says, is the way "we do it in the West," while the third way is the way "the Easterners do it." On first reflection, one might naturally think that he was referring here to his own West Syrian, Jacobite, Church and to the East Syrian, Nestorian Church, but that can hardly be what he intends. By "the West" he must mean the patriarchate, that part of the West Syrian Church which is immediately subject to the Jacobite patriarch of Antioch, while "the Easterners" must be the Jacobite Christians of the maphrianate, the Eastern part of the West Syrian Church, geographically situated in the formerly Persian territory, subject to the Jacobite patriarch, but having the maphrian closer at hand to perform many of the patriarchal functions. This understanding of Barhebraeus' distinction is not contradicted by his including himself, the maphrian of the Jacobite East for the last twenty-two years of his life, among the Westerners. He was actually from the western part of his church, and it was in its western dioceses that he lived continually until shortly before he became maphrian.[71] He may, in fact, have produced his *Nomocanon,* or part of it, including this part, while he was still living in the Jacobite West.[72]

So by the late thirteenth century the consecrated bread was no longer placed in the communicant's hands in the West Syrian

[70] He does say elsewhere that a spoon should be used in communicating: see *Disciplina antiochena antica,* Siri, 3:193, n. 1.

[71] Born in Melitene in 1225, Barhebraeus studied in Antioch and in Syrian Tripolis, and he was bishop of Gubba, then of Akko, and finally of Aleppo—dioceses which were all in the western, patriarchal, part of the church—until the arrival of the Mongols in 1260 led to his move to Maraga in Azerbaijan. In 1264 he was appointed maphrian of the East. For the biographical details, see Vööbus, *Syrische Kanonessammlungen,* 1/1B:499–501. For the geographical locations of the places mentioned by Vööbus, see the fold-out map of Jacobite dioceses between 1150 and 1280 at the end of the volume by Peter Kawerau, *Die jakobitische Kirche im Zeitalter der syrischen Renaissance: Idee und Wirklichkeit* (Berlin: Akademie-Verlag, 1960), which also shows the boundary between the patriarchal territory and the territory of the maphrianate. Gubba (or Gubos), not on the map, was near Melitene (ibid., 111, n. 23).

[72] See Vööbus, *Syrische Kanonessammlungen,* 1/1/B:506–507.

Church. Two other ways of giving Communion to lay persons had supplanted it in the two major regions of the Church.

In the western region, immediately subject to the patriarch, priests were giving Communion by taking a particle of consecrated bread from the paten, dipping it into the consecrated wine of the chalice held by a deacon at the priest's right hand, and then conveying it directly to the communicant's mouth. To do this, priests perhaps usually used a spoon.

In the Church's eastern zone, subject to the maphrian, however, priests were giving Communion without using the chalice at all, by taking from the paten a particle broken from the consecrated loaf at the fraction, after it had been moistened with consecrated wine, and conveying the moistened particle directly to the communicant's mouth, probably without the use of a spoon. One of these two ways of giving Communion continues as the universal practice of the West Syrian Church today.

V. THE TWENTIETH CENTURY

In our own times, lay people do receive Communion in their hands in the Syrian East, not in the West Syrian Church, however, but in the East Syrian Church (now called correctly the Church of the East, more popularly the Assyrian Church, less desirably, in the preference of its own members, the Nestorian Church). Their manner of doing so is essentially the first of the three ways described by Barhebraeus in the thirteenth century, the way which he did not then find characteristic of either the western or the eastern part of his own Church.[73]

---

[73] When the faithful receive Communion in the Church of the East, they first purify their hands and their faces by bringing the palms of their hands close to a censer placed at the priest's left and wafting some of the smoke toward their faces; they then present themselves before the priest, with their hands crossed in the manner prescribed in the ancient texts. The priest places a piece of the consecrated bread in the hand of each communicant, who conveys it to his or her mouth and then moves on to stand before a deacon standing at the priest's right, holding a chalice which he proffers to the communicant and a red cloth with which the communicant, after drinking, wipes his or her mouth and the deacon wipes the rim of the chalice. Since almost everyone present for the Eucharistic *qūrbānā* receives Communion, there are usually several deacons with chalices, lined up in a row at the priest's right.

It is interesting to note that in the West Syrian Church of our own times (the Syrian Orthodox Church) the manner of giving Communion to nonclerical persons is that of Barhebraeus' third way. In his own age, this was not the way characteristic of the western part of his Church, the region immediately subject to the Jacobite patriarch of Antioch, within which such historic centers as Edessa and Antioch itself lay. It was rather the way characteristic of the eastern part of the Church, the maphrianate, whose territory corresponded roughly to that of modern Iraq.[74]

The priest no longer places the Lord's body on the communicant's hand as he did in Philoxenus' time, but the formula which he pronounces today as he gives the body and blood to the faithful people,

"The atoning *gmourto* of the Body and Blood of Christ our God is given to the faithful [the communicant's name is pronounced] for the remission of offenses and for the forgiveness of sins in both worlds forever and ever,"[75]

retains the words which Philoxenus himself pronounced as believers approached him to receive in their hands a *gᵉmūrtō*, a fiery

[74] At the end of the rite of fraction and intinction, the Syrian Orthodox priest today uses one of the pearls of the consecrated loaf of bread to moisten the others by dipping it into the chalice as often as is necessary and touching it, while it is quite wet with the consecrated wine, to each of the pearls still attached to one another as the loaf lies on the paten. At the Communion of the faithful, he breaks off the number of pearls needed, brings them on the paten to the communicants (without the chalice) and places one of the pearls previously moistened with the precious blood directly in the mouth of each communicant. The liturgical spoon is used in the Communion of the celebrant and other clerics, but not of the lay people. See Aelred Cody, "L'eucharistie et les heures canoniales chez les Syriens jacobites: une description des cérémonies," *L'Orient syrien* 12 (1967) 169–170, 176, 184–185.

[75] *Anaphoras: The Book of the Divine Liturgies According to the Rite of the Syrian Orthodox Church of Antioch*, translated from the original Syriac by Archdeacon Murad Saliba Barsom, (place of publication not indicated; edited and published by Metropolitan Mar Athanasius Yeshue Samuel, Archbishop of the Syrian Orthodox Church in the United States of America and Canada, 1991) p. 142 (the corresponding Syriac text is on p. 141). The historic importance of this volume should not be overlooked. The Syrian Orthodox Church has never allowed the altar texts for the Holy Liturgy or the texts of sacramental and pontifical rites to be printed. It has continued to insist on the use of

coal,[76] and to drink from the chalice. We know that those words were essentially these,

"The body of God for the forgiveness of sins, and the blood of the Son of God for the remission of offenses,"

because he quoted them in one of his discourses.[77]

---

manuscripts for them. The wise, open, and far-sighted Mar Athanasius Yeshue Samuel, who has done much for his Church in general and who is its founder and organizer in North America, has convinced his fellow hierarchs that this finely printed book of the anaphoras in Syriac and English, and other bilingual volumes with the sacramental rituals, are necessary if the Church's liturgical heritage is to flourish in the diaspora. For this, and for many other things, those of us who belong to sister churches and who have enjoyed association with Mar Athanasius Yeshue are also grateful. I know that Fr. Aidan Kavanagh, to whom this collection of essays is presented, will join me in saying that.

[76] See n. 26 above.

[77] A. Tanghe, "Memra de Philoxène de Mabboug sur l'inhabitation du Saint-Esprit," Le Muséon 73 (1960) 45 (Syriac) 61 (French translation).

Joanne M. Pierce

5. Early Medieval Vesting Prayers in the *ordo missae* of Sigebert of Minden (1022–1036)

The liturgical reforms of Vatican II ushered in a number of significant changes in the way the Roman liturgy was to be celebrated. However, in that process, a certain number of ritual moments were either eliminated completely, or have fallen into disuse by being made "optional." One of these moments is the presider's recitation of prayers as he dons the liturgical vestments for the celebration of the Eucharist: the vesting prayers.

These texts (as well as the liturgical vestments they accompanied) were considered an essential element of sacerdotal (and ministerial) spirituality and ritual activity in the medieval period, and provide an important way of accessing some key moments and insights. Some modern authors have treated these texts dismissively, as "not of great interest."[1] However, others do not take the significance of liturgical vesture so lightly. As Aidan Kavanagh, o.s.b., writes: "The vestment is a garment, not a costume. Its sacredness in turn derives from the nature of the events in which it is worn. Since these events are not trivial, neither can the sacred garment afford to be trivial."[2]

---

[1] Robert Cabié, *The Church at Prayer, Volume II: The Eucharist* (Collegeville: The Liturgical Press, 1986) 150.

[2] Aidan Kavanagh, o.s.b., "Liturgical Vesture in the Roman Catholic Tradition," in Christa C. Mayer-Thurman, Raiment for the Lord's Service: A Thousand Years of Western Vestments (Chicago: The Art Institute of Chicago, 1975) 13–15; here, 13. He was a key figure in organizing the entire exhibit, and has indeed been a key figure in the entire area of liturgical studies in the United States. I might add that his influence in my own educational career, as my

Certainly, for Christians of the early medieval period (here, the ninth through the eleventh centuries), neither liturgical events nor liturgical vestments were regarded as trivial. As Kavanagh points out, all sacraments (including the Eucharist) were originally treated as "unsettling encounters between living presences divine and human in the here and now."[3] It is therefore understandable that the donning of the liturgical vestments[4] was considered an important ritual transition moment before offering the "Holy Sacrifice," and the words and gestures which accompanied this liminal moment testify to several different ways of apprehending and entering into another reality, this public but intimate encounter with the Other.[5]

---

professor and advisor at Yale Divinity School, helped to shape my own interest in a pursuit of a career as a professor of historical and liturgical theology.

[3] Aidan Kavanagh, o.s.b., *On Liturgical Theology* (Collegeville: The Liturgical Press/Pueblo, 1984) 82. Citing Robert Taft, s.j., Kavanagh further points out that the medieval use of allegory in liturgical commentary does mark an initial moment in the "shift from structure to interpretation," leading to the Reformation and modern problem of secondary theology "determining rather than interpreting liturgical text and form," 80–81. See also Robert Taft, s.j., "The Structural Analysis of Liturgical Units: An Essay in Methodology," *Worship* 52 (1978) 314–329; here, 315–317.

[4] A complete bibliography on the history of liturgical vestiture would be an article in itself. In addition to the important *Raiment for the Lord's Service* cited above, a few of the more recent general works to note include: W. Jardine Grisbrooke, "Vestments," in Cheslyn Jones, *et al.*, *The Study of Liturgy* (New York: Oxford University Press, 1978, 1992) 542–547; Gilbert Cope, "Vestments," in J. G. Davis, ed., *The New Westminster Dictionary of Liturgy and Worship* (Philadelphia: Westminster, 1986) 521–540; John D. Laurence, S.J., "Vestments, Liturgical," in Peter E. Fink, S.J., ed., *The New Dictionary of Sacramental Worship* (Collegeville: The Liturgical Press/Michael Glazier, 1990) 1305–1314; Robert Lesage, *Vestments and Church Furniture*, transl. Fergus Murphy (New York: Hawthorn, 1960; *Twentieth Century Encyclopedia of Catholicism*, Section X, Volume 114); Janet Mayo, *A History of Ecclesiastical Dress* (London: Batsford, 1984); Cyril E. Pocknee, *Liturgical Vesture: Its Origins and Development* (London: Mowbray, 1960); Roger Reynolds, "Vestments, Liturgical," in *Dictionary of the Middle Ages* 12 (1989) 397–404; and Rudolf Suntrup, *Die Bedeutung der liturgischen Gebärden und Bewegungen in lateinischen und deutschen Auslegungen des 9.bis 13. Jahrhunderts* (München: Wilhelm Fink Verlag, 1978; Münstersche Mittelalter-Schriften, Band 37). All of these contain further bibliography on the subject.

[5] See, for example, Joseph Jungmann, *The Mass of the Roman Rite: Its Origins and Development*, trans. Francis A. Brunner (Westminster: Christian Clas-

The task of analyzing these medieval prayer texts is more complex than might appear at first glance.[6] The actual wording of these prayers is highly variable, and seems to change according to time of composition and place of use. Jungmann notes that in general these prayers seem to fall into three categories, which stress different allegorical or symbolic themes: the earliest, which focuses on the moral or ethical expectations for the presider; a later shift to the connection between the priest and the person of Christ; and last, an emphasis on elements of Christ's passion commemorated in the Mass.[7]

The task may be simplified by choosing one particular set of early medieval vesting prayers as a focus. Perhaps the most complete collection can be found in the early eleventh-century *ordo missae* produced for the use of Sigebert, bishop of the German city of Minden (1022–1036).[8] An examination of these Minden prayers

sics, 1986; reprint of the second edition, 1951) Volume I, 280: "the priest in a sense leaves this earth and enters another world, the shimmer of which is mirrored in his vesture . . . each piece of clothing [had] a particular relation to that other world." This standard work in the history of the Mass will hereafter be referred to as MRR I (or II, for Volume II).

[6] A complete study of the evolution and significance of the vesting rite would include examination of several areas beyond the scope of this article. The vesting prayers at Mass should be set in the context of other medieval liturgical moments, including the prayers for the dedication of vestments, and prayers to accompany other vesting rituals, e.g. ordinations and coronations. In addition, a wider ritual studies approach should include an analysis of the cultural codes implied in vesting and vestiture in general.

[7] Jungmann, MRR I, 280–281.

[8] This (incomplete) manuscript, which contains an *ordo missae* as well as an *ordo* for the veneration of the Cross, and the beginning of a series of daily prayers, is actually a *libellus precum,* or book(let) of prayers. It is one of a set of nine liturgical books prepared for Sigebert about the year 1030, and, judging from the generally excellent physical condition of the manuscript, may well have been used as a source book or guide for a master of ceremonies. For a more complete discussion of its significance, see Joanne Pierce, "New Research Directions in Medieval Liturgy: The Liturgical Books of Sigebert of Minden (1022–1036)," in Gerard Austin, O.P., ed., *Fountain of Life* (Washington: The Pastoral Press, 1991) 51–67. The original manuscript is held in the collection of the Herzog August Bibliothek in Wolfenbüttel, in the former West Germany, under the signature *Codex Helmstadiensis* 1151. The eucharistic section of the manuscript was edited in 1557 by Matthias Flacius Illyricus, and the *ordo missae* became known as the Missa Illyrica. This edition can most easily

in the light of those found in earlier and slightly later *ordines missae* may yield some deeper insights into the various streams of medieval spirituality which prompted their composition and use.[9]

The actual vesting rite in the Minden *ordo* can be subdivided into three distinct parts: the preparation for vesting; the actual donning of each piece of liturgical vesture; and prayers after vesting.[10] Each of these sections contains a series of related psalms, versicles, *preces*, and longer, oration-style, prayer texts. While the pre-and post-vesting structures will be discussed briefly, the main focus of this article will be on the actual vesting process, with the accompanying prayers.

The preparation for vesting at Minden would have been rather lengthy if followed in its totality. The priest or bishop *(sacerdos)*[11]

be found in Edmond Martène, *De antiquis Ecclesiae ritibus* (1737; reprinted Hildesheim: G. Olms, 1967), *Lib. I, Cap. IV, Ordo IV*, cols. 489–528. (All further references to *ordines* found in Martène can be found in this book and chapter unless otherwise noted.) It should be noted that the Martène edition should not be used without consulting two additional works by Aimé-Georges Martimort: *La documentation liturgique de Dom Edmond Martène. Étude codicologique.* (Città del Vaticano: Biblioteca Apostolica Vaticana, 1978; *Studi e Testi* 279); and "Additions et corrections à *La documentation liturgique de Dom Edmond Martène*," *Ecclesia Orans* 3 (1986) 81–105. A fresh edition of the entire manuscript has been done by Joanne M. Pierce, *Sacerdotal Spirituality at Mass: The Prayerbook of Sigebert of Minden (1022–1036)* (unpublished Ph.D. dissertation: University of Notre Dame, 1988); it is presently under revision for possible publication in the *Medieval Studies* series of the Medieval Institute, University of Notre Dame. See also Joanne M. Pierce, "Early Medieval Liturgy: Some Implications for Contemporary Liturgical Practice," *Worship* 65 (1991) 509–522; Wolfgang Minde, "Die Handschriften des Bischofs Sigebert von Minden," in Martin Klöckener, ed., *Lectionarium: Berlin, Ehem, Preussische Staatsbibliothek, Ms. theol. lat. qu. 1 (z. Zt. Kraków Biblioteka Jagiellónska, Depositum)* (München: Edition Helga Lengenfelder, 1993); *Codices illuminati mediiaevi* 18, 7–25.

[9] I would like to thank my colleagues in both the Medieval Liturgy Seminar of the North American Academy of Liturgy, and the Medieval Liturgy Group at the University of Notre Dame, for their helpful comments on these prayers as this article was being written.

[10] See also Pierce, *Sacerdotal Spirituality*, 289–319, for overall commentary.

[11] The terminology used to refer to the presider is not consistent in the manuscript. While the more general and inclusive word *sacerdos* (for a bishop or priest celebrant) is used frequently (here in the rubrics at the very beginning of the *ordo*, for example), in some instances the rubrics refer more specifically to the bishop *(episcopus)*. This duality of meaning referring to the liturgical presider was certainly true in the Carolingian period, although by the elev-

enters the sacristy to vest after first kneeling at the altar to recite a series of psalms, the *Pater noster* and the *Credo*, several versicles, and probably one or two from a series of five other *orationes*[12] depending on the time and place (the rubrics specifically note "if time permits").[13]

He then enters the sacristy to put on the vestments.[14] After a prayer requesting God's assistance by the intervention of all the saints and chosen ones[15] (an augmented version of the *Actiones*

---

enth century *sacerdos* was taken more and more to refer to the priest alone; see Pierre-Marie Gy, o.p., "Notes on the Early Terminology of the Christian Priesthood," in Bernard Botte, *et. al.*, eds, *The Sacrament of Holy Orders* (Collegeville: The Liturgical Press, 1962) 98–115; here, 107 and 115. See also "Early Medieval Prayers Addressed to the Trinity in the *ordo missae* of Sigebert of Minden (1022–1036)," to appear in *Traditio* 51 (1996).

[12] Fernand Cabrol seems to assume that every prayer text in an *Alia* series (such as this one) would indeed be recited; there are several in the complete Minden *ordo missae*. Indeed, Cabrol estimated that the celebration would have lasted from cockcrow to noon. See Cabrol, "La messe latine de Flacius Illyricus," RB 22 (1905) 151–165; here, 153. I disagree; even though this is an *ordo missae* clearly designed for large and lengthy celebrations involving the bishop and entire diocese of Minden, the time required to recite every prayer text in the complete *ordo* seems excessive. The *Alia* directive should be interpreted as meaning "another," implying a choice within a series, not "next" in the sense of unalterable links in a chain. See Pierce, *Sacerdotal Spirituality*, 449–450, and "Early Medieval Prayers Addressed to the Trinity."

[13] Pierce, *Sacerdotal Spirituality*, nos. 1–8, 149–155; the rubrical direction is found in no. 1, 149. These texts and the texts for the vesting prayers discussed in the body of this article can also be found in Martène, cols. 490–494.

[14] See Pierce, *Sacerdotal Spirituality*, no. 9, 156. In fact, the sacristy is not mentioned at this point; the rubric simply states that "he gets up to put on the priestly vestments."

However, at the close of the vesting rite, another rubric clearly mentions the sacristy: after incense is prepared and the gospel-book is kissed, the bishop (*episcopus*) is directed to recite a series of versicles as he leaves the sacristy (*de sacrario*). See Pierce, *Sacerdotal Spirituality*, no. 38, 166.

[15] The prayer reads:

"Interuenientibus pro nobis omnibus
sanctis et electis tuis.
actiones nostras quaesumus Domine
et aspirando preueni. et
adiuuando prosequere. ut omnis oratio
et cuncta nostra operatio.
et a te semper incipiat.
et per te coepta finiatur. Per."

nostras prayer which in Minden closes the thanksgiving rite after Mass in the sacristy[16]), the presider then washes his hands with the versicle *Lavabo inter innocentes*[17] and the prayer *Largire sensibus nostris:*

"Largire sensibus nostris omnipotens Deus. ut sicut hic exterius abluuntur inquinamenta manuum. sic a te mundentur interius pollutiones mentium. et crescat in nobis augmentum sanctarum uirtutum."[18]

The explicit connection made in this prayer between exterior washing of the body (hands) and both interior purification of the mind as well as growth in holiness sets the tone for the rest of the

---

The text can be found in Pierce, *Sacerdotal Spirituality*, no. 10, 156. Texts from the Minden *ordo* will be cited using spelling and punctuation as it appears in the manuscript. This particular prayer can also be found at the beginning of the *ordo missae* in the sacramentary of Amiens (variously dated from the ninth or tenth century). See the edition by Victor Leroquais, "L'*ordo missae* du sacramentaire d'Amiens," *Ephemerides Liturgicae* (EL) 41 (1927) 435–445; here, 439.

[16] "Actiones nostras quaesumus Domine et
aspirando preueni. et aduiuando
prosequere. ut omnis oratio et cuncta
nostra operatio. et a te semper incipiat.
et per te cepta finiatur. Per"

See Pierce, *Sacerdotal Spirituality*, no. 204, 259. This form of the prayer is found widely in the Gregorian and Gelasian sacramentary traditions, and in the contemporary *ordines missae* from the tenth and eleventh centuries. It was retained, with minor changes, as part of the thanksgiving after Mass in the *Missale Romanum*.

[17] Pierce, *Sacerdotal Spirituality*, no. 11, 156. The line is taken from Ps 25(26):6, and is found in the same relative position in several of the contemporary *ordines:* Amiens (Leroquais, "Amiens," 439); Troyes (Martène, *Ordo* VI, col. 528, with the *Asperges* verse, Ps 50:9); St. Martin of Tours (Martène, *Ordo* VII, col. 534, with the *Asperges*); and in the sacramentary of Figeac (for the use of Moissac; Martène, *Ordo* VIII, col. 537). Tirot notes that the *Lavabo* is the oldest prayer text used with liturgical handwashing, first to begin the vesting process, and later, at the offertory. See Paul Tirot, "Les prières d'offertoire du VIIe au XVIe siècle," EL 98 (1984) 148–197; here, 176–177.

[18] See Pierce, *Sacerdotal Spirituality*, no. 12, 156. It is also found at the offertory in the Minden *ordo*, and accompanies liturgical handwashings in many of the earlier and contemporary *ordines*. For a more complete discussion, see Tirot, "Les prières d'offertoire," 176–177; Jungmann, MRR I, 277; and Pierce, *Sacerdotal Spirituality*, 290–294.

vesting actions and prayers to follow, which may account for its widespread use in earlier and contemporary *ordines*.[19] As Jungmann notes, in early medieval liturgical celebration, "the preparation of the outer man was apparently a very serious concern";[20] thus, as will be seen even more clearly later, practical actions are often allegorized by the addition of accompanying prayer texts.[21]

This preparation for vesting is concluded by the presider's "ritual putting-off of the outer clothing"[22] while reciting a short prayer: *"Conscinde Domine saccum meum. et circumda me laetitia salutari."*[23] The verse is taken from Ps 29(30): 12 (you have loosed

[19] It is used again in the Minden *ordo* at the offertory; see Pierce, *Sacerdotal Spirituality*, no. 98, 205–206. Incipit phrases of the prayer are found in the Gregorian and Gelasian traditions among the Holy Thursday orations; others from this text can be found in some of the eighth-century Gelasian sacramentaries among the prayers for the visitation of a monastery. The contemporary *ordines* all use a text identical with the Minden version for sacerdotal handwashings at various points during the Mass. Primary examples include the *ordo missae* of Warmund of Ivrea, edited by Bonifacio Baroffio and Ferdinand Dell'Oro, "L'*ordo missae* del vescovo Warmundo d'Ivrea," in *Studi Medievali*, ser. 3, 16 (1975) 795–824, here, no. 25; the *ordo missae* from Reichenau, edited by Joaquim Bragança, "O 'Ordo Missae' de Reichenau" *Didaskalia* 1 (1971) 137–161, here, no. 11; the Hamburg *ordo* edited by Niels Rasmussen, o.p. in "An Early *ordo missae* from Hamburg with a *litania abecedaria* addressed to Christ (Rome, Bibl. Vallicelliana, Cod. B 141, XI cent.)," EL 98 (1984) 198–211, here, no. 6; and the pontifical of Hugh of Salins, edited by Jean Lemarié, "Le pontifical d'Hugues de Salines, son 'ordo missae' et son 'libellus precum,'" in *Studi Medievali*, ser. 3, 19 (1978) 363–425, no. 01. The prayer text is also found in several of the *ordines* edited along with the Minden *ordo* by Martène. For further discussion, see Pierce, *Sacerdotal Spirituality*, 291–294.

[20] Jungmann, MRR, I, 277–278.

[21] See Noele Maurice Denis-Boulet, "Rites and Prayers," in Aimé-Georges Martimort, Noele Maurice Denis-Boulet, and Roger Beraudy, eds. *The Church at Prayer, Volume II: The Eucharist* (New York: Herder and Herder, 1973) 126. This is the earlier first edition of *The Church at Prayer;* Cabié's commentary mentioned above in note 1 is found in the later second edition prepared in the mid-1980s.

[22] Jungmann, MRR, I, 278. For further discussion, see Pierce, *Sacerdotal Spirituality*, 294–295.

[23] Pierce, *Sacerdotal Spirituality*, no. 13, 157. The verse is used in a few of the contemporary sources to accompany the alb (the *ordo* of St.-Denis, Martène, *Ordo* V, col. 518) or the amice (the ordo of Stavelot, Martène, *Ordo* XV, col. 583; the *ordo* of Nonantola, in Pierre Salmon, "L'*Ordo missae* dans dix manuscrits du Xe au XVe siècle," in *Analecta Liturgica: Extraits des manuscrits*

my sackcloth and girded me with gladness); the reference is clearly applicable to the doffing of the presider's daily clothing ("sackcloth") in preparation for dressing for the celebration of the Mass (note that the verse here speaks explicitly of "the joy of salvation"). Next, the assisting ministers are directed to chant certain psalms (Pss. 83 [84]–87 [88], 115 [116], 131 [132]); Jungmann notes that the first three are the core of the original form of the priestly preparation for vesting and Mass[24]) while the presider (here explicitly referred to as *episcopus*[25]) vests himself.[26]

The first of the vestments to be donned in the Minden *ordo* is the amice, also referred to as the *ephot*, or ephod (in reference to the ancient Jewish priestly vestment[27]). The amice (not always used today) is a thin cotton rectangle which encircles the neck; long, narrow cotton ribbons or strings are attached to the two opposite corners, allowing the presider to secure the amice more tightly by tying the strings across his chest and around his waist. However, Jungmann notes that "vesting did not always occur in the precise order now followed," and observes that the medieval

---

liturgiques de la Bibliothèque Vaticane (Città del Vaticano: Biblioteca Apostolica Vaticana, 1974; *Studi e Testi* 273) 196–221; here, 199).

[24] Jungmann, MRR, I, 272–273. They are indeed found in several contemporary *ordines*, including Nonantola (Salmon, 198); Reichenau (Bragança, no. 7); Ivrea (Baroffio and Dell'Oro, no. 1); Hamburg (Rasmussen, nos. 1 and 2); and Salins (Lemarié, no. 02).

[25] As mentioned in note 7, above, the Minden rubrics refer more specifically to the bishop (*episcopus*) on occasion. This is probably the case here because the vesting prayers listed include texts to accompany episcopal vesture (the *rationale*, the gloves, and the ring) as well as simple priestly vestments (the stole and the chasuble, for example).

[26] Pierce, *Sacerdotal Spirituality*, no. 14, 157.

[27] The use of the term *ephot* for the amice is fairly common in medieval texts from about the eighth century; see Joseph Braun, *Die liturgische Gewandung im Occident und Orient* (Freiburg im Breisgau: Herder, 1907) 23 and 45 (for a complete discussion of the vestment, see 21–52). Interestingly, the rubric introducing the prayer uses this term first when referring to the vestment *(Ad ephot uel amictum induendum)*. See Pierce, *Sacerdotal Spirituality*, no. 15, 157. An interesting discussion of (ancient) Jewish and Christian liturgical vestiture in terms of the concept of "memorial" can be found in the classic book by Max Thurian, *The Eucharistic Memorial*. Part 1. *The Old Testament* (London: Lutterworth Press, 1960; *Ecumenical Studies in Worship* No. 7) 57–73. A much condensed piece (in English) by Braun on vestments can be found in *The Catholic Encyclopedia*, Vol. XV (1912) 388–392. See also Reynolds, "Vestments," 397.

custom was often to put the amice on after the alb, "as would be natural with a scarf or neck-cloth."[28]

The vesting prayer itself reads:

"Humeros meos sancti spiritus gratia tege Domine. renesque meos uiciis omnibus expulsis precinge ad sacrificandum tibi uiuenti et regnanti in saecula saeculorum."[29]

Notice that the prayer is of the ethical/moral type, and contains both a "positive" request that the Lord "cover" the presider's shoulders with the Spirit's grace and a "negative" request that the presider's heart (the "seat of the affections," lit. "kidneys") be girded or encircled by the expulsion of all vices in preparation for the "Sacrifice." Jungmann dates this text to the eleventh century, but it is found in at least one tenth-century *ordo*;[30] he also notes that the primary allegorical focus seems to have been the above-mentioned linen bands tied around the waist.[31]

The alb[32] is the next vestment mentioned in the Minden *ordo*, and, like a few other vestments (the stole and the chasuble, perhaps considered major, more important vesture), is accompanied by both a short text *(Ad albam)* and a longer prayer *(Oratio ad albam)*.[33] The shorter vesting prayer again has a moral theme, comparing the floor-length, white linen robe or gown to the "armor of

---

[28] Jungmann, MRR, I, 278–279.

[29] Pierce, *Sacerdotal Spirituality*, no. 15, 157.

[30] Nonantola (Salmon, p. 199); it is also found in the eleventh-century *ordo* from Reichenau (Bragança, no. 1).

[31] Jungmann, MRR, I, 281; see n. 33 for other sources. Amalarius, in his *Liber Officialis* (823), connects the amice to the allegorical virtue of control over or purification of the voice *(castigatio vocis)* since it is tied around the neck, see J. M. Hanssens, *Amalarii Episcopi Opera Liturgica Omnia*, Tomus II, *Liber Officialis* (Vatican City: Biblioteca Apostolica Vaticana, 1948; Studi e Testi 139), l. I, c. 17, 239. Reynolds, however, notes that "the vesting" prayer refers to the "helmet of salvation," perhaps because it was often draped over the head like a hood while the other vestments were put on; see "Vestments," 397. He appears to be referring to the prayer which eventually became standard in the *Missale Romanum*. See also Braun, *Gewandung*, 711.

[32] For more on the history and development of the alb, see Braun, *Gewandung*, 59–101, and Reynolds, "Vestments," 397–398.

[33] See Pierce, *Sacerdotal Spirituality*, nos. 16 and 17, 158.

faith"[34] which protects against the "arrows of injustice," and assists in maintaining the presider's equity and righteousness:

"Circumda me Domine fidei armis. ut
ab iniquitatum sagittis erutus.
ualeam aequitatem et iustitiam
custodire."[35]

The longer oration, (addressed to God, *Deus*, not the Lord, *Dominus*) stresses a slightly different idea: the whiteness and purity of the garment. The strong and powerful symbolism of the "white garment" at baptism was appreciated from Christian antiquity:[36] the linen fabric (derived from plant, not animal, matter) and white color were understood in Hellenistic culture to speak of purity and immortality, making it a garment which "has nothing of death in itself."[37] Since "the alb worn by newly baptized Christians . . . was the standard liturgical undergarment of clerics,"[38] it offered to the presider as well a tangible and visible contrast between the darkness and "dirtiness" of sin and the clarity and cleanliness of God (and of divine light, life, and love[39]). The Minden text reads:

"Omnipotens sempiterne Deus te
suppliciter exoro. ut fraude omnium
obfuscatorum exutus. alba ueste

[34] "The spiritual warrior . . . in the armor of faith," Jungmann, MRR, I, 282.

[35] Pierce, *Sacerdotal Spirituality*, no. 16, 158. A few sources assign this text to the amice (e.g., Saint-Denis, Martène, col. 518; Troyes, col. 529).

[36] See, for example, Johannes Quasten, "The Garment of Immortality: A Study of the 'Accipe vestem candidam,'" in *Miscellanea Liturgica in onore di sua eminenza il Cardinale Giacomo Lercaro*, Volume primo (Paris: Desclée, 1966) 391–401.

[37] Ibid., 391–394. The quote is taken from Jerome, *Epistula* 64, 19 (CSEL 54, 610: *nihil in se mortis habente*) see Quasten, 391.

[38] Reynolds, "Vestments," 398. He does note, however, that medieval albs were made of wool (or silk, on occasion) as well as linen.

[39] In noting this contrast, Jungmann suggests a possible scriptural allusion to Rev 7:14 (those dressed in white who have washed their robes in the blood of the Lamb), MRR, I, 282; see n. 37 for other sources for the prayer.
Amalarius interprets the meaning of the alb as a reference to control or purification of the body (*Lib. Off.* l. II, c. 18, 3; Hanssens, 240) or of the other lower or inferior senses (*Lib. Off.* l. II, c. 26, 1; Hanssens, 254).

indutus te sequi merear ad regna ubi
uera sunt gaudia."[40]

The next garment to be donned in the Minden *ordo* is, logically, the cincture (*cingulum*, often referred to in medieval texts as the *zona*, or "belt"), a linen cord or girdle fastened around the waist to secure the alb more closely to the body. Not surprisingly, the text alloted for it also has a moral focus: it is interpreted as the "belt of justice" which spiritually "circumcises" the presider's heart and body of vice as it physically "girds" his loins[41]:

"Circumcinge lumbos meos Domine zona
iustitiae. et circumcide uicia cordis
et corporis mei."[42]

The reference to the girding of the loins alludes to more than one scriptural passage (Luke 12:35; 1 Pet 1:13), as does the idea of circumcision of the heart (Jer 4:4; Rom 2:29). The Minden text seems to be a conflation of two different texts cited by Jungmann,[43] and, as noted above, several variants were in use during the tenth and eleventh centuries.

The prayer accompanying the cincture is followed immediately by another for the *precinctorium*. Braun theorized that this rather rare word is used in the Minden *ordo* for the pontifical vestment known as the *subcinctorium*, a kind of decorated cincture worn over the plain white cincture.[44] The prayer is a more "positive"

[40] Pierce, *Sacerdotal Spirituality*, no. 17, 158. It is found in the Nonantola (Salmon, 199) and Stavelot *ordines* (Martène, col. 583).

[41] According to Amalarius, the cincture signifies the control of reason over the sensuality of the flesh, *Lib. Off.*, l. II, c. 26, 1; Hanssens, 254.

[42] Pierce, *Sacerdotal Spirituality*, no. 18, 158. Versions of the prayer are found frequently in earlier and contemporary sources as a cincture prayer. Examples include the Carolinian *Libellus Coloniensis*, edited by André Wilmart in *Precum libelli quattuor aevi karolini* (Rome: Ephemerides Liturgicae, 1940) 49–59 (here, no. 5); Nonantola (Salmon, 199); Amiens (Leroquais, 440); Salins (Lemarié, no. 08), and several of the *ordines* found in Martène. At least two have the identical text: Reichenau (Bragança, no. 3) and Stavelot (Martène, col. 583).

[43] Jungmann, MRR, I, 283.

[44] Braun, *Gewandung*, 120–122. Like the amice, the *subcinctorium* was often referred to by another scriptural term linked with ancient Jewish vestments worn by the high priests: here, the *balteus*, meaning "belt" or (in Carolingian times) "swordbelt." Reynolds notes that it was "perhaps originally intended to secure the stole to the cincture," in "Vestments," 398.

90

prayer, a request that God encircle or gird the presider with virtue and make his "way" pure:

"Precinge me Domine uirtute. et pone
inmaculatam uiam meam."[45]

This prayer is more rarely seen in other sources, since it does accompany an episcopal, not presbyteral, vestment, which was often fastened on the waist at the same time as the cincture[46]; at least three include the text (or a version) as a cincture prayer[47] and one[48] lists it as a prayer for the maniple (possibly because of the connection between the origin of that vestment as a small towel and the reference to "making clean/pure"). This is an interesting development, especially in light of the later evolution of the *precinctorium* itself: Braun notes that in later centuries, the garment shifted shape from a belt to a piece of cloth shaped more like a maniple (a shorter strip of gold or decorated cloth designed to be draped over the wrist), which was worn draped over or hung from the cincture.[49]

Next in the Minden vesting order comes the stole (or *orarium*[50]). Like the alb, above, the stole is accompanied by the shorter vesting prayer, and a longer oratio. The first, shorter text is a combination of a "positive" and a "negative" request, that the Lord might encircle the presider's neck with the "stole of justice" and purify his mind from all "corruption of sin":

"Stola iustitiae circumda Domine
ceruicem meam. et ab omni corruptione
peccati purifica mentem meam."[51]

---

[45] Pierce, *Sacerdotal Spirituality*, n. 19, 158.

[46] Braun, *Gewanding*, 723.

[47] Nonantola (Salmon, 199), Stavelot (Martène, col. 583) and Troyes (Martène, col. 529).

[48] Saint-Denis (Martène, col. 519).

[49] Braun, *Gewandung*, 117–120.

[50] The word *stola* was used in northern Europe during this period, but in Rome (and in the East in general) the ancient word *orarium* was still in use, see Reynolds, "Vestments," 403.

[51] Pierce, *Sacerdotal Spirituality*, n. 20, 159.

This prayer is used widely in the contemporary ordines to accompany the stole in the vesting process.[52]

The longer prayer also takes the eradication of sin as its starting point, that by freeing the presider from the "chains" of his sins, he might more worthily serve the Lord with "fear and reverence":

"Disrumpe Domine uincula peccatorum
meorum. ut iugo tuae seruitutis
innixus ualeam tibi cum timore et
reuerentia famulari."[53]

The use of the *"iugo"* (*jugum*, yoke) is worthy of note here: the allusion to the "easy yoke"[54] of Matt 11:29-30 is often explicitly spelled out in some versions as "the texts of our Lord from Matthew have been added, and that at a very early time."[55] The scriptural connection is fairly obvious for this prayer; what is perhaps less obvious is its connection with prayers for protection against temptation in some of the early sacramentaries. The incipit of the prayer appears in early manuscripts of the Gregorian Sacramentary and the eighth-century Sacramentary of Angoulême.[56]

---

[52] Some sources have the identical text (Nonantola, Reichenau, and Stavelot, among others) while others use some version of it (e.g., Amiens and Troyes). See Pierce, *Sacerdotal Spirituality*, 302–304.

[53] Pierce, *Sacerdotal Spirituality*, n. 21, 159.

[54] Amalarius, too, makes this connection in his discussion of the stole: it signifies the yoke of Matt 11:29, which means, in his interpretation, the gospel. See *Lib. Off.* l. II, c. 20, 1, and c. 26, 2; Hanssens, 242–243, and 254.

[55] Jungmann, MRR, I, 285; see notes 58 and 59 for more complete lists of sources for these prayers. At least two contemporary *ordines* contain this longer prayer: St-Denis (Martène, col. 519), which does add the actual words of Jesus from the Matthean text (for my yoke is easy and my burden is light); and Stavelot (Martène, col. 583), which does not. In the *Missale Romanum*, this verse is incorporated into the vesting prayer for the chasuble.

[56] GrD 2321: *Missa pro temptatione carnis (Super oblata)*; and An 2295 (the same). All references to the Gregorian sacramentary tradition can be found in the edition by Jean Deshusses, *Le sacramentaire grégorien*, 3 volumes (Fribourg: Éditions Universitaires, 1971, 1979, 1982; *Spicilegium Friburgense* 16, 24, 28). The most recent edition of the sacramentary of Angoulême is by Patrick Saint-Roch, *Liber sacramentorum Engolismensis* (Turnhout: Brepols, 1987; *Corpus Christianorum* 159 C).

The bishop next dons three layers of vestments assigned to three "lower" orders of ordained ministry: the tunicle (subdeacon[57]); the dalmatic (deacon); and the chasuble (priest and bishop). The first is the tunicle (called here the *subtile*, the term used in *ordines* from German-influenced areas such as Minden; the word *tunicella* is used elsewhere[58]), a sleeved overtunic with rather limited ornamentation. The prayer which accompanies it reads:

"Indue me Domine uestimente salutis et
circumda me lorica fortitudinis."[59]

Interestingly, this prayer appears in most other contemporary sources to accompany the white linen alb,[60] possibly because the reference to the "vestment/garment of salvation" calls to mind the scriptural and baptismal "white garment."[61] Like the amice prayer, the image it calls to mind is that of spiritual armor (echoing 1 Thess 5:8, and Eph 6:14-17, especially in the use of the "breastplate," or *lorica*, image).[62]

---

[57] For an interesting discussion of this office (and others of the minor orders) in terms of its proper vestiture, see Roger Reynolds, "The Portrait of the Ecclesiastical Officers in the *Raganaldus Sacramentary* and its Liturgico-Canonical Significance," *Speculum* 46 (1971) 432-442, esp. 441. This article is one of several Reynolds has written on medieval illuminations of vested ecclesiastical ministers in liturgical and canonical documents. Others include "Image and Text: A Carolingian Illustration of Modifications in the Early Roman Eucharistic Ordines," *Viator* 14 (1983) 59-75; "Image and Text: The Liturgy of Clerical Ordination in Early Medieval Art," *Gesta* XXII (1983) 27-38; and "Rites and Signs of Conciliar Decisions in the Early Middle Ages," in *Segni e Riti nella Chiesa altomedievale occidentale* (Spoleto: Presso la Sede del Centro, 1987; Settimane di Studio del Centro Italiano di Studi sull'alto medioevo XXXIII), Tomo primo, 207-244.

[58] Braun, *Gewandung*, 287, note 5; he refers explicitly to Germany, Switzerland, and Hungary.

[59] Pierce, *Sacerdotal Spirituality*, n. 22, 159.

[60] Several sources use a form of this prayer to accompany the tunicle (Salins, Lemarié, no. 011), the cincture (Hamburg, Rasmussen, no. 8), the alb (e.g., Troyes, col. 529, among several of the Martène *ordines*), or as a general vesting prayer (Wilmart, the Cologne *libellus* 4). Some use an identical text, but for the alb (Reichenau, Bragança, no. 2), or the alb and amice together (Amiens, Leroquais, 439).

[61] See the discussion of the alb, above.

[62] See also Jungmann, MRR, I, 282. Amalarius connects the tunicle more generally with the most profound virtues of the soul, or the works of the

The dalmatic, a more elaborately decorated tunic with sleeves, was the normal vestment worn by the deacon (or priest taking the role of deacon) at Mass.[63] Here, it is worn over the tunicle and under the priestly chasuble. Prayers to accompany the donning of the dalmatic seem to be rare in the Middle Ages, and the Minden text is perhaps the best and most accessible example[64]:

"Indumento hoc typico priscorum
patrum ritu in modum crucis
tramitibus purpureis contexto
uestitus humiliter postulo. ut ex
commemoratione passionis tuae fiam
tibi Domine Iesu Christe iugiter
gratiosus. Qui vivis."

For the first time in this series of vesting prayers, the allegorical focus is not an ethical or moral one,[65] but rather Christological—more specifically, to the Mass as commemoration of Christ's passion (Jungmann's third category, marking it as a somewhat later composition than the other vesting prayers). The long, full sleeves of the vestment do, in fact, lead one to notice its cross-like shape; here, it is seen as a "type" of the Cross handed on by the rite or use of the ancient Fathers in a "blood-red" (purpureis) context. This leads to the wider request that the presider be continually/ perpetually "filled with grace" or grateful to Christ by the commemoration of his passion. These references are somewhat unusual in light of the more common medieval association of the dalmatic with festivity[66] and rejoicing; it was seen "as a garment

---

mind (opera mentis); see Lib. Off. l. II, c. 22, 1, and c. 26, 2, Hanssens, 246–247 and 254.

[63] For a more complete discussion of the history and role of the dalmatic, see Braun, Gewandung, 247–305, and Reynolds, "Vestments," 399.

[64] Braun, Gewandung, 725; he lists three other manuscripts in which a form of the prayer appears: Vat. lat. 4746; Vat. Ottob. 27; and Vat. lat. 1145.

[65] Unlike the interpretation provided by Amalarius, who holds that the dalmatic signifies works of charity and mercy to our neighbors, especially widows and orphans; see Lib. Off. l. II, c. 21, 1, and c. 26, 2, Hanssens 243–244 and 254.

[66] The penitential nature of the prayer itself does fit in with the theological agenda of the compiler of the Minden libellus precum: large numbers of penitential prayers called sacerdotal apologiae are included at several points

of praise and joy . . . omitted in penitential seasons [by the twelfth century]."[67]

Like the alb and stole, the chasuble[68] is assigned two vesting prayers, one brief, the second, a longer *oratio*. Both begin with the same words *(Indue* ("cover, envelop") *me Domine)*, a possible reference (according to Jungmann) to the shape of the large, enveloping, poncho-like garment, which ". . . like Christian love, covers everything, and encloses everything. . . ."[69] The shorter text reads:

---

during the *ordo missae*, and other prayer texts have been reshaped to emphasize the themes of sin and repentance, see Pierce, *Sacerdotal Spirituality*, 451, and "New Research Directions," 57–62. Several specific questions arise about the context of this prayer: would a vesting prayer to be recited as a deacon donned the dalmatic differ from the one recited as a priest or bishop put on the vestment? Is the color a reference to the violet (or penitential) vestments worn on the Ember Days, the traditional times for ordinations, or does it refer to the first "deacon-martyrs" (Stephen and Lawrence)? It is even possible that the prayer contains a deliberate echo of the *Vexilla regis*, a hymn by Venantius Fortunatus, used at Holy Week Vespers and on the feast of the Exaltation of the Holy Cross (September 14). Stanza 5 describes the "tree" of the Cross as: "Arbor decora et fulgida, ornata regis purpura," the word "purple" or "blood-red" referring both to "Christ's royal dignity (the purple robe befitting a king; cf. Mark 15, 17) and to Christ's Blood reddening the Cross;" see Joseph Szöverffy, *Hymns of the Holy Cross* (Leyden: Brill, Brookline: Classical Folia Editions, 1976; *Medieval Classics: Texts and Studies* 7) 17. This last idea is made even more plausible by the attention paid to the service of the veneration of the Cross in the Minden *libellus precum*; after the *ordo missae* section comes a detailed order *ad crucem salutandam*. See Pierce, *Sacerdotal Spirituality*, nos. 206–221, 260–268 and 431–438. The cathedral treasury at Minden contains a large, bronze crucifix probably used for the public veneration of the cross about the year 1080; see Hans Butzmann, "Einige Fragen zum Mindener Kreuz und die Adoratio Crucis des Bischofs Sigebert," in *Zwischen Dom und Rathaus. Beiträge zur Kunst-und Kulturgeschichte det Stadt Minden* (Minden: J.C.C. Bruns, 1977) 61–70.

[67] Reynolds, "Vestments," 399. He refers here again to "the vesting prayer," most probably the text retained in the *Missale Romanum*, which does indeed refer to it as the *vestimento laetitiae* and *dalmatica justitiae*.

[68] For a more complete discussion of the chasuble, see Braun, *Gewandung*, 149–247.

[69] Jungmann, MRR, I, 286.

"Indue me Domine sacerdotali
iustitia ut induci merear in
tabernacula sempiterna."[70]

It appears in a number of the contemporary *ordines*, and seems to
be used for the alb just as often as for the chasuble.[71] In fact, the
actual wording of this prayer (and of the one which follows) is
quite variable, perhaps because the various authors and compilers
"differ[ing] in their concept of the garment."[72] The priestly
"right/justification" is seen here as necessary for the presider to
be made worthy to enter the "eternal temple/tabernacle" (an allusion to the imminent entrance into the sanctuary of the cathedral
to celebrate Mass).

The longer oration expresses a different idea: it, too, deals with
moral allegory, but in a more "negative" way, requesting the
Lord's protection (through the "ornament" of humility and charity) against "the insidious enemy" so that the presider might
praise the Lord's name with a pure heart and chaste body.[73] The
full text in the Minden *ordo* runs as follows:

"Indue me Domine ornamento
humilitatis et caritatis. et
concede mihi protectionem contra
hostem insidiatorem ut ualeam puro
corde. et casto corpore laudare
nomen tuum sanctum in saecula
saeculorum amen."[74]

---

[70] Pierce, *Sacerdotal Spirituality*, n. 24, 160.

[71] The Saint-Denis *ordo* has the identical text for the chasuble (Martène, col.
519), while Reichenau (among others) has a text closer to that of the Minden
oratio (Bragança, no. 5). Several others of the Martène *ordines* have texts which
more or less approximate the Minden version, but for the alb (e.g., Stavelot,
Martène, col. 583).

[72] Jungmann, MRR, I, 286.

[73] Amalarius, too, interprets the meaning of the chasuble along similar
lines: it signifies what might be called the "corporal works of mercy" or
"justice," as well as bodily chastity; *Lib. Off.* l. II, c. 18, 1 and 2, and c. 26, 2,
Hanssens, 241, 254.

[74] Pierce, *Sacerdotal Spirituality*, n. 25, 160.

This text, too, is found in a number of contemporary sources as a chasuble prayer, but with a significant number of variations; interestingly, one even uses a form of the text for the stole.[75]

The last of the more usual vestments, the maniple, deriving from a simple "handkerchief or napkin,"[76] was a strip or band of ornamented cloth worn around the wrist.[77] The Minden *ordo* lists two prayers for this vestment, one to be recited while "taking" or holding the maniple *(Cum mappulam acceperit)*, the second, as the maniple is put on *(Cum mappulam induerit)*. The first text reads:

"Inuestione istius mappulae subnixe
deprecor Domine ut sic operer in
temporali conuersatione quatinus
exemplo priorum patrum in futuro
merear. perenniter gaudere. Per Dominum."

According to Jungmann, the maniple in this text is allegorized "as a badge of honor with which one was 'invested' and which one wore even at work."[78] Here, as obliquely in the dalmatic prayer, it is the example of the early fathers which is to guide the daily interactions of the presider, in such a way as to lead him to eternal joy.

The use of the second text, with its focus on "wiping" away uncleansed stain (of sin) by virtue that the presider might serve God without "pollution of mind and body," appears to hint at the original function of the maniple.[79] It reads:

---

[75] The closest version is found in the Hamburg *ordo* (Rasmussen, no. 11); others include Reichenau (Bragança, no. 5) and Stavelot (Martène, col. 583, for the stole).

[76] Jungmann, MRR, I, 283. For a more complete list of manuscript sources and parallels, see Jungmann, 284, and Braun, *Gewandung*, 715–716.

[77] "Until the twelfth century the maniple might be worn on the wrist, left or right, or carried in the hand or fingers," Reynolds, "Vestments," 401.

[78] Jungmann, MRR, I, 284.

[79] It may also hint at Ps 24:3-4 (who shall stand in [the Lord's] holy place? He who has clean hands and a pure heart). Amalarius uses another term for this vestment, *sudarium*, and explicitly parallels the use of a handkerchief to wipe away overflow from the eyes, nose and lips, with the wiping away of the "sweat," "plague," or "trouble" of spiritual weariness *(tedium)* through works of piety; see *Lib. Off.* l. II, c. 22, 1–5, and c. 26, 2, Hanssens, 249–251, 254.

"Da Domine uirtutem manibus meis ad
abstergendam omnem maculam inmundam
et sine pollutione mentis et corporis
ualeam tibi seruire amen."

The contemporary sources and parallels provide one clue: a few
entitle this prayer *ad mappam,* that is, to accompany the drying of
the hands on a towel *(mappa)* after the prevesting ablution.[80] The
maniple was originally a small towel, and the Minden diminutive
(mappula) represents a stage in the evolution of the terminology
used for this vestment (the later word *manipulus,* used in the contemporary Hamburg *ordo).*[81]

The maniple was normally donned before the stole; however, in
one contemporary source (Hamburg), it is the last vestment put
on before leaving the sacristy to celebrate Mass.[82] Here (and in
several of the eleventh-century sources[83]), it is the last of the
"ordinary" vestments to be assumed; the next, and final series of
texts accompany a small group of specifically episcopal garments.[84]

The final three prayers to accompany specific vestments deal
with three[85] associated only with the bishop: the gloves, the ring,
and a short ornamented band of cloth worn on the chest (the

[80] One example is an *ordo* for the use of the monastery of St. Vincenzo al
Volturno (Martène, *Ordo XII,* col. 568). The Stavelot *ordo* lists this prayer *ad
fanonem* (Martène, col. 583).

[81] Rasmussen, no. 12. See also Jungmann, MRR, I, 284; and Braun, *Gewandung,* 517–519. Braun further notes that another word for this vestment, *fano,*
comes from earlier words (Latin *pannus,* Greek *panos,* Anglo-Saxon/Gothic
fana, and High German *fano)* which refer more generally to different kinds of
cloths or veils (e.g., the cloth covering the chalice, the corporal, the amice).
Reynolds notes the evolution of a separate neckpiece called the *fanon* (or
anabolagium) at Rome, "a piece of material with a head hole in the center,"
which was a papal vestment from the twelfth century; "Vestments," 397.

[82] Rasmussen, 207.

[83] For example, Stavelot, St. Vincenzo al Volturno, and Troyes (between
the stole and the chasuble).

[84] The later episcopal order of vesting places the donning of the maniple
after the entry into the church and the prayers at the foot of the altar; see
Rasmussen, 207, and Jungmann, MRR, I, 290.

[85] Interestingly, other pontifical vestments are not mentioned in this list of
vesting prayers, e.g. the pontifical shoes and stockings (*sandalia* and *udones* or
caligae), or the miter and crosier.

rationale). The pontifical gloves (*chirothecae*[86]) are not explicitly mentioned in the Minden *ordo;* the prayer is entitled "At the covering of the hands" (*Ad induendas manus):*

"Creator totius creaturae dignare
me indignum famulum tuum indumentis
iustitiae et laetitiae induere ut
puris mentibus ante conspectum tuum
assistere merear mundus. Per"[87]

Another moral/allegorical prayer, it asks God (the "creator of all creatures") to cover (*induere*) the bishop (the "unworthy servant") with the garments of justification and joy that his mind (or "thoughts"[88]) might be pure as he stands in God's sight.

The bishop next puts on the episcopal ring (on top of his glove) with the prayer:

"Circumda Domine digitos meos
uirtute et decora sanctificatione."[89]

This short prayer is yet another moral allegory, in which the bishop asks that the Lord encircle (surround) his fingers with virtue and sanctifying propriety (*decora*). Like the *precinctorium,* and the dalmatic, medieval prayers to accompany the episcopal ring are rather rare. However, the late tenth-century Sacramentary of Corbie does provide a short text for the bishop as he slips on his ring (handed to him by an assisting minister with the request *"Jube Domine benedicere."*) The bishop responds with a more Christological and eucharistic reference:

"Digna manus nostras Christi custodia servet,
ut tractare queant nostrae monumenta salutis."[90]

---

[86] Reynolds traces their use from France to Rome by the tenth century, and notes that they were "knitted or made of woven white material [and the] backs [were] often highly ornamented"; "Vestments," 403.

[87] Pierce, *Sacerdotal Spirituality,* n. 28, 161.

[88] It is possible that the text here should read "manibus" for "mentibus," since the prayer for the gloves could logically refer to the hands themselves. This would also continue the allusion noted earlier with the maniple to Ps 24:3-4. Since there do not seem to be any parallels or earlier sources for the prayer among the documents studied here, this would be difficult to confirm.

[89] Pierce, *Sacerdotal Spirituality,* n. 29, 102.

[90] Martène, *Ordo* XI, col. 564.

Perhaps the most interesting of all these vesting prayers is the one provided for the vestment known as the *rationale*. First mentioned in the late tenth century, it was a short, ornamental sash, worn over the chasuble on the shoulder and/or chest.[91] At Minden, it stretched across the chest, and was fastened at each shoulder on the chasuble by large round clasps; small fringed ends hung down from each clasp.[92] Originally worn only by a few bishops of German cities, it was used in the later medieval period by certain French bishops as well.[93]

The prayer text reads as follows:

"Da mihi Domine ueritatem tuam
firmiter retinere et doctrinam
ueritatis plebi tuae digne aperire."[94]

[91] Braun, *Gewandung*, 676–677. See also Klemens Honselmann, *Das Rationale der Bischöfe* (Paderborn: Selbstverlag des Vereins für Geschichte und Altertumskunde Westfalens, 1975) 29. A discussion of the general history of the *rationale* can be found in Beda Kleinschmidt, o.f.m., "Das *Rationale* in der abendländischen Kirche," *Archiv für Christliche Kunst* 22 (1904) 9–11, 22–27, 39–42, 52–56, 64–68, 78–80, 88–92. A short summary on the *rationale* in English can be found by Joseph Braun in the article "Rationale," *The Catholic Encyclopedia*, Vol. XII (1911) 651–652.

[92] Honselmann, *Rationale*, 51, 53. He notes that the ivory carving of Bishop Sigebert of Minden (originally used to decorate the cover of the manuscript containing the *ordo missae*) and the full-page painted portrait of Sigebert (originally part of this same manuscript) are among the earliest known depictions of this vestment. See also Beda Kleinschmidt, o.f.m., "Das Rationale von Minden," *Der Kunstfreund* 22 (1906) 65–69. Reynolds notes that the *rationale* was "like a Y- or T-shaped pallium . . . at times trimmed with small bells," "Vestments," 403. Interestingly, the Old Testament Aaronic vestment known as the *ephod*, allegorically connected with the *rationale* as will be seen, seems to have also been trimmed with bells (Ex 28:343–35, and 39:25–26). Thurian notes a dual emphasis in the Old Testament on the ringing of the *ephod* bells in liturgical action: protection for the priest (Ex 28:35) and as a "memorial" for the people (Eccl 45:9); see Thurian, 70.

[93] See Klemens Honselmann, "Das Rationale der Bischöfe von Minden. Ein kostbares mittelalterliches Ornatstück," in *Zwischen Dom und Rathaus. Beiträge zur Kunst-und Kulturgeschichte der Stadt Minden* (Minden: J.C.C. Bruns, 1977) 71–83; here, 72–73. He notes that the use of the vestment continued into the early 20th century in the cities of Eichstatt, Crakow, Paderborn, and Toul.

[94] Pierce, *Sacerdotal Spirituality*, n. 30, 161. For a more complete discussion, see 312–315. An earlier, and quite different prayer to accompany the *rationale* can be found in the tenth-century sacramentary of Corbie (Martène, col. 564).

The allegorical meaning of this prayer can best be understood in the light of yet another set of ancient Jewish vestments: the ephod and the *choschen* worn by the high priests. Two stones were kept in the *choschen*, on which were written the characters *urim* and *thummin;* they were cast or rolled on certain occasions in order to determine the will of God on particular matters or questions.[95] In the Vulgate, the names of the two vestments were translated as *superhumerale* (see the above discussion on the amice) and *rationale,*[96] and those of the two stones, as *doctrina* and *veritas.*[97] The references in the prayer, then, to holding firmly to the truth and teaching that truth to the people, are clearer when understood in this scriptural context: the meaning of this episcopal vestment was often interpreted in terms of the bishop's responsibility for teaching correct doctrine and safeguarding the truth.[98]

The actual action of vesting ended after the *rationale* was affixed to the chasuble. The Minden *ordo* then concludes this vesting rite with a short series of prayers and versicles[99]; incense is then placed in the thurible with a short prayer, the gospel book is formally kissed (with another short prayer), and then the bishop leaves the sacristy while reciting a series of psalm verses.[100]

---

[95] Ex 28:30; see also Thurian, 58.

[96] Amalarius connects another episcopal vestment, the pallium (like a "necklace" or "collar"), with the episcopal duties of preaching and teaching, although he refers to the Old Testament *humerale; Lib. Off.* l. II, c. 23, 1–3, and c. 26, 2, Hanssens, 248–249 and 254. On the connection between the Old Testament *rationale* and the pallium, see Odilo Engels, "Der Pontifikatsantritt und seine Zeichen," in *Segni e Riti,* Tomo secondo, 707–766; here, 736.

[97] Honselmann, "Das Rationale der Bischöfe," 71–72.

[98] Honselmann, "Das Rationale der Bischöfe," 76. For a more complete discussion of the wider use of the term *rationale* in theological documents, see Timothy Thibodeau, "*Enigmata Figurarum:* Biblical Exegesis and Liturgical Exposition in Durand's *Rationale,*" *Harvard Theological Review* 86 (1/1993) 65–79; here, 70–71. See also his dissertation, *A Study of William Durand's (circa 1230–1296) Commentary on the Divine Office in Book V of the Rationale Divinorum Officiorum* (unpublished Ph.D. dissertation, Department of History, University of Notre Dame, 1988). Thibodeau and Anselme Davril are currently preparing a critical edition of Durand's *Rationale* for *Corpus Christianorum Continuatio Mediaevalis;* the first volume has already appeared, *Guillelmi Durandi Rationale Divinorum Officiorum I–V* (Turnholt: Brepols, 1995; CCCM vol. 140).

[99] Pierce, *Sacerdotal Spirituality,* nos. 31–35, 162–165.

[100] Pierce, *Sacerdotal Spirituality,* nos. 36–40, 166–167.

Perhaps it would be best to close this discussion of the Minden vesting prayers by discussing two especially interesting examples of these postvesting prayers. The first of these prayers is specifically designated to be recited by the presider immediately after the vesting is finished *(Postquam infulatus fuerit dicat hanc orationem):*

"Rogo te altissime sabaoth Pater
sancte ut me tunica castitatis
digneris accingere et meos lumbos
baltheo tui amoris ambire. ac renes
cordis et corporis mei caritatis igne
perurere. quatinus pro peccatis meis
possim digne intercedere. et
asstantis populi peccatorum ueniam
promereri. ac pacificas singulorum
hostias immolare. me quoque audacter
Domine ad te accedentem non sinas
perire. sed dignare me mundare lauare.
ornare. et leniter ac benigne suscipere.
Pater sanctissime. Qui cum Filio
et Spiritu Sancto uiuis et regnas
Deus in saecula saeculorum amen."[101]

This prayer is quite commonly found in *ordines* of the tenth and eleventh centuries: it can be found at the end of the vesting prayers (as at Minden and Stavelot); as the presider approaches the altar to begin Mass (San Vincenzo al Volturno, Ivrea, and probably Nonantola); to accompany the tunicle (Amiens and Troyes) or the cincture (*subcinctorium* or *balteus,* as at Salins and Corbie),[102] possibly prompted by the use of certain words in the prayer text (e.g., *tunica, accingere, baltheo*). However, the prayer is actually found in earlier collections: it appears in the Gregorian tradition among the *apologiae* included in certain codices, as well as the Irish/Celtic Stowe Missal.[103]

[101] Pierce, *Sacerdotal Spirituality,* n. 31, 162.

[102] Stavelot (Martène, col. 584); Volturno (Martène, col. 569); Amiens (Leroquais, 440); Troyes (Martène, col. 529); Salins (Lemarié, no. 09); Corbie (Martène, col. 563); Ivrea (Baroffio and Dell'Oro, no. 19); Nonantola (Salmon, 199, very similar incipit).

[103] GrD 4381; Sir George F. Warner, ed., *The Stowe Missal* (Suffolk: The Boydell Press, 1906 and 1915, repr. 1989; Henry Bradshaw Society, vols. 31–32)

Jungmann notes the penitential character of the prayer, expressing "intercession for the people";[104] the presider prays to be made worthy to intercede not only for his sins but those of the gathered community. The Father's ennobling forgiveness is expressed in terms of the presider's being clothed with the garments of various virtues (the "tunic" of chastity, the "belt" of divine love), and of his being gently and benevolently cleaned, adorned, and accepted as worthy. This first "concluding prayer" to the ritual of vesting caps the vesting actions by recapitulating them and their moral/penitential allegorical significance and directing the focus to the coming sacrificial action of the Mass.

The last of the prayers from the Minden vesting rite to be examined here is a text which Jungmann considers to be the classic "general" vesting prayer, used at earlier stages in the evolution of the *ordo missae*[105] to accompany the vesting activity before the assignment of individual prayer texts to each piece of vesture.[106] In the Minden *ordo*, the prayer follows the *Rogo te* text after another oration and a series of versicles and responses. The prayer is prefaced by an *oremus* (the first to be so headed in the vesting rite proper), and the text reads as follows:

3-4. See also Frederick Edward Warren, *The Liturgy and Ritual of the Catholic Church* (Oxford: Clarendon Press, 1881) 250, note 7.

[104] Jungmann, MRR, I, 298, n. 3.

[105] The elaboration of the *ordo missae*, particularly by the addition of sacerdotal *apologiae* (private penitential prayers by the priest), versicles, and gestures at a number of "quiet" points in the service, has been studies by theologian Boniface Luykx. He has theorized that the *ordo missae* passes through three general stages of evolution from the ninth through the eleventh centuries, based on the degree of augmentation. The broad category which is the latest stage, named the Rhenish *ordo missae* after the area (the Rhineland of Germany) in which Luykx believes it originates, is the category in which the Minden *ordo missae* falls, according to his classification. See Boniface Luykx, "Der Ursprung der gleichbleibenden Teile der heiligen Messe," in *Priestertum und Mönchtum*, volume 29 of *Liturgie und Mönchtum* (1961) 72–119. Jungmann incorporated Luykx's work into the fifth edition (1962) of his *Missarum Solemnia*, available only in the German original. See also Joanne M. Pierce, "The Evolution of the *ordo missae* in the Early Middle Ages," in Lizette Larson-Miller, ed., *Essays in Medieval Liturgy* (New York: Garland Press, forthcoming, 1996) 3–25.

[106] Jungmann, MS I, 286–287.

"Fac me quaeso omnipotens Deus. ita iusticia indui.
ut in sanctorum tuorum merear exultatione laetari.
quatenus emundatus ab omnibus sordibus peccatorum
consortium adipiscar tibi placentium sacerdotum.
meque tua misericordia a uiciis omnibus exuat. quem
reatus propriae conscientiae grauat. Qui uiuis."[107]

This prayer is another fairly early text, found originally in the
Gregorian sacramentary tradition in formularies for votive masses
on behalf of the priest.[108] It is also found in many of the contemporary *ordines*, either as a more general vesting prayer,[109] or to
accompany the chasuble.[110] Jungmann notes that this prayer becomes a characteristic of the later, Rhenish *ordo missae* group, and
often concludes the vesting rite or "access" psalmody.[111] It is typi-
cally followed by the *Aures tuae pietatis* prayer (as is the case in the
Minden *ordo*[112]), another characteristic of the Rhenish *ordo missae*.[113]
Note that the *Fac me quaeso* text also refers to vesting in a general
way, by carrying on the allegory of "putting on" justice and
being cleansed of all sin, placed in priestly fellowship, and freed
of all vice by God's mercy.

These early medieval vesting prayers allow us to tap into a
particular stream of liturgical spirituality: the clear focus on the
parallelism between the outer and the inner, the exterior and the
interior, a movement which does not permit any preparatory ac-

---

[107] Pierce, *Sacerdotal Spirituality*, no. 34, 165.

[108] GrD 1281, 2112, 2117.

[109] Salins (Lemarié, no. 04), Hamburg (Rasmussen, no. 4), Reichenau
(Bragança, no. 9), and Ivrea (Baroffio and Dell'Oro, no. 4).

[110] Saint-Denis (col. 519); Troyes specifically directs that it be recited after the
chasuble is put on (col. 530), and Stavelot implies this position (col. 583).

[111] Jungmann, MS I (fifth edition, 1962) 372–373.

[112] Pierce, *Sacerdotal Spirituality*, no. 35, 165.

[113] Jungmann, MS I (fifth edition, 1962) 356, note 14. Although rooted in the
Gregorian sacramentary tradition and widely attested in the contemporary
ordines, the *Aures tuae pietatis* prayer does not explicitly allude to vesting, but
is instead a more general prayer for God's assistance in making the presider
worthy to celebrate the sacred mysteries. God is asked to listen to the
presider's prayers and illuminate his heart with the grace of the Holy Spirit,
that he might both minister God's mysteries and love God with eternal
love/charity.

tion to be regarded as minor or unimportant in the face of the overwhelming significance of the liturgical activity to be celebrated. An intense concentration is demanded, even more striking when one considers the bustling atmosphere of a major cathedral and the busy preoccupation of its bishop and clergy in preparation for a major pontifical liturgy. In addition, the strong emphasis on sinfulness, penitence, vice, and virtue often makes these prayers sound extreme and harsh to modern ears. Even the prayer for the dalmatic, Christological as it is, takes the passion and cross, rather than festivity and rejoicing, as its theme.

As Aidan Kavanagh has noted:

"Liturgical history does not deal with the past . . . but with tradition . . . 'a genetic vision of the present,' a present conditioned by the way in which it understands its roots. . . . The purpose of doing liturgical history is to understand present liturgy, which, because it has a history, can only be properly understood in motion, just as the only way to understand a top is to spin it."[114]

Perhaps what a study of these prayers calls to our attention is neither the need to discard them entirely, nor the necessity for reappropriating an allegorical world of "hidden meaning" alien to a contemporary worldview. Perhaps what a study of this element of the tradition reveals is a need to recover the sense of transcendent mystery which should pervade the entire stress-filled life of the Christian, ordained and lay, a mystery which can and should be felt most strongly in the preparation for and celebration of the liturgical "mysteries" which lie at the heart of the Church's identity in and for the world.

[114] Kavanagh, *On Liturgical Theology*, 131.

Regis Duffy, O.F.M.

6. The *Medicus* and Its Transformation from Its Patristic to Its Medieval and Tridentine Usages

Benedict in his *Regula Monachorum* reminds his monks:

"Let the abbot exercise all diligence in his care for erring brethren, for 'they that are in health need not a physician, but they that are sick' (Matt 9:12). He ought, therefore, as a wise physician, to use every remedy in his power."[1]

It is, then, *dignum et justum* that this article which pays warm tribute to a son of Benedict, Aidan Kavanagh, O.S.B., should resonate with the image of *medicus* to which the founder refers. The concept of Christ as the "physician of souls" and the eventual application of this image to the pastoral care of the Christian community have invited some attention from both scriptural and patristic scholars.[2] My particular interest in this article is the more specific penitential dimensions of the image as one moves from canonical penance to Irish tariff penance and its consequences as seen in the Tridentine debates on the necessity of the integrity of confession. The argument that I propose is this: the image of *medicus* as a result of the Irish penance begins to be equated with the image of *judex* (judge) and thus, undergoes a radical change of meaning. The reasoning behind these changes is found in this analogy: just

---

[1] Benedict, St., *The Rule of Saint Benedict*. Abbot Justin McCann, tr. (London: Burns Oates, 1952) chapter 27, 77.

[2] In particular, A. von Harnack, "Medicinisches aus der Ältesten Kirchengeschichte," *Texte und Untersuchungen zur Geschichte der altchristlichen Literatur* 8 (1892) 37–147.

as the sick person must show their wounds so that the doctor might diagnose the illness and prescribe the appropriate medicine, so must the penitent show their sins (in their specific number and circumstances) if the confessor is to judge the appropriate penance. After surveying the scriptural and patristic usage of *medicus* and its related terms, the major part of the article will deal with the medieval and Tridentine discussions.

THE ORIGINS OF THE MEDICAL ANALOGY

Sickness, even in our scientific age, is still described as a mystery that questions human meaning and destiny. It should be no surprise, then, that the scriptures offer no ready-made solution for the problem. The Hebrew Scriptures make sense of the medical problems of Tobit and Job, for example, by interpreting them as signs of their fidelity to God. On the other hand, the sufferings of God's servant in Isaiah 53 are understood as expiating the sins of the nation. The psalms move in a different direction by connecting sickness and sin: "There is no soundness in my flesh because of your indignation; there is no health in my bones because of my sin" (Ps 38:3; also, Ps 107:17). This same connection is still being made in Christ's time as the conversation over the cause of the young man's blindness reveals, a connection Christ repudiates (John 9:2).[3]

It would probably be a mistake to derive the positive image of God as healer from these connections of sickness and sin. The covenant faithfulness of God provides the context for the description "I am the Lord who heals you" (Exod 15:26). It is this image (or perhaps, a Greek proverb) that suggests the closing lines of Mark's account: "Those who are well have no need of a *physician* but those who are sick. I have come to call not the righteous but sinners" (Mark 2:17).[4] Christ had earlier in Mark 2 cured the paralytic and then called Levi, the tax collector, to discipleship. Mark

---

[3] See R. E. Brown, *The Gospel According to John I–XII* (Garden City: Doubleday, 1966) 371. On another occasion when a similar connection is made, Christ does not directly address the issue (Luke 13:2); see J. A. Fitzmyer, *The Gospel According to Luke* (X–XXIV) (New York: Doubleday, 1985) 1007.

[4] So J. Gnilka, *Das Evangelium nach Markus* (Mark 1–8, 26) (Zürich: Benziger, 1978) 109.

then recounts what will be a familiar scene, Jesus at table in Levi's house with "many tax collectors and sinners" (Mark 2:15). In defense of his tableship with such guests, Christ draws the medical analogy cited above. It is important to note that the context for the Markan saying is conversion.

The obvious theological counterpart of such a meal is the eschatological banquet at the end of time. Jesus is seen as the messianic host who had cured the paralytic as a sign of forgiveness (Mark 2:9-14) and now eats with religious outcasts as the messianic host.[5] Thus, at the beginning of his gospel, Mark clearly proclaims the redemptive mission of Christ in his meal with sinners: Jesus had come not to call the upright but sinners (Mark 2:17c). (The Lucan reformulation (Luke 5:28), as J. Fitzmyer notes, stressed a more radical notion of conversion by depicting Levi as having "left everything."[6]) Within this context of meals with outcasts, the emphasis in the analogy of doctor/sick moves from the former to the latter: "It is decisive that the inviting call now goes out to sinners and outcasts. The invitation connects the meal to the time of salvation whose proleptic introduction is the meal with tax collectors. The host is Jesus while Levi is the symbol of the called sinner."[7]

In brief, the image of Christ as the doctor finds its meaning in the redemptive and eschatological themes of a festal meal with sinners. The conversion of Levi and his guests concretizes these themes and focuses the image of Christ the physician. The scene resonates with the familiar descriptions of a healing God: "I will seek the lost, and I will bring back the strayed, and I will bind up the injured, and I will strengthen the weak" (Ezek 34:16). "Christus medicus," then, sums up the pastoral care of the Savior and provides a normative example for his disciples.

This notion of Christ as doctor was no doubt given new impetus in the Greek-speaking world to counteract the widespread cult of Aesculapius, the god-doctor of the Greco-Roman world. The sick clients of this god were customarily left in his temples overnight (in an incubation hall attached to the temple area) so that the god

[5] W. L. Lane, *Commentary on the Gospel of Mark* (Grand Rapids: Eerdmans, 1973) 106.

[6] J. A. Fitzmyer, *The Gospel According to Luke* I–IX (New York: Doubleday, 1981) 589.

[7] Gnilka, *Markus*, 109.

might cure them.[8] Aesculapius was considered a savior by the sick of the ancient world. Christian apologists, for example, such as Justin Martyr felt compelled to challenge this cult since it defined on a practical level what the term "savior" meant.[9] Ignatius of Antioch refers to Christ as a doctor and to the Eucharist as the "immortal drug."[10] Origen pictures the church as "the room of healing" in which "Jesus the physician . . . applies, not juices of herbs, but the sacraments of the Word to their diseases."[11] In a logical extension of the medical analogy, he also compares sin to a disease that requires radical treatment to be cured.[12]

MEDICUS IN A CONTINUING TRADITION

Thus far we have seen a wide range of related meanings attached to the notion of *medicus* from the first moments of conversion to the goal of salvation. The *Apostolic Constitutions* captures this overall understanding in its exhortation to the head of the community: "Heal, O bishop, like a compassionate physician, all who have sinned, and employ methods that promote saving health. Do not confine yourself to cutting or cauterizing . . . but employ bandages. . . . Use mild and healing drugs and sprinkle words of comfort as a soothing balm."[13]

Within this constellation of medical analogies, sin is often referred to as a "wound" or a "disease." Ambrose, for example, employs such terms in describing the penance of the Church as "confessing her wounds, wishing to be cured."[14] Chromatius of Aquilea speaks in much the same terms: "In what does he show

---

[8] See M. Honecker, "Christus medicus," *Kerygma und Dogma* 31 (1985) 307–323.

[9] Ibid., 311–13.

[10] Ephesians 7, 2, and 20, 2. For other patristic references, see G. Dumeige, "Médecin (le Christ)," *Dictionnaire de la Spiritualité*, vol. 10, c. 891–901.

[11] Origen, Homily 8 on Leviticus, as cited by A. von Harnack, *The Mission and Expansion of Christianity in the First Three Centuries*, J. Moffatt, trans. (Gloucester: P. Smith, 1963) n. 4, 100.

[12] "Do you not believe that our sin resembles a tumor and it does not only take a touch of iron or cauterization. It requires both to remove it." *Commentary on Matt 18:4* in Dumeige, *Médecin*, 896, my translation.

[13] Cited with similar examples in von Harnack, *Mission*, 114–116.

[14] *De paenitentia* 1, 7, 20; Ambroise de Milan, *La Pénitence*, R. Gryson, ed., *Sources Chrétiennes* (Paris: Cerf, 1971) 80; also *De paenit.* 1, 7, 2530 (SC 179:78).

himself the true and heavenly doctor who had come to cure the wounds of the human race and prove the infidelity of the scribes who when caught in the serious sickness of sin, inflated by intellectual pride, thought themselves to be healthy. . . ."[15] The terms for medicine (medicina, medicamentum), in line with these developments, are regularly used to describe Christ's healing power, or, more specifically, to refer to the sacraments.[16]

Patristic writers such as Ambrose and Augustine make regular use of these medical images. In a typical passage Ambrose cites the Matthaean version of the "doctor" saying (Matt 9:12) and then says, "Show the doctor your wound so that you may be cured . . . wash your wounds with your tears."[17] Augustine evocatively calls Christ "the complete physician of our wounds"[18] and describes how Christ reacts to Peter's denial by noting that he took the pulse of Peter's heart.[19] The Scholastics continue this medical usage. Hugh of St. Victor in response to the question of when the sacraments were instituted replies: "As long as there is sickness, there is time for medicine."[20] As late as the thirteenth

---

[15] Chromatius of Aquilea, e.g., says: "In quo se verum ac caelestem medicum ostendit, qui ad sananda humani generis vulnera venerat, et scribarum infidelitatem arguit, qui cum in gravi infirmitate peccati iacerent, superbia mentis inflati, sanos se esse putabant . . . "Tractatus in Mathaeum. 45, 34, my translation. The liturgy for penitents in the Gelasian sacramentary employs similar language: "sana vulnera eiusque remitte peccata," Liber Sacramentorum Romanae Aeclesiae Ordinis Anni Circuli, edited by C. Mohlberg (Rome: Herder, 1968), #80; also, "da indulgentiam reis et medicina tribue vulneratis . . .," Ibid., #362.

[16] For typical patristic citations, see J. Hubner, "Christus medicus. Ein Symbol des Erlösungsgeschehens und ein Modell ärtlichen Handelns," Kerygma und Dogma 31 (1985) 324-335, esp. 327-328 and G. Mueller, "Arzt, Kranker und Krankheit bei Ambrosius von Mailand (334-397)," Sudhoffs Archiv für Geschichte der Medizin und der Naturwissenschaften 51 (1967) 193-216.

[17] "Ostende igitur medico vulnus tuum, ut sanari possis . . . Absterge lacrimis cicatrices tuas." De paenit. 2,8-20-22 (SC 179:174), my translation.

[18] In Joh. evangel. 3.2 as cited in R. Arbesmann, "The Concept of 'Christus medicus' in St. Augustine," Traditio 10 (1954) 1-28, here 13. In a computer search of Corpus scriptorum christianorum (in what is so far available on CD-ROM), some 240 references were found which employ one of the medical terms discussed, sometimes in relation to sacrament.

[19] Sermo guelferb. 17.1, as in Arbesmann, "Christus medicus," 19.

[20] PL 176, 313 D, as cited in W. Knoch, Die Einsetzung der Sakramenten durch Christus (Münster: Aschendorff, 1983) 84-85, my translation.

century, St. Bonaventure insightfully discusses the sacraments in a chapter on "Sacramental Medicine."[21]

Two centuries after Ambrose, the Irish penitentials also retain this medical vocabulary to designate the pastoral care needed by sinners: "So also should spiritual doctors treat with diverse kinds of cures the wounds of souls, their sicknesses, pains, ailments, and infirmities."[22] The Penitential of Cummean refers to the "remedies of wounds" in its prologue "on the medicine for the salvation of souls."[23] The Bigotian penitential develops the medical analogy by noting that the physician of penitents must be aware of the specific circumstances of "age and sex of the sinner, what instruction he has received, what is his strength, by what trouble he has been driven to sin, with what kind of passion he is assailed . . ." in order to heal the wounds of sinners.[24] (We will return to this extension of the analogy in discussing the Tridentine usage.)

There is no need to multiply citations. There is a widespread and consistent use of the scripturally inspired *medicus* image. In its broadest use, it refers to a quality of pastoral care grounded in the compassion of Christ. This same metaphor sometimes connotes the more specific healing of the sacraments. But the goal of this healing continues to be the ongoing conversion of the baptized.

A DIFFERENT KIND OF DOCTOR?

Irish tariff penance, so different from the earlier canonical penance on the continent, seems to have been influenced by Eastern monasticism.[25] The Irish Church quickly became a monastic Church after Patrick's evangelization of the island. The monk's confession to his abbot or "soul-friend" with its detailed listing of

---

[21] *Omnia Opera* (Quarracchi: Collegium St. Bonaventura, 1891) 5:265–80. For a summary of this use in Bonventure, see J. Finkenzeller, *Die Lehre von den Sakramenten im allgemeinen* (Freiburg: Herder, 1980) 161–162.

[22] *Penitential of St. Columban* in *The Irish Penitentials*, L. Bieler, ed. (Dublin: The Dublin Institute for Advanced Studies, 1963) 99.

[23] *Penitential of Cummean*, in *The Irish Penitentials*, 109.

[24] *Bigotian Penitential*, in *The Irish Penitentials*, 199.

[25] For a good overview, see J. Dallen, *The Reconciling Community. The Rite of Penance* (New York: Pueblo, 1986), esp. 102–110 and T. Oakley, "Celtic Penance: Its Sources, Affiliations, and Influence," *Irish Ecclesiastical Review* 52 (1938) 581–601.

sins and a penance assigned for each sin became the model for the laity. The penitentials that document these penances for specific sins remain a fascinating witness to a notably different conception of pastoral care, no doubt prompted by the unique social and religious situation of the Irish Church.

Given the monastic context of Irish penance, it is not surprising to find the abbot described as the physician of monks as early as the beginning of the sixth century.[26] Somewhat later, Columban (c. 600) speaks of "spiritual physicians (who) ought to heal with various sorts of treatment the wounds, fevers, transgressions, sorrows, sicknesses, and infirmities of souls."[27] Similar references can be found in Basil and other Eastern fathers.[28] The confessor was to share the penance of the penitent since "no physician can treat wounds of the sick unless he comes in contact with their foulness."[29]

But there is also an interesting shift in the use of medical images in the Irish penitentials. The most striking one is the use of the principle of the "contraries" in which a cure is effected by doing the contrary.[30] Finnian cites the principle in his early (c. 525–550) penitential: "But by contraries, as we said, let us make haste to cure contraries . . . patience must arise from wrathfulness, kindliness, or the love of God and one's neighbor, for envy. . . ."[31] McNeill, in attributing this principle of contraries to the influence of John Cassian (*Collations* XIX, 14, 15), compares this conception of the doctor to modern psychiatrists who must identify with their patients.[32] Implicit in the medical analogy and its expression in the

[26] *Penitential of Gildas*, #18 in *Medieval Handbooks of Penance*, J. T. McNeill and H. M. Gamer, trans. (New York: Octagon, 1965) 177.

[27] *Penitential of Columban*, B in McNeill and Gamer, *Handbooks*, 251.

[28] G. Mitchell cites Basil in PG 31:1236, in "The Origins of Irish Penance," *Irish Theological Quarterly* 22 (1955) 1–14, here 11, n. 2.

[29] *St. Gall Penitential* in McNeill and Gamer, *Handbooks*, 283. Although this is a continental penitential, it may have Irish sources (*Cummean*), ibid., 282. The same phrase can be found in the so-called *Roman Penitential* in ibid., 297.

[30] For the principle's Greek roots and its mediation through John Cassian's Colloquies, see J. T. McNeill, *The Celtic Churches. A History* A.D. *200 to 1200* (Chicago: University of Chicago, 1974) 84.

[31] *The Penitential of Finnian*, #29 in McNeill and Gamer, *Handbooks*, 92.

[32] McNeill and Gamer, *Handbooks*, 46. His succinct treatment of "Medicine for Sin" (ibid., 44–46), is quite comprehensive though the concerns are not the same as those studied in this article.

principle of contraries is the need for a doctor's diagnostic skills which is a form of judgment. Although the earlier penitentials seem only to imply this, by the time of Bede (eighth century) the similarity of skills required of both doctors and judges is being noted: "physicians of bodies pursue diverse remedies . . . (as do) the judges of secular cases. Therefore, those who are good and just weigh and set forth diverse decisions, even as they judge rightly . . . between one case and another. How much more, therefore, O priests of God, is it proper to weigh and set forth for men the diverse remedies of their invisible souls."[33]

To complete the picture, another possible source of the penitentials themselves may well be the early Irish civil law which already shows Christian influences.[34] The commutations or equivalent ways of performing large penances which the penitentials assigned seem to reflect similar civil law solutions.[35]

There are two important characteristics of tariff penance to note. First, the possibility of more frequent penance also encourages a short-range view of conversion in contrast to that of canonical penance. The canonical penitent usually supported the effects of penance until death, even though reconciled to the Church. The tariff penitent remained such only until the penance was performed. Second, as Cyril Vogel pointed out, the detailed admission of sins in tariff penance had a different meaning than for later confessional practice: "In the tariff system the 'confession' was the indispensable *means* to allow taxation, but the means only, since expiation remained the essential act."[36]

This emphasis on the proper tariff and its satisfaction did shift the perspective from the revelation of one's spiritual condition to

[33] Bede's remarks are given in McNeill and Gamer, *Handbooks*, 221–222. Alcuin, an important witness in this same period to the continuing opposition to tariff penance on the continent, speaks of the priest as a judge and gives the familiar argument about the need to know the sin in order to reconcile the sinner; see C. Vogel, *Le Pécheur et la Pénitence au Moyen-Age* (Paris: Cerf, 1969) 143–146.

[34] See the extracts from *Senchus Mor* (c. mid-5th c.) in McNeill and Gamer, *Handbooks*, 370–371, and the editors' remarks, ibid., 8.

[35] See T. Oakley, "Commutations and Redemptions of Penances in the Penitentials," *Catholic Historical Review*, 18 (1932–1933) 341–351 and ibid., "Alleviations of Penance in Continental Penitentials," *Speculum* 12 (1937) 488–502.

[36] Vogel, *Le Pécheur*, 28, author's emphasis.

facilitate ongoing conversion to an almost Pelagian notion that confused satisfaction with conversion. In the latter case, the image of judge rather than doctor might seem the more appropriate metaphor.

THE MEDIEVAL TRANSFORMATION

Kilian McDonnell, with good reason, has recently suggested that the notion of integrity of confession (the accounting of all serious sins in their number and species) assumed an increasingly rigorist interpretation in the tradition of the medieval *Summae Confessorum*.[37] These manuals put great responsibility on the confessor's interrogation of the penitent and seem to model the confessor's role on that of a secular judge. McDonnell finds the source of this juridical emphasis in the patristic age.[38] I should like to nuance that statement.

Certainly canonical penance deprived penitents of Eucharistic participation, a literal "excommunication." This temporary exclusion from the Eucharist accurately mirrored the condition of someone who had separated herself from the body of Christ, the Church.[39] Such an excommunication was viewed as a medicinal penance to bring the sinner to a deepened awareness of Christian discipleship. Although there was probably a private meeting between the bishop and the penitent, there seems little evidence to suggest that this resembled the detailed confession of tariff penance.[40]

[37] K. McDonnell, "The Summae Confessorum on the Integrity of Confession as Prolegomena of Luther and Trent," *Theological Studies* 54 (1993) 405–426.

[38] Ibid., 420.

[39] For a thorough patristic survey, see K. Hein, *Eucharist and Excommunication.* (Bern: H. Lang, 1975). Some authors move too quickly from the notion of excommunication to theorizing about a "juridical structure" in the medieval sense, as e.g., A. Ziegenaus, *Umkehr, Versöhnung, Friede* (Freiburg-im-Breisgau: Herder, 1975) 187.

[40] The debate on this point occupied a number of theologians earlier in this century. For a summary, see B. Poschmann, *Penance and Anointing of the Sick* (New York: Herder and Herder, 1964) 85–87, esp. n. 128, 129. See also J. Dallen, *The Reconciling Community,* 66–67. For a good example of such a meeting, see R. Gryson's remarks on Ambrose's ministry in his edition of *La Pénitence,* 33–35.

Canonical penance itself was premised on the biblical warrant of "binding and loosing" (Matt 16:15-19, 18:15-18, John 20:19-23) which would imply some notion of judgment. But again, the judgment can be interpreted in a medicinal way as when Ambrose, in writing on penance, employs a play on words and connects *ligare* (to bind) and *alligare* (to bandage), thus recalling the Good Samaritan who binds up the wounds of the injured.[41] Therefore, the juridical image is present in the pastoral praxis of the patristic period. The juridical image, however, was not attached to the later notion of integrity but should be understood, as Karl Adam long ago suggested, as showing the complementarity of the external and internal dimensions of belonging to the body of Christ.[42] To put it differently, in the patristic period, the juridical aspect of penance was firmly rooted in the continuing medicinal need for conversion.

More importantly, canonical penance was ecclesial in character and thus, the penitent was "reconciled" (not "absolved" in the more restricted understanding of tariff penance).[43] Even when Origen, for example, speaks of the priest as the "judge of souls," it is usually, implicitly or explicitly, contextualized by the healing or medical analogy.[44] Moreover, in the more rigorous Tertullian, we find a movement from the medicinal view of excommunication in his Catholic period to a vindictive or juridical view in his Montanist period.[45]

[41] Ambrose, *De paenitentia*, I, 7, and Gryson's remarks, ibid., 39–40.

[42] K. Adam, "Die abendländische Kirchenbusse im Ausgang des christlichen Altertums," *Theologische Quartalschrift* 110 (1929) 1–66, esp. 20–21. Thus Ziegenaus (*Umkehr*, 221–226) while strongly insisting on the juridical character of penance, contextualizes it within the larger teaching of God's mercy, but he does not allude to the medicinal image. In the well known debates between Karl Adam and Bernard Poschmann, earlier in this century, on whether certain historical periods of penance could be understood as sacramental, Adam returns several times to his contention that the therapeutic and juridical do not exclude one another. He does insist on the juridical in order to argue against Poschmann that fifth and sixth century practices were sacramental rather than simply spiritual direction; again, see Poschmann, as cited in n. 40.

[43] See Mohlberg, ed., *Liber sacramentorum*, #352–363; also, W. LentzenDeis, *Busse als Bekenntnisvollzug* (Freiburg: Herder, 1969) 30–38.

[44] See J. Grotz, *Die Entwicklung des Busstufenwesens in der vornicänischen Kirche* (Freiburg: Herder, 1955) 214–215.

[45] Ibid., 356–365.

These remarks, however, do not contest the fact that the juridical description of the confessor is already evident in the early medieval theologians such as Alan of Lille and Peter Le Chantre.[46] Are we to assume that these theologians derived the juridical analogy from the contemporary practice of a detailed confession? Possibly, but there is also a patristic tradition that might partially account for the comparison: the commentaries on Christ's healing of the lepers and the raising of Lazarus.

Paul Anciaux, in his classic study of the theology of penance in the twelfth century, for example, notes that all the theologians of the period, influenced by the commentaries of Jerome and Gregory, interpreted Christ's curing of the lepers and the raising of Lazarus as paradigms for the confessor's role of interrogating the sinner and, on this basis, accorded them absolution.[47] He cites Honorius of Autun, Hervie of Bourg-Dieu, Anselm of Laon, and others to illustrate this point.[48]

Certainly these scholastic connections are influenced by the patristic commentaries on the gospel pericopes. John Chrysostom, for example, uses the example of the power of the Jewish priests to declare lepers cured to highlight the power of Christian priests "to remove altogether leprosy of the soul. . . ."[49] But it would seem that Jerome's commentary on the pericope was much more influential: "Thus, just as the priest makes the leper clean or unclean, so, in our case, the bishop or priest neither binds the innocent nor does he loose the guilty, but in accordance with his

---

[46] The most famous example that predates these early scholastics is the influential "Letter to a woman religious on true and false penance" (beginning of eleventh century) which insists on integrity of confession (#14) (but for the sake of correct expiation) and refers to the confessor as the "spiritual judge" (#20). Vogel, in giving the text, points out that the very fact of it being incorporated into the decretals of Gratian and the Sentences of Peter Lombard attests to its authority; see Vogel, *Le Pécheur*, 162–173.

[47] P. Anciaux, *La Théologie du Sacrement de Pénitence au XIIe siècle* (Louvain: Nauwelaerts, 1949) 279. For the texts, see *Faith of the Early Fathers*, W. Jurgen, ed. (Collegeville: The Liturgical Press, 1979) vol. 2, 202 (#1386, Jerome) and *Sacraments and Forgiveness*, P. Palmer, ed. (Westminster: Newman, 1959) 138–139 (#16, Gregory).

[48] Ibid., 171–175.

[49] *On the Priesthood*, 3, 6, (PG 48, 643f.) text in P. Palmer *Sacraments and Forgiveness* (Westminster: Newman, 1959) 83.

office, when he had heard the circumstances of the sins, he knows whom to bind and whom to loose."[50] When Peter Le Chantre urges sinners to confess their sins openly and from the heart "with all their circumstances," he cites the scriptural example of the priest's judgment in the case of the lepers.[51] J-A. Dugauquier in his critical edition of Peter's *Summa*, cites Jerome's commentary as a source for Peter's text.[52]

Alan Lille takes up the familiar *medicus* theme in describing the confessor "as if a doctor while the sinner approaches him as if a spiritually sick person." The priest's care facilitates the penitent's honest confession. Alan then cites the example of Jesus telling the cured lepers to show themselves to the priest which means that spiritual lepers should "show themselves" by the confession of their sin.[53] Although he does not specifically mention the obligation to confess the circumstances of such sins, the rest of the treatise deals with such specific situations.

Gregory the Great's commentary on the raising of Lazarus likewise became a *locus classicus* for medieval theologians writing on penance. (The context of Gregory's thought, however, which is often missed, is that absolution follows the revivification of the sinner by grace.) The famous line is: "Absolution will only be efficacious if it follows the decision of the interior judge." The pope then gives the Lazarus pericope as the proof of his statement: Christ had already raised Lazarus to life before he told him to come out from the tomb and the penitent does this in confessing his sins. Gregory then comments on the question of "binding and loosing." (Cyril Vogel reminds scholars that Gregory speaks from the practice he knows at Rome and that it would be bad methodology to generalize from this citation.)[54]

---

[50] *Commentary on Matthew*, 16, 19 (PL 26, 122); text in Palmer, *Sacraments*, 110. Obviously the citation should not be read in terms of the later tariff penance as Palmer does.

[51] Pierre le Chantre, *Summa de sacramentis et animae consiliis*, III, 515, J-A. Dugauquier, ed. (Louvain: Nauwelaerts, 1957) 279–280.

[52] Ibid., N.14, 280.

[53] *Liber Poenitentialis* I, 3; in the critical edition of the text prepared by J. Longere (Louvain: Nauwelaerts, 1965) vol. II, 26.

[54] Vogel, *Le Pécheur*, 132.

In its final decree on penance (Nov. 25, 1551), the Council of Trent summarized the development of the juridical metaphor from its sources in these words: "If a sick person should blush to reveal a wound to the *doctor*, then medicine cannot cure what it is ignorant of. Thus, it makes sense that those circumstances which change the species of the sin must be detailed in confession since without them neither are the sins themselves fully set forth by the penitent, nor are they known to the *judge* so that he might rightly judge the seriousness of the sins and to impose a fitting penance on the penitents."[55]

The transition in the above citation from the medical to the juridical metaphor is made quite easily and has a certain logic to it, if not examined too closely. Several days before that intervention, one theologian had put is even more baldly: the priest is a judge whom the sinner it obliged to obey as a guilty party must secular judges. Even though a judge is not competent in all cases and therefore, cannot absolve all sins, absolution is a judicial act and not a "bare" *(nudum)* ministry.[56] The decree itself, of course, was the end result of a long series of discussions at Bologna and at Trent. To appreciate this final position, we need to follow these earlier discussions, if only briefly.

In the sessions at Bologna (1547), theologians presented their views on the Reformers' articles on penance. Simon Gromerius

---

[55] "Si enim erubescat aegrotus vulnus medico detergere, quod ignorat, medicina non curat. Colligitur praeterea, etiam eas circunstantias (sic) in confessione (explicandas esse), quae (speciem peccati mutant), quod sine illis peccata ipsa nec a poenitentibus integre exponantur, nec *iudicibus* innotescant, et fieri nequeat, ut de gravitate criminum recte censere possint, et poenam, quam oportet, pro illis poenitentibus imponere." *Concilii Tridentini Actorum,* Tomus Septimus, Partis Quartae, Volumen Prius (Friburg: Herder, 1961) 7 (1) 348 (line 17) - 49 (=CT), my emphasis. (In the Goerres edition Tomes 6 and 7 have volumes 1 and 2. The volume is indicated in parenthesis after the Tome number.) The decree then goes on to discuss and briefly illustrate the "circumstances" to be revealed (349). See also n. 1 on the same page.

[56] "Judexque est sacerdos, cui obedire tenetur peccator, ut rei iudicibus saecularibus. Ergo satisfactiones faciendae sunt. Et quilibet iudex non est legitimus omnium causarum . . . ergo non omnis omnia peccata absolvere potest. Absolutio igitur iudicialis est et non nudum ministerium." CT 7 (1) 311 (lines 14–19), (Elnensis, Nov. 11, 1551). For a similar argument, see CT 7 (1) 276 (lines 10–19), (Franciscus de Toro, Oct. 27, 1551).

notes that in the Hebrew Scriptures the leper is obliged to show himself to the priest (Lev 14:2) which he regards as a figure of confession. He does not develop the connection further.[57] Several months later, the Council took up the pastoral issues connected to penance in sessions on the use and abuse of the sacrament (June 11, July 26, August 29, 1547).

The second proposition on such abuses states that the confessor is the "doctor of souls" and as such, should, with special expertise, know well both the character of the sick and their diseases, a task that the untrained cannot perform.[58] Once again, integrity of confession is not directly dealt with but the implications for its defense are there. In this proposition, however, the juridical extension is not made.[59] In a summary statement of the conventual friars' response to the propositions, the confessor is simply described as a judge, without any medical allusions, and Augustine's use of Lazarus being loosened from his bindings refers to the similar task of the confessor for the penitent.[60] In other words, by this time the doctor/judge metaphors are sometimes found together and, at other times, separated.[61]

One of the great Tridentine theologians, Melchior Cano, O.P., best sums up how the sixteenth-century Church expounded integrity with the two metaphors: Christ would have instituted a "stupid judgment if the priest were to judge without any knowl-

[57] CT 6 (1) 23–24 (April 2, 1547); also, CT 6 (2) 9–12 (April 15, 1547) where the Jerome reference is employed.

[58] ". . . .qui peritia propria et naturam infirmarum et infirmatum qualitates optime agnosceret, ut cuilibet infirmo congruam et opportunam medicinam exhibere sciret et valeret, quod imperiti nullo modo adimplere possunt." CT 6 (1) 403. For an earlier version of the proposition, see CT 6 (2) 25, #26: "Quod medici medicent infirmos, antequam infirmi vocaverint medicas animarum et ab eis fuerint absoluti a peccatis et susceperint sacramentum eucharistiae . . ."

[59] In commenting on this proposition some weeks later (Nov. 9, 1547), one theologian attacked the idea that the unskilled confessor/doctor is not able to "give medicine" since a priest with jurisdiction is able to absolve. CT 6 (1) 580, Aquensis (Gallus) & 587 (line 48) - 588.

[60] CT 6 (2) 44 (lines 26–29), 45 (lines 5–13).

[61] Sometimes the medical metaphor is alluded to by a verb such as "diagnose." (CT 7 (1) 244 (lines 1–2), 256 (lines 3, 4) and 257 (lines 36, 38), 311 (lines 16, 18), 322 (lines 30–31). For the clearest use of the secular judgement process offered as a parallel for the spiritual process, see CT 7 (1) 262 (lines 29–31).

edge of the causes; nor is he able to know what should be done about the sinner unless he first hears his sins. Nor is the doctor able to cure unless he first knows the sickness."[62] As in his earlier interventions, Cano is an eloquent witness to a tradition that has been only partially retained.

Although the conciliar participants were reacting to the positions of the reformers on the questions of integrity and absolution, it would be simplistic to regard Trent's position concerning the confessor as judge as a polemical exaggeration of one aspect of the complex penitential process. As noted in several places, the juridical dimension of penance has scriptural and patristic overtones. But the understanding of *judex*, linked to the notion of integrity, had gradually become isolated from the metaphor of *Christus medicus* and its biblical implications of ongoing conversion. This development did not exclude the pastoral concerns of the council as will be mentioned below. But there is a tendency either to reduce the therapeutic ideal to one of pastoral kindness or to use it as an adjunct metaphor to justify the judicial emphasis of the sacrament.

SOME CONCLUDING REMARKS

The concerns about "judging" and "healing" have been prevalent in pastoral praxis and theological writing since the time of the first Christian communities. The very use of the *medicus* image often connotes the complementary diagnostic (judging) skills. In canonical penance, excommunication from the body of Christ, both Eucharistic and ecclesial, entailed some form of judgment but the penitential process was a medicinal one with ongoing conversion as its goal. Once the *medicus* tradition came in contact with the tariff penance, however, the diagnostic dimension was more easily interpreted in a juridical way. The penitentials with their juridical sentences encouraged such a view. More important than any explicit development and use of the term "judge" was the tariff system itself which functioned in some of the ways that Irish clan law seemed to have been practiced. In the meantime, the

---

[62] "Alius Christus instituisset stultum iudicium, si absque causae cognitione sacerdos iudicaret; neque cognoscere potest, quid facturus sit de peccatore, sacerdos, nisi eius peccata prius audiat. Neque medicus curare potest, nisi prius morbum noscat." CT 7 (1) 263 (lines 14–17) see also his earlier discussion in the same talk, ibid., 262 (lines 7–13, 28–32).

juridical "invasion" of sacramental and liturgical theology by canon law in the early medieval period and its later expression in the *summae confessorum* set the stage for an explicit development of the notion of the confessor as judge, given the necessity of the integrity of confession.

The Council of Trent was no less pastoral in its theology and praxis than previous councils of the Church. The polemical tone of its discussions did not exclude the desire for sacramental renewal and reform. This is best shown in the sessions on the "use and abuse" of each sacrament which were designed to complement the dogmatic sessions of the same sacrament. The Tridentine dogmatic sessions on the sacraments have too often been interpreted apart from these complementary discussions which in some ways represent the *lex orandi* of the late medieval period.

The conciliar participants were aware that even the most pastorally sensitive understanding of integrity of confession would be thwarted by inadequate or unskilled "doctors." On November 12, 1547, for example, the work of St. Antoninus, bishop of Florence (1389-1459), on the art of being a good confessor was warmly recommended as a compendium for those who received faculties.[63] The call for confessors whose lives reflected the counsel they gave others was also often heard.[64] The fact that trained confessors were in short supply was repeatedly lamented by council participants.[65] The proposed conciliar catechism was discussed as a possible manual for confessors. Even the problem of how to prevent priests from sleeping while hearing confessions was discussed.[66] These concerns perhaps account for the more patristic tone of the Roman Ritual which issued from the canons on penance at Trent: "Let the confessor remember to support the penitent equally as both judge and doctor; established by God as a minister, at the one and same time, of divine justice and mercy. . . ."[67]

With the renewal of ecclesiology at Vatican II, the nature of conversion within the ecclesial community has also been reexamined.

[63] CT 6 (1) 588 (line 8); for a similar recommendation made earlier, see CT 6 (1) 404 (line 22).

[64] See, e.g., CT 6 (1) 404 (lines 1–8).

[65] See, e.g., CT 6 (1) 683 (lines 20–23).

[66] CT 6 (1) 581 (lines 13–14).

[67] *Rituale Romanum Pauli Pontificis Maximi* (Paris: n.p., 1863), #78.

The sacrament of penance, as the other sacraments, has benefited from this reexamination since the complementary aspects of ecclesial and personal penance and reconciliation recall some of the classical insights of the *medicus* metaphor. The results of this retrieval are perhaps best seen in the introduction to the post-conciliar rite of penance and reconciliation: "In order to fulfill his ministry properly and faithfully the confessor should understand the disorders of souls and apply the appropriate remedies to them. He should fulfill his office of judge wisely and should acquire the knowledge and prudence necessary for this task. . . . By receiving the repentant sinner and leading him to the light of the truth the confessor fulfills a paternal function: he reveals the heart of the Father and shows the image of Christ the Good Shepherd."[68] This reminder to the confessor retrieves some of the classical balance in the use of the *judex* metaphor in the light of the *medicus* metaphor.

[68] "Rite of Penance, The Rites of the Catholic Church as Revised by the Second Vatican Ecumenical Council (New York: Pueblo, 1976) 348, #10 a, c.

John F. Baldovin, s.j.

7. *Accepit Panem:* The Gestures of the Priest at the Institution Narrative of the Eucharist

"On the night he was betrayed he took bread. . . ." These familiar words open the institution narrative which for most Western Christian piety and theology forms the central core of the Eucharistic prayer. The words are accompanied by gestures performed by the presiding priest, namely, taking the bread while bending slightly and saying the words, genuflecting, and then showing the bread to the assembled faithful before replacing it on the paten, and then doing the same with the cup. These gestures are often referred to as the manual acts. The purpose of the present essay is to analyze these gestures in the light of liturgical history, the practice of other Christian Churches, recent theology of the Eucharist and particularly the Eucharistic prayer, and finally to make some observations on the dynamics of these gestures vis-à-vis the rest of the worshipping assembly in order to come to some better understanding of what is at stake in this nonverbal aspect of liturgy.

While much has been written on the history of the texts of the Eucharistic prayer, scholars have tended to pay little attention to their enactment. From a liturgical point of view this lacuna is unsatisfactory since liturgy, as embodied worship, is a physical activity in the context of which words are spoken.[1] Liturgy, in a

[1] Notable exceptions include R. Kevin Seasoltz, "Non-verbal Symbols and the Eucharistic Prayer," in F. C. Senn, ed., *New Eucharistic Prayers: An Ecumenical Study of Their Development and Structure,* (New York: Paulist, 1987) 214–236; Cesare Giraudo, *Preghiere eucaristiche per la chiesa di oggi: Riflessioni in margine al commento del canone svizzero-romano = Aloisiana* 23 (Naples: Morcelliana, 1993) 107–131; Michael Merz, *Liturgisches Gebet als Geschehen:*

word, is a holistic experience and its analysis requires investigation not only of words and ideas but also of gesture. This essay is a limited attempt to analyze one set of gestures within the complex of actions that constitute the Eucharistic prayer. A number of gestures or actions like the *orans* position, the extension of hands over the gifts and accompanying sign of the Cross at the *epiclesis*, the lifting up of the gifts at the doxology, as well as the sign of the Cross the priest makes on himself at the words "may be filled with every grace and blessing" and the striking of the breast at "though we are sinners . . ." in the first Eucharistic prayer, not to mention the posture and gesture of the rest of the assembly are omitted here in the interest of space and to provide some focus. This analysis will relate to the rest of the complex of actions in the Eucharistic prayer at least by inference since all of these actions depend on what is understood to take place at the institution narrative.

This analysis must also be made in the context of the five times that the priest handles the gifts in the course of the Eucharist proper, namely the preparation of the table, the narrative itself, the doxology and Amen, the fraction, and the invitation to Communion. In particular, the first of these actions is liable to misinterpretation in the contemporary Roman Rite. The rubrics at this point in the Missal of Paul VI differ from those of the Missal of Pius V in an important respect. At the Offertory of the Tridentine Mass the priest was explicitly directed to make a gesture of offering: *Sacerdos ipse accipit Patenam cum Hostia, quam offerans, dicit. . . .* and after the mixture of water with the wine and accompanying prayer: *Postea accipit Calicem, et offert dicens. . . ."*[2]

Liturgiewissentschaftlich-linguistische Studie anhand der Gebetsgattung eucharistisches Hochgebet = *Liturgiewissenschaftliche Quellen und Forschungen 70*, (Münster: Aschendorff, 1988) 133–134; Bernard Botte, "*Et elevatis oculis in caelum*. Etude sur les récits liturgiques de la Dernière Cene," Burkhard Neunheuser, "Les gestes de la prière a genoux et de la genuflexion dans les Eglises de rite romain," in *Gestes et Paroles dans les Diverses Familles Liturgiques* = *Conferences Saint-Serge xxive semaine d'études liturgiques*, (Rome: Centro Liturgico Vincenziano, 1978) 77–86, 153–166.

[2] "The priest takes the paten with the bread which he offers saying. . . . After this he takes the chalice and offers it saying. . . ." *Missale Romanum ex decreto sacrosancti concilii Tridentini resitutum,* 1570 and subsequent editions.

In the new rite, however, the priest is not directed to offer the bread and the wine but rather to hold each in turn slightly above the altar *(aliquantulum elevatam super altare tenet)* while saying the formula "Blessed are You, Lord God of all creation . . ." inaudibly.[3] In practice, however, the gesture of offering the gifts up to God has been retained by many, thus obscuring the intent of the reformed rite of the Eucharist, which clearly limited the sacrificial gesture to the doxology and Amen at the end of the Eucharistic prayer.

Thus, in the contemporary Roman Rite, there are three levels at which the gifts are held: 1) slightly above the altar in a gesture of placing—at the preparation of the gifts and during the recitation of the words of the Lord at the institution narrative; 2) the showing *(ostendit)* to the people, usually at chest height—at the end of each section of the institution narrative and at the invitation to Communion; and 3) elevating the gifts at the doxology and Amen—concluding the Eucharistic prayer.

In itself, retaining the gesture of offering at the preparation of the gifts, despite the clear indications of the rubrics as well as the directives of the *General Instruction of the Roman Missal*,[4] represents an obvious misunderstanding of the Roman Catholic reform of the Eucharist as well as the power of actions of words, in the liturgy; i.e., the words of the blessing prayers do not connote offering, but the action of lifting the gifts on high does.

But the focus of the present essay is on the actions of the priest during the institution narrative, especially in the context of the reform in which, instead of facing in the same direction as the assembly, the priest faces them directly. The first task to be undertaken is a survey of the origins of these actions.

A BRIEF SURVEY OF ORIGINS

In his monumental history of the eucharist in the Roman Rite, Josef Jungmann argued that during the first millenium the priest was not directed to touch the bread or the chalice during the insti-

---

[3] *The Roman Missal Revised by Decree of the Second Vatican Council, 1969, 1975.* The priest may also say the formula aloud.

[4] Second edition, Vatican City, 1975, #102.

tution narrative.[5] The first mention of such a manual act is found in a Cluniac Customary of 1068 by the monk Bernhard who recounts that the priest holds the host in his first four fingers before the words of institution. Jungmann finds similar evidence throughout the late eleventh century.

While Jungmann seems to be correct with regard to liturgical books, he may have neglected a mention of the manual acts some two centuries earlier. In his description of the Eucharistic prayer Amalar of Metz states quite clearly that "the priest takes bread into his hands after the example Christ. . . . and the same way with the chalice."[6] Without corroborative evidence there is no way of knowing whether Amalar is describing an isolated instance in Carolingian France or widespread practice. It would not be surprising if the manual acts were an innovation of the Carolingian period in which the dramatic aspects of the liturgy as well as an allegorical approach to Christ in the liturgy came to the fore.

From the twelfth century on we have a number of indications of the manual acts. During the twelfth century the priest was accustomed in some places to replace the host on the corporal after making the sign of the Cross (benedixit) over it, and only then to recite the words of consecration. In other places he would hold it aloft as soon as he spoke those words.[7] In order to avoid adoration of the host by the faithful before the words of consecration, in 1210 the bishop of Paris ordered that the elevation not take place until the words had been said. Jungmann corroborates this with evidence from the Cistercians (1210) and the Carthusians (1222).[8] A similar elevation of the chalice was not universally mandated, however, until the Missal of Pius V (1570). Presumably the reason for not elevating the chalice was the inability to see the consecrated wine. Moreover the faithful were not accustomed to

[5] Josef A. Jungmann, *Missarum Sollemnia: The Mass of the Roman Rite,* vol. 2, trans. by Francis A. Brunner (New York: Benziger, 1955) 205 (hereafter MRR).

[6] Amalar of Metz, *Liber Officialis* 1.III.24.4 - "Quo ordinis id perficiendum sit, ex Domini institutione addiscitur. Accipit sacerdos manibus suis exemplo Christi de quo dictum est: 'Accepti panem in sanctas ac venerabiles manus suas,' et reliqua. Similiter et calicem . . ." J. M. Hanssens, ed., *Amalarii Episcopi Opera Liturgica Omnia,* vol. II, = Studi e Testi 139. (Vatican City: Bibliotheca Apostolica Vaticana, 1948) 338.

[7] MRR II, 206.

[8] MRR II, 207.

receive from the chalice. Hence the importance of the elevation of the chalice in Luther's *Formula Missae et Communionis* of 1523.

The elevation of the host can be related to two important medieval issues: the desire for ocular Communion[9] and debates about when the consecration of each of the elements took place; i.e., was the host transformed into the Body of Christ immediately after the words *"Hoc est enim corpus meum,"* or only after the institution narrative as a whole?[10] The elevation of the host after the words over the bread certainly resolved this question in the liturgical realm, as did the accompanying genuflexion for which there is evidence from the fourteenth century on. St. Thomas Aquinas, for example, used the liturgy itself as an argument for the consecration of the host immediately after the words *"Hoc est enim corpus meum."*[11] Genuflexions that both preceded and followed the elevations were only made definitive in the Missal of Pius V.[12] With the exception of the signs of the cross made over the gifts (which multiplied from the eighth century on)[13] and the cracking of the bread or miming of the fraction during the institution narrative, these are the gestures that accompanied the recitation of the Last Supper narrative in the medieval Roman Mass.

What of the practice prior to the ninth century, where we have found the first recorded instance of the priest touching the gifts during the narrative? Other than the description of Amalar of Metz cited above, there is no mention of the priest touching the gifts during the first millenium. The *Ordo Romanus Primus* (c. 750), which is quite detailed in its rubrical prescriptions makes no mention at all of such actions. This does not mean, of course, that priests made no gestures at all during the institution narrative. As Jungmann demonstrated, it was customary for the priest to make oratorical pointing gestures during the Eucharistic prayer, gestures that later became signs of the cross. The argument could also be

[9] See the classic study of Edouard Dumoutet, *Le desir de voir l'hostie,* (Paris: Beauchesne, 1926) and Nathan Mitchell, *Cult and Controversy: The Worship of the Eucharist Outside Mass,* (New York: Pueblo, 1982) 367–389; see MRR II, 208.

[10] See Mitchell, *Cult and Controversy,* 151–157.

[11] St. Thomas Aquinas, *Summa Theologiae* IIIa, Q. 78, a. 6 Resp.

[12] MRR II, 213.

[13] See Mario Righetti, *Manuale di Storia Liturgica,* vol. III, 3rd ed. (Milan: Ancora, 1966) 426–430. Jungmann argues (MRR II, 145–147) that these signs of the Cross probably originated from indicative gestures during the prayer.

made that touching the bread and the cup during the institution narrative were so familiar that they need not be written down. Early liturgical texts are notorious for what they take for granted.[14] The fact, however, that a document as detailed as the *Ordo Romanus I* fails to mention the manual acts does at least suggest that they were not employed until after the mid-eighth century. Without seeming to argue that what is earliest is best simply because it is earliest, one might bring some critical analysis to the question of why the actions of the priest, and especially the elevation of the Host, eventually formed part of Roman Eucharistic ritual.

Without specific documentary evidence we can only theorize as to why the manual acts were introduced into the institution narrative. The following developments come to mind as possible reasons: 1) the increasing infrequency of lay Communion from at least the sixth century, if not well before; 2) the Carolingian movement toward Old Testament models of kingship and priesthood; 3) the heightened devotion to the Eucharistic elements, especially after the eleventh century Berengarian controversy and various movements like the Albigensians who questioned the real presence; 4) the substitution of spiritual, or ocular Communion to replace eating and drinking the Body and Blood of Christ; and 5) the focus on the institution narrative as the moment of consecration of the elements and the drama associated with that moment—a movement which began as early as the fourth century as represented by Ambrose of Milan and John Chrysostom.

THE PRACTICE OF OTHER CHURCHES

We have already seen that Martin Luther retained the elevation of the consecrated bread and introduced the elevation of the cup in his *Formula Missae* (1523).[15] Luther was in many ways a true child of medieval Western piety and therefore adoration of the real presence of Christ in the Eucharistic species remained important for him. But eventually the only aspect of the Roman Canon he retained was the institution narrative since it alone communicated

[14] See Paul Bradshaw, *The Search for the Origins of Christian Worship* (New York: Oxford University Press, 1992) 76–77.

[15] Though the elevation of the chalice may already have been a custom in the usage that Luther knew. See *Formula Missae et Communionis* in Bard Thompson, *Liturgies of the Western Church* (New York: World, 1961) 112.

the gospel promise of forgiveness. Similarly Zwingli, Bucer and Calvin scorned the Roman Canon and removed the institution narrative completely from the context of Eucharistic prayer.[16] Cranmer represents a somewhat different approach, for he retained the Eucharistic prayer and manual acts but eliminated the elevation in the 1549 *Book of Common Prayer*. In the 1552 *Book of Common Prayer* Cranmer rearranged the Eucharistic prayer and removed the manual acts from the rubrics.[17] The integrity of the Eucharistic prayer and the manual acts were restored in the 1637 Scottish *Book of Common Prayer*, an ancestor of the American Episcopal book.[18]

What of the Eastern churches? Jungmann claims that the Byzantine Rite alone fails to provide for any handling of the elements by the priest at the institution narrative.[19] Instead, the deacon points to the bread and the cup with his stole at appropriate times during the narrative and again later during the epiclesis. The deacon also lifts the gifts at the oblation which concludes the anamnesis.[20] Jungmann concurs with the judgement of J. M. Hanssens that the manual acts were once employed in the Byzantine Rite but were removed to stress the consecratory nature of the epiclesis on account of theological controversy.[21] One might regard the position of Jungmann and Hanssens as highly speculative given the lack of documentary or icongraphic evidence for such gestures by the priest as well as the relatively late entrance of similar gestures into the Roman Rite. Moreover, the Armenian Rite rubrics indicate a slight elevation of the gifts by the priest at the oblation concluding the anamnesis but no manual acts during the institution narrative itself.[22] Likewise the Maronite Rite indicates no handling of the gifts during the institution narrative, but the priest does pass his

[16] See Thompson, *Liturgies*, 155, 177, 205.

[17] Thompson, *Liturgies*, 258, 280.

[18] See, Bryan D. Stuhlman, *Eucharistic Celebration, 1789–1979* (New York: Church Hymnal Corp., 1988) 32–40.

[19] MRR II, 202–203.

[20] See Isabel Hapgood, *The Service Book of the Holy Orthodox Catholic Apostolic Church*, revised ed. (Englewood, NJ: Antiochian Orthodox Christian Archdiocese, 1975) 104–105.

[21] J. M. Hanssens, *Institutiones Liturgicae de ritibus orientalibus*, vol. III, (Rome: 1932) 446.

[22] *Divine Liturgy of the Armenian Apostolic Orthodox Church*, trans. Tiran Narsoyan, 4th ed. revised (New York: John XXIII Center, 1970) 36–38.

hands and makes a sign of the cross over them a number of times.[23] On the other hand, the liturgy of the Syrian Orthodox Church does indicate that the priest picks up the host and the chalice during the narrative.[24] As has already been mentioned, the West Syrians and the Copts imitate the fraction during the institution narrative by miming it but not breaking the bread.

Having surveyed the practice of the Christian Churches of the East and the reformed liturgies of the sixteenth century, what can be said of the fate of the manual acts in the wake of the liturgical reform of the twentieth century among Protestant and Anglican churches?

The *Lutheran Book of Worship* retains the manual acts but mandates only one elevation—at the doxology concluding the Eucharistic prayer.[25] An earlier rubric, however, notes the appropriateness of the *orans* position for the minister from the preface through the doxology, presumably without prejudice to the institution narrative.[26] The American *Book of Common Prayer* includes the following rubric in the Eucharistic prayer for Rite I:

"At the following words concerning the bread, the Celebrant is to hold it, or lay a hand upon it; and at the words concerning the cup, to hold or place a hand upon the cup and any other vessel containing wine to be consecrated."[27]

This rubric, repeated in the four Eucharistic prayers of Rite II, allows the same latitude in the actions of the priest but does not call for elevating the gifts. The Church of England's *Alternative Service Book* allows for some latitude as well. The first rite (Rite A) is intended to recapture the fourfold shape advocated by Gregory Dix (of which more will be said below) and includes a handling of the gifts at the preparation rite. The rubrical notes, however, allow for the use of the "traditional manual acts" during the Eucharistic

---

[23] *The Divine Liturgy according to the Maronite Antiochian Rite*, Francis M. Zayek, ed., (Detroit: Maronite Church, 1969).

[24] *The Divine Liturgy of St. James, the First Bishop of Jerusalem*, Mar Athanasius Yeshue Samuel, ed., (Hackensack, NJ, 1967) 38–39.

[25] *Lutheran Book of Worship (Minister's Desk Edition)* (Minneapolis: Augsburg, 1978) 29.

[26] Ibid., 28.

[27] *The Book of Common Prayer . . . According to the Use of the Episcopal Church* (New York: Seabury, 1979) 334.

prayer.[28] Rite B, on the other hand, directs the priest to pick up the bread and cup at the appropriate moments in the institution narrative.[29] Neither of these rites provide for any elevation.

The *United Methodist Book of Worship* represents another contemporary attempt to ritualize Dix's fourfold shape.[30] In line with the Methodists' broad tradition, rubrics for the manual acts as well as the *orans* position are all put in the subjunctive mood: "The pastor may hold hands, palms down, over the bread, or touch the bread, or lift the bread."

To conclude this brief (and admittedly incomplete) survey it may be instructive to consider the ecumenical rite proposed by the World Council of Churches' Commission on Faith and Order—the so-called Lima Liturgy. This rite was intended to represent ritually the convergence marked by the statement *Baptism, Eucharist, and Ministry*. The text of the Eucharistic prayer of the Lima Liturgy attempts to emphasize the theological gains of increased attention to anamnesis and epiclesis as well as to respect the Roman Rite's addition of an epiclesis prior to the institution narrative.[31] No rubrics are provided for the Lima Liturgy's Eucharistic prayer.[32] There are several possible reasons for this omission. The architects of the rite may have wished the liturgy to be adaptable to the ritual practices of many different churches. On the other hand, it may not have occurred to them that including ritual actions was as important as the theological meaning of the text. In either case one might note the ritual naiveté that has characterized the contemporary reform of worship; i.e., an intellectualist bias that dis-

[28] *The Alternative Service Book* (London: Hodder and Stoughton, 1980) 130, 117.

[29] Ibid., 194. I am grateful to Canon Donald Gray for allowing me to use his commentary on this aspect of the *Alternative Service Book*: "Manual Acts in the Eucharistic Prayer," unpublished paper, delivered at the International Anglican Liturgical Consultation, Untermarchtal, Germany, August, 1993.

[30] *United Methodist Book of Worship* (Nashville: United Methodist Publishing House, 1992) 27-30.

[31] On the novelty of this "consecratory epiclesis" see Thomas J. Talley, "Future Directions for Eucharistic Revisions," unpublished paper, International Anglican Liturgical Consultation, Untermarchtal, Germany, August, 1993.

[32] The liturgy is printed in Max Thurian and Geoffrey Wainwright, eds., *Baptism and Eucharist: Ecumenical Convergence in Celebration* (Grand Rapids: Eerdman's, 1983) 241-255.

regards the importance of gesture. In fact, a liturgy on paper with no rubrical directions is no liturgy at all.

A MODERN THEOLOGY OF THE EUCHARIST
AND THE EUCHARISTIC PRAYER

Disembodied worship is merely a figment of the imagination. But neither do liturgical gestures occur in a vacuum. They correspond to some intended meaning of the rite even as they embody that meaning in ways that words alone cannot achieve. In other words, the gestures of the liturgy are related to theology; and nowhere are theological issues more at stake than in the Eucharistic Prayer and, in particular, in the role of the priest who prays it.

Some fifty years ago the Anglican Benedictine Gregory Dix brought out a monumental study of the Eucharist entitled *The Shape of the Liturgy*.[33] This work shaped the attitudes of a generation of scholars. Despite the misgivings one might have with the details of the argument,[34] Dix succeeded in demonstrating that the Eucharistic action as a whole (taking, blessing, breaking, giving) represents obedience to the dominical command: "Do this as my memorial." Thus he counteracted a tendency to view what was essential about the Eucharist solely in terms of the priest's words and activity during the Eucharistic Prayer. In other words, the meaning of the Eucharist is fundamentally an ecclesial act; i.e., communal. Moreover, argued Dix, attempts to isolate a moment of consecration during the Eucharistic Prayer (whether at the institution narrative as in the West or at the epiclesis as in the East) were fundamentally misguided and ignored the central function of the prayer as an outgrowth of a series of thanksgivings. Indeed, the institution narrative itself may not have figured in a number of early Eucharistic prayers, finding its undisputed place only in the

[33] Gregory Dix, *The Shape of the Liturgy* (London: Dacre, 1945).

[34] For example, the nature of early Christian architecture, the status of *Didache* 9-10 as a Eucharistic Prayer, the Last Supper as a *chaburah*, and the meaning of the "offertory." See Kenneth Stevenson, *Gregory Dix: Twenty-five Years On = Grove Liturgical Study* 10, Bramcote (Nottingham: Grove Books, 1977); David Tripp, "Shape and Liturgy," and Richard Buxton, "The Shape of the Eucharist: A Survey and Appraisal," in K. Stevenson, ed., *Liturgy Reshaped* (London: SPCK, 1982) 65-82, 83-93.

fourth century.[35] If Dix was correct about the development of the fourfold shape as a communal act, there are profound theological consequences with regard to the role of the priest in the Eucharist as a whole and the Eucharistic Prayer in particular. Convinced as I am of the basic correctness of Dix's insight that the Eucharist is ecclesial, I will lay out some theological implications of the centrality of the fourfold shape.

The Church hears the command of Christ to *do* something, namely to take, bless, break and give as his memorial. The form which the memorial takes is apt because it recapitulates the person (presence) and activity (sacrifice) of Christ in, as it were, a ritual nutshell; i.e., Jesus is the one who enacts perfect prayer to the Father by accepting his life (taking), blessing or acknowledging God with that life (blessing), allowing himself to be broken and poured out (breaking) and giving himself freely and completely for the life of the world. The Eucharistic meal (presentation of gifts, Eucharistic prayer, fraction, Communion) plays out this presence and activity of Jesus in ritual form in order that the Body of Christ (the Church) might become who Christ is by doing what he did. This approach captures the biblical and patristic themes of perfect sacrifice of self (Rom 12:1-2; Mal 1:11; Phil 2:6-11),[36] the centrality of thanksgiving as the acknowledgement of God's mighty acts in Christ, a realistic notion of identification with Christ (real presence) and the corporate activity of the Church (Eucharist as Communion and foretaste of the eschatological banquet). The only aspect that needs to be added (and with emphasis) is that the Church can do this only in the power of the Holy Spirit, who con-

---

[35] Recent scholarship has followed Dix here. See, for example, Louis Ligier, "From the Last Supper to the Eucharist," in L. C. Sheppard, ed., *The New Liturgy*, London: Darton, Longman and Todd, 1970, 113-150; idem., "The Origins of the Eucharistic Prayer," *Studia Liturgica* 9 (1973) 161-185; Cesare Giraudo, *La struttura letteraria della preghiera eucaristica = Analecta Biblica 92*, (Rome: Biblical Inst. Press, 1981); idem., *Preghiere*, 111; Hans-Bernard Meyer, *Eucharistie: Geschichte, Theologie, Pastoral = Gottesdienst der Kirche 4* (Regensburg: Pustet, 1989) 99-100.

[36] It is important today to recognize the metaphorical and ironic use of the term sacrifice both for the death of Christ and the Eucharist. See the masterful treatment by Gordon Lathrop, *Holy Things: A Liturgical Theology* (Minneapolis: Fortress, 1993) 139-158.

vokes the *ecclesia* (assembly) in the first place. Further this approach based on the ritual action of the Eucharist avoids a static understanding of the presence of Christ in the elements in favor of showing why Christ is present and how his presence and activity are inextricably interrelated. Thus this approach also remedies scholastic theology's tendency to divorce the questions of real presence and sacrifice from one another and to make the sacrifice dependent on Christ present in the elements, instead of showing that the presence of Christ in the elements flows from the activity itself.[37]

The theological approach to the Eucharist I have outlined here avoids concentrating on the institution narrative as the moment of consecration in favor of understanding the entirety of the Eucharistic action as consecratory.[38] What, then, is the function of this narrative of institution? It simply acts to provide the warrant for the whole of the Eucharist in the context of one of its essential elements—prayer. This position on the meaning of the narrative may well explain its absence in a number of primitive prayers. An explicit proclamation of the warrant for the pattern of the Eucharist was not necessary when the meaning of that pattern could be presumed.

This ritual theology of the Eucharist cuts through a number of traditional "Gordian knots" in controversial theology, but it must be compared with contemporary official Roman Catholic Eucharistic theology in order to understand what is at stake in the gestures of the priest. I will limit my observations to Pope John Paul II's 1980 Holy Thursday letter to priests *(Domincae Cenae)*, which admirably summarizes the official theology.

For John Paul "the Eucharist is the principal and central *raison d'etre* of the sacrament of the priesthood, which effectively came

[37] Interestingly enough Thomas Talley has attempted to demonstrate that St. Thomas (ST IIIa, q. 83, a. 4) gave a temporal priority to sacrifice in the eucharist, albeit locating it at the medieval offertory, see his "Future Revisions," 6–7.

[38] How this is related to the Liturgy of the Word would be another topic. My approach here is not meant to slight the proclamation of the Word but rather to focus on the precise meaning and function of the Eucharistic Prayer in an effort to understand the gestures of the priest.

into being at the moment of the institution of the Eucharist and together with it."[39]

Several aspects of this statement are worthy of note. First, the Pope makes the closest possible link between Eucharist and priesthood. Second, he makes the specific historical claim that the Christian priesthood came into being at the Last Supper. Given the complex relation between Eucharist and liturgical presidency in the first three centuries, the origins of the priesthood do not seem so simple.[40] Rather the link between Eucharist and priesthood seems to come about through a gradual process of sacralization, reinterpreting Christian ministry in light of the priesthood of Israel. Third, the Pope treats the relation, priest-Eucharist, before dealing with the relation, Church-Eucharist. The sequence is significant (even in a letter written specifically to priests) for much hangs on the issue of whether the priesthood is somehow prior to the Church. In other words, could the priest be understood somehow to be acting independently of the Church? At issue here is the question of the precise meaning of the distinction between the ministerial priesthood and that of the faithful drawn by Vatican II.[41] However the "essential difference" between the priesthood of the faithful and ministerial priesthood is understood, it would be an error to fail to understand ministerial priesthood in the context of the Church.[42]

Another crucial aspect of *Dominicae Cenae* is the affirmation that the priest acts in the person of Christ *(in persona Christi)* at the Eucharist and that this role "means more than offering 'in the name of' or 'in the place of' Christ. *'In persona'* here means in specific sacramental identification with the 'eternal High Priest' who is the author and principal subject of this sacrifice of his, a sacrifice in

[39] John Paul II, "The Mystery and Worship of the Eucharist *(Dominicae Cenae),"* in Edward J. Kilmartin, *Church, Eucharist and Priesthood,* (New York: Paulist, 1981) #2.

[40] See, for example, Paul F. Bradshaw, *Liturgical Presidency in the Early Church* = *Grove Liturgical Study 26,* Bramcote (Nottingham: Grove Books, 1983).

[41] Dogmatic Constitution on the Church *(Lumen Gentium)* #10.

[42] Hence the by-now nearly classic formulation of Aidan Kavanagh: "The Church baptizes to priesthood; it ordains to episcopacy, presbyterate and diaconate," *The Shape of Baptism* (New York: Pueblo, 1978) 188.

which, in truth, nobody can take his place."[43] The same concern for sacramental representation of Christ is expressed in the 1987 response by the Secretariat for Promoting Christian Unity in collaboration with the Congregation for the Doctrine of the Faith to the Lima Document of the World Council of Churches' Faith and Order Commission.[44] I would argue that the priest acts in the person of Christ in the context of acting in the person of the Church, for he is representing the faith of the whole Church. To reduce this representation either to the words of Christ at the institution narrative (thus misunderstanding the role of the narrative in the prayer) or to a specific moment of sacrificial offering (thus misunderstanding the sacrificial character of the Eucharist as a whole) would inevitably undermine the communal nature of the Eucharist.

Here one comes face to face with the ambiguity of the post-Vatican II liturgical reform. On the one hand, both the rubrics for the Eucharistic celebration and the theological foundations of the *General Instruction on the Roman Missal* repeat the traditional notion that the priest offers the sacrifice.[45] On the other hand, the aim of the Council and other aspects of the *General Instruction* point to a more communal understanding of the Eucharist as well as to a broader understanding of the presence of Christ in the liturgy.[46] Just as historical theologians argue over positions taken by St. Augustine, which at times seem to contradict one another, so too modern commentators gravitate toward those texts in the liturgy and official documents which suit their arguments best. Current papal teaching on the Eucharist clearly favors the more traditional aspects of Eucharistic worship, although to be fair there are many moving and profound statements about the communal dimension and spiritual meaning of the Eucharist in the Pope's 1980 letter.

This essay cannot settle the theological question of the role of the priest in the Eucharist, but I trust that my bias in favor of a

[43] *Dominicae Cenae* #8. Astute readers will note here the theological foundation for the argument against the ordination of women.

[44] "Roman Catholic Church: Response," in M. Thurian, ed., *Churches Respond to BEM*, vol. VI = *Faith and Order Paper 114*, (Geneva: World Council of Churches, 1988) 129.

[45] See the introduction and first chapter of the *General Instruction on the Roman Missal*, 2nd ed., 1975.

[46] *General Instruction* #14, 8 respectively.

fundamentally communal understanding of the Eucharist based on Dix's fourfold shape is apparent. That the priest plays an essential role in the celebration is not, to my mind, an issue for debate. He is the official articulator of the Church's faith both in preaching and especially in the Eucharistic Prayer. Without this crucial element the Eucharist would not exist as an act of the Church. This is not precisely the same, however, as saying that the priest consecrates the bread and wine by repeating the words of Christ. In other words, although the priest's leadership in the person of Christ is indispensable to the celebration, one neglects the communal dimension of the Eucharist if the representative role of the priest is tied too closely to the institution narrative. What are the consequences of this approach for the gestures of the priest during the narrative?

THE MANUAL ACTS

The preceding historical and theological considerations serve as a framework for understanding the issues surrounding the gestures of the priest during the institution narrative. At this point we shall discuss the practical and communicative aspects of the manual acts.

First, it should be noted that the meaning of the manual acts has been altered by the shift in the position of the priest, who now faces the people during the celebration. Ironically a shift intended to emphasize the communal-meal nature of the Eucharist has had the unintended result of focusing more attention on the person (even personality) of the priest.[47] Previously most of the actions of the priest were obscured.[48]

People could see the genuflexions and elevations, of course, but not the acts of picking up the gifts and pronouncing the words over them. This shift in the position of the priest is all the more ironic in that it emphasizes the *in persona Christi* character of the rite even while a number of proponents of that theology prefer

[47] See Ralph Keifer, *To Give Thanks and Praise: General Instruction on the Roman Missal with Commentary for Musicians and Priests* (Washington: Pastoral Press, 1980) 98 for an excellent commentary on this liturgical shift to a "priest-centered" rite.

[48] So much so that Gregory Dix's grandmother could think that the Roman Catholic Mass was a matter of the priest letting loose a crab on the altar and then trying to keep it from the view of the congregation, *Shape*, 145.

the previous posture.[49] The post-Vatican II liturgical reform was rather naive when it came to perceiving how the various changes would alter what and how the ritual communicates to an assembly. It seems to me that by being able to see the priest during the Eucharistic Prayer, the notion is reinforced that during the institution narrative the priest is doing precisely what Christ did at the Last Supper.

Little wonder, then, that in the course of the reform many priests began to break the host during the narrative. Little wonder as well that, given the medieval theology of a moment of consecration, sixteenth century reformers like Luther and Cranmer introduced Communion after each part of the institution narrative, so that Christ's actions could be more faithfully imitated. What was lost was the fourfold shape in which the entire assembly became ritually involved in making Eucharist.

An alternative to the present rubrics might have the priest continue to hold his hands in the *orans* position throughout the prayer (perhaps with the exception of the epiclesis), lifting up the gifts in a true gesture of offering only at the doxology. Cesare Giraudo has suggested that it is only after the doxology and "Amen" that the priest might be directed to genuflect in adoration—a suggestion I find agreeable.[50] Needless to say other considerations would have to be introduced if such a change in the rubrics were to take place, namely the posture and gesture of the assembly as a whole.

No doubt numerous objections could be raised with regard to any proposal aimed at eliminating the manual acts. The piety of Catholics since the Middle Ages has been focused on the elevations during the institution narrative. Would eliminating these not promote further disintegration of the worship and belief in Christ's real presence in the elements? Perhaps this undesirable outcome might be avoided by a greater attention to reverence which often seems lacking in contemporary Eucharistic celebration. Perhaps more attention could be given to the elevation at the doxology (followed by the genuflexion proposed by Giraudo) and the adora-

---

[49] On the issue of *versus populum* celebration, see Jaime Lara, "*Versus Populum* Revisited," *Worship* 68 (1994) 210–221.

[50] *Preghiere*, 110.

tion of the gifts after the fraction as in the 1979 Episcopal *Book of Common Prayer*.

Another objection might be raised against the perceived rationalization of the reformed Roman Rite in which so many gestures and actions have been eliminated only to be replaced by over-verbalization. Would removing the manual acts not exacerbate this tendency? Moreover, would it not be strange to have the gifts spoken of so directly during the Eucharistic Prayer without their having been touched or at least pointed to?

To the first of these objections one can only agree that Catholic liturgy has been rationalized in the course of the reform and that we must seek a new "choreography" for the ritual, but one that corresponds to a more communal understanding of the Eucharist. As to the second, it would indeed take a great deal of time for people to get used to perceiving the Eucharistic Prayer as a prayer rather than a mimesis of Christ's actions, but it is a prayer that articulates the Lord's self-donating and self-sacrificial love in the context of a larger action.

CONCLUSION

In his *On Liturgical Theology*, Aidan Kavanagh adopted Erving Goffman's typology of social relationships to liturgy. There he argued that the liturgy is best characterized as a relationship of many-to-many rather than one-to-one or one-to-many. A proposal to eliminate the manual acts at the institution narrative could well enhance the many-to-many character of the rite both theologically and in terms of ritual communication. After all, the Spirit of Christ calls the entire assembly to give thanks and praise and to participate in the meal that represents Christ's self-gift for the life of the world.

This essay has been intended not so much as advocacy for future revisions in the Roman Rite as analysis of what the gestures of the priest during the Eucharistic institution narrative communicate with regard to the meaning of the Eucharist. Whether or not these rubrics are altered must depend on a determination of the meaning of the Eucharist as a whole and the role of the priest in relation to it.

Peter S. Hawkins

8. Crossing Over: Dante's Purgatorial Threshold

Among the many contributions made by cultural anthropologists to the study of religion, few have proved as useful as the notion of liminality. The term itself, deriving from limen, the Latin for threshold, comes from Arnold van Gennep's pioneering *Les Rites de passage* (1908). In his study of tribal rituals that mark transitions "from group to group or from one social situation to the next,"[1] van Gennep identified three successive but distinct stages: a *separation* from the everyday world, an entrance into ritual time and space called the "margin" or *limen,* and a *reaggregation* into mundane existence. A half century later Victor Turner seized upon the middle term of this sequence as the very heart of the ritual process. But whereas van Gennep conceived of a finite moment within the processural form of traditional rites of passage, Turner saw more extensive, even revolutionary, implications. His discovery of liminality was like a pebble tossed into a pool; its widening circles drew him beyond the small, preindustrial societies with which he had been initially concerned, leading him to consider the place of "margins" or "thresholds" in large-scale civilizations such as our own. He came to think, in fact, that the notion of liminality was applicable to "all phases of decisive cultural change, in which previous orderings of thought and behavior are subject to revision and criticism, when hitherto unprecedented modes of ordering relations between ideas and people become possible and desirable."[2]

[1] Arnold van Gennep, *Rites of Passage,* trans. Monika B. Vizedom and Gabrielle L. Carfee (Chicago: University of Chicago, 1960).

[2] Victor and Edith Turner, *Image and Pilgrimage in Christian Culture: Anthropological Perspectives* (New York: Columbia University, 1978) 2. Other

Instead of a delimited stage in the ritual of preindustrial societies, he found a "potentiality" at play in our own world.

But at play where? Turner suggested that liminal moments throughout Western history have given birth to a wide variety of "margins": utopias, new philosophical systems, political programs, even scientific hypotheses. He also saw in Christian monasticism an effort to turn the ritual threshold into a way of life, that is, into "a very long threshold, a corridor, almost, or a tunnel."[3] But the form of liminality that finally claimed his interest was not the stabilized margin represented by monastic enclosure; it was, rather, the ancient and enduring phenomenon of pilgrimage. For Catholic Christians throughout the ages, he argued, the journey to and from a shrine or sacred place offered the laity "the great liminal experience of the religious life": "While monastic contemplatives and mystics could daily make interior salvific journeys, those in the world had to exteriorize theirs in the infrequent adventure of pilgrimage."[4]

The ways in which the pilgrim's "adventure" resembles many elements of the traditional rite of passage (separation, *limen*, reaggregation) is explored at length in the introduction to Turner's *Image and Pilgrimage* (1978).[5] The journey begins, of course, with an

---

relevant works by Turner are "The Center Out There: Pilgrim's Goal," *History of Religions* 12.3 (Feb. 1973) 191–230; *Dramas, Fields, and Metaphors: Symbolic Action in Human Society* (Ithaca, NY: Cornell, 1974); "Liminality and Communitas," *The Ritual Process: Structure and Anti-structure* (Chicago: Aldine, 1974) 94–130, "Variations on a Theme of Liminality," *Secular Ritual*, eds. Sally F. Moore and Barbara G. Meyerhoff (Amsterdam: Van Gorcum, 1977) 36–52 and, again with Edith Turner, "Religious Celebrations," *Celebration: Studies in Festivity and Ritual*, ed. Victor Turner (Washington: Smithsonian Institution Press, 1982) 201–219. Critical assessment of Turner's methods and conclusions can be found in the essays collected in *Contesting the Sacred: The Anthropology of Christian Pilgrimage*, eds. John Earle and Michael J. Sailnow (New York: Routledge, 1991).

[3] "Variations on a Theme of Liminality," 37: "A *limen* is a threshold but at least in case of protracted initiation rites or major seasonal festivals it is a very long threshold, a corridor, almost, or a tunnel which may indeed become a pilgrim's road or, passing from dynamics to statics, may cease to be a mere transition and become a set way of life, a state, that of an anchorite or monk."

[4] *Image and Pilgrimage*, 6–7.

[5] Despite the free-ranging aspect of his analysis in *Image and Pilgrimage* of pilgrimage as a rite of passage, Turner is careful to qualify his use of van

act of separation, as the pilgrim not only leaves the familiar geography of home but also the structures and priorities of mundane life. Gradually, the markers of class and status also loosen their hold, as a more egalitarian *communitas* develops between fellow travelers on their way to a common spiritual destination. Daily life itself is increasingly spiritualized, transformed by the reality of those *sacra*, or sacred things, that are revealed to the pilgrim in the holy places and expounded through various kinds of instruction and exhortation. Physical discomfort or actual ordeal are also part of this extended initiation, for the way of a Christian pilgrim is inevitably experienced as a *via crucis*. Indeed, suffering has its intended purpose, either as a purgation of the "old" self or as the birth pangs associated with the emergence of a "new," more authentic person. Whereas reaching the sacred site at first seems like the primary goal of the journey, what gradually emerges in importance is the pilgrim's new and deeper level of existence. What really matters is the crossing of a spiritual rather than a physical threshold; the "end" of the journey is a renewed heart and mind. Finally, once the pilgrimage is completed, the rounds of daily life resume within the familiar structures of home. But things are not the same as they were before the journey. Like Eliot's *Magi*, the pilgrim is "no longer at ease here, in the old dispensation." Encounter with the sacred has destabilized the structures of secular life and altered the status quo; it has opened the "windows of perception" onto something new.

Working from this generic model of pilgrimage, Turner goes on to identify four main types—prototypical, archaic, medieval, and modern. In subsequent chapters he analyzes several contemporary instances of each, ranging from St. Patrick's purgatory in Lough Derg, Ireland, to Lourdes, to a number of sites in Mexico. But throughout this discussion the cultural anthropologist never mentions what may well be the most important pilgrimage in all of

---

Gennep. Because pilgrimage is voluntary, "not an obligatory social mechanism to mark the transition of an individual or group from one state or status to another within the mundane sphere, pilgrimage is probably better thought of as 'liminoid' or 'quasi-liminal,' rather than as 'liminal' in van Gennep's full sense (34–35). Likewise, though pilgrimage has initiatory features, it is not, strictly speaking, initiatory (that is, "an irreversible, singular ritual instrument for effecting a permanent, visible cultural transformation of the subject" (31).

Christian tradition, a sacred journey undertaken precisely as a liminal experience of transformation—the one Dante describes in the pages of his *Commedia*. There are, of course, other notable literary treatments of pilgrims and pilgrimages that reflect different aspects of this "liminoid phenomenon": other poems, such as Chaucer's *Canterbury Tales*, Tasso's *Gerusalemme Liberata*, the first book of the *Faerie Queene*; or such prose works as Petrarch's "familiar letters" on fourteenth century pilgrims or the descriptions of holy sites in the anonymous medieval *Mirablia urbis Romae*. None of these works, however, comes close to approaching either the depth or the extent of Dante's reflections on pilgrimage; nor does any yield the poet's insights into the fundamental place of Christian ritual in the experience of liminal transformation. In other words, while cultural anthropology offers the reader of Dante a lens through which to see anew the entire enterprise of the *Commedia*—and most especially that of the poem's own middle space, the *Purgatorio*—the *Commedia* in its turn brings the notion of liminality to life.

In the following pages I want to argue that Dante conceives of the whole of his poem as a pilgrimage text written "for the reason that the pilgrim's staff is brought back wreathed with palm" (33.77-778), that is, both to testify to a process completed and to inspire others to undertake the same. On one level, the *Commedia* presents Dante's experience as an actual itinerary through real (if otherworldly) space, not as a dream vision from which the poet wakes up into reality. Yet this allegorical work is also an *itinerarium mentis*, the journey of a soul from death to life, or, as Beatrice puts it in the Paradiso, from Egypt to Jerusalem (Par. 25.55-56). In the fiction of the poem, Dante is rescued from the "dark wood" of spiritual malaise and led through the three realms of the afterlife by a series of divinely-appointed guides. Separated from the mundane world of Florence, he crosses over one boundary after another; in so doing, he learns the mysteries of hell, purgatory, and paradise, and is transformed by what he sees. Toward the end of this progress he is told to make his entire vision known to the world: "*tutta tua visïon fa manifesta*" (Par. 17.128). The *Commedia* itself, therefore, is to be memory's witness, the memoir of the poet's crossing over "to the divine from the human, to the eternal from time . . . from Florence to a people just and sane" (Par. 31.37-39).

Yet, at the same time that Dante makes so singular a claim, he is also at pains to underscore a commonality between this unique itinerary through the afterlife and those sacred journeys undertaken, at home or abroad, by other Christians. For this reason, he invokes the particulars of pilgrimage—what Turner called the laity's "great liminal experience of the religious life"—in order to join his voyage to those taken by so many of his contemporaries to Jerusalem, Rome, or Compostella.[6] He does this in the first place by setting his journey in 1300, during the Jubilee "holy year" promulgated by Pope Boniface VIII, when Christians making a pilgrimage to the sacred sites of Rome were offered the same spiritual benefits of a pilgrimage to Jerusalem ("not only a full and copious, but the most full pardon of all their sins").[7] Because the Holy Land was no longer in Christian hands, and in any case stood at too great a distance for most people to visit, the popular response to Boniface's offer of plenary indulgence was enormous. The resulting influx of people into Rome, estimated variously between two hundred thousand and two million,[8] is explicitly

[6] For a general consideration of "pilgrim" and "pilgrimage" in all of Dante's works, see the entry "pellegrino" in the *Enciclopedia Dantesca* (Rome: Istituto della Enciclopedia Italiana, 1971) 4:369–70. The most extensive treatment of the *Commedia* in the context of pilgrimage is John Demaray, *The Invention of Dante's 'Commedia'* (New Haven and London: Yale University, 1974). Demaray argues that the "Great Circle" pilgrimage route from Rome to Egypt/Sinai to Jerusalem and back to Rome again underwrites the structure of the three *cantiche* and provides a "key" to interpreting the poem. While Demaray's thesis strikes me as far-fetched, he offers many useful insights about the importance of actual pilgrimage to the *Commedia*. For other treatments of medieval pilgrimage, see Jonathan Sumption, *Pilgrimage: An Image of Medieval Religion* (Totowa, N.J.: Rowman & Littlefield, 1975), Christian K. Zacher, *Curiosity and Pilgrimage: The Literature of Pilgrimage in Fourteenth Century England* (Baltimore: Johns Hopkins University, 1976), Margaret Wade Labarge, *Medieval Travelers* (London: Hamish Hamilton, 1982), *Sacred Journeys: The Anthropology of Pilgrimage*, ed. Alan Morninis (Westport, Conn.: Greenwood Press, 1992), and L. K. Davidson and M. Dunn-Wood, *Pilgrimage in the Middle Ages: A Research Guide* (New York: Garland, 1993).

[7] In addition to Demaray, 37–43, see Herbert Thurston, *The Holy Year of Jubilee* (London: Sands & Company, 1900); also Jacques LeGoff, *The Birth of Purgatory*, 1981, trans. Arthur Goldhammer (Chicago: University of Chicago, 1984) 330–331.

[8] The fourteenth century chronicler, Giovanni Villani, reports that Rome was filled with "200,000 pilgrims" who came from "distant and diverse coun-

recalled at one point in the *Commedia,* in a context rich in irony. When in *Inferno* 18 the poet looks down into a ditch that is packed with panders and seducers, he notes that the damned are crowded together in a single passageway but move past one another in opposite directions. Despite the presumed difference between the ditches of hell and the pilgrim-thronged streets of Christian Rome, this two way flow of traffic reminds Dante (as no doubt it would have reminded many of his contemporary readers) of efforts made at crowd control during the holy year: "thus the Romans, because of the great throng, in the year of the Jubilee, have taken measures for the people to pass over the bridge, so that on one side all face toward the Castle and go on to St. Peter's and on the other they go on toward the Mount" (28–33).[9]

If this is the *Commedia's* one explicit recollection of the holy year, it is by no means the only remembrance of Roman pilgrimage. When Dante enters the Empyrean, for instance, he is as wonderstruck as some northern "barbarian" first setting foot in Rome, seeing the Lateran rise up, and agog at the architectural wonders of the city ("*Roma e l'ardüa sua opra,*" *Par.* 31.34). Taking in the *civitas Dei,* he is "like a pilgrim who is refreshed within the temple of his vow as he looks around, and already hopes to tell again how it was" (43–45). When he finds himself in the presence of St. Bernard, moreover, he is as amazed as any visitor to St. Peter's who makes his way to the chapel of the Veronica Veil and there beholds the imprint of Christ "face to face": "As is he who comes perchance from Croatia to look on our Veronica, and whose old hunger is not sated, but says in thought so long as it is shown,

tries, both far and near" (*Villani's Chronicle,* trans. Rose E. Selfe, ed. Philip H. Wicksteed [London, 1906]: 320). The estimate of two million pilgrims for the first Jubilee year is given by Henri Daniel Rops, *Cathedral and Crusade,* trans. John Warrington (London: Dent, 1957) 64.

[9] Citations of the *Commedia* are based on the Petrocchi text as found in *The Divine Comedy,* translated, with a commentary, by Charles S. Singleton, 3 vols. in 2 parts, Bollingen Series 80 (Princeton: Princeton University, 1970–1975). In his commentary on these verses, Singleton cites the consensus that Dante was himself in Rome during the holy year and saw the "remarkable organization" (315) that he describes in the poem. The bridge mentioned was the only one in Dante's day to serve the Trastevere section of the city where St. Peter's is located. The "Castle" is the Castel Sant'Angelo, the "Mount" Monte Giordano.

'My Lord Jesus Christ, true God, was then your semblance like to this?' such was I'' (Par. 31.103–109).

While the whole of the *Commedia* can be said to represent a pilgrimage from the city of man to the city of God, it is quite specifically in the *Purgatorio* that the poet undertakes his major exploration of liminality. There are a number of reasons why this should be the case. In the first place, and in contrast to the eternal states of beatitude or damnation, purgatory is a temporal realm; it is governed by time and characterized by process and change. Standing betwixt and between the eternal, it presents the Catholic imagination with a more open middle term, a threshold to be traversed after death by those who, while not in a state of mortal sin, are still not ready for the beatific vision.[10] What they require is a period of transformation, a *limen* that may extend for centuries—a ''margin'' for renewal in the afterlife.

In addition to being temporal, purgatory is also a temporary realm coterminous with the age of grace. ''Born'' after the death and resurrection of Christ—born, that is, as one of the first fruits of the redemption—it will also pass away at the time of the Last Judgment, when purgation finds its fulfillment in beatitude. For this reason purgatory is (like Turner's understanding of the *limen*) more a phase or a process than a state; for this reason, too, its residents are, in fact, only sojourners. Assisted by the suffrages of those who are still alive in the Church Militant—the faithful who keep fasts, make prayer, give alms, and most especially have masses offered up—the penitents make their expiation in hope rather than despair. For although the souls endure pains that are virtually the same as those of hell, they look forward to an eventual release from their misery. The Church Suffering will end as the Church Triumphant.

Jacques LeGoff counts the mid-thirteenth century as the definitive ''birth'' of purgatory and the Jubilee year of 1300 as its theo-

---

[10] For the history of purgatory's theological formulation and popular reception, see Jacques LeGoff, *The Birth of Purgatory*, passim. Of all the theologians LeGoff studies, Bonaventure (250–256) is most interesting in connection with Dante's own purgatorial ''innovations,'' e.g. the greater proximity of purgatory to heaven than to hell, the direction of penance by angels rather than demons, and the liberation of the soul from purgatory prior to the Last Judgment.

logical and social triumph; he also celebrates Dante for giving purgatory its "noblest representation," that is, for making "an enduring selection from among the possible and at times competing images whose choice the Church, while affirming the essence of the dogma, left to the sensibility and imagination of individual Christians" (334). There is no doubt that the poet did indeed take full advantage of this imaginative liberty. In the first place, he resolved the vexed whereabouts of the *locus purgatorius* as had nobody else before him. He brought it up from the horrors of the underworld, turned it into a seven story mountain at the antipodes from Jerusalem, and placed it in the bright light of day. He also crowned it with Eden, the "place chosen for nest of the human race" (*Purg.* 28.77–78). With geography ultimately made the handmaiden to theology, Dante showed the place of penance to border Eden rather than hell, thus suggesting that penitence itself culminates in the restoration of innocence and joy.[11] The end of the purgatorial pilgrimage, therefore, is for the soul to be as guiltless as Adam and Eve before the Fall; it is to be born again.

Although Dante was bound by dogma to present the experience of purgatory in terms of suffering, he nonetheless took the received notion of purgatorial punishment and turned it into the dynamic of spiritual growth. The endurance of pain becomes instead the pangs of a maturation process whereby the human worm struggles to become the angelic butterfly (*"noi siam vermi/nati a formar l'angelica farfalla,"* *Purg.* 10.124–125). Dramatically countering the strong fourteenth-century tendency to infernalize purgatory, he transformed what others had imagined as a torture chamber into a hospital of the spirit where (to recall Psalm 51) broken bones come to rejoice; he also made purgatory a school where souls engage in the strenuous business of learning beatitude. "Heed not the form of the pain," the poet tells the reader on the first terrace of the mountain, "think what follows" (*Purg.* 10.109–110).

---

[11] For Dante's theological geography, his decisions with regard to mapping both this world (Eden) as well as the world of the afterlife (purgatory), see my essay " 'Out upon Circumference': Discovery in Dante," *Discovering New Worlds: Essays on Medieval Exploration and Imagination,* ed. Scott D. Westrem (New York: Garland, 1991) 193–263, viz. 196–198. See also Alison Morgan, *Dante and the Medieval Other World* (Cambridge and New York: Cambridge University Press, 1990) 144–165.

But most importantly for our purposes, Dante transformed the middle term of the afterlife into an extended threshold between earth and heaven, a "margin" within which souls move from one order of being to another, until in time they are reborn in God. Indeed, among the poet's most valuable contributions to Catholic theology was his explicit cultivation of that dimension of liminality which, while inherent in any notion of purgatory, nonetheless remained undeveloped in earlier (not to mention later) representations. What he portrayed in the central *cantica* of his poem was exactly what the Church's teaching on penitence had long required as a theological redress—a sense of health and excitement to be found in the refining fire, of exhilaration over new discoveries awaiting the broken and contrite heart. For in Dante's vision the point of purgatory was not so much to "serve time" in a place of temporal suffering as it was to enter into a process of transformation, to become someone new. In short, the poet took what was popularly imagined as an upper chamber of hell and turned it into an extended passage to heaven. His purgatory is the *limen* of the afterlife, a threshold crossing in which (to quote Turner again) "previous orderings of thought and behavior are subject to revision and criticism, when hitherto unprecedented modes of ordering relations between ideas and people become possible."

In Dante's purgatory this process of revision, the discovery of a new way of ordering reality, is the result not only of God's grace but of human prayer. In this regard, of course, the *Commedia* simply reflects what the Church had taught, namely, that within the communion of saints, the trials of the dead could be lightened by the intercessory prayers of the faithful on earth. This belief is demonstrated throughout the *Purgatorio* as the souls either ask to be remembered by relatives and friends, or recall those suffrages once made on their behalf that sped them on their way up the mountain: "I sought peace with God on the brink of my life," says one of the envious, "and my debt would not yet be reduced by penitence, had not Pier Pettinaio remembered me in his holy prayers, who in his charity did grieve for me," 13.124–129). The souls also approach Dante for intercessions, as when Arnaut Daniel calls out from the fires on the terrace of lust and asks to be remembered in his pain, *"sovegna vos a temps de ma dolor!"* (26.147).

At least once, moreover, the poet himself makes an authorial request for prayer, bidding his audience to turn their reading of the *Commedia* into a suffrage for the souls in purgatory. In *Purgatorio* 11, after reporting that the penitents on the terrace of pride pray for those who remain behind on earth, the poet asks his readers, "If there they always ask good for us, what can here be said or done, by those who have their will rooted in good? Truly we ought to help them wash away the stains they have borne thence, so that pure and light they may go forth to the starry wheels" (11.31-36).

If Dante inherited a traditional belief in the efficacy of prayer for the faithful departed, he was in other respects quite innovative. For in addition to the economy of intercessory prayer, he imagined another connection between the Church Militant on earth and the Church Suffering in purgatory: he transferred to the *limen* of the afterlife those ritual aids to spiritual formation and transformation that are characteristic of ordinary Christians. In his hands, therefore, purgatory became a worshipping community, with prayer and praise shown to constitute the souls' penance far more than the mechanics of their pain. LeGoff reminds us that the scholastic theologians who effectively "systematized" purgatory had almost entirely kept the liturgy out of their writings (249). So too, by and large, did the preaching friars and other popularizers, who exhorted the living to acts of piety on behalf of the dead but did not imagine the souls themselves as engaged in ritual process. Apparently in this regard, as in so many others, the poet discovered his own way: in his vision of purgatory not only does the liturgy of the Church on earth assist the dead, it also informs the souls' own practice of purgation in the afterlife. They worship themselves clean.

To signify the importance of liturgy both as the medium for penance and as the agent of personal transformation, Dante filled the thirty-three cantos of *Purgatorio* with liturgical song, prayer, ceremony, and drama. Thus, even though his penitents work out their salvation through physical suffering and ordeal—as the proud are bowed down by the stones they carry (10.112–120) and the lustful process along a "burning road" (26.28)—it is rather their participation in Christian worship that renews and reorders them, that indicates their newfound orientation. While some of these rites

Dante invents for the poem's occasion, they are not without evident parallels to ecclesiastical practice. When he first approaches the "holy mountain," for instance, he enacts a kind of *Asperges* by washing his face and girding himself with a rush (1.94–105, 121–129); likewise, when he completes his journey, he is immersed in two Edenic rivers, emerging from their sacramental bath "pure and ready to rise to the stars" (33.145). Liturgical invention, however, is not the norm; rather, the souls in purgatory sing their way up the mountain in familiar songs that are taken from the daily liturgical action of the Mass and the Divine Office: the *"Miserere"* and the *"Agnus Dei,"* the *"Salve Regina"* and *"Te Deum laudamus,"* and the psalms.[12]

This reliance on the texts and rituals of the Church Militant is put in the foreground at the outset of the *cantica* when Dante hears new arrivals to purgatory chanting the words of Psalm 113(114): " '*In exitu Israel de Aegypto*' all of them were singing together with one voice, with the rest of that psalm as it is written" (2.46–48). By immediately drawing attention to this unison perfor-

---

[12] Louis M. La Favia, " '. . . Che quivi per canti . . .' (*Purg.*, XII, 113), Dante's Programmatic Use of Psalms and Hymns in the Purgatorio," *Studies in Iconology* 10 (1984–1986) 53–65, argues that by means of the psalms and hymns cited throughout the *Purgatorio* the poet intended a program of parallels between the canonical hours of an earthly day and Dante's experience of purgatory. La Favia offers a useful summary of the liturgical texts cited: "From the Mass Dante mentions the *Asperges* (*Purg.*, XXXI, 98), *Gloria in excelsis* (*Purg.*, XX, 136), *Benedictus* (*Purg.*, XXX, 19), *Osanna* (*Purg.*, XXIX, 51), and *Agnus Dei* (*Purg.*, XVI, 19). From the Divine Office he mentions the following psalms: *In exitu Israel de Aegypto* (*Purg.*, II, 46), *Miserere* (*Purg.*, V, 24), *Adhaesit pavimento anima mea* (*Purg.*, XIX, 73), *Labia mea, Domine* (*Purg.*, XXIII, 11), *Delectasti* (*Purg.*, XXVIII, 80), *Beati quorum tecta sunt peccata* (*Purg.*, XXIX, 3), *In te Domine speravi* (*Purg.*, XXX, 83), and *Deus venerunt gentes* (*Purg.*, XXXIII, 1). From the hymns of the Divine Office, he refers to the *Salve Regina* (*Purg.*, VIII, 82), *Te lucis ante* (*Purg.*, VII, 13), *Te Deum laudamus* (*Purg.*, IX, 140), and *Summae Deus clementiae* (*Purg.*, XXV, 121). It should be noted how the poet distributes the single songs along his journey, actually according to the liturgical time of the Church: the parts of the Mass are proclaimed in the morning hours; the first two mentioned hymns, which belong to Compline, are sung in the evening hours, and the other two, which belong to Matins, in the early morning hours; and the psalms are recited variously during the entire day. Consequently, all the liturgical parts respect the same liturgical time as on earth" (55). See also Erminia Ardissino, "I Canti liturgici nel *Purgatorio* dantesco," *Dante Studies*, 108 (1990) 39–65.

mance, the poet alerts us to the great gulf fixed between hell and purgatory: whereas the damned knew nothing about corporate song, the redeemed here unite themselves *"ad una voce,"* finding their private speech become the corporate word of Scripture. But the particular choice of this psalm is also telling, for in keeping with venerable allegorical interpretation, *"In exitu Israel de Aegypto"* invokes both the Old Testament's Exodus and the New Testament's redemption in Christ—the two salvation events that underwrite Dante's entire journey in the *Commedia*. The psalm also has its place in the ancient baptismal liturgy of Easter Eve, where Israel's passing through the Red Sea is conflated with the sacrament of Christian initiation.[13] Dante draws a connection, therefore, between two spiritual rites of passage, for just as on earth the newly baptized cross over into the Body of Christ, so the souls in purgatory also move *in exitu de Aegypto* across the threshold of their sanctification. As on earth so in purgatory, the redeemed become pilgrims *in via*.

In *Purgatorio* Dante structures our experience of this crossing in three quite distinct stages. Each one is given its own location on the mountain; each also explores a distinctive moment of spiritual transformation that correlates quite remarkably to the stages of van Gennep's rites of passage. The first, commonly identified by contemporary Dante critics as "Ante-purgatory," corresponds to the initial phase of separation. Located at the base of the holy mountain and standing outside the gates of purgatory proper, the poet presents a kind of limbo for all those not yet ready to begin their ascent, who must first "ripen" in preparation. These include a number of categories: excommunicates (who remain here thirty years for every year outside the Church), the spiritually slothful, those who repented only *in articulo mortis*, and souls whose lives were preoccupied with worldly rather than spiritual matters. What characterizes all of them is their deep attachment to what they have so suddenly or so incompletely left behind in the world.

---

[13] See Charles S. Singleton, *"In exitu Israel de Aegypto,"* in John Freccero, ed., *Dante, A Collection of Critical Essays* (Englewood-Cliffs, NJ: Prentice Hall, 1965) 102–121; Dunstan J. Tucker, *" 'In exitu Israel'* . . . The *Divine Comedy* in the Light of the Easter Liturgy," American Benedictine Review, 11 (1960) 43–61; also Jean Daniélou, *"Les Figures du Baptême: la traversée de la mer rouge,"* Bible et Liturgie (Paris: Editions du Cerf, 1958) 119–135.

Therefore, they point to their mortal wounds or describe the circumstances of their death, preoccupied with their bodies, the places they once lived, and with all that brought them to their end: "Siena made me, Maremma unmade me, as he knows who with his ring had plighted me to him in wedlock" (5.134–136).

Yet in the midst of preoccupation over how they conducted or ended their lives on earth, the poet suggests the ways in which they are even now finding another existence; he gives glimpses of the new self they will actively discover in purgatory. Thus the late repentant who died violent deaths are "singing *Miserere* verse by verse" (5.24), thereby taking on the psalm's cry of penitence even as they themselves learn to ask God for mercy. Likewise, the souls who died in a state of excommunication from the Church, who were spiritual sheep without a shepherd to guide them, are compared in an extended simile to a "fortunate flock" (*"mandra fortunata,"* 3.86) all huddled together and "bending eyes and muzzle to the ground" (81). It is as if they too are in the first stages of becoming a community.

Among all the pilgrims-in-the-making within Ante-purgatory, however, the group most interesting to Dante are those who because of political cares neglected their spiritual condition. To represent them the poet chose a number of thirteenth-century European rulers who were bitter enemies in life but who are now shown comforting one another in common grief over a failed past. Behind this group portrait of monarchs involved in a penitential healing process, there may well stand, as LeGoff suggests (118–122, 190–193), two precursor texts. In the vision of purgation ascribed to Charles the Fat, for instance, a living man sees his father's lords "and the lords of my uncles and brothers" poised between two pools, one boiling and the other cool. He learns that these princely ancestors can be rescued from the agony of the former by "masses, offerings, psalmodies, vigils and alms" (120). Likewise, in the vision of Tondal, once warring kings of Ireland—legendary enemies like Domachus and Conchobar—are no longer at war as they were in life; instead, Tondal sees them gently reconciled to one another in friendship.

What is striking about the "Valley of Princes" (*Purg.* 7–8) that Dante describes, especially when viewed in contrast to these earlier representations of monarchs in purgatory, is not only the paradisical beauty of his setting—"Nature had not only painted there, but of the sweetness of a thousand scents she had made their one unknown to us and blended" (7.79-84)—but also the profoundly liturgical dimension of his entire treatment. Here princes become monks, their days spent in prayer, song, and the regulated labor of mourning. Thus, as the sun sets on the poet's first day in purgatory, he sees the princes interrupt their sorrow over things done and left undone in order to sing the evening antiphon, "Salve Regina." In doing so, presumably, they remind themselves "in hac lacrimarum valle" that they are children of Eve in exile from their true patria in heaven.[14]

Later on, one of their company rises up, assumes the orans position, and sings the compline hymn, "Te lucis ante": "Then the rest joined him sweetly and devoutly through the whole hymn, keeping their eyes fixed on the supernal wheels" (8.16-18). The poet does not include the text of the hymn in his poem; he counts instead that the reader will supply those familiar words attributed to St. Ambrose and commonly invoked to protect against the terrors of the night:

"Procul recedant somnia
Et noctium phantasmata;
Hostemque nostrum comprime,
Ne polluantur corpora.

From all ill dreams defend our eyes,
From nightly fears and fantasies;
Tread under foot our ghostly foe,
That no pollution we may know."[15]

Even before the princes close their eyes in sleep, however, the petition of the "Te lucis ante" is fulfilled. This is demonstrated in a liturgical drama that immediately unfolds, as if it were a kind of nightly homily bidden by the words of the hymn. Dante sees two

[14] Ardissino (52) notes the penitential character of the "Salve Regina" and its assignment to the office of Holy Saturday eve, after vespers. If the antiphon was relatively recent in Dante's day, it became extremely popular through introduction into the Office by the Franciscans toward the middle of the thirteenth century.

[15] Matthew Britt, O.S.B., ed., The Hymns of the Breviary, rev. ed. (New York: Benziger Brothers, 1955) 39-40.

angels with flaming swords descend from the "bosom of Mary" (8.37) and take positions before the assembled princes, awaiting "our adversary," "a snake perhaps such as gave to Eve the bitter food" (98–99). In this brief pageant, with its reenactment of heaven's conquest of evil, the angels cleave the air with their wings and repel the serpent. In so doing they remind the princes that the petition of the compline hymn, *"Hostemque nostrum comprime,"* has indeed been granted.

In Ante-purgatory, therefore, the poet shows the power of ritual to foster a separation from secular reality, to inaugurate life in the sacred. The hymns they sing become the dramas they watch, the redemption in which they trust. Moreover, by singing hymns that were left unsung in life, by reminding themselves of their status as *"exsules filii Evae,"* by viewing again and again a pageant of their redemption—in short, by learning to see themselves not as powerful men of the world but as souls rescued from *"nostro avversaro"* (8.95)—the souls begin to let go of the past and to long for the future. When the time comes that they burn to know what awaits them (*"nobis post hoc exsilium"*—to recall once again the *"Salve Regina"*), they will be ready to enter purgatory proper.

That entrance is strongly marked by a literal threshold that signals the *Purgatorio's* second and liminal stage: there is a gate, three steps leading up to it, and an angelic guardian who wields a brilliant sword. As Dante sees his true spiritual likeness mirrored in the steps of the angel's throne, he is prepared for his initiation into purgatory by what amounts to a ritual scarring: the angel inscribes on his forehead seven P's, one for each of the deadly sins. Thus marked by the "courteous doorkeeper" (9.92) and prepared for the gradual erasure that will take place along the terraces of the mountain—"See that you wash away these wounds when you are within" (9.114)—Dante crosses over into purgatory proper as the sound of the *"Te Deum laudamus"* rings in his ear. Again the choice of liturgical text is important in context. Believed to have been composed by Ambrose and Augustine at the occasion of the latter's baptism, this hymn was sung in Dante's day (according to one of the poet's fourteenth-century commentators) "when a man departs from this world and enters a religious order."[16] Sounded

---

[16] Francesco da Buti (1385–95), cited by Singleton, 2.2, 195.

at this particular threshold, therefore, it commemorates more than one ritual initiation into a sacred life.

Once inside the gate, the poem begins its exploration of liminal transformation in earnest, as Dante's "pilgrim" joins vicariously in a purgatorial program that stretches from cantos 10–27. Throughout the seven terraces of the mountain, each redressing one of the deadly sins, he and the souls learn the realities of a new life in God. Together they separate from worldly identifications and detach themselves from old definitions of self and society. As the newcomer to this reorientation, Dante is inevitably the initiate who stands to be corrected. For instance, when he asks on the terrace of envy if there are any Italians for whom he might make intercession, one of the souls takes it upon herself to set him straight. As a former Sienese speaking to a present Florentine, it is clear that Sapia does not reach out to him on the basis of earthly kinship; rather, it is in the new spirit of purgatory's *communitas* that she addresses Dante as "brother," as if the two of them were monks in a common order or fellow travelers on a common way:

"O frate mio, ciascuna è cittadina
d'una vera città; ma tu vuo' dire
che vivesse in Italia peregrina" (13.94–96).

"O my brother, each one here is a citizen
of a true city: but you mean one that
lived in Italy while a pilgrim."

Using the same civic distinctions between temporary and absolute citizenship that Augustine deploys in *City of God* 15, Sapia makes a crucial shift in verb tense to bring home her point. Is anyone on the terrace of envy an Italian? The answer is both yes and no: she is ("*è*") a citizen of heaven's true city even though she once *lived* ("*vivesse*") in Italy as a pilgrim. Far more forcefully than on earth, however, she now knows that her citizenship (to recall St. Paul in Phil 3:20) is in heaven.[17]

---

[17] For Dante's use of Augustine to suggest purgatory's reorientation of civic values (as well as the poet's dramatic transformation of the Bishop of Hippo's ideas about the earthly city), see my essay "Divide and Conquer: Augustine in the *Divine Comedy*," *PMLA*, 106/3 (May 1991) 471–482.

If liminality is experienced in this gradual distancing from former social or civic identifications, it is also evident in manifestations of what Turner calls "homogenization" (*Image and Pilgrimage* 34), that is, in the separation of the pilgrim or initiate from prior notions of status and position. On the terrace of the avaricious and prodigal, for instance, when Dante kneels to reverence the soul of Pope Adrian V, he uses the honorific "you" (*"voi"*) in addressing the former pontiff. Adrian at once reminds him, however, that he has crossed over the threshold of purgatory and is now in a realm of redeemed *communitas*. "Straighten up your legs, rise up, brother," the pope tells him, "do not err: I am a fellow servant with you and the others unto one Power" (19.133–135). Here we find what Turner speaks of as the margin's "leveling process."[18] Pope and layman are each "brothers," united by a spiritual bond quite over and above the formal social hierarchies that once differentiated them from one another.[19]

While, as we have seen, the terraces of *Purgatorio* give ample demonstration of two of the three major components of the liminal process—the "recombination of cultural traits and constituents" and the fostering of *communitas*—so too do they give even more attention to the third, to what Turner calls "the communication of the *sacra*" ("Religious Celebration," 202–206). In discussing the latter, he borrows classicist Jane Harrison's division of *sacra* into three kinds: exhibitions ("what is shown"), actions ("what is

[18] In "Religious Celebrations," Turner notes that in *communitas* "there is a direct, total confrontation of human identities which is rather more than the casual camaraderie of ordinary social life. It may be found in the mutual relationships of neophytes in initiation, where *communitas* is sacred and serious, and in the great seasonal celebrations" (205). In this instance, Dante and Adrian are both purgatorial neophytes, but whereas Dante's transformation is only provisional and "initiator," Adrian is undergoing a true initiation, that is, "an irreversible, singular ritual instrument for effecting a permanent, visible cultural transformation of the subject" (Turner, *Image and Pilgrimage*, 31).

[19] Adrian cites scripture in support of this new *communitas:* "If ever you have understood that holy gospel which says, 'Neque nubent,' you may well see why I speak thus" (19.136–138). Part of the power of this interaction with a former pope is the parallel conversation with the soul of Nicholas IV in *Inferno* 19. There, in the inverted world of the simonists, the layman poet plays the role of prophet and priest to a pontiff likened in simile to an assassin. "*Neque nubent*" in hell as well as in purgatory.

156

done"), and instructions ("what is said"). Thus, for instance, an initiate may be shown holy objects or relics, may witness or even participate in the performance of sacred drama, and may formally receive the teaching of spiritual guides or adepts. Initiation, therefore, entails the handing on of lore, the movement from skills to wisdom; it is "a kind of catechumenate."[20]

Perhaps the most striking feature of the *Commedia's* purgatory is the way attention to the *sacra* claims more of our attention than the mechanics or even the experience of penitential pain. This might be seen as part of the poet's refusal to infernalize purgatory, his choice to view the suffering as one element in expiation's rite of passage rather than as its predominant feature. It may also represent his interest in the power of art—his own very much included—both to transform people and to mediate sacred reality to them. By privileging the communication of the *sacra* on the terraces of the holy mountain, Dante is not only inventing a liminal purgatory, so to speak, he is also underwriting his own enterprise in art. In any event, Jane Harrison's tripartite classification is helpful in seeing how the purgatorial process of Dante's terraces "works." To take the terrace of pride, for instance, "what is shown" is a series of art works created by God, the divine craftsman, that illustrate first the virtue of humility and then the vice of *superbia*. To exemplify the former there are bas-reliefs (or "intaglios") that show Mary at the Annunciation, David dancing naked before the Ark, and the emperor Trajan administering justice to a widow. All are made with such skill and perfection that "not only Polycletus but Nature herself would be put to shame" (10.32–33). To portray the wages of pride, on the other hand, the penitents look down at their feet at a carved pavement recalling the "storiated" tombstones covering the floors of some medieval churches; it is covered with images of the mighty who have fallen.[21] In their purgation,

---

[20] I am grateful to Paul V. Marshall for his reading of my essay in manuscript as well as for this particular insight.

[21] Dante was counting on the reader's familiarity not only with a feature of medieval churches but with the pious uses that were put to them: "As, in order that there be memory of them, the stones in the church floor over the buried dead bear figured what they were before (*"portan segnato quel ch'elli eran pria"*), wherefore many a time men weep for them there, at the prick of memory that spurs only the faithful: so I saw sculpted there, but of better

therefore, the souls are both called to look up and aspire to the representations of depicted virtue, and then to look down upon and to trample under foot those of vice. What they see informs who they will become.

On this same terrace, and in addition to the acts of continuous viewing, "What is done" by the penitents is the shouldering of a heavy stone weight, a burden that seems to signify for Dante what Iris Murdoch has called the "fat relentless ego."[22] The souls must bear the weight of themselves for as long as they are burdened by pride; when they are no longer so afflicted, they are released from their burdens and stand tall. At that moment they presumably experience the same erasure of the forehead *peccati* that Dante comes to know at the conclusion of each round of purgation. At those threshold crossings, an appropriate Beatitude is sung ("*Beati pauperes spiritu*" [12.110]) and a brush of an angel's wing effaces the mark of sin.

Finally, "What is said" on the terraces ranges widely. There is instruction given in conversation by the penitent souls, as when the artist Oderisi speaks at length about the folly of artistic fame or "*nominanza.*" Elsewhere on the mountain sight is impeded, and so instructional oracles are heard in passing or "rain down" without mediation from heaven's own light of imagination (17.13–18). Then, of course, there is the continuous teaching offered by Dante's purgatorial guides—Virgil for the most part, but also Sordello, Statius, Matelda, and finally Beatrice. Each of these "adepts" imparts a different degree of revelation, affording another glimpse of the "eternal view" ("*veduta etterna,*" 25.31) into which all of purgatory is an initiation. Each of them guides Dante's pilgrimage to an appointed end.[23]

---

semblance in respect of skill, all that for the pathway juts out from the mountain." (12.16–24)

[22] *The Sovereignty of Good* (New York: Schocken Books, 1971) 53. "In the moral life the enemy is the fat relentless ego."

[23] The release of a soul from its entire purgatorial work is shown through the figure of Statius. In *Purg.* 20 the mountain trembles and all the penitents cry out "Gloria in excelsis Deo," thus conflating the earthquake at the time of Christ's passion with the song of the angels at his nativity. Statius explains that the mountain quakes whenever "some soul feels itself pure" (21.58–72). Statius has spent "five hundred years and more" (21.68) on the terrace of avarice/prodigality and "for more than four centuries" (22.93) on that of sloth.

This communication of the *sacra* along the various terraces is completed in the third and final stage of the purgatorial pilgrimage, when the penitents emerge free of their sin and are able to enter the Garden of Eden (*Purg* 27–33). At the end of this journey of transformation, in other words, the original birthplace of humanity becomes the site of the soul's rebirth. Yet Eden also continues the terraces' work of exhibition, action, and instruction, thereby filling the earthly paradise with psalms and liturgical songs, as well as with a wide variety of theological drama. For it is here that Dante sees an allegorical pageant of revelation (canto 29), watches a symbolic reenactment of Christ's redemption (canto 32), and receives a vision of apocalypse (canto 32). Here too he learns for the first time that the purpose of his pilgrimage is not limited to himself. Rather, he is charged upon his return to earth to write down everything that he has seen "for profit of the world that lives ill" (32.103). His liminal transformation, as recorded in the *Purgatorio*, is meant to transform others as well.

In addition to all that Dante is shown or told in Eden, moreover, there are also ritual acts that the pilgrim must undergo, two quasi-sacramental washings that effectively complete his initiation. First, he is cleansed of all guilty memory in the waters of the river Lethe, even as the *"Asperges me"* is sung (31.98); later, immersed in the river Eunoe and swallowing its "sweet draught" (*"il dolce ber,"* 33.138), he is "restored to the memory of every good deed" (28.129; 33.115–129). At the conclusion of purgatory's liminal process, therefore, we find the symbolic enactment of birth and renewal that Turner identifies as typical of reaggregation rites ("Religious Celebration," 202). Only here in Eden, instead of being readied as a pilgrim prepared to return once again to the mundane world, Dante is made "pure and disposed to rise to the stars" (33.145). He has still to cross over the final boundary into humanity's true home, into the heavenly *patria* for which all of purgatory has been but the preparation. "For a little time," Beatrice tells him in *Purg.* 32.100–102, he will be a "forester" in the Garden; his eternal goal, however, is heaven, "that Rome where

---

He spends almost no time on the remaining terraces of gluttony and lust before entering Eden and, like Dante, passing through the waters of Lethe and Eunoe.

Christ is a Roman.'' Purgatory functions, therefore, as the margin between two cities, the earthly and the paradisal. At the end of his pilgrimage the transformed pilgrim returns to the world he left behind for as long as his mortal life; but he knows precisely as a result of his journey that ultimately he belongs elsewhere, in that "Rome" which is above and free.

In a dedicatory letter to his patron, *Can Grande della Scala*, Dante claimed that his poem was intended "to remove those living in this life from the state of misery and to lead them to the state of happiness." For this reason he wanted it to be considered as a branch of moral philosophy or ethics, inasmuch as the whole and the part have been conceived for the sake of practical results, not for the sake of speculation.''[24] What he might equally have said, however, is that he meant the *Comedia* to lead his readers through a Christian rite of passage, to offer them a pilgrimage through the life to come that is, in fact, an initiation into a more conscious and God-centered understanding of the life already at hand. For to read the poet's text on its own evangelical terms—that is, to follow Dante's lead in undertaking the spiritual journey he describes—is in essence to become an initiate and pilgrim oneself. It is to enter the *Commedia*'s "betwixt and between" in order to discover a mystery of spiritual transformation that begins in a dark wood of confusion and ends in the Blessed Trinity's light. The "practical results" of such a journey will inevitably vary from person to person. Pilgrims do not remember the temple of their vow in the same way, any more than they see it with the same eyes. But no doubt it was the poet's hope that the reader who crosses over the threshold of his *Commedia* might in the end be changed by the experience: might be dislodged from the status quo, exposed to a new ordering of reality, even brought closer to the eternal one "who is blessed in the world without end.''[25]

[24] *Literary Criticism of Dante Alighieri*, trans. Robert S. Hailer (Lincoln: University of Nebraska, 1973) 102.

[25] The letter to Can Grande ends as follows, with a description of the "aim" of the *Paradiso* that gives as well the trajectory of the entire *Commedia*: "And since, having reached the beginning or first cause, which is God, there is nothing further to seek, he being Alpha and Omega, or the first and the last (as he is designated in John's vision), the treatise comes to an end in God himself, who is blessed in the world without end" (111).

Kenneth Stevenson

9. The *Mensa Mystica* of Simon Patrick (1626–1707): A Case Study in Restoration Eucharistic Piety

INTRODUCTION

The seventeenth century was a veritable cauldron for Eucharistic theology, particularly in England, where rival groups fought for control of the Established Church. A particular focus for that controversy was the Civil War, leading into the Commonwealth, and the imposition of the *Westminster Confession of Faith*, in 1645, followed by the restoration of the monarchy in 1660, and the imposition of the *Book of Common Prayer* in 1662. In the long run, there were gains and losses for all sides, in both the severe actions of 1645 and 1662.

But how did the vicissitudes—political, theological, and liturgical—of these times affect that almost caricature figure of these islands, the scholar-pastor? One example is to be found in the writings of Simon Patrick. Never regarded in the top rank of theologians, he nevertheless embodies many of those characteristics which came to be identified with classical Anglicanism. He was a faithful son of the Reformation; he sought for the truth in a common mean between two extremes; he was well-versed in the Fathers; he was—above all—nourished by the Book of Common Prayer. Theologically, he stood within that tradition of broad Calvinism nuanced considerably by firm attachment to an ordered liturgy as well as by the commitment to reason that he learned at Cambridge when he came under the Platonist spell. He was also a quasi-ecumenical figure, for though Anglican and episcopal in ecclesiology, he had friendships of a comprehensive kind:

161

"He has left behind him the record of a faithful parish priest, an exemplary bishop, an effective preacher and a copious writer of theology, especially on its devotional side."[1]

So wrote Jocelyn Perkins. In his nine-volume edition of Patrick's main writings, Alexander Taylor includes his autobiography, which Perkins describes as "a work of the most entertaining character, as fresh and readable as if it had been written yesterday."[2] (Perkins had reason to admire Patrick, for he was a Canon of his beloved Westminster Abbey for seventeen years.) The autobiography is a fine example of Patrick's simple, fluent, and unpretentious style, and from it, and from other evidence, the following picture of his life emerges.[3]

Patrick was born in Gainsborough, Lincolnshire, on 8 September, 1626, the son of a landowner, and died on 31 May 1707, as Bishop of Ely. His grandfather, also a Lincolnshire landowner, and also called Simon Patrick, had published some translations of contemporary French literary works, and it may be that the young scion of this family inherited his literary flair from his forebear. In 1644, he was admitted at Queens' College, Cambridge, where he came under the influence of John Smith (1618–1652), the noted Cambridge Platonist, and at whose funeral, in 1652, Patrick preached the sermon. That year, Patrick had been ordained a Presbyterian, the only public option for him, if he was to enter upon a Fellowship at his College, under the Commonwealth. But already, the Platonism of Cambridge was being mingled with another influence, that of a wider tradition as expounded in the writings of Henry Hammond (1605–1660) and Herbert Thorndike (1598–1672), both of whom had been deposed from their church posts because of their defence of episcopacy. This led Patrick

---

[1] Jocelyn Perkins, *Westminster Abbey—Its Worship and Ornaments* II (Alcuin Club Collections 34) (London: Milford, 1940) 99.

[2] Ibid., 99; see also 98, "that excellent man, Symon Patrick, not the least eminent of the later Caroline divines." Patrick usually signed his name "Symon," but the modern spelling is normally employed.

[3] See *The Works of Simon Patrick, D. D., including his Autobiography*, Alexander Taylor, ed., 9 vols. (Oxford: University Press, 1858). The Autobiography is in vol. 9, 405ff. Hereafter cited as "Patrick." See also Henry Horwit, *Parliamentary Policy and Politics in the Reign of William III* (Manchester: University Press, 1977).

(along with others) to seek ordination from a bishop, which took place in 1654 at the hands of Joseph Hall (1574–1656), the deprived Bishop of Norwich. The two strands of toleration and reason (on the one hand) and historic continuity within the Church (on the other) were to run right through Patrick's ministry, his theological and political thought, and his personal and public actions.

In the following year, he moved away from academe to become domestic chaplain to the influential Royalist, Sir Walter St. John, at Battersea Manor, and in 1657, he was presented by St. John, as Patron, to the living as Vicar of St. Mary's, Battersea, a post which he held until 1675. Anglican clergy often held more than one appointment, and at the Restoration, in 1660, Patrick was able to spread his wings, for in 1662, he became Rector of St. Paul's, Covent Garden, London, just a few miles from Battersea, north of the River Thames. (St. Paul's was a prestigious church, designed 30 years before by Inigo Jones.) This, however, was only after the unfortunate episode of the Presidency of Queens' College, Cambridge, to which he was elected by the Fellows, but on whom Charles II imposed Anthony Sparrow (1612–1685), who had been expelled from his Fellowship of Queens' by the Puritans in 1644. Patrick retained the living of Covent Garden right up until 1689, when he was made Bishop of Chichester. Meanwhile, Patrick was becoming a well-known figure, and in 1671 was made a Chaplain to the King, and in 1672, a Canon of Westminster; he made his mark in the latter post, for in 1675 he became Canon-Treasurer, and moved to a new house in the Abbey precincts, which is probably why he relinquished Battersea in that year. In 1679, he turned down the Archdeaconry of Huntingdon, only later that year to be made Dean of Peterborough. He preached on numerous special occasions, including the meeting of the Convocation of Canterbury in 1680. He had already observed King James II's attitude at his coronation in 1685, noting it to be perhaps a harbinger of problems for the Church of England, and he was subsequently drawn into theological discussions, together with William Jane (1695–1707), the Regius Professor of Divinity at Oxford, in company with the King himself on the matter of his religion, because of the King's Roman Catholicism.

Matters came to a head in 1688 when James II tried to impose a Declaration of Indulgence, which would have allowed complete religious freedom in the land. Patrick, and several prominent London clergy, took this as an affront to the Church by law established and refused to read it. James II's political position soon became untenable, with the result that William of Orange invaded the country in the "Glorious Revolution" of 1689. Patrick sided with the new regime, and was soon made Bishop of Chichester, together with two others of a similar political (though not necessarily theological) standpoints, Gilbert Ironside (1632–1701) of Bristol, and Edward Stillingfleet (1635–1699) of Worcester. Two years later, he was translated to the much better endowed bishopric of Ely to succeed Francis Turner (1637–1700). That in itself was a firm commitment to the new joint monarchy of William III and Mary II, for Turner did not die in office; he was deprived of his bishopric for refusing to take the oath of obedience to the new sovereignty. Turner had been a staunch ally of James II, and a prominent High Churchman.

Patrick's episcopate was as distinguished as the rest of his ministry. He combined the diocesan-pastoral and government-political roles expected of bishops at the time, visiting in his diocese, preaching frequently at Whitehall before the King. In 1695, Patrick was appointed to join the small group of bishops set up that year by the King to deal with all matters of church patronage, which is some testimony to the standing in which he was held. In 1702, he voted against the (unsuccessful) Bill (eventually passed in 1711 but repealed in 1719) of Occasional Conformity, which would have tampered with the rights of Dissenters seeking public office in a way unacceptable to the "Whig" element.[4] In 1702, he purchased Dalham Hall, in Suffolk, in the Norwich Diocese, for his widow, Penelope Jephson (1646–1725) after his death. In 1705, he confesses that he began to look back on his life. It was indeed a long and full one.

HIS THEOLOGICAL WORKS AND THEIR CONTEXT

Patrick's life spanned a crucial time in the life of his country. It is hard for those who live in such a different political and religious

---

[4] See G. V. Bennett, "King William III and the Episcopate," in G. V. Bennett and J. D. Walsh, eds., *Essays in Modern English Church History in Memory of Norman Sykes* (London: A. & C. Black, 1966) 124. For whole essay, and the patronage Simon Patrick and others enjoyed, see 104–131. See also N. Sykes, *Church and State in the XVIIIth Century* (Cambridge: University Press, 1934) 34ff.

climate to understand the close connections between Church and state that accrued at the time. For example, political loyalty was intricately bound up with what kind of understanding of the Church one had—including its worship. Patrick will have been brought up as a child on the *Book of Common Prayer* (1604)—that of King James VI and I (1566-1625). As the Civil War wore on before and after his arrival at Cambridge, the use of the Prayer Book became more and more suspect, so that for virtually all his time at Cambridge, until his third year at Battersea as vicar (1645-1660) it was outlawed; any persons found using it in public were liable for payment of a fine. Exactly what form of liturgy Patrick used, whether at Cambridge or at Battersea during those years, is impossible to tell. The *Westminster Directory* (1645) only gives guidance (not set liturgical texts) to ministers conducting public worship, though Horton Davies in his exhaustive history of worship and church life in these years uncovers interesting byways of clandestine Anglican liturgical life.[5] It could be that Patrick used the Prayer Book in private as the domestic Chaplain to the St. Johns of Battersea—a role he continued to fulfil after taking over as Vicar there. He does note in his autobiography that on 22 July 1660, he "read Common Prayer publicly in Church, Battersea," which suggests an enthusiastic relief on the part of one who had deliberately sought episcopal ordination a few years before. The Prayer Book in question would have been, again, that of 1604.

The year 1662 saw Patrick appointed also to Covent Garden, the year in which the Restoration Prayer Book was imposed on St. Bartholomew's Day (August 24), a command Patrick meekly obeyed. For most clerics of the time, the liturgical tale ended there. But this was not the case for Patrick. One of William of Orange's desires, as a Dutch Calvinist intent on securing as broad a base of support within the Church of England as possible, was to enable at least a body of Dissenters to conform to the Established Church. Between 1662 and 1689, the climate had changed. It

---

[5] See Ian Breward, ed., *The Westminster Directory* (Grove Liturgical Study 21) (Bramcote: Grove, 1980). This was imposed on all churches in England, Scotland, and Ireland, by law, and represents the triumph of Presbyterian polity and liturgy in the Commonwealth. On clandestine Anglican worship; see Horton Davies, *Worship and Theology in England, II, From Andrewes to Baxter and Fox (1603-1690)* (Princeton: University Press, 1975) 352ff.

was easier for an Anglican to be magnanimous towards Dissent from a position of strength in the latter year, for by that time Anglicanism had triumphed and was increasingly mature in its ethos and life. Accordingly, a group of Bishops and prominent clergy put forward proposals in 1689 for revising the Prayer Book and for making it more flexible. Patrick was heavily involved in this project, and is reputed to have been responsible for redrafting the Collects so that they agreed more with the Epistles—a process that is barely discernible in the liturgical work of Thomas Cranmer (1489-1556) in the First Prayer Book (1549) or the revision in 1662.[6] Why was Patrick part of this move? The answer is most likely partly political and partly liturgical. He was known to support the new monarchy, and was at the time nearing the end of his days as Dean of Peterborough, and about to be made Bishop of Chichester. On the other hand, he was by this time well-known as a theological writer with a strongly devotional slant, having written many prayers for private and personal use, in the lengthy and flowery *genre* of the time. It is worth noting at this point, however, the evolutionary and changing character of the worship Patrick himself experienced throughout his life, since it explains in large measure the passion and the power of the prayers he wrote to accompany *Mensa Mystica* in 1684.

Mensa Mystica ("A Discourse Concerning the Lord's Supper")[7] itself was first published in 1660. On the face of it, the work was a sequel to Patrick's first published work, his *Aqua Genitalis* ("A Discourse Concerning Baptism"),[8] which had appeared in 1658 and was an expanded version of a sermon preached at the baptism of the son of a friend. But its significance is infinitely greater than that. Sixteen-sixty was a key-year for the Anglican Church, which was rising from years of persecution and in dire need of good, broadly-based doctrinal teaching that would be accessible not just to other clergy but to the ever-increasing laity who were taking a

---

[6] See E. Cardwell, *A History of Conferences and other Proceedings connected with the revision of the Book of Common Prayer* (Oxford: University Press, 1840) 392ff. and T. J. Fawcett, *The Book of Comprehension* (Alcuin Club Collections 54) (Great Wakering: Mayhew McCrimmon, 1973) 174, pass.

[7] See Patrick, vol. 1, 65-318.

[8] Ibid., 1-64.

prominent part in Church life.[9] It was written at the home of Sir Walter and Lady St. John, as the dedicatory preface makes clear. Patrick tells us two significant things about its character. First, it was written at the suggestion of John Worthington (1618–1671), who had been Vice-Chancellor of Cambridge during the Commonwealth, and who in 1660 was deprived of the Mastership of Jesus College. Secondly, Patrick notes the impact the book had on Bishop Matthew Wren (1585–1667), Bishop of Ely from 1638–1667, but who had been imprisoned in the Tower of London because of his collaboration with Archbishop William Laud (1573–1645), who was executed for high treason. Wren said "he did not think any among the Presbyterians could have written such a book."[10] One senses that Patrick enjoyed both the sponsorship of the Platonist Worthington and the enthusiastic approbation of the High Churchman Wren.

Patrick wrote consistently and persistently about the Eucharist. While *Mensa Mystica* was the most systematic and academic of all, he wrote *Christian Sacrifice*[11] in 1670 in a more obviously devotional style, adding yet more prayers in the 1672 edition. In 1679 followed *A Book for Beginners*,[12] intended to help young communicants in their Eucharistic nurture. (He had only married Anna Jephson in 1675, and their first child, a son, had died the year before, but another son, Simon, was born in 1680.) In 1684, moreover, he published a series of sermons which he had preached the year before in Peterborough Cathedral as *A Treatise of the Necessity and Frequency of receiving the Holy Communion*.[13] The purpose of the course of sermons was to inaugurate in his Cathedral congregation at Pentecost 1683 a weekly celebration of the Eucharist as the norm, which in those days was unusual.[14]

Nor was Patrick's enthusiasm for the Eucharist confined to his Peterborough ministry. It is significant in itself that his second

[9] See C. W. Dugmore, *Eucharistic Doctrine in England from Hooker to Waterland* (London: S.P.C.K., 1942) 111ff.

[10] See Patrick, vol. 1, pp. lix ff., on the origins of *Mensa Mystica*, also vol. 9, 430f.

[11] See Patrick, vol. 1, 319–588; the bulk of this is prayers.

[12] Ibid., vol. 1, 589ff.

[13] Ibid., vol. 1, 1–92.

[14] Ibid., vol. 9, 483; quoted by Perkins, *Westminster Abbey*, III (Alcuin Club Collections 38) (London: Cumber, 1952) 134.

published treatise should have been on the Eucharist. In 1680, he noted that the great congregations at Communion at Covent Garden had built up a large body of church funds (the collection of alms and offerings in those days only took place when the Eucharist was celebrated), and he succeeded in persuading his churchwardens to spend the money on endowing a curate, who would be able to lead public worship and preach in his absence. As a member, too, of the Chapter of Westminster Abbey, he was with his colleagues responsible for raising the standard of reverence in worship.[15] After his consecration as Bishop of Chichester at Fulham on 13 October 1689, Patrick notes (in an age which knew no liturgy for the enthronement of new diocesan bishops) that he went to Chichester and in the Cathedral "preached and gave Communion," on 14 November, thus inaugurating his ministry in the manner which he thought supremely appropriate. His episcopal ministry demonstrates a similar commitment to increase the frequency of Eucharistic services, at a time when it had fallen into neglect. In his first Visitation Articles in Chichester in 1690, he asks about the local incumbent, "doth he celebrate the sacrament of the Lord's Supper so often, that every parishioner may receive it thrice at least in every year?" And of the laity, he asks, "are there any who profess to live in the communion of the Church of England, who neglect to come to the sacrament of the Lord's Supper, being of age fit to receive it?"[16] At Ely in 1692 he writes to his clergy that they should envisage monthly Communions as the norm.[17] The story of his public actions backing up his published and spoken words ends with his will:

"My Communion plate, viz. a gilt flagon, a chalice with a cover, a paten and a bason, I give to the parish of Dalham in Suffolk for their use in the administration of the sacrament of Christ's body and blood, of which I pray God they may frequently partake."[18]

[15] Ibid., 130ff. The Restoration Chapter at Westminster were a formidable band of like-minded men, including Herbert Thorndike, who died in the year Patrick took up his Canonry (1672) see 113ff.

[16] Patrick, vol. 9, 333, 335.

[17] Ibid., 550f.

[18] Ibid., 675. The communion plate is still in the possession of Dalham Parish Church, but is kept in a bank in Newmarket. The pieces consisting of alms basin, chalice, small paten, and large paten were generous of design and

Comparing *Mensa Mystica* with *Aqua Genitalis,* Patrick's nine-teenth century editor, Alexander Taylor, has this to say:

"It is both longer and more systematic than its sister treatise, entering fully and deeply into every aspect of its sacred subject, both dogmatic and practical, and supplying under every head those devotional aids which a careful pastor would wish to see in familiar use among the members of his flock but which were scantily provided in the religious manuals of the time. Its reception was such that a second edition was issued in 1667, in company with a reprint of *Aqua Genitalis;* followed by others in rapid succession. The fifth of these appeared in 1684, the sixth and last during the author's lifetime in 1702, the seventh in 1717, and the demand never discontinued down to the present time (1858)."[19]

Taylor certainly expresses much of the method and the atmosphere of the work. It comes in five main sections and like so much of Patrick's writings is clearly laid out and fluently written. The scheme is as follows:[20]

"• the epistle dedicatory (to Sir Walter and Lady St. John)
 • Introduction
 • Section I—Introduction (the main theological part)
   Chapter 1—preliminaries *[sic]*
   Chapter 2—1st reason for eucharist—remembrance of Christ
   Chapter 3—2nd reason—remembrance with thanksgiving
   Chapter 4—3rd reason—a holy rite to enter covenant with God
   Chapter 5—4th reason—sign and seal of remission of sins
   Chapter 6—5th reason—means of nearer union with Christ
   Chapter 7—6th reason—means of nearer union with each other
   Chapter 8—conclusion

---

typical of the period and made of silver gilt, hallmarked 1691, the year of Patrick's translation to Ely. A large matching flagon is part of the set, hallmarked 1712, and thought to have been added by Patrick's widow. The whole set is in good condition. I am grateful to the Rev. Brian Hayes, Vicar of Gazeley with Dalham and Moulton with Kentford, for this information.

[19] Patrick, vol. 1, lx.

[20] Ibid., 67ff. The 1684 ed., bound with *Aqua Genitalis* (London: Tyton, 1684), summarizes each section and chapter, in a separate part before the "epistle dedicatory."

Patrick uses every opportunity to explain, illustrate, teach, and exhort, and one can see why, in an age in which devotional manuals abounded, this particular one was so successful. In scholarship, too, Patrick is well-versed, quoting the Fathers, as well as recent writers who have clearly been an influence on him, like Ralph Cudworth (1617-1688), another Cambridge Platonist, Jeremy Taylor (1613-1667), who had to live in seclusion for the latter part of the Commonwealth and then emerged as Bishop of Down and Connor in Ireland, in addition to Richard Hooker (c. 1554-1600), that classical exponent of Anglicanism, as well as Thorndike, whom we have mentioned before. But others appear, like Theodore Beza (1519-1605), and the great Maimonides (1135-1204) himself. They have all left their mark on his thinking, which, though giving the appearance of being framed in systematic fashion, is at root that of the historical theologian with a big pastoral heart. From the Fathers he has learnt of the deep traditions of the Church, though he is far from being enslaved by their thought patterns, and in this he follows Jeremy Taylor.[21] His quotations

21 Both Patrick and Taylor set great store by reason: cf. Patrick, ''God hath given us the use of reason, which if we will blindly resign to any pretended authority, what is it but to shut our eyes when we should open them.'' (*A Sermon Preached Before the King*, 1675, 25, quoted in Paul Avis, *Anglicanism and*

and citations with the names of Cyprian, Augustine, Chrysostom, Theodoret and others demonstrate a man at home in Patristics. From the Cambridge Platonists he has learnt the importance of biblical studies, notably the Jewish background to Christian faith and practice, as well as the need for tolerance and breadth of vision for this new age of Anglicanism about to be born. And from the classical Anglicans he has learnt something of the developing method of historical theology itself, and that Anglicanism is a part of a larger whole, with its own ethos and style. The resulting whole is far from lacking conviction: It is no mere pragmatic performance, for it has a cutting edge, and though the style is easy-going, we are left in no doubt about where Patrick stands on controversial matters.

We shall discuss later the *Mensa Mystica* prayers, which only appear in the 1684 edition. Meanwhile, because of its importance, it is appropriate to discuss in a little more detail what Patrick actually says about Eucharistic faith and practice, before he gives his readers words to pray some of his thoughts. The "epistle dedicatory" is a florid piece, eulogizing the home in which he wrote the treatise. In the introduction, he begins with a statement about the nature of God, revelation, and incarnation:

"God, who is simple and removed far from all sense, considering the weakness of man's soul, and how unable he is to conceive of things spiritual purely and nakedly in themselves; and yet having a mind to be better known unto us, and to make himself more manifest than ever, was pleased in his infinite goodness to dwell in flesh, and appear here in the person of his Son, who was made like to man, to shew what God is in our nature."[22]

---

the Christian Church (Edinburgh: T. & T. Clark, 1989) 280; and Taylor, "They that are dead some ages before we were born, have a reverence due to them, yet more is due to truth that shall never die; and God is not wanting to our industry any more than to theirs; but blesses every age with the understanding of his truths." *The Complete Works of Jeremy Taylor*, W. Jacobson, ed. (Oxford: University Press, 1884), *Deus Justificatus*, vol. 9, 342, quoted in Henry McAdoo, *The Eucharistic Theology of Jeremy Taylor Today* (Norwich: Canterbury Press, 1988) 31. Admittedly, Taylor takes a more belligerent line than Patrick, but, as McAdoo shows, this is from the context of theological controversy in which Patrick was not involved.
[22] Patrick, vol. I, 71.

From that starting point, divine nature, rather than the sin of man, he constructs his theology of the Eucharist. "We profess ourselves federates of God" is a recurring theme, and one which finds expression in one of the prayers. He is firm about the solemn and transcendental character of the Lord's Supper: ". . . let all Protestants take heed how they do irreverently behave themselves in participation of these holy mysteries, lest we give them occasion to say that we have nothing but common bread and wine empty of all sacrament."[23]

The meat of the treatise, however, is in Section I, the first eight chapters. His Anglicanism is expressed almost in caricature form: "The truth commonly lieth between two extremes, and being a peaceable thing, cannot join itself with either of the directly opposite parties. And therefore I shall seek for her in a middle path. . . ." In thus looking for a definition of the Eucharistic memorial (his "first end"), he firmly states ". . . *anamnesis* doth not signify barely '*recordatio*,' recording or registering of his favours in our mind; but '*commemoratio*,' 'a solemn declaration,'" . . . And: "We keep it, as it were, in his memory, and plead before him the sacrifice of his Son, which we show unto him, humbly requiring that grace and pardon, with all other benefits of it, may be bestowed on us." And again: "such an unbloody sacrifice, which is only rememorative, and in representation, we all acknowledge."[24]

In describing the thanksgiving aspect (his "second end"), he gives the Jewish liturgical background to the Last Supper, a rarity in his time and in this kind of literature, delighting in the theme of spiritual sacrifices (I Peter 2:5), but he is anxious to avoid turning this notion into no more than a form of mental prayer: ". . . I would not be so mistaken, as if I thought the Christian thanksgiving consisted only in inward thoughts and outward words. For there are eucharistical actions also whereby we perform a most

[23] Ibid., 77, 85.
[24] Ibid., 94, 99f., 100, 102. On this latter, see Kenneth Stevenson, " 'The Unbloody Sacrifice': The Origins and Development of a Description of the Eucharist," in G. Austin, ed., *Fountain of Life: In Memory of Niels K. Rasmussen, O.P.* (Washington: Pastoral Press, 1991) 116ff. and nn. (for whole essay, see pp. 103–130). It is interesting that Patrick quotes Origen's description of the eucharist as "reasonable and unsmoky sacrifice," Patrick, vol. 1, 115.

delightful (a key word for Patrick!) sacrifice unto God." He links self-oblation and the offering of alms and the bread and wine: ". . . the spiritual sacrifice of ourselves, and the corporal sacrifice of our goods to him, may teach the papists that we are sacrificers as well as they, and are 'made kings and priests unto God.' "[25] This is a key point of liturgy, for in the 1662 revision of the Eucharist, the words "and oblations" were added after "alms" at the beginning of the Prayer for the Church, after the preparation of the Table. As Bishop John Dowden (1890–1910) of Edinburgh, a noted liturgical scholar, has observed, Patrick was the first to identify "oblations" with the bread and wine, itself a matter of some dispute at the time and subsequently.[26] Patrick added, in the 1667 edition: "We pray him therefore, in our Communion service, to accept our 'oblations' (meaning those of bread and wine), as well as our 'alms.' " And in 1670, in *Christian Sacrifice*, he was able to develop this further:

"These ("alms" and "oblations") are things distinct; and the former (alms) signifying that which was given for the relief of the poor, the latter (oblations) can signify nothing else but (according to the style of the ancient church) this bread and wine presented to God in a thankful remembrance of our food both dry and liquid (as Justin Martyr speaks), which he, the Creator of the world, hath made and given unto us."[27]

It is interesting to note the consistency of thought between these two passages, the 1667 insertion into the main text of *Mensa Mystica*, (which, as it happens, flowed out from an allusion to Justin's account of the Eucharist in his time), and the *de novo* treatment of the theme in 1670 in *Christian Sacrifice*. Patrick clearly espouses the early patristic notion of offering bread and wine to God for consecration to his use.

Patrick's "third end" is a holy rite to enter covenant with God, and it is in this and the following chapter that the "federal" ethos

[25] Ibid., 114, 114f.

[26] See John Dowden, "What is the Meaning of 'Our Alms and Oblations'? An Historical Study," in *Further Studies in the Prayer Book* (London: Methuen, 1908) 178. (quotation from *Mensa Mystica*), and 220 (quotation from *Christian Sacrifice*).

[27] Ibid., 377.

is explored. "What is there more in the desire of a holy soul than to cease to be its own?" "This eating and drinking is a federal rite." It is at this point, too, that Patrick openly acknowledges his debt to Cudworth in seeing the Eucharist as a "feast upon a sacrifice," and "a renewal of our covenant with God." He goes on to discuss the different kinds of Old Testament sacrifices, explaining how the Eucharist is distinctive, in having the characteristics of all of them, but in being unique. "Our approach to this table is but more strongly to tie the knot, and to bind us in deeper promises to continual friendship with him."[28] His "fourth end" is "a sign and seal of remission of sins." Here he develops his covenant theology further, by drawing together strands from his previous treatment; the movement of the liturgy from offertory, through consecration and Communion is a feast upon a sin offering, where *all* eat and drink, since all are priests and kings, a "federal rite" (again!), where the sacrament sets the seal on the covenant of grace. The two final "ends" are union with Christ and with one another. He follows Hooker in his view of Eucharistic presence: "the real presence is not to be sought in the bread and wine, but in those that receive them, according as learned Hooker speaks." Communion and self-oblation, as in the Prayer Book rite, are inextricably linked: "we are, though not transubstantiated into another body, yet metamorphosed and transformed into another likeness, by the offering up of our bodies to God, which is a piece of this service, Romans 12:1,2." He shrinks from any receptionism: "this presence is the bread, though in it." And he warns, "other union than this (by Christ's Spirit) I know no use of, though we should believe that which we do not understand." The marriage-covenant lurks behind these chapters and, as we shall see, some of the accompanying prayers.

Of brotherly love, Patrick writes with warmth and depth, treating of the Farewell Discourses of the Fourth Gospel, as well as the kiss of peace in antiquity, taking Communion to those unable to be present, the offering of alms, and feasting together as "entertainment": "we must think that we enter into a mutual covenant

[28] Ibid., 119, 122f., 126. There are three citations to Cudworth's *Discourse concerning the true notion of the Lord's Supper* (1642) which Taylor notes in his edition, 92, 122, 156. On Cudworth, see below.

with our brethren by eating of the same bread and drinking of the same cup."[29]

What does all this amount to in theological terms? Like Jeremy Taylor, Patrick brings together Eucharistic presence and sacrifice. He is firm that the Eucharist is an objective action of the Church. The way in which these six "ends" are splayed out runs the risk of fragmenting a theology which is essentially unitive.[30] He holds it all together. Patrick wants his treatment of sacrifice to be grounded in Scripture and the Fathers, while remaining faithful to Reformation convictions about the unique character of Christ's sacrifice on the cross, hence the intricate move towards the "memorial-sacrifice" of the Eucharist. In this, Patrick is not original, but he synthesises judiciously, always bringing his sources to heel, and never being burdened by them.

The remainder of the treatise demonstrates Patrick at his most pastoral. The language is even more fluent, the sources far fewer. One has the feeling of a writer who can expand himself, having set the doctrinal scene in the crucial introductory chapters. He seems to be aiming at monthly Communion as the norm, as we have seen in his letter to the Ely clergy in 1692. In preparation, we come across telling sentences again: "Prayer makes a Christian live holily, and a holy life makes us fit to pray fervently." "The better we know ourselves and our own wants, the more hungry we shall be; and the more knowledge we have of our own sincerity, with the greater comfort and sweetness we shall eat." "Advise with a spiritual pastor and director in the way of life."[31]

Of the hope of heaven, he quotes the end of the Prayer for the Church (albeit it with a Eucharistic parenthesis of his own!) in its 1549 version, and as it appeared in the Scottish 1637 Prayer Book, and also proposed in 1662 by one group in the Church of England, without success: "Come, you blessed of my Father, (you who have loved me, and kept my commandments, you that did what I bid you in remembrance of me), and inherit the kingdom pre-

---

[29] Ibid., 151f., 158, 160, 167. The Hooker quotation is given by Taylor in a footnote, ibid., 151 n.: "The real presence of Christ's most blessed body and blood is not therefore to be sought for in the sacrament, but in the worthy receiver of the sacrament," *Laws of Ecclesiastical Polity*, Book 5, ch. 657, par. vi.

[30] See above n. 9.

[31] Ibid., 186, 209, 213.

pared for you." One wonders if Patrick's familiarity with this liturgical text resulted in his actual use of it in Church. In 1662, the 1549–1637 ending would probably have been too difficult to gain official approval, given the anti-Catholic atmosphere prevailing, but it is significant that the 1662 Prayer for the Church, which in England since 1552 had simply ended with the suffering, did gain an eschatological conclusion, about all the faithful departed being made "partakers of thy heavenly kingdom."[32] The material in Section III deals with the thoughts of the communicant during the actual service. The entire sweep of his writing starts with earth and ends in heaven, with the *Sanctus*, and a citation to Thorndike.[33]

In Section IV, Patrick discusses different attitudes on the part of people after Communion, carefully delineating the stages of faith people might be at, and quoting Ambrose, Bernard of Clairvaux, and Jeremy Taylor (whose *Great Exemplar*, the first such life of Christ, was published in 1649, and whose *Holy Living* appeared the following year—both of which deal with the Eucharist). The final Section, V, gives the slight impression of a writer in overdrive, but there is still space for *aperçus:* "we taste not only what he is to our souls at present, but what he will be for ever." "We taste of the fruit of his death, and of the fruit of his resurrection also, yea, and of his coming again to raise us from the dead too." "By a right use of this holy sacrament, all the faculties and parts of the soul are nourished and enlarged. The understanding becomes more full and clear in its perceptions of truth; the affections more heavenly and divine, more forward and compliant with our wills; the passions more regular and orderly, under better government and command."[34]

It is, however, at the very end, that the scholar-pastor who has learnt of the Fathers, and of tolerance, and of Anglicanism in its

---

[32] Ibid., 220. On this text, see F. E. Brightman, *The English Rite*, II (London: Rivingtons, 1915) 690. (1549) and 665 (1552 and 1662). See also Gordon Donaldson, *The Making of the Scottish Prayer Book of 1637* (Edinburgh: University Press, 1954) 190, and G. J. Cuming, ed., *The Durham Book, Being the First Draft of the Revision of the Book of Common Prayer in 1661* (London: Oxford University Press, 1961) 148–151.

[33] Ibid., 261, note, "See the Learned Mr. Thorndike in His *Religious Assemblies.*"

[34] Ibid., 291, 293.

earlier forms, but who has had to suffer the excesses of the Commonwealth, finally speaks from the heart:

"And let me but tell you these two truths, and I shall put an end to this discourse: the way to have reformed us would not have been to leave off communion, but to make them more frequent. Nor, secondly, to unite and consolidate parishes, but to make more pastors in greater churches, that, by more personal instruction, men might be better fitted for frequent communion. But so it is that zeal oftimes hath too much passion in it, and too little knowledge. The good Lord pardon us, and be gracious to us. Amen."[35]

THE *MENSA MYSTICA* PRAYERS

In 1684, the fifth edition of the treatise appeared, this time described as having "several Prayers and Thanksgivings, not extant before, in any of the former Editions . . . to make it of more general use." As has been pointed out, Patrick was a great prayer-writer, and frequently added them at the end of his sermons, for example when he gave Penelope Jephson, later to become his wife, a copy of his sermons, "each with a prayer." Nor was the custom of accompanying treatises with prayers a new one. It was known in antiquity, in the Middle Ages, and among the Anglican divines. John Donne (1571–1631) for example, the famous poet and preacher, ended his *Essays in Divinity* with prayers, and Jeremy Taylor intercalated his writings with similar compositions. It is, surely, part of the Anglican literary heritage that such a development took place.

But why were these prayers added in 1684? It was, it will be remembered, the year in which the series of sermons on the Eucharist preached the previous year in Peterborough Cathedral were published. And he had in 1683 introduced a weekly Eucharist in the Cathedral, the sermons of which were preached in order to encourage his congregation. At the time, he noted the recommendation, no doubt greatly to his own liking, from Archbishop Sancroft, that Cathedrals and Collegiate Churches should celebrate

[35] Ibid., 317f.

the Eucharist every Sunday.[36] The coincidence of 1684 as the year
of publication of his sermons *and* of the fifth edition of *Mensa
Mystica*—both works concerned with a subject dear to his heart,
namely the faith and practice of the Eucharist—is too great. We
may, guardedly or not, conclude that there is no coincidence at
all, and that the prayers and sermons were all part of the same
movement—to bring the eucharist into the heart of Caroline Anglican worship.

We have noted Patrick's grandfather as a translator. He had a
cousin, John Patrick (1632–1695), also a graduate of Queen's College, Cambridge, who was a champion of Protestantism in James
II's reign, and of a different theological hue from Simon. His hey-
day was as "preacher" of Charterhouse, London, but he was also
a Prebendary (Canon) of Peterborough for the last decade of his
life, while his cousin was Dean. He, moreover, had literary gifts,
too, for he published his *Century of Select Psalms* (1679), which were
popular among Dissenters.[37] The Patrick clan, it would seem, had
the pen of a ready writer.

But there is nothing metrical about the *Mensa Mystica* prayers.
There are, in all, thirteen, each coming, approximately, at the end
of a chapter. Space prevents a treatment of all. For convenience's
sake, we shall limit ourselves to the six which come at the end of
the chapters which explain the six reasons (or "ends") for the Eucharist. As a block of prayers, they form a liturgical "unit" but
there is no standard length. Patrick wants to say what he wants to
say, and he feels under no constraints as he would, for instance,
in writing a Collect. Each has a direct relation to the material in
the book that precedes. It is a curious, and unique, example of
doctrine and private liturgy (if there is such a thing!) blending to-

---

[36] See above, n. 14, where Perkins expresses the view that Patrick is referring to a directive from Sancroft which is now lost. Alexander Taylor, however, suggests that Patrick is putting into practice a much earlier
recommendation dating from 1670, see ibid., p. lxi, n. However in his
magisterial study, John Spurr traces the directive to a meeting of Bishops in
1683, though he points out that there were pressures from influential clergy
for a weekly Eucharist; see *The Restoration Church of England, 1646–1689* (New
Haven/London: Yale University Press, 1991) 364, and nn. 166–168; cf. also
p. 86.

[37] See Horton Davies, op. cit., 278.

gether: of the *lex credendi* of 1660 being supplemented with the *lex orandi* of 1684. And the material itself was a blending of Prayer Book, Bible, and Patrick's own thinking and style.

Prayer 1: "Remembrance of Christ"[38] *(at the end of Chapter 2)*
"Blessed Lord, who hast outlined this holy feast for a solemn and affectionate commemoration of the condescending kindness of our most gracious Lord and Master, in taking our nature upon him; but especially, in laying down his life, nay, suffering the death of the cross for us: possess my soul, I beseech thee beforehand, with such lively thoughts of him, and of his love to me; and with such ardent love to him, who hath given himself for me; that when I come to *do this in remembrance of him,* I may want none of those devout affections which become his presence, and ought to attend upon him: but may so magnify and praise his inestimable benefit, and make such a representation of it unto thy Divine Majesty, that may obtain all that mercy and grace from thee, which he purchased by the sacrifice of his most blessed body and blood.

"Which, I beseech thee, give me grace to commemorate, with such supplications and prayers, such intercessions and thanksgivings, that I may offer up unto thee spiritual sacrifices, acceptable unto thee, through Christ Jesus. Amen."

The prayer brings together the fact of redemption, the place of the Eucharist within it (encapsulated by the reference to "do this," in italics) and the response of the believer, in preparation. As the second paragraph makes clear, the response is in the first place the liturgical one of praying the service. Patrick's broad understanding of Eucharistic sacrifice ("spiritual sacrifices, acceptable unto thee"—1 Pet 2:5) he is about to elaborate in the next chapter. Allusions to the Prayer Book permeate the prayer: "Blessed Lord" (cf. Collect of Advent II); "taking our nature upon him," (cf. Collect for Christmas Day); "suffering the death of the cross" (cf. Consecration Prayer); "inestimable benefit" (cf. Collect for Easter II); "thy Divine Majesty" (cf. Prayer for the Church); "his most blessed body and blood" (cf. Consecration Prayer).

[38] See Patrick, vol. 1, 103. See above n. 24.

Prayer 2: "Remembrance with Thanksgiving"[39] *(at the end of Chapter 3)*
"Blessed be thy name, O Lord, who hast made our religion such
a cheerful service of thee; and hast given us such abundant cause
to give thee praise and thanks perpetually; or rather to sing joyful
hymns in honour of thy holy name, who hast not thought thy
Son too great a gift to bestow upon us; and in honour of our
blessed Saviour and Redeemer, who hath not thought his own life
too much to part with for us.

"Yea, we ought to give thanks and rejoice, that thou hast instituted this holy feast, to be an everlasting thanksgiving for him,
and to him: and especially, then to have our hearts as full of joy
as they can hold, when we come to partake of it; to think that we
are so highly favoured by him, and beloved of him.

"Blessed be thy name that I am already thus disposed to bless
and praise Thee, which is an earnest of the power of thy holy
Spirit to be with me, to excite and stir me up to the highest degree of joy and thankfulness, when I come into thy presence, to
feast with him at thy holy table.

"O fill me then with admiring thoughts of his astonishing grace;
that I may be filled, as the apostles were, with gladness of heart:
triumphing in the honour thou hast done me, in making me so
nearly related to the Lord of life and glory. Of which had I a full
sense, I know it would transport my spirit from all these little
things here, and fill me with joy unspeakable and full of glory.

"Vouchsafe me as much of this as thou in thy wise goodness
shalt think fit to impart unto one that is unworthy of the least of
thy mercies. For all which, enable me then, as I do now, to bless
and praise thee; and with a cheerful heart to make thee, together
with the oblation of myself, both soul and body, the oblation of
some part of these good things which thou hast blessed me
withal; as an earnest that I intend not to forget to do good and to
communicate: with which sacrifices, I know, thou art well pleased,
through Christ Jesus.

"To whom, with the Father and the Holy Ghost, be endless
praises. Amen."

[39] Ibid., 117. See above nn. 25, 26, 27.

Joy and thankfulness are the dominant notes of this prayer, hence "cheerfulness," "joyful," "full of joy," "admiring thoughts," "gladness of heart," "transport my spirit," "joy unspeakable," "cheerful heart." And once again we have the fact of redemption and the response of the believer juxtaposed. That response is, therefore, not just to sing hymns, but to offer self and gifts, as he has made clear in the pages immediately preceding. The doxology at the end is not a liturgical convention; it is fitted by context, the mood of this remarkable prayer.

There appear to be fewer direct Prayer Book parallels: "we ought" (cf. Eucharistic Preface); and, at the end, the "oblation of myself" (cf. the Prayer of Oblation after Communion), "the oblation of some part of those good things which thou hast blessed me withal" (cf. the offering of alms, Prayer for the Church). The major part of the prayer is a kind of personal Eucharistic preface, complete with the link of earthly and heavenly in the *Sanctus*.

Prayer 3: "Holy Rite, to Enter Covenant with God"[40]
   (at the end of Chapter 4)
"I acknowledge with all thankfulness, O Lord of heaven and earth, that as I am thine by having received my being from thee, so I was early devoted and engaged to thee in a solemn covenant; by which I stand bound to do thee all faithful service.

"I have too much neglected it, I confess, and have presumed to dispose of myself according to my own will and pleasure; when I ought to have had no other thoughts but what would be pleasing unto Thee.

"And yet, such is thy goodness, thou art not willing to let me be undone by following the devices and desires of my own heart; but invitest me to come and renew my covenant with thee; and, sorrowfully bewailing what is past, to resolve to be more firm and steadfast in my duty for the time to come.

"That is the desire of my soul, O Lord, which thou (blessed be thy name for it) hast wrought in me. Which encourages me to hope, that thou wilt make me so sensible of my obligations to thee, when I commemorate the dying love of our Saviour for me,

---

[40] Ibid., 131. See above n. 28.

that I shall never hereafter start from thee; who tiest me unto thee in the strictest bonds of love and friendship, and layest such obligations upon me as infinitely excel all others that I can receive from any in this world.

"For thou hast already given thy blessed Son to be a sacrifice for me; and now thou invitest me to partake of that sacrifice, and to feast upon his body and blood; that Christ may dwell in me and I in him; that he may be one with me and I with him.

"O how great, how precious is this grace, which thou vouchsafest to me! How freely ought I to give myself to him, to be his entirely.

"How careful ought I to be, never to revolt from him! but to keep my faith with him, and abide in his love, by continuing firm and unmoveable in his obedience.

"Far be it from me to do anything contrary to my holy religion; and to those sacred bonds that are upon me, and wherein I am going to engage myself again, as I ought to do, with the most forward affection and devotion to him.

"For what greater happiness can be conceived, than to be a friend of God, a confederate with Christ; an habitation of the Holy Ghost; and to be bound by living in perfect agreement with his holy will here, to live with him in endless love in the other world.

"For which I beseech thee to prepare me by holy communion with thee at present, and at last to translate me, according to thy gracious covenant with us, into thy heavenly kingdom, through Christ Jesus our Lord. To whom, & c."

Covenant theology runs through this prayer, hence the reference at the start to being "early devoted and engaged to thee in a solemn covenant," i.e. baptism. That covenant is one which is renewed in the Eucharist—"thou invitest me to come and renew my covenant with thee," an expression which emphasizes the ecclesial dimension of the Eucharist ("*come* and renew . . ."). It is no light undertaking, as Patrick asks for "my obligations" to be spelt out again, and in the particular circumstances as these change; the repetition of the word "obligations" does not seem anything but deliberate, specific, and for devotional emphasis. The covenant is wrought by the sacrifice of Christ, hence the theme of Eucharistic sacrifice applied to the memorial, the "feast upon a sacrifice," as he had explained, by reference to Cudworth. To be "a confederate with Christ," then, is to be bound in Holy Communion. The marriage-covenant, never far from the surface in this part of the treatise, also appears in this and the following prayers.

Prayer Book sources also recur: "faithful service" (cf. "true and laudable service," Collect for Trinity XIII); "let me be undone by following the devices and desires of my own heart" (cf. Confession at Morning and Evening Prayer); "sorrowfully bewailing what is past" (cf. Confession at Holy Communion); "that Christ may dwell in me" (cf. Prayer of Humble Access at Holy Communion); "abide in his love" (cf. the first of the altar prayers at Marriage). "Firm and unmoveable" comes fittingly from I Cor 15:58. It is interesting to note the two clear echoes of the Prayer Book *Confessions* near the start of this prayer, compared with the (corresponding) echoes from the Prayer Book *Absolutions* near the beginning of the next prayer.

Prayer 4: "Sign and Seal of Remission of Sins"[41]
      (at the end of Chapter 5)
"O Lord, the Father of mercies, and the God of all consolation, who hast not only most graciously promised forgiveness to all them that with hearty repentance and true faith turn unto thee; but also made a new covenant with us in the blood of Christ, for the remission of sins; which thou likewise sealest to us in the sacrament of it; I most humbly beseech thee to make me thoroughly sensible of the greatness and the riches of this grace, that so I may neither neglect it nor be unthankful for it; but go unto that holy feast, to which thou invitest me, upon his body and blood, there to present myself unto thee with a lively faith and unfeigned repentance; and then to receive the assurances that thou wilt be merciful to my sins, and remember them no more; and then to bless and praise thee for such strong assurance as thou hast given us by the blood of thy dear Son, who sacrificed himself for our sins; and by making us partakers of that sacrifice, in the commemoration of it, which thou thyself hast ordained for our fuller satisfaction.

[41] Ibid., 141f. See above n. 29.

"And what greater satisfaction can we have than to be assured that we are reconciled unto thee, and at peace with thee; and thereby to be eased of that intolerable burden of our sins, which should it lie upon us, would press us down to hell?

"O make me more deeply sensible of the weight of their guilt, that so I may the more admire the exceeding riches of thy grace, which will deliver me from that load.

"For the obtaining of which deliverance, I ought to be willing to submit to anything which thou shalt demand of me; and to think no conditions hard or uneasy, but be as ready ever to forgive freely, even the greatest offences against me, as I am desirous thou wouldst forgive all my offences against thee.

"O Lord, dispose my soul, I beseech thee, unto this grace, as an earnest of the other. Root out all hatred, enmity, and ill will: cleanse me so perfectly from the least relic of them, and possess me with such hearty love and kindness towards all men, even towards my bitterest enemies, that I may more comfortably expect to receive perfect remission and forgiveness from thee, by those pledges of thy love which I receive from the hands of thy minister.

"Whose absolution here pronounced on earth, I beseech thee, ratify in heaven; through our Lord Jesus Christ, who lives for ever to make intercession for us. To whom with thee, O Father, and the Holy Ghost, be everlasting praises. Amen.''

This is perhaps the most rhetorical of the prayers, given that it expresses one of the chief priorities of the Reformation, the forgiveness of sins, and the reality of this forgiveness in the context of Eucharist. It is, however, void of that introspection for which some Reformation piety is justly charged. The starting point is the greatness of God's love,[42] from which true penitence flows, not as God's manipulation of us to make us feel sinful, but as our sense of dependence upon him; there is a truly Augustinian approach whereby penitence is our response to God's loving nature. Moreover, this response is seen closely connected with the Eucharist, for it is in the sacrifice of Christ that we find our home, in the

---

[42] Cf. the very opening to *Mensa Mystica*, quoted earlier, above n. 22.

184

feast, the celebration, "for our fuller satisfaction." History and eternity are brought together at the Lord's Table. Only then comes the self-searching, the pouring out of conscious and unconscious sin, as the communicant approaches (N.B. the reference earlier to "*go* unto that holy feast") the altar. In the Prayer Book rite, the confession and absolution come just before the consecration, hence its close and intimate connection, in Patrick's scheme, with Communion itself. The doxology, once again, is deliberate, and carefully placed here.

Prayer Book allusions abound: "who hast not only . . . unto thee" (cf. Absolution at Holy Communion); "lively faith and unfeigned repentance" (cf. Absolution at Morning and Evening prayer); "which thou hast ordained" (cf. Introduction to Marriage Service); "the riches of thy grace" (first blessing of couple at Marriage); "intolerable burden" (cf. Confession at Holy Communion); "perfect remission and forgiveness" (cf. Collect for Ash Wednesday). Covenant theology again recurs, both at the start, in that key reference to the Eucharist as a sealing, and the penultimate paragraph, which evokes the (later) Methodist Covenant Service prayer, with its (equally Augustinian) love for God's uncertain future.[43] One can see here the cross-fertilisation that was going on between Anglican and Puritans in a way that makes traditional labels sometimes difficult to use. Another such theological theme present in the prayer is the heavenly intercession of Christ (Heb 7:26).[44]

Prayer 5: "A Means of Nearer Union with Christ"[45]
       (at the end of Chapter 6)
"O God, who, by faith in thy Son Jesus Christ, hath incorporated us into him, and made us members of him; and by the increase of that faith and of love and of hope, doth knit us more perfectly unto him, and make us more entirely one with him; I bless and praise thee that thou hast ordained a holy feast upon his body

---

[43] Cf. the traditional form, used by Methodists since the late eighteenth century, "And the covenant which I have made on earth, let it be ratified in heaven," *The Methodist Service Book* (London: Methodist Publishing House, 1975) 110. On the history of this rite, see David H. Tripp, *The Renewal of the Covenant in the Methodist Tradition* (London: Epworth, 1969).

[44] See above n. 21, McAdoo, op. cit.

[45] See Patrick, vol. 1, 153f. See above n. 29.

and blood, for the nourishment and growth of these, and for my stronger and closer union with him.

"What an honour is this, that not only our nature should be assumed unto an union with the divine, but that thou shouldest take every particular person of us, who obediently believe on thy Son Jesus, into such a near conjunction with him as testifies his most tender affection towards us, though unworthy of the least respect from him.

"O that I may never prove ungrateful for it, nor vainly presume of it, while I am a stranger to it. But my will being perfectly made one with his will (so that what pleases him pleases me), I may feel that I am really and truly made one spirit with him; and may comfortably hope that being thus united to him, death itself shall not separate me from him; but that he will quicken even this mortal body, at the last day, by his Spirit which dwelleth in me.

"And I most humbly beseech thee, daily to quicken this faith and hope in me, that by the power of it I may overcome the world and all the temptations of it. Make me to feel a living virtue continually flowing from Christ my head unto me, that I may continue a lively member of his body; steadfastly walking in this world as Christ walked, and never doing any thing unbecoming the relation I have to him; but by doing him all the honour I am able, may be at last preferred to the honour of dwelling with him for ever. Which I humbly beg for his sake, who hath undertaken to be our advocate with thee: to whom with thee, O Father, and the Holy Ghost, be all honour and glory now and eternally. Amen."

This prayer seems to be a kind of expanded version of the "Prayer of Humble Access" (just before the Consecration Prayer), beginning with the well-known words, "we do not presume to come to this thy table. . . ." The union of the believers (for the prayer is corporate in focus) in Christ is the starting point, to which the human response is made. The movement is what we have seen again and again thus far: the fact of redemption and the human response to it. "What an honour is this" leads into a consideration of how that union may work yet more closely. That union is eternal, for not even death can separate us (Rom 8:38f).

And again, we see the same repetition of the worshipper in the sanctuary and the practical Christian working out that faith in daily living.

Prayer Book sources occur still: the first paragraph is a catena of material, "incorporated" (cf. Thanksgiving prayer after Communion); "increase of faith and of love and of hope" (cf. Collect for Trinity XIV); "knit us" (cf. Collect for All Saints Day); "continue a lively member" (cf. Thanksgiving Prayer after Communion); "our advocate with thee" (cf. end of Prayer for the Church). Again a doxology, leading naturally from the intercession of Christ in heaven.

Prayer 6: "A Means of Union with Each Other"[46]
(at the end of Chapter 7)

"O Lord, who art good, and who doest good; who art love, and delightest to see us all live in love; and for that end, among others, hast instituted this holy feast, that our hearts may be knit by love, one to another, as well as unto thee: inspire me, I beseech thee, with a powerful sense of thy goodness, who wouldst have us all so happy, happy in the love of thee, and happy in the love one of another. And help me so deeply to lay to heart the design of thy love, that I may never be averse to it, nor cross my own happiness; but most forwardly comply with thy gracious intentions, having all Christians as my brethren, and living in peace with them.

"We are too prone, I am sensible, not only to be angry upon small occasions, but to quarrel and strive; which too often ends in enmities and hatreds. And therefore preserve in me always, I beseech thee, such a lively remembrance of my Saviour's love, and the profession I make at this holy feast, of love to him, and to all that belong to him, that I may presently suppress all such unchristian passions; especially all the beginnings of hatred and ill will, that they may never settle in my heart; but I may easily forgive others, as thou, O Lord, for Christ's sake hast forgiven me.

"And work in me, most gracious God, not only the affection of love, but excite me to all the actions of it; by doing good, and studying how others may be the better for me: for my knowledge,

---

[46] Ibid., 172f.

187

my riches, my interest, my friends; for every thing whereby they may receive any benefit from me, or by my means. That being endued with this blessed charity, expressing itself not merely in word and tongue, but in deed and truth; not only in some pang of devotion, but in the constant course of my life, I may have a good hope of coming at last into the holy society of saints and angels, to live with them in undisturbed love and friendship, world without end, Amen.''

This prayer shows Patrick at his most human, both at the personal and the corporate levels. It is not a pious collection of nice thoughts, for it represents a profoundly social understanding of the nature of the Eucharist, which runs very much along the lines of what Rowan Williams described as "Imagining the Kingdom,"[47] seeing the Lord's Supper not as a separate, ecclesiastical action, cut off from the world, but as a powerful vehicle for the judgment of the Kingdom of God upon the world. It sums up the chapter which it seeks to illuminate, and it also (again) avoids the individualism which this kind of devotional writing runs the risk of encouraging: "We are too prone, I am sensible . . ." If God is great and good, and that makes us aware of our dependence on his grace, then let the human race bask in renewal and forgiveness, starting with a real awareness of the other members of it. There is, too, a deep understanding of the different kinds of feelings which may build up; "all the beginnings of hatred and ill will." There is, too, a sense of deep devotion, "not only in some pang of devotion, but in the constant course of my life." There are no direct Prayer Book allusions, except "lay to heart," from the prayer for unity, in the service for use on the occasion of the Accession of the Sovereign.[48] That prayer, by the way, seems to lie behind much of this composition; the unity is a social one, it is corporate; it is about repentance, and the work of Christ in the community.

[47] Rowan D. Williams, "Imagining the Kingdom: Some Questions for Anglican Worship Today," in Kenneth Stevenson and Bryan Spinks, eds., *The Identity of Anglican Worship* (London: Mowbrays, 1991) 1–13.

[48] Ibid., 5, where Williams draws attention to the national, social origin of the prayer, which is nowadays recited out of its original context, to sound far more "churchy" than intended!

From this study of his thought and prayers, certain features stand out. First of all, the relationship between discourse and prayer, even though separated by a period of twenty-four years, is one where the latter are written in order to inculcate the devotion and teaching of the former. But it is not a case of the dogmatic tail wagging the liturgical dog! Already the treatise is part of an applied theology, of an historico-devotional kind, intended to edify but also to help people to pray. The *lex orandi-lex credendi* relationship is a mutual one.[49] The six prayers reflect the six "ends" of the Eucharist, and in both media, reading the treatise and praying the prayers, reason and affection, understanding and will (to use some of the parts of the personality enumerated by Patrick towards the end of the treatise)[50] are used *together*. It is not a case of the head being fed in the former, the heart in the latter. Patrick sees right theology as an orthodoxy, a right praise.[51] Moreover, the way he fashions his doctrine is a careful blend of the tradition of the Church across the centuries, recent thinking included; time and again he grounds his reflections on the Prayer Book rite of Holy Communion as chief *locus* of tradition and piety.

Secondly, these are private prayers, which have a corporate focus. They are, moreover, inspired by Prayer Book language and the Bible, but they have not been written self-consciously to include these references. Patrick's method of liturgiography is not a

[49] This is precisely the point made by Henry McAdoo in *The Spirit of Anglicanism—A Survey of Anglican Theological Method in the Seventeenth Century* (London: A. C. Black, 1965) 190: ". . . Patrick's thought moves naturally within the setting of the liturgy of the Church. It is not that Tillotson and Stillingfleet neglected to deal with such matters, but that Patrick seems more involved in the day-to-day actuality of its realized corporateness." See also pp. 189–198 on Patrick in general, though not specifically on his Eucharistic thought. For a modern discussion of this subject, see Geoffrey Wainwright, *Doxology: A Systematic Theology* (London: Epworth, 1980), and Aidan Kavanagh, *On Liturgical Theology* (New York: Pueblo, 1984).

[50] See above n. 34.

[51] This theme has been taken up repeatedly by scholars on an ecumenical scale, from Alexander Schmemann, *Introduction to Liturgical Theology* (London: Faith Press, 1966), through Geoffrey Wainwright, *Doxology*, cited above, to Aidan Kavanagh himself, *On Liturgical Theology*, cited above. It has since been explored on a Danish Lutheran front by Jens-Holger Schjørring, *Grundtvig og Påsken* (Copenhagen: Gad, 1987).

tired, slavish usage of ancient or modern models. He sets out to write what he wants to write, and the only stylistic point of methodology is the one we have noted, namely that Patrick places redemption before the reader and evokes a response. Perhaps this is the kind of writing in which he excelled, and explains why his own suggested Collects in the proposed revisions of 1689 were not altogether happy ones.[52] Although the Collects written in 1662 to replace a few of Cranmer's weaker compositions were already getting longer than Cranmer's standard norm,[53] Patrick was in quite another league altogether—that of the rambling evocation of God and humanity facing each other and exploring their relationship. Prayer writing had moved on, and however much Patrick protests in these prayers a kindly nudge towards seeing these prayers as corporate, not individual, they belong at home, not in the sanctuary, and Patrick was better suited to write for that context.

Thirdly, the kind of theology exemplified in this work, treatise and prayers alike, is that of the Restoration Church of England in general, and of a flavour which is not easy to label in particular. Patrick has been described as "Latitudinarian," but Gareth Bennett has shown that this is not altogether an accurate description, specially of Patrick himself.[54] Paul Avis, in his study of Anglicanism, uses labels easily, in order to show the variety of theological opinion from the first years of the Church of England, but even he shrinks from giving one to Patrick. We have pointed to the mixture of influences on Patrick,[55] and how these remained consistently with him for the whole of his ministry. He was very much

[52] Cf. John Dowden's verdict on them: "It is indeed true that we have reason to be grateful for what we have escaped," in *The Workmanship of the Prayer Book* (London: Methuen, 1902) 139.

[53] See G. J. Cuming, *The Godly Order* (Alcuin Club Collections 65) (London: 1983) 56ff. There were many minor corrections and additions to the Collects in 1662, but the two completely new ones were for Advent III and Epiphany VI, see Brightman, op. cit., 209ff., 273.

[54] See above Bennett, art. cit., n. 5. Cuming repeats the "Latitudinarian" theme in *A History of Anglican Liturgy*, 2nd ed. (London: Macmillan, 1982) 132.

[55] See Avis, op. cit., 280, in a paragraph in which Taylor is called a Liberal Catholic, Gilbert Burnet (1643-1715) a Liberal Protestant, and William Laud a High Churchman; Patrick is simply referred to as "in the seventeenth century!"

his own man, theologically and politically. But if he is to be given a label, then he would be more accurately called a "Liberal Catholic" Anglican, like Jeremy Taylor, than a "Central Churchman," like Edward Stillingfleet, the man who was consecrated bishop of Worcester the same day Patrick was made bishop of Chichester. In his Eucharistic theology alone, Patrick has the same priorities as Taylor; a depth of patristic reading, a strong touch of Platonism from the Cambridge of his student days, and a quiet but firm determination to rebuild, in the tradition of Hooker and others, the Church of England after the dismal years of the Commonwealth. And, as we have seen by his innovations at Peterborough, his pastoral ministry in Chichester and Ely, and even by his last will and testament for his own Communion plate, he burned with a passion for his Church to meet more frequently, and with greater understanding and devotion, for the celebration of the Lord's Supper. The way, too, that he handled controversial issues, like Eucharistic sacrifice and presence, showed that he was, essentially, a man who looked with reason on tradition and scripture, and applied the method of the broad approach, moving from the general to the particular.[56]

Fourthly, are there features of his Eucharistic theology that could be regarded as peculiarly his? This is always a rash quest, because precedents can be found for most new ideas. We have noted Patrick's accent on Eucharistic sacrifice; and his stress on the self-oblation of the worshipper is derived, doubtless, from the Prayer of Oblation at the end of the Prayer Book Communion rite. Charles Gore (1853–1932) was to take a similar line, and from the same source, in his classic treatment of Eucharistic doctrine, *The Body of Christ* (1901), where, moreover, he shows a comparable predilection for the expression "pleading" Christ's sacrifice as a description of the Eucharistic memorial.[57] But there is one feature

[56] See, for example, a similar approach in Kenneth Stevenson, *Eucharist and Offering* (New York: Pueblo, 1986).

[57] See Charles Gore, *The Body of Christ—An Enquiry into the Institution and Doctrine of Holy Communion* (London: Murray, 1901) 213; cf. Stevenson, *Eucharist and Offering*, 188f., 326. For "Plead," see Gore, op. cit., 165, 193, 198, 201, 286, 301; cf. Bryan Spinks, "The Ascension and Vicarious Humanity of Christ: The Christology and Soteriology Behind the Church of Scotland's Anamnesis and Epiklesis," in J. Neil Alexander, ed., *Time and Community* (Washington: Pastoral Press, 1990) 185–201.

of Patrick's discussion which we have already mentioned but which deserves special focus. Several times in the *Mensa Mystica*, he refers to the Eucharist as a "federal rite," or in some cognate expression.[58] The whole area of Federal Theology is being subjected to increasing scrutiny. Bryan Spinks,[59] for example, has recently made an examination of the influence of "federalism" on such distinct figures as Richard Baxter (1615–1691) and Jeremy Taylor (1613–1667), where it is a prominent theme in their writings and liturgical provisions for baptism but not Eucharist. (Taylor's liturgy was an unofficial form, for use during the Commonwealth.) Dugmore points to the influence of Ralph Cudworth, that prominent Cambridge Platonist, on Patrick's view of the Eucharist as "a feast upon a sacrifice."[60]

But where is the link with Patrick's Eucharistic federalism? It is to be found in two places. First, in his own writing on Baptism, the *Aqua Genitalis* (1658), the very work which so impressed the Platonist, Thomas Worthington, that he suggested Patrick write on the Eucharist as well. *Aqua Genitalis* is littered with references to baptism as a covenant sacrament, and it ends with a call to Christian living that made it almost inevitable that the covenant-theme would hold at least a prominent place in any subsequent discussion of the Eucharist: "And therefore let us live with them all as our Confederates, as those that are tied together in the same bonds, and united in the same Covenant. . . ."[61] In the second

[58] See above n. 40.

[59] See Bryan Spinks, "Two Seventeenth-Century Examples of *Lex Credendi, Lex Orandi:* The Baptismal and Eucharistic Theologies and Liturgies of Jeremy Taylor and Richard Baxter," *Studia Liturgica* 21 (1991) 165–189.

[60] See above n. 40.

[61] See Patrick, vol. 1, 59. The theme recurs, for example in the following somewhat lyrical and pastoral passage: "(Holy Communion) increases our love to God and our love to man, which is the sum of all our duty . . . It is a little epitomy of the whole gospel, for it shows what God will do for us, and what we must do for him; and it affords strength unto us for to do it. And therefore it is called the new testament of covenant in his blood, because here the whole new covenant is represented; God giving his Son and all blessings unto us, and we giving of ourselves and our best service unto him . . . By this God sets to his seal, that all things contained in the covenant shall be done for us; and we also set to our seal, and openly profess ourselves to belong to the covenant, and that we esteem and highly value all those blessings, and will do anything for to obtain them." Ibid., 174.

place, right at the end of Cudworth's *Discourse Concerning the True Notion of the Lord's Supper* (1642), a short work written when he was only twenty-five, he makes the title of his fifth and final chapter, "The Lord's Supper Is a Federal Rite."[62] Cudworth's aim is distinct from Patrick's; for the former is concerned with discussing Jewish origins, and the religious world into which the early Eucharist was born, whereas the latter is expounding at far greater length the history of Eucharistic theology within his own scheme (the "six ends"), and applying it to worshippers today. Both men worked within the same theological climate. Cudworth explained origins, distancing himself from extremists who would either teach transubstantiation or play down the Eucharist altogether. Patrick takes hold of this theological approach and applies it much more widely, using deliberate echoes from the marriage service and human experience as if to reaffirm the very contemporaneous character of the sacraments, thus producing a coherent approach to the Eucharist that maintained its inner dynamic of divine initiative and human response. It is entirely consistent with such a pattern of thought that Cudworth's exposition in 1642 should be followed by Patrick's baptismal covenant-theology in 1658; and this is rightly followed up in 1660 with the third "end" of Holy Communion, "a holy rite, to enter covenant with God," which, in turn, is given devotional expression in the accompanying prayer of 1684, near the end of which we come across the telling words:

"For what greater happiness can be conceived, than to be a friend of God, a confederate with Christ; an habitation of the Holy Ghost; and to be bound by living in perfect agreement with his holy will here, to live with him in endless love in the other world."[63]

---

[62] See Thomas Birch, ed., *The Works of Ralph Cudworth in Four Volumes*, vol. 4 (Oxford: Talboys, 1829) 276ff. (whole work, 215–286). On Cudworth in general, see G. P. H. Pawson, *The Cambridge Platonists and Their Place in Religious Thought* (London: S.P.C.K., 1930) 70–81 (esp. 70ff., on the "Discourse"). See also McAdoo, *The Spirit*, pass.

[63] See above n. 40. Patrick propounds a covenant theology that envisages spiritual growth as a real goal: "Is Christ's death to excuse us from holy living? No, it is to teach us to take up our cross and follow him." (*The Hearts Ease*, in Patrick, vol. 4, 506, quoted in Spurr, op. cit., 302.)

Here is a covenant theology that is begun at baptism, and nourished at the Lord's Table, awaiting its final fruition in heaven. It need hardly be said that it was biblical as well as social concerns that made Federal Theology such a feature of seventeenth-century England.

Finally, both the treatise and the prayers demonstrate that fine literary tradition that was already secure in the Church of England. It has its limitations, for people who are overconscious of the book do not necessarily wait upon the Lord expectantly. The seventeenth-century churches in England continued to debate the issue of set liturgy versus liberty of prophesying. But we are clear on which side Patrick stood, and if he was in favour of some liturgical latitude in 1689, it was probably inspired by a generous spirit, as well as a conviction that the liturgy, unlike the Bible, does not have canonical status, and should change from time to time.[64] The literary tradition which fed him is none the poorer for his work. In our own day, there is a different set of priorities, for since Patrick's time, hymn singing has become much more central to Anglican culture, and liturgical texts are produced with a rapidity that would have shocked those divines who had liturgical interests in that particular time. Patrick, however, as part of that tradition, emerges from our study as both quintessentially an Englishman of his time, but also a man of many ages, traditions, and thought patterns, because of the width of his reading, the depth of his piety, and the carefully nuanced style in which he brought together different truths about the Lord's Supper; his purpose in doing this was to do justice to an action of the Church on which he so wholly depended that he knew it to be a reality beyond his own, or anybody else's, words.

CONCLUSION

Where, then, is Patrick to be placed? The conventional labels, we have observed, do not really work. He could be described by that all-embracing jargon as an exponent of "liberal orthodoxy," and one can certainly see within him the tensions and the promise

[64] Cf. Kenneth Stevenson, "Anglican Identity: A Chapter of Accidents," in Stevenson/Spinks, eds., op. cit., 184–196.

of later theologians, such as the *Lux Mundi* school.[65] One can also see in the liturgical background to his writings a firm conviction that the Prayer Book occupies in his mind a place of strength and authority. Patrick's theology is not "confessional" in the conventional sense of the term, and for that reason he has to stand apart from formal Calvinism or Lutheranism. The kind of theology we encounter here is the pastor's mélange of historical theology, presented in the way that best suits him, within the context of worship.[66]

It was the narrow conception of the Church of the extreme Puritans, and their exclusive, world-rejecting attitudes to the Sacraments that provoked in Patrick a firm conviction, fed by his "latitude" thinking, that the Church of England needed breadth as well as depth. He was an ecumenist before his time in his desire for "comprehension," not sectarianism. It is not for nothing that *Aqua Genitalis* grew from a sermon preached at the baptism of the son of a clerical colleague in 1658 whose name does not appear on the Restoration lists, from which one supposes that he could not subscribe to the 1662 Act of Uniformity.[67] Furthermore, towards the end of *Aqua Genitalis*, Patrick calls in not only Richard Baxter (1615–1691) but also Jonathan Hanmer (1606–1687) with overt enthusiasm when he is emphasizing the importance of public profession of faith before receiving Communion.[68] Both Baxter and Hanmer left the Establishment in 1662, Hanmer to found the first Nonconformist congregation in Barnstaple.

We have mentioned, too, other writers concerned about the Eucharist. Of these, Thorndike[69] stands out as one cited by Patrick,

[65] See, for example, Geoffrey Rowell, "Historical Retrospect: Lux Mundi 1889," in Robert Morgan, ed., *The Religion of the Incarnation: Anglican Essays in Commemoration of Lux Mundi* (Bristol: Classical Press, 1989) 205–217, for a discussion of the context in which *Lux Mundi* was written, and the background to its original intention on the part of its authors.

[66] See, for example, Kenneth Stevenson, "Lex Orandi and Lex Credendi— Strange Bed-Fellows?: Some Reflections on Worship and Doctrine," *Scottish Journal of Theology* 39 (1986) 225–241.

[67] See Patrick, vol. 1, 1, for E. Vaughan's letter to the Reader, and note a. Vaughan was "a minister in Lombard Street."

[68] Ibid., 47. See also following pages for further discussion, and the Appendix, added, 60–64.

[69] See E. C. Miller, "The Doctrine of the Church in the Thought of Herbert

and who, like Patrick, followed Cudworth's lead in developing a strongly federal approach to Eucharistic doctrine; and he also is cautious about anything suggesting transubstantiation, but strong on Eucharistic sacrifice. Thorndike is probably more of a conscious High Churchman than Patrick, as is also George Bull (1634–1710), a parish priest, later Archdeacon of Llandaff, who in 1705 became Bishop of St. Davids.[70] But the theologian he most resembles is Jeremy Taylor.

Both had Platonist tendencies, loved patristics and writing prayers, and both were naturally interested in the doctrine and practice of the Eucharist. Both inherited the mantle of theological federalism as enunciated by the Platonists, thus avoiding the exclusivism of the Puritan conceptions of covenant[71] and ensuring a strongly objective character to the sacraments of baptism and Eucharist. There are, of course, differences. Taylor never got the English see he should have been given, remaining in Ireland as Bishop there at the start of the Restoration, until his death in 1667.[72] (The reason for this may well have been the controversy surrounding Taylor's view of original sin, in which he took a decidedly anti-Augustine line.)[73] Both, however, are nuanced on Eucharistic presence, exploratory on sacrifice, though Taylor in-

---

Thorndike (1598–1672)," unpublished D. Phil. thesis, Oxford University, 1990, for an interesting discussion of the way in which Thorndike moulds the term "covenant" to apply to a strong understanding of the sacraments of baptism and Eucharist. Patrick will have been familiar with Thorndike's writings, but Cudworth seems to have been the starting-off point.

[70] See above n. 9.

[71] Patrick's enthusiasm for federalism and covenant theology must not, however, be taken as wholesale endorsement of its popular usage; in fact, he ridicules it, see A Friendly Debate between a Conformist and a Nonconformist (1668) and A Continuation of the Friendly Debate (1669), in Patrick, vol. 5, 253ff., 435ff. See also Horton Davies, op. cit., 174f.

[72] See F. R. Bolton, The Caroline Tradition of the Church of Ireland With Particular Reference to Bishop Jeremy Taylor (London: S.P.C.K., 1958), pass., and also 118, 165, 209, for reference to Patrick's order of service of the Consecration of St. Katharine's Hall, Cambridge (For full text, see Patrick, vol. 9, 249–257), and its influence on Irish Church use; and also to Bishop Richard Mant (1776–1848) and his use of Patrick's Christian Sacrifice in one of his Diocesan Charges, at Killaloe, in 1822 (it is to do with the interpretation of the word "oblations," for which, see above n. 27).

[73] See McAdoo, Eucharistic Theology of Jeremy Taylor, 27ff.

dulges himself in the high priestly ministry of Christ here; on the other hand, Patrick prefers the simpler conceptual imagery of the Fathers, Anglican admirers of whom found the view of "memorial-sacrifice" consonant with tradition and with Reformation sensitivites. In short, both want to be faithful to tradition, but to use their powers of reason to interpret that tradition.

In his recent study of the Restoration Church, John Spurr describes Patrick as "the doyen of the devotional writers on the sacrament," and suggests that Patrick's devotional writings reached a far wider public than the better-known names who have constantly gained the attention of subsequent generations.[74] Indeed he ventures to say that Patrick has been neglected by scholars. He does not, of course, stand in the same league as Lancelot Andrewes (1555–1626), John Cosin (1594–1672), or Jeremy Taylor (1613–1667). Nor is his medium the same. Andrewes is best known for his preaching, and for the *Preces Privatae*[75] (a work which, by its very title, Andrewes did not intend for publication!), Cosin for his *Collection of Private Devotions*[76] (1627), and for his detailed interest in the revision of the Prayer Book, and Taylor for his many doctrinal works, his devotional writings—*Holy Living* (1650), *Holy Dying* (1651)—and (among liturgists) his *Book of Offices*[77] (1658). Unlike Andrewes, Patrick does not produce his own private prayers which others happen to want to bring before the general public; unlike Cosin, Patrick does not issue an unofficial book of prayers for daily use, in the succession of the *Primers* of the previous century; and unlike Taylor, Patrick is far from writing an underground Anglican liturgy. On the other hand, Patrick's concerns were very wide indeed, as the list of works drawn together by Alexander Taylor, albeit selected, demonstrate, in their nine volumes. He exercised

[74] John Spurr, *The Restoration Church of England*, 397.

[75] See Nicholas Lossky, *Lancelot Andrewes The Preacher (1555–1626): The Origins of the Mystical Theology of the Church of England* (Oxford: Clarendon Press, 1991); and F. E. Brightman, tr., *The Preces Privatae of Lancelot Andrewes, Bishop of Winchester* (London: Methuen, 1903).

[76] See P. G. Stanwood, ed., *John Cosin: A Collection of Private Devotions* (Oxford: Clarendon Press, 1967); see also Kenneth Stevenson, "The Liturgical Work of John Cosin: A Study in Method," paper delivered at John Cosin Conference, Durham University, July 1993.

[77] See *The Whole Works of the Right Revd. Jeremy Taylor*, vol. 8 (London: Longmans, 1850) 573–701 (Book of Offices); see also H. Boone Porter, *Jeremy Taylor—Liturgist* (Alcuin Club Collections 61) (London: S.P.C.K., 1979).

himself in a whole host of theological and apologetic areas, including the defence of Anglicanism, and the journey of the soul, both of which are typical of Restoration Anglicanism. As far as the *Mensa Mystica* is concerned, he works on a more modest level than Andrewes, Cosin, or Jeremy Taylor, expounding a rich theology that strove to put the Eucharist back into the heart of the Church's life.

In one sense, Patrick could only have been a seventeenth century Anglican, living in an age when his own kind of "liturgical theology" could find its own climate, through the sheer accessibility of his writings, with their deliberately targeted markets and inner consistency.[78] Further, the way in which he brings the past into the present, scrutinizes it,[79] and represents it afresh through exposition, pastoral challenge, and prayerful nourishment, makes him appear an attractive figure to us who live at a time when the Western Churches have all produced fine new liturgies but are beginning to wonder what might be missing. Is there, too, a theological hermeneutic for Patrick's "dynamic federalism?" Some recent explorations into Eucharistic faith and practice show marked affinities with Patrick and those other more open federal theologies of his time. He shows an unusual blend of sacrificial motifs, too, in the unbloody unity of the oblations of bread and wine with the self-oblation of the worshippers in a Communion that affirms and redeems, rather than rejects and revokes life, so touching it with the cross;[80] nor does he forget the real hope of heaven.

"The encounter at the burning bush was no seminar," said

[78] See Kenneth Stevenson, "The Eucharistic Theology of Simon Patrick," in *Ordet, kirken og kulturen* (Århus: Universitetsforlag, 1993) 300–313. See also Kenneth Stevenson, *Covenant of Grace Renewed: A Vision of the Eucharist in the Seventeenth Century* (London: Darton, Longman, and Todd, 1994), 136–163, on Thorndike and Patrick.

[79] For example, Patrick's sensitivity to a less reactive and more constructive view of Eucharistic sacrifice may well have borne fruit in the tiny emendations in this direction which were proposed in the 1689 "Liturgy of Comprehension"; Christ's Body and Blood in the Eucharist are referred to as "the sacrifice" both in the Prayer of Humble Access, before Communion, and in the Catechism. For the texts, but not the suggestion, see Fawcett, op. cit., 110, 131. The resulting formulae would have come close to the "feast upon a sacrifice" notion we have explored in Patrick's theology.

[80] See, for example, David N. Power, *The Eucharistic Mystery: Revitalizing the Tradition* (New York: Crossroad, 1992), a book which opens up many areas for fresh examination, and poses more questions than it answers. It would in-

Aidan Kavanagh in one of his idiosyncratic asides[81] during a paper he delivered at the 1983 meeting of the *Societas Liturgica* in Vienna. Kavanagh has done a great deal to deepen our understanding of the reciprocal nature of the relationship between liturgy and historical theology—a relationship which at its healthiest is the private preserve neither of the Churches of the Reformation nor of the Roman Catholic Church. In this short study, we have highlighted some of the issues which arise when a given liturgy—that of the 1662 Prayer Book with all its rich ambiguity, was interpreted afresh by a creative thinker who was in touch not only with a remarkable array of writers across the ages but also with the worshipping life of his Church—a life which he sought to renew sacramentally. And it is of the utmost significance that the original text of the *Mensa Mystica* of 1660 gained in the course of time a series of prayers (a common device at the time) in order to give the work a fuller measure of coherence, and thus embody that reciprocal relationship in a vital manner. All of this, however, ultimately has to leave Simon Patrick, together with his prolix and quaintly dated prayers,[82] very much where he lived and worked in Caroline England. But his special combination of synthesis and application, comprehensiveness and ecumenical vision, as well as discernment and love of tradition causes him to stand out before a much wider audience, the Church Catholic, as the scholar-pastor of every age, a man in whom zeal lived and grew, untrammelled by passion, and fed abundantly on knowledge.[83]

----

deed be fruitful for a Roman Catholic theologian to examine the federal theologies of baptism and Eucharist in seventeenth century England, Patrick included.

[81] A conscious (?) echo of the following which subsequently appeared in print, though not of the printed version of the lecture; "It was presence, not faith, which drew Moses to the burning bush, and what happened there was a revelation, not a seminar." See *On Liturgical Theology*, 92. Cf. "Nothing alters us so much as serious prayer, which puts a new mind into us, and for the present makes us a quite another sort of creatures," *The Hearts Ease*, Patrick, vol. 4, 652, quoted from Spurr, op. cit., 334, n. 17.

[82] Of his work for the revision of the collects in 1689, the caustic historian Macaulay wrote, "whether he was or was not qualified to make the collects better, no man that ever lived was more competent to make them longer," T. B. Macaulay, *A History of England* III (London: 1856) 476, quoted from Horton Davies, op. cit., 400, n. 83. See above n. 52 for Dowden's view.

[83] See above n. 35, for the final sentences of *Mensa Mystica*.

Louis Weil

10. **Aspects of the Issue of** *Per Saltum* **Ordination: An Anglican Perspective**

An aspect of the life of the Church in late medieval Christianity which was retained in the English Church at the time of the Reformation was the canonical norm of sequential ordinations. Although this norm had attained a fixity only during the later centuries of the Middle Ages, it had come to be generally assumed that a person who aspired to ordination to the presbyterate would pass through a series of ordinations to what were called "minor orders." This was in its effect a process of socialization to the hierarchical structuring of the Church's authority, and it led, with ordination to the subdiaconate, into the "major orders," where it culminated in ordination to the sacramental priesthood. In late medieval theology, it was this order which was viewed as the pinnacle of ordained ministry in the Church.

As it were with the stroke of a pen, Archbishop Thomas Cranmer abolished the minor orders and, along with them, the subdiaconate; and, in his Ordinal (1550), he reasserted the patristic model of Holy Orders as comprising bishops, priests, and deacons. Within Cranmer's model, however, there remained some of the presuppositions of the late medieval pattern, and specifically the maintenance of the sequence by the candidate's passing through an "inferior order" before being ordained to a "higher order." It was thus firmly established in canon law and normative practice that a man must be ordained deacon before he might be ordained priest, and ordained priest before he might be ordained bishop. When the situation was seen to require it, however, the sequence might be telescoped, so that the candidate would remain in the inferior orders for a far shorter time than the canons required.

Although the balance will shift at some time in the later 1990s, it remains true at the present that the majority of the clergy of the Episcopal Church were ordained according to the rites of the American Book of Common Prayer of 1928. This means that, in their own ordination process, the rites still stated, in the language of Cranmer's reworking of the medieval Sarum text, that they were serving as deacons in an inferior order which was a kind of testing period during which they were to show themselves "worthy to be called unto the higher Ministries in thy Church."[1] In the corresponding collect of the rite for the Ordination of a Deacon in the 1979 BCP, the idea of inferior status is completely eliminated, and the newly ordained deacon is referred to as "an effective example" with whom the whole people may together serve God. There is clearly here a significant shift of focus which must be linked to the introductory rubric at the Ordination of a Priest, and which states that "The ordinand is to be vested in surplice or alb, without stole, tippet, or other vesture distinctive of ecclesiastical or academic rank or order."[2] In other words, the rites suggest in these texts a recovery of a sense of the theological integrity of each order, seeing no order as merely a testing ground for another, "higher," order.[3] In all these rites, the candidate enters

[1] Collect after Communion at the Ordering of Deacons, BCP (1928) 535. Cranmer based this text upon the rite in the Sarum Pontifical where the passage indicated occurs in the final part of the ordination prayer itself. It is found in that place as part of the traditional diaconal ordination formula from as early as the tenth century, when it appears in the manuscripts of the Romano-Germanic pontifical. See C. Vogel, *Le Pontifical Romano-Germanique du Dixième Siècle*, I, p. 26, lines 23–26. (Studi e Testi 226), (Vatican City: 1963). Earlier documentation shows no such pattern of sequential ordination. Cf. C. Vogel, *Medieval Liturgy. An Introduction to the Sources*. Trans. and rev. by W. Storey and N. K. Rasmussen. (Washington: 1986) 174–176.

[2] BCP (1979), 524. It is to be noted that this same rubric, with minor modifications, appears also among the introductory rubrics for the Ordination of a Bishop (511) and for the Ordination of a Deacon (536).

[3] Note the comment in *Prayer Book Studies* 20 (New York: 1970, 23), published during the preparatory stages of the 1979 BCP: "Each order is presented as a distinctive vocation, having its own characteristics. This avoids the misleading impression that the three orders are simply in an ascending scale of promotions." I am reminded of a newly-ordained deacon who said to

the assembly precisely as a candidate chosen for a specific ministerial order, not wearing the vesture of another office which is
being put aside or subsumed.

As we shall see later in this essay, these seemingly minor ritual
changes are indicative of a significant and deepened awareness of
the relation of all particular vocations to the common life of the
baptized. Such changes in the rites are signs of a growing awareness that Holy Order cannot be studied as a reality unto itself,
with its own self-contained history and meaning. Our understanding of ordained ministry must be grounded in ecclesiology, for it
is our understanding of the nature of the Church which offers the
most fruitful context for sorting through the various issues surrounding ordination.[4]

DIRECT ORDINATION:
THE LARGER PERSPECTIVE

When we turn to history to help us with the specific issue of
whether or not the introduction of direct *(per saltum)* ordination
would be appropriate for the Church today, it provides no easy
answer. Let us begin by looking once again at Cranmer's achieve-
ment, at its medieval background, and at its patristic affinities.
Archbishop Cranmer's Ordinal was a brilliant recovery of the normative, classical pattern of the threefold ministry. He maintained
continuity by a kind of backward leap, a reassertion of the patristic model of the bishop as the fount of order within the life of the
Church. We forget too easily that this was a startling recovery of
an understanding of order which had become obscured as, in the
later Middle Ages, the meaning of ordained ministry had come to
be narrowly linked to the celebration of the Eucharist. The
delegated priesthood of the presbyterate, because of its preeminent identification with the offering of the sacrifice of the Mass,
had come to be seen as the summit of Holy Orders. It was this
development to which H. Boone Porter referred as the emergence
of the "omnivorous priesthood." Those in minor orders, and in

---

me at the reception following the ordination, "Well, that's one down and two
to go."

[4] L. Wm. Countryman, *The Language of Ordination* (Philadelphia: Trinity
Press International, 1992), offers a useful discussion of the ecclesial foundations of holy order; see especially 29–41.

the "inferior" major orders of subdeacon or deacon, were seen as being in transit toward the priesthood.[5]

As to the episcopate, St. Thomas Aquinas taught that it was not an order. In effect, Aquinas teaches a bishop is a priest who has been given the power to ordain; otherwise, in regard to the authority to consecrate the Body and Blood of Christ, a bishop, and even a pope, is no different from an ordinary priest. Consistent with this, Aquinas comments that in episcopal ordination no distinct character is received by the ordinand; rather, the ordination of a bishop establishes a new relation to the Body of Christ which is expressed in pastoral oversight. In other words, a bishop is quite simply a priest with added responsibilities.[6] When we see clearly the pattern of order presumed by Aquinas, we are able to recognize the radical aspects of Cranmer's Ordinal. Yet, even as Cranmer's work reclaimed the patristic model, we can see how his rites were also influenced by the late medieval experience, which presumed and expected a sequential pattern linking the three orders.

The issue of direct ordination, however, emerges from within the same patristic period from which Anglicanism claims to take its norms. The patristic evidence itself is not uniform, and an obligatory sequential pattern for ordination emerged very slowly. Gregory Dix characterizes the understanding of orders in the pre-Nicene Church as organic, each ministerial function relating directly to the whole Christian society, rather than relating to other ministerial functions in some defined, sequential pattern.[7] In this context, direct ordination occurred when a local church discerned gifts for a particular ministry in a person, then elected and ordained that person without requiring some transitional ordinations along the way.

Yet, in a sense, the idea of a flexible, sequential pattern already existed in the early Church. A person who served in one ministry

[5] H. Boone Porter, "A Traditional Reflection on Diaconate in Relation to 'Omnivorous Priesthood,' " *Living Worship* 12 no. 9 (November 1976).

[6] It is useful to consider the teaching of St. Thomas Aquinas on these matters as characteristic of the later medieval understanding of orders. It is summed up in the Supplement to the *Summa Theologiae*, questions 34–40. Regarding the issue discussed here, see especially questions 37–38.

[7] Gregory Dix, "The Ministry in the Early Church," in *The Apostolic Ministry*, ed. K. E. Kirk (London: 1946) 284.

(especially as lector or deacon, according to the historical evidence) might be recognized at a later time as having, or as having developed during years of service, the appropriate gifts for election to the episcopate. In practice, this meant that generally the person had served a number of years as, for example, a lector or deacon, and certainly had no anticipation of some inevitable call to a "higher order." The earlier ministry became, though unintentionally, the opportunity for the community to share the benefit of those gifts and to come to discern the potential for another form of ministry at a later date.

It is here that we see the clear distinction between the "organic" pattern of the early centuries, and the later, sequential pattern which developed within medieval society. The Church's sequences were imaged within the structure of the secular model of authority; there, persons rose, usually gradually, through a series of levels, each of which offered an opportunity for testing their capacity to move on to a higher level of responsibility. In the Church's life, this accepted pattern was modeled in the transition through minor orders in what I called earlier a process of socialization. At each level, certain expectations were imposed which, if not fulfilled, would deny access to the higher rank. Once a candidate had passed through the minor orders, the arrival at major orders marked the acceptance of those lifetime commitments which characterized clerical life: the personal obligation to recite the daily office, and celibacy, both of which were already implicit in the lower orders.

As we seek to sort out these matters in regard to the question of a pattern of ordination appropriate to our understanding of the nature of the Church and with respect for the principles which have characterized the Anglican tradition for over four centuries, we need to be conscious of this larger historical picture. Whereas our debt to the patristic period for the pattern of ordained ministry which Cranmer reclaimed is evident, it is also true that we carry our *whole* history, and that the significance of medieval Christianity for Anglican identity is very deep. We must be careful not to treat history like a buffet from which we choose only the dishes we find agreeable to our taste. Our deliberation must take into account the whole tradition, including its ambiguities and inconsistencies, and at the same time look with a clear eye at the realities of our own time. We cannot choose an ideal in the past, lift it out of its historical framework, whether patristic, medieval, or Reformation, and impose it upon our situation in the present.[8] Hence our deliberation about direct ordination must take many factors into account, and not merely our knowledge that such ordinations did take place in the past and, in fact, may even be called "normative" in the pre-Nicene Church.

THE CASE OF AMBROSE OF MILAN

The historical data regarding the early evolution of ordained ministry may be found in many publications from the beginning of this century to the present.[9] Within the Episcopal Church, some recent articles have summed up the historical material and spare us the repetition of that material here.[10] Instead of surveying the whole history of the issue, I want rather to take one specific and quite famous example from history, the ordination of Ambrose as bishop of Milan in December, 373. At the time of his election, although born into a Christian family at Trier, Germany, the thirty-five year old Ambrose had not yet been baptized. The case of Ambrose's consecration is probably the best known example of direct ordination, and with careful attention it offers us an excellent focus for reflection on the issue as it might commend itself for implementation in the Church today.

[8] This was the essence of the Cambridge Movement in the nineteenth century, which, in a complementary effort to the Oxford Movement, set forth rigid ideals for the architecture and appointments of church buildings based on idealized medieval models. The method of the leaders of the movement was highly eclectic, not to say idiosyncratic, and the architectural features thus conflated had never actually coincided in history. See Kenneth Clark, *The Gothic Revival* (New York: 1928), and James F. White, *The Cambridge Movement* (Cambridge: 1962).

[9] See, for example, T. M. Lindsay, *The Church and the Ministry in the Early Centuries* (London: 1903); H. B. Swete, ed., *Essays on the Early History of the Church and the Ministry* (London: 1918); K. E. Kirk, ed., The Apostolic Ministry, which includes the long essay of Gregory Dix cited above (183-303), and an essay by T. G. Talland on "The Doctrine of the Parity of Ministers" with a concluding note on "The Decline of the Diaconate" (305-349); both of these contain material of special relevance to our subject.

[10] See J. M. Barnett, "Direct Ordination and Catholic Order," *Diakoneo* 12 no. 5 (November 1990), and Ormonde Plater, "Direct Ordination: The Historical Evidence," *Open* 37, no. 4 (Winter 1992) 1-3.

The distinguished German liturgical scholar, Balthasar Fischer, also of Trier, Germany, has written a very useful article concerning Ambrose's ordination to the episcopate.[11] Fischer offers significant insight into the question of direct ordination by confronting the assumption, voiced by such well-known authors as F. H. Dudden, Gregory Dix, and Henry Chadwick, that Ambrose received a series of transitional ordinations during the week between his baptism and his ordination as bishop.[12] This assumption indicates the danger of reading backward into an earlier period a practice which dates from a much later time. Our information concerning these events comes from a document written about twenty-five years after the death of Ambrose, by his former secretary, Paulinus. The sentence concerning the events following the election of Ambrose and his episcopal ordination reads as follows:

"Baptizatus itaque fertus omnia ecclesiastica officia implesse, atque octavo die episcopus, ordinatus est summa gratia et laetitia cunctorum.[13]

"Upon being baptized he is said to have fulfilled all the ecclesiastical offices, and on the eighth day was ordained bishop with the greatest favor and joy of all."

In his biography of Ambrose, F. H. Dudden interpreted this sentence as referring to an intervening series of ordinations prior to that to the episcopate. Dudden writes that Ambrose

"was baptized on the 24th of November; he was apparently made to pass formally through the successive grades of the ministry;

[11] Balthasar Fischer, "Hat Ambrosius von Mailand in der Woche zwischen seiner Taufe und seiner Bischofskonsekration andere Weihe empfangen?" in *Kyriakon*, vol. 2, P. Granfield and J. A. Jungmann, eds. (Münster im Westfalen: Aschendorff, 1970) 527–531.

[12] F. H. Dudden, *The Life and Times of St. Ambrose* (Oxford: 1935) 72–74; Gregory Dix, "The Ministry in the Early Church," 284; H. Chadwick, *The Early Church* (London: 1967) 167. In the midst of otherwise useful material, Dix feels able to assert that "St. Ambrose, elected as a catechumen to the bishopric of Milan, received baptism and confirmation, the minor orders, diaconate, and presbyterate on successive days before receiving the episcopate."

[13] *Vita Ambrosii*, ed. M. Pellegrino (Rome: 1961) 9, 8–10, p. 62.

and finally on the eighth day after his baptism, that is, on Sunday, the 1st of December, A.D. 373, he was consecrated bishop."[14]

Dudden's words, "apparently made to pass," at least imply some doubt as to precisely what happened between the baptism and the episcopal ordination. In an extended note which need not be quoted here, Dudden spells out his interpretation of the sentence from the *Vita Ambrosii* in elaborate detail, reminding his readers of the second canon of the Council of Nicea "which prohibited ecclesiastical promotion without adequate probation," but he later admits that the quick sequence of ordinations according to his interpretation of Paulinus fulfilled the spirit of the canon in a merely formal way.[15] In another article, Professor Fischer makes an observation which is important for our consideration of these matters. He writes: "It is interesting to observe how a biographer of the quality of F. H. Dudden projects this formalism of the tenth century backward and discovers it in the fourth century in the career of Saint Ambrose."[16]

Since it is acknowledged that Ambrose was not even baptized at the time of his election, Dudden, Dix, and Chadwick do not take note of the then much more common practice of electing a lector or deacon directly to the episcopate. Rather than recognizing in Ambrose a special case of the latter practice, that is, a direct ordination from baptism to episcopate, the writers impose the later model of a long sequence of transitional ordinations. Such a sequence would not have been generally presupposed before about the tenth century. Of even greater concern to me, and relevant to our current reflections, is the failure to recognize the reciprocity between liturgical/sacramental practice, and theology. The assertion that the intermediary ordinations took place ignores the fact that such a practice would have been totally incompatible with the theological understanding of the nature of Holy Orders in the life of the Church at the time of Ambrose.

I have focused on the case of Ambrose because, first, of its notoriety as an example of direct ordination; and second, because

---

[14] Dudden, vol. 1, 68.

[15] Ibid., 72–74.

[16] Balthasar Fischer, "Esquisse historique sur les Ordres mineurs," *La Maison-Dieu* 61 (1960) 65.

of the importance of considering the issue in its own historical context with regard to how Holy Order was understood in relation to the nature of the Church at the time. Without such attention to the total picture, as Fisher points out, even a skilled writer such as F. H. Dudden is capable of reading the theological presuppositions of one era backward (or forward!) into another context. Unfortunately, Dudden's conjecture was picked up uncritically by others and thus entered the realm of commonly accepted opinion. This has only served to cloud and confuse the debate on direct ordination by feeding our discussion with both fact and fiction.

What Dudden did not appreciate regarding the nature of the Church at the time of Ambrose was its "organic" character with respect to the understanding of Holy Orders. Although Gregory Dix attributes this characteristic, as we observed earlier, only to the pre-Nicene Church, the facts indicate otherwise. Dix presumes a dramatic shift towards the pattern of sequential ordinations in the second half of the fourth century; he therefore follows Dudden's interpretation of the sentence from Paulinus' biography of Ambrose, and assumes that the candidate passed through a week of daily ordinations prior to his consecration as a bishop.[17]

In his useful summary of the historical evidence regarding direct ordination, Ormonde Plater says that the first known example of a man elected to the episcopate who was required to receive a rapid sequence of ordinations leading to the episcopate was Photius, when he was elected Patriarch of Constantinople in 858. It is generally recognized that from the election of Pope Gregory VII, in 1073, the sequential pattern became a normative expectation which was eventually established in canon law.[18] Thus, contrary to Dix, the idea of a fixed pattern of sequential ordinations was not a development of the later fourth century, but rather of the high Middle Ages. As Plater comments, "Throughout the ancient church, the episcopate usually followed years of service as an ordinary Christian, deacon, or presbyter."

THE ISSUE OF "ADEQUATE PROBATION"

This sorting out of the case of Ambrose permits us to assert with confidence that his ordination as bishop of Milan was an ex-

[17] Dix, 284.
[18] Plater, 1–2.

ample of direct ordination, and reflected a fulfillment of the community's discernment of the gifts of pastoral leadership. The case, however, cannot be taken as a blanket justification in our own time for direct ordination to become established as normative. As noted earlier, the second Nicene canon prohibited ecclesiastical promotion without adequate probation. Ambrose must have been aware of that canon, or at least have been imbued with its sense from personal observation. In his study of Ambrose, Hans von Campenhausen reminds us that the career of Ambrose prior to his election cannot be regarded as adequate preparation for high ecclesiastical office. At first Ambrose tried to avoid election, and later asked that his ordination be postponed.[19] This seems indicative on Ambrose's part of an awareness of a lack, to say the least, of "adequate probation." Certainly the spirit of the canon could not be seen as being fulfilled by submitting to a series of "purely formal" ordinations in the span of a week. More commonly, "adequate probation" was fulfilled through long and tested service in another ministry, most often the diaconate.

Adequate probation continues to be an appropriate expectation for those who present themselves for ordination. The question for us is whether adequate probation and a transitional diaconate are appropriately and fruitfully linked. Certainly a common view in the Episcopal Church is that the transitional diaconate is a period of apprenticeship, a time for practical pastoral experience without full pastoral responsibility, a time to learn from a mature and experienced priest in a hands-on situation. There is also the aspect of probation in that, albeit rarely, a person's time as deacon may be extended, even greatly extended, because of misgivings about their suitability for ordination at that time to the presbyterate. Even more rare, perhaps, but certainly a reality in my experience of over thirty years of contact with seminarians passing through the process, there are those persons who realize during their diaconate that they have not discerned their own vocational call correctly and choose not to move on to presbyteral ordination.

My own experience as a deacon has had a considerable influence upon my thinking about these matters. Having been or-

[19] Hans von Campenhausen, *Men Who Shaped the Western Church* (New York: 1965) 92.

dained a deacon three days earlier, I left my home diocese in Texas to begin pastoral work as a missionary in the Diocese of Puerto Rico. I was immediately given pastoral responsibility for three small missions in the mountains of Puerto Rico. I realized quickly that the ministry I was needed for (and hence "called to") in that situation was the full sacramental ministry of the presbyterate. I was a deacon canonically, but pastorally I was a "prepriest." My work full time was the normal pastoral ministry of a parish priest, except that I was not authorized to celebrate the central sacramental signs. For that, the nearest priest, who served a cluster of missions in the next mountain range, would come over as time permitted, celebrate the Eucharist in one of my mission stations, and leave me abundantly supplied with a ciborium full of consecrated hosts.

The problems with this model, or with similar variations on it which can be found in this country today without looking overseas, are numerous and serious. I was obliged on many occasions to give Communion outside the normal context of a celebration of the Eucharist, and thus to propagate a deprived model of Eucharistic celebration. In a culture with a strong rooting in Eucharistic piety, to have substituted Morning Prayer during the months prior to my ordination to the presbyterate would have shown a serious disrespect for the piety of the people. But the solution, since there were six mission stations in that mountain area, was to meet the expectation of Eucharist on Sunday with a deprived model of celebration. Further, it required my neighboring priest to leave the normal pastoral context of his own regular sacramental ministry to become something of a "sacrament machine" for the communities I was serving. One may say that I was being given "adequate probation" in that my first year was an engagement with ordained ministry not unlike a baptism by fire, but this was at a serious cost to the integrity of the sacramental signs. Baptism and Eucharist are not commodities to be made available by an ordained supplier; they are the basic faith-actions of Christian identity and are most fully expressive of their meaning when celebrated within a community in the context of consistent pastoral care.[20]

[20] See H.-M. Legrand, "The Presidency of the Eucharist According to the Ancient Tradition," in *Living Bread, Saving Cup,* ed. R. K. Seasoltz (College-

It would be a mistake to dismiss this example as an anomaly from the mission field. In three decades with seminarians, I have been regularly asked to supply guidelines for about-to-be-ordained transitional deacons who will be in similar situations to that described above and who will be obliged to officiate at "a deacon's Mass." The situation suggests that our pattern itself is awry: we are ordaining people and sending them into pastoral situations to which their transitional diaconate is inappropriate to the needs of the community.

Earlier in this century it was more common for the newly ordained deacon to serve as a curate in a parish with a rector and perhaps other priests on the staff. In such situations, it was, of course, rare for the scheduling of "a deacon's Mass" to be necessary. Again, based on years of observation and close contact with former students, this period as a transitional deacon was often a time of treading water, a time of feeling rather useless, while awaiting ordination to the priesthood. In their experience, these deacons felt like "prepriests," often quite misunderstood by some members of the congregation who would express confusion at the coming of a second ordination. This time of waiting, frequently reduced to six months to shorten the candidate's ordeal, was often experienced as a time of suspension, a ministry without focus. Adequate probation is certainly an important and needed testing of the capacity and gifts to fulfill the ministry to which one is called. But the model as I have often seen it in practice, with deacons as curates, has seldom dealt very effectively with that purpose. There must be other ways to achieve adequate probation than to use a formalistic transition through an "inferior" order merely to fulfill the letter of the law.

It would be absurd to suggest that all transitional deacons who have served as curates have had the anomalous type of experience

---

ville: The Liturgical Press, 1982) 196–221. Legrand offers an illuminating discussion of the origins of sacramental leadership in the Church, and sees this as a public expression of the shared signs of faith under the leadership (or "presidency") of the one who oversees the general pastoral care of the community. To preside at the Eucharist is thus not an expression of power but rather an articulation through words and signs of the underlying commitment of pastoral responsibility. The ordained priest on this view is not some kind of sacramental studhorse who makes sacred commodities available!

which I had during my six months as a deacon. For some, the transitional period may serve a fruitful purpose in engaged pastoral experience, in accomplishing the legitimate need for adequate probation. But again, does the person need to be an ordained deacon for these goals to be achieved? Two obvious solutions have often been suggested by a variety of writers: first, that seminarians might be ordained to the diaconate for the whole of their final year of study, and second, that persons ordained to the diaconate with the expectation of later ordination to the presbyterate would nevertheless serve in the order of deacon for a substantial length of time, say, two or three years. I have had the opportunity to observe both these models at close hand. In the midwest it was fairly common for certain bishops to ordain their candidates in the first semester of the final year, and thus to permit them a rather full experience of diaconal ministry both in the daily liturgical life of the seminary and also in the larger scope of pastoral ministry in parishes where they worked on weekends. There is no question in my mind that, given the canonical requirements inherent in sequential ordination, this system at least permitted a vigorous experience of diaconate. As to the second, the substantial lengthening of the term of the diaconate, this did not, in the cases I know, solve the problem of being caught up in getting on to the priesthood. It merely lengthened the process.

Adequate probation remains an appropriate concern of the Church for those who are called to leadership. In most dioceses, however, we already have the elements of a system other than diaconate which serves the goal of adequate probation, and might serve it better if it were seen as a whole ordered toward that purpose. From the time a person expresses the idea that he or she might have a call to ordination, some form of scrutiny begins and then takes more formal shape during postulancy and candidacy. The years in seminary (or in some other program of academic formation) clearly expand the opportunities for probation, and might serve this purpose more fruitfully if greater cooperation between the Commission on Ministry and the seminary faculty might be fostered. A curacy with an experienced priest who has been trained to develop particular skills for this type of cooperative ministry could be an invaluable complement to all that went before, but there is certainly no reason evident to me why a person who has arrived at the point of serving as a curate needs to be a transitional deacon. What we have in practice is an almost accidental joining of two elements which show no integral reason to be linked.

"ONCE A DEACON . . ."

Whenever the subject of direct ordination is raised, it is, in my experience, almost inevitable that someone—usually a priest—will say, "Once a deacon, always a deacon." I want to know where and when this phrase was first uttered. It is clearly the fruit not only of a sequential pattern of ordination, but also of a model of ordination in which a "higher" order swallows up a "lower" order. The latter phenomenon is not necessarily inherent in a sequential pattern in itself; a deacon of many years might be elected bishop on the basis of the testing of the gifts which had taken place during the earlier and distinct, but not necessarily inferior, ministry as a deacon.

The "once a deacon" idea has contributed to an abusive liturgical practice in which a member of one order vests in the liturgical vesture of another order. This is seen most often when a priest assists another priest who is presiding at the Eucharist. All too frequently, instead of being what he or she is, namely, an assisting priest, this person will cross the stole in the style of a deacon, or even, in some places, wear a dalmatic. When questioned about this, the person will explain that they are not really a deacon, but are serving as "the liturgical deacon." Then comes the inevitable refrain: "After all, once a deacon, always a deacon."

This strikes me as an example of an appalling trivialization of an outward symbol (a vestment) which does not correspond to the interior reality. It would be wise to remember that both the Orthodox and Roman Catholic Churches canonically inhibit a minister of one order from wearing the vesture of another order. Since Anglicans claim to share with those two traditions a concern for the maintenance of the threefold pattern of ordained ministry, even a slight degree of humility would suggest that these traditions understand vesture not merely as a surface decoration, but rather as corresponding to the reality of the person's place in the community. This is not a liturgical charade.

The seriousness of this seemingly trivial occurrence can perhaps be brought home with an explicit example which throws the issue into a deeper perspective. Let us assume that a priest is vested as a deacon for a celebration of the Eucharist at which he or she will assist the presider. A parishioner comes up and says, "I would like to take a few minutes before the celebration to make a confession." Does the priest-vested-as-deacon respond, "I can't right now because I am in the person of a deacon," or perhaps, "You're welcome to make your confession, so long as you're happy with a Declaration of Forgiveness instead of a full-scale Absolution," or even, "Yes, if you can give me a moment to shift my stole"? The example is somewhat humorous and perhaps unlikely, but it does make the point: as an ordained person, what am I really? Even if I have undergone two ordinations, which ordination defines my "place" in the community of faith? My ministry is, for the sake of its integrity, defined by that identity established by the ordination out of which my ministry is most distinctively exercised. These identities are not masks to be alternated back and forth. My ordination establishes who I am in a lived relationship with the ecclesial community.

These comments alone are sufficient to reveal the anomaly of a brief transitional diaconate en route to the presbyterate. For those called to the presbyterate, the diaconate is not the "place," the personal context, in which that person's vocation within the community will be lived out. And, at least as importantly, for those called to the diaconate, the definition and ecclesial recognition of their "place," their personal context, is made much more difficult by its being cluttered up by short-term, perhaps confused or resentful, "prepriestly" transients.

As a justification for maintaining the sequential pattern, it has been suggested by Robert Wright and others that a required ordination to the diaconate (for those called to presbyterate or episcopate) constitutes "an endorsement that the basis for all ordained ministry is service." When applied to the question of direct ordination, this leads to the idea that without ordination to the diaconate, a person would lose this dimension of the nature of ministry. Yet Wright himself says that the idea that service is the basis of all ordained ministry begins "for all the people of God in

Baptism."[21] It seems to me that this latter phrase is the key to the issue. The call to servanthood begins at baptism, and it is the shared vocation of every Christian to live out that servanthood in ways appropriate to our individual lives.

From within that Christian society of servants, those who are called to be deacons, priests, or bishops clearly continue to be called to a life of *diakonia* in ways appropriate to their vocation, but all three orders are called to live out those ministries on the basis of the common baptismal vocation to service. The error, I believe, is to place a particular emphasis upon the deacon as the sole witness to this shared character, and thus to fall into a confusion between *diakonia* (service), and *diakonos* (deacon). This confusion is, I believe, at the heart of the adage, "Once a deacon, always a deacon." Behind this phrase lies the certain truth that servanthood is a fundamental imperative for the Christian person, and that often the deacon has, in selfless service, reminded others of that common vocation. But such service has by no means always been a characteristic of all deacons, who are sometimes as prone as many others, both lay and ordained, to playing power games in the Church. The assertion by priests of their continuing identity as deacons does not inoculate priests against the danger of ignoring in practice the servanthood they are claiming in principle. The order of *diakonos*, of deacon, is a specific, designated ministry whose distinct character we are painfully trying to discover anew for our time. *Diakonia*, or service, on the other hand, is a basic aspect of the vocation of every Christian in the image of the one who said, "I am among you as one who serves." It is not univocally the characteristic of one order, but rather the common ground for all forms of Christian ministry.

WHAT KIND OF CHURCH?

From all that has been said above, it would seem that I am leading toward a passionate call for the abolition of sequential ordinations and the adoption of direct ordination as soon as possible.

---

[21] J. R. Wright, "Sequential or Cumulative Orders vs. Direct Ordination," *Anglican Theological Review* 75 (1993) 249. See the recent response to Wright: John St. H. Gibault, "Sequential Ordination in Historical Perspective: A Response to J. Robert Wright," *Anglican Theological Review* 77 (1995) 367–391.

But that is not the case. Certainly it is already evident that I find no historical or theological barrier to the modification of canons which would permit direct ordination in those unusual circumstances in which the electing community discerned in a person the gifts for a particular ordained ministry. In such a case, the trivialization of the transitional diaconate through a rapid sequence of ordinations is too obvious an anomaly to need discussion here. We already have enough experience with the six-month diaconate to make us aware of the problem.

On the other hand, while we are becoming aware of the practice of direct ordination during the early centuries of Christianity, as in the case of Ambrose, we must not overlook the concern during that same period for adequate probation. We would have accomplished little with the abolition of the transitional diaconate if all that we achieved was an even more weakened pattern for the scrutiny of candidates for the presbyterate. Stewardship of the Church regarding the testing of candidates for ordination is a primary obligation of the Church's leadership. If, as I have suggested, the transitional diaconate is not often well-suited to the task of testing for priesthood, then the challenge is all the greater for us to develop a pattern of probation that is more effective.

A further concern I have about a precipitous decision is one which I share with Robert Wright concerning the ecumenical aspects of this question.[22] As Professor Wright notes, the issue of the ordination of women has already contributed to a very stressful ecumenical context. The way ahead on the issue of direct ordination, it would seem to me, is to have the issue made an intentional agenda item in Anglican dialogues with both Roman Catholics and the Eastern Orthodox. Since we share with them the tradition of the threefold pattern of Holy Orders, should we not explore with them a question which is an aspect of our common heritage regarding ordination? The historical evidence is remarkably well documented, and it seems that such direct ordinations as we see in history do not present problems about validity. No one is saying that Ambrose's ordination, for example, was invalid, even though a similar direct ordination today would not be permitted by the canons and would not be licit. Perhaps we could

[22] Ibid., no. 3, 248–249.

engage in an ecumenical conversation which would result in changes in the canonical norms, that would once again allow for direct ordination in our various traditions.

This issue has arisen within the Episcopal Church because of a deepened awareness of the relation of all particular vocations to the common life of the baptized. This suggests to me that the underlying question is ecclesiological: what kind of Church do we want to be? We do not, of course, have complete control of that, but our decisions and choices all contribute to the shaping of the life of the Church in which we find ourselves. When I think of the Church which Gregory Dix referred to as "organic," I find it profoundly attractive, a Church which manifests a mutuality within the fabric of a common life, in which the chief characteristic of the leadership is service rather than power. But we carry our whole history, and much of the hierarchical experience of Christianity still lives on in us, in our structures and traditions. We need to engage the issue of direct ordination in this larger context, as one aspect of the more fundamental question: as the People of God, what Church are we *called* to be?

Within a fixed system of ordination theory, the only question that can be asked in response to proposed change is, "What has been done in the past?" But when the issue is seen in the context of the nature of the Church and the baptismal foundation of all ministry, then the horizon expands so that past heritage and present imperatives may work in counterpoint as a source of new insight. In this way, there is an ongoing evolution of the Christian tradition as a living testimony to God's continual leading of the Church in new situations for which the answers of the past alone may be inadequate. We can see this process at work not only among Anglicans but also in the larger ecumenical context with regard to the ordination of women. The ecumenical context is also important for the issue of direct ordination, and it will be a major influence upon any policies we may shape. It will involve conversation among the traditions of Christianity who share the common heritage of the threefold ministry, even when that relation is impaired by institutional separation; and it may also involve conversation with nonepiscopal traditions, which may offer complementary insights from within quite different approaches to questions of ordained ministry.

Bryan D. Spinks

11. "Freely by His Grace": Baptismal Doctrine and the Reform of the Baptismal Liturgy in the Church of Scotland, 1953-1994

INTRODUCTION

In 1929, with the reunion of the United Free Church of Scotland (itself a union between the United Church of Scotland and the Free Church of Scotland in 1900) with the Church of Scotland, the major rifts within the Scottish Presbyterian tradition were formally healed. There were theological differences, but in ethos rather than substance, and mainly related to the status of the Established Church, and, arguably, the doctrine of the Atonement. As regards baptism, however, both Churches broadly shared the Presbyterian inheritance of the Reformation. Infant baptism was the norm and promises were made by the parents, based on covenant theology. The two uniting Churches had each issued liturgies in 1928 and 1929 for the guidance of ministers, though the liturgical freedom allowed by "Knox's" *Book of Common Order* 1562 had become almost a dogma after the 1644 *Directory*, and was steadfastly maintained by ministers as a "Reformation heritage."

In 1940 the Church of Scotland issued a new *Book of Common Order* for ministers. Its baptismal rite was carefully modelled on previous rites of the two uniting Churches, together with material from the influential *Euchologion* of the Church Service Society.[1] The rite itself seems to have caused little stir. Reflecting Reforma-

---

[1] For details of the baptismal rites in pre-1940 liturgical compilations, see W. D. Bailie, "The Rites of Baptism and Admission of Catechumens according to the Liturgy and History of the Church of Scotland," Unpublished Ph.D. thesis, Queen's University, Belfast, 1959.

tion covenant theology of baptism, specific promises were required of the parents rather than godparents, and their commitment to the Christian faith was assumed. However, The Act of Assembly 1933, vii, stated: "A child has a right to Baptism (1) whose parents, one or both, having been themselves baptized, profess the Christian religion, or (2) who, being of unknown parentage or otherwise separated from its parents, is under Christian care and guardianship."

The words "profess the Christian religion" were widely interpreted, from meaning communicants in good standing to simply desiring the child to be baptised. In an effort to clarify the intention of this Act, a new Act was passed in 1951, but this proved capable of just as many different interpretations. As a direct result of a request from the Presbytery of Glasgow in 1953, a Special Commission was appointed to guide thought and study, and allow the Church to find theological agreement and uniform practice. It is the purpose of this study to review the reports of this Special Commission, and that of the subsequent Panel on Doctrine, and to examine the resulting revisions of the baptismal rite. For the sake of convenience it is useful to divide the forty-year period into two: From 1953 to 1979, and from 1980 to 1994.

I. 1953–1979

The Special Commission first met in Edinburgh on October 27, 1953. Consisting of twenty-five members, its Convener was Professor T. F. Torrance and the Secretary was John Heron.[2] The way of

[2] The original list of members was as follows: The Revs. Professor T. F. Torrance, D. Cairns, D. Baillie, I. Henderson; the Revs. J. MacInnes, G. S. Gunn, J. Wilson Baird, R. S. Wallace, D.G.M. Mackay, J.S.M'Ewen, D.H.S. Read, D.F.S. Dick, R. S. Louden, T. D. Stewart Brown, H. C. Donaldson, G. F. Cox, William Barclay, Johnston R.M'Kay, John Heron, Ian A. Muirhead, J.A.M'Fadden, W.C.V. Smith; and James Adair Esq., J. R. Philip Esq. and G. Grant Esq.

Professor T. F. Torrance explains: "However, quite a few of these resigned or fell away, but we were given powers by the Assembly to add to it numbers of people of different types—"biblical and patristic scholars, Ministers of experience as Foreign Missionaries, Ministers at large in Scotland, and laymen expert in the fields of education and youth work. . . . The hard working core, however, came from those who were connected in some way or other with the Scottish Church Society, the Church Service Society, the Scottish

proceeding, if the task was to be thorough, was to compile and present to the General Assembly a series of "Interim" reports. The first of these appeared in 1955, and the final report appeared in 1962. In practice much of the drafting was in the hands of the Convener for whom it could be claimed that he was not only the Church of Scotland's leading theologian, but also the United Kingdom's, and whose knowledge of historical theology was probably unsurpassed; indeed, a "Torrance flavour" to these reports is not too difficult to discern.[3]

(1) 1955 Interim Report:
The New Testament Doctrine of Baptism[4]

This interim report was prefaced by what the Commission regarded as the four-fold task ahead. Since the Church of Scotland was in the Reformed tradition, then the study of scriptural teaching about baptism was necessary "in order that the doctrine and practice of the Church may have a solid Biblical foundation." There would also need to be a thorough examination of the Scottish tradition and its Reformed roots. These researches must then form the basis of a constructive formulation of the doctrine of baptism. Guidance of the Spirit would be needed to put the results into readily understood language, and its application to the life of the Church. This preface served notice that the Special Commission was determined to do a thorough survey, and that no quick summary was to be expected.

Since the Reformed tradition places importance on the authority of Scripture, this report on the New Testament was to form the cornerstone of the whole task, and thus needs to be considered at some length.

Church Theology Society, and particularly from those who were connected in some way or other with the Scottish Journal of Theology." I am grateful to Professor Torrance for this information (letter February 12, 1993). For some unknown reason the names of the Commissioners were not recorded in the *Reports to the General Assembly.*

[3] Cf. T. F. Torrance, "The Sacrament of Baptism," in *Conflict and Agreement in the Church*, vol. 2. The Ministry and the Sacraments of the Gospel. (London: Lutterworth Press, 1960); "The One Baptism Common to Christ and His Church," in *Theology in Reconciliation*, (London: Geoffrey Chapman, 1975); *The Mediation of Christ*, 2nd ed. (Edinburgh: T & T Clark, 1992).

[4] *Reports to the General Assembly* (Hereafter *RGA*) 1955, 609ff.

The opening pages considered the then current position of biblical studies, with such names as A. M. Hunter, W. Manson, Hoskyns and Davey, Matthew Black and Kittel, and (common in this era of "biblical theology," but much qualified in more recent scholarship) contrasted the Hebraic and Hellenistic minds. At this stage, however, the report stated: "The doctrine of Baptism is grounded in the Person and Work of Christ. What He was, what He taught, and what He did are the facts that determine and shape the Sacrament of Baptism and give it its significance."[5]

These words actually sum up the entire work of the Commission: the doctrine of Baptism was given a firm Christological basis, and the one baptism of Christ and its salvific implications were to be the hermeneutical key to unlock subsequent discussion.

Next the institution of baptism was considered, and here its Trinitarian dimension was stressed. At the Jordan the Word of the Father is heard addressing the Son; the Spirit of God descends upon him, confirming his Sonship. Thus baptism into the name of Christ and baptism into the name of the Trinity are alternative ways of referring to the same thing. The report also seized upon the New Testament use of *baptisma* rather than *baptismos*, suggesting that it is similar to kerygma, and describes an event of God. The word refers not only to the rite in water, but the sacrificial death of Christ: "The Baptisma of which the New Testament speaks is the *One Baptism* of vicarious sacrifice on the Cross." Appealing to J.A.T. Robinson, the report asserted: "In the New Testament the Sacrament of Baptism and the Vicarious Baptism of Christ are spoken of so indivisibly that it is impossible to distinguish what has been done for us by the Cross and resurrection and what by the Sacrament of that Baptism."[6]

The section dealing with baptism in the Apostolic Church spoke of the Spirit bringing redemption and creation together, and that on the rite of baptism argued that it was an act of obedience of initiation into the new covenant. Jewish proselytes baptized themselves, but children were baptized by someone. In Christian baptism all are baptized in the manner of children. Baptism is also in the Name. This means that baptism is into the sphere where the

[5] *RGA* 1955, 611.
[6] *RGA* 1955, 618; cf. J.A.T. Robinson in *Scottish Journal of Theology* 6 (1953) 257–274.

mighty acts of God in the incarnation, birth, life, death, resurrection, and ascension are operative for our salvation.

"This does not mean, of course, that the Sacrament of Baptism automatically saves us, but that it places us in Christ, where His death and resurrection are operative, though we may fall away from Him with terrible consequences (1 Corinthians 10:1-12). Baptism requires the response of faith, and a whole life of faith, for we cannot be saved without faith; yet Baptism tells us that it is not our faith that saves us but Christ Himself alone."[7]

Infant baptism was defended, appealing to Acts 2:38, the promise to you "and your children," and on the grounds that baptism is not the sacrament of our repentance, nor our faith, but of God's adoption and His promise of the Spirit.

The strong Christological approach of this report was further strengthened in a section on "The Apostolic Interpretation of Baptism." Here baptism is described as a sacrament of the incarnation:

"In the actual administration of Baptism by the Apostolic Church the candidates descended into the waters and after being immersed in them in death, they ascended out of them in resurrection to newness of life. That language of descent and ascent described the descent of Christ into the death of the Cross and His ascent out of it in His resurrection, but it was also used to describe the descent of the Son of God into our mortal humanity and His ascent in our resurrected humanity to the right hand of God the Father Almighty. Thus behind Baptism into Jesus Christ lies the whole Incarnation and Ascension of the Son of God, spoken of as the Descent and Ascent of the Son of Man (for example, in John 3:13; Ephesians 4:9f.).

"Ultimately the Sacrament of Baptism is grounded in the Incarnation, in which the Eternal Son of God immersed Himself in our mortal humanity and assumed it into oneness with Himself that He might heal it and through the whole course of His obedience reconcile us to God."[8]

[7] RGA 1955, 626.
[8] RGA 1955, 637.

The report also explored baptism as common to Christ and the Church, as participation in the Mystery of Christ, and in his death and resurrection, as well as a cleansing in the blood of Christ.

The final section of the report was headed "The Formulation of the Doctrine of Baptism." It concluded that there are two primary and related issues involved which needed further elucidation: (a) The relation between God's Covenant faithfulness and our faith; and (b) the Christological pattern of the doctrine.

With regard to (a) the report argued for an analogy between creation and baptism. Creation is by God's Word, and God also calls humans into a responsible relationship. It was not of our choosing that we were born and made in the image of God to respond to Him, but we cannot disclaim that responsibility. In baptism we are re-created, and summoned to confess his name. However, this takes place within the context of the biblical witness that while God keeps truth and faith with humans, they in turn are unfaithful. Thus our salvation does not depend on our faithfulness, else who would be saved? The ground of baptism is not our faith but the faithfulness of Christ. In him God has kept covenant and faith with His people and the promise is to us and to our children. "Baptism is not therefore a Sacrament of our faith, or a Sacrament of our repentance or our experience of Christ, but a Sacrament of the gospel, a Sacrament in which salvation is bestowed upon us from beyond us by pure grace."[9] In baptism Christ stands surety for us.

There followed a crucial discussion on covenant, where a distinction was made between the Old and New dispensations. While in the Old Covenant our approach is on the basis of God's demand, in the New Testament our approach is on the basis of what God has done for us in Jesus Christ. In subsequent reports the development of Federal Theology and the idea of a bilateral covenant would be seen as a distortion of the New Testament faith and the authentic (Genevan rather than Zurich and South Germany) Reformed theology. Baptism here is understood as a sacrament of pure free grace, without condition. As to the need for a response, this was acknowledged, but the report pointed out that in the New Testament Jesus demanded different levels of response from

[9] *RGA* 1955, 658.

different individuals, and from some he demanded none at all. "We can be sure that He does act in Baptism and will act precisely as he acted during His ministry in Judea and Galilee sometimes requiring prior faith, sometimes acting through the faith of parent or even master, and sometimes without any prior response to His Word of re-creation and blessing and peace."[10] A final warning was given against trying to divide in the sacrament what was the act of God and what was a human act.

Since this report was to be the cornerstone of the Commission's work, it was perhaps no surprise that it was re-written and published in book form under the title *The Biblical Doctrine of Baptism* in 1958. The earlier material was simplified and rearranged, but there is no change in emphasis: baptism is related to the new humanity brought into being by the incarnation, and it is related to the Christ's self-offering of an obedient life:

"Our salvation ultimately depends upon something other than our faithfulness within the covenant relationship: that would be a salvation by works, and who then would be saved? To be baptized is to be baptized out of self and into another, into Christ. It is He who saves us, and He alone. The ground of Baptism is therefore not our faith, but the faithfulness of Christ."[11]

However, more attention was now given to the place of human faith—of the recipient, the congregation, parents, and child. Faith is itself a gift of God, and it is faith in a promise which lies in the future. The faith of the congregation provides an atmosphere of faith analogous to that in which some of Jesus' miracles took place; the parents' faith is important because of their influence on the child; and just as from its early days a child responds to stimuli, particularly that of a mother's love, so a child can respond to God.

In this elucidation we see a response to a criticism of the 1955 report as being too free with grace, and ignoring the New Testament concern for faith. However, although giving more space to human faith, the book made no concessions to semi-pelagianism or Federalism:

[10] *RGA* 1955, 660.
[11] *The Biblical Doctrine of Baptism*, (Edinburgh: Saint Andrew Press, 1958) 58.

"All these responses of faith, however, are genuine only in so far as they share in the faith of Jesus Christ, 'the faithful AMEN of man to God.' This is the language used in the New Testament of Christ and His response, rather than of us and of our response. Baptism in the setting of the One Baptism reminds us that we have no answer to God except the answer of Christ Himself: "Nothing in my hand I bring. Simply to Thy Cross I cling." He died for us, and it is on that ground alone that we are baptized and call upon the name of the Lord. Jesus Christ is not only the revelation of the faithfulness of God, on which we have rightly laid such emphasis: He as man, in perfect obedience even unto the death of the cross, made the only adequate response of faith to the faithfulness of the Heavenly Father. When the Holy Spirit was given on the day of Pentecost, all who received the promised Baptism of the Spirit were incorporated into the body of Christ, so that His faith became theirs. Every child received in Baptism into that same body becomes a sharer in the faith of Christ. This is why S. Paul can say: 'Yet not I, but Christ liveth in me.' His faith *is* Christ's faith."[12]

(2) *The Interim Reports 1956–1963*

The subsequent interim reports—all substantial and valuable pieces of work in their own right—mapped out the key stages in the subsequent history of the Church, and particularly its development with the Scottish Presbyterian tradition. All developments were tested against the findings of the New Testament doctrine. Only a brief summary of these reports can be given here.

(a) The 1956 report looked at the early Church, including the influence of Judaism and Hellenism, and writers such as Athanasius, Leo, and Ephraim. These particular writers were regarded as being in harmony with the thrust of New Testament doctrine. It was stressed that "regeneration" in the New Testament refers to what had already happened in the incarnation and which will not be final until the Parousia. An Epiphany Hymn attributed to Ephraim was quoted with approval:

"His birth flowed on and was joined to His Baptism,
His Baptism again flowed on to his Death.

[12] Ibid., 61–62.

His Death led on and reached to His Rising.
He made of these four a bridge to His Kingdom,
And lo, His sheep pass over behind Him."[13]

Observing that the Fathers grounded baptism not just upon
Romans 6 but also Ephesians, Galatians, and the Johannine teachings, the report noted:

"The modern doctrine of Baptism, which often rests almost exclusively on the death and resurrection of Christ and is understood as a dying and rising with Him, tends to make of the
Sacrament of Baptism a rite of timeless significance, abstracted
from the actual historical events of the life of Jesus."[14]

(b) The report of 1957 considered baptism in the medieval West
and the Reformation, and included Augustine, Lombard, Aquinas
and the Schoolmen, Luther, Calvin, and the Anglican tradition.
As regards Calvin, the report found that for him "Baptism is essentially the sacrament of what Christ has done for the Church,
and must be celebrated as a corporate sacrament in the midst of
the Church."[15] Infant baptism was perceived as more clearly
representing that the promise of God precedes all faith, and that
faith can only follow and depend on that prior promise.

(c) The 1958 report concerned itself with the Scottish tradition
from the thirteenth-century Statutes of the Diocese of Aberdeen,
and John Major (who is alleged to have influenced Calvin)
through the Scottish tradition to the nineteenth century. Knox and
the Scots' Confession are regarded as continuing the Biblical doctrine. Thus Knox wrote that "the effect and signification of Baptism is that, of His free grace, we are received in the household of
God." But a gradual distortion of the classical Reformed doctrine
was detected at some points in John Craig, John Davidson, and
Robert Bruce; more drastic distortion was discovered in the writings of Robert Rollick, Robert Boyd, and John Forbes. Notions of
feeling were introduced, together with a division between justification and sanctification, and the importance of a life of good
works. Ultimately the older Covenant Theology developed into full

[13] *RGA* 1956, 636.
[14] *RGA* 1956, 638.
[15] *RGA* 1957, 683.

226

blown Federal Theology with a pronounced emphasis on experiential faith and personal covenanting.

(d) The report of 1959 covered the various strands of theology in the fragmented Presbyterian Church in Scotland. Principal David Cairns is cited from the United Presbyterian tradition, Andrew Bonar, James Bannerman and James Candlish from the Free Church, and Principal Dewar, Thomas Crawford, and Wotherspoon and Kirkpatrick from the Church of Scotland.

(e) In 1961 a further report summed up the response from the Presbyteries, pinpointing certain tensions and outlining a theology of baptism in the light of the discussions. It also made suggestions for altering the rite in the 1940 *Book of Common Order,* and proposed that a new Act of Assembly be passed.

(f) In 1962 the report of 1961 was slightly revised, and set out with a new Act of Assembly. This latter—Act XVII—was concerned with infant baptism, and stated that in all cases one of the parents must themselves have been baptized and must have professed the Christian faith, and understood to give or allow the Christian upbringing of the child. The Act was passed in 1963. The report of 1962 was reprinted in 1966 as representing the Church of Scotland's mind on Baptism.[16]

(3) From Lex Credendi to Lex Orandi: *A failure of Nerve?*

It is possible to identify several key theological emphases or concerns which ran through these various interim reports and which serve as a unifying thread.

(i) Christology is the hermeneutical key to the meaning of the sacrament of baptism. This is found—albeit with different approaches—in a number of modern theologians, such as Schillebeeckx, Rahner and, arguably, Karl Barth. Such an approach (which some might regard as Christomonism) contrasts with the Reformed Scholastic tradition which made covenant, or in its more pronounced form, Federalism, the setting for baptism. In the latter it tended to be regarded as an adjunct to assurance of faith and the duties of the covenant.

(ii) The Christology is the high Christology of neo-orthodoxy, "from above." Here is Barth's Christ as the Divine Word, the second person of the Trinity, the Son of God who journeys into a far

---

[16] *The Doctrine of Baptism,* (Edinburgh: Saint Andrew Press, 1966).

227

country, and the exaltation of the Son. There is a stress on the vicarious life and death, and resurrection and ascension. Here God incarnate acts for us and in our place. The *katabasis* of God is balanced by the *anabasis* of humanity.[17]

(iii) The grace of God in the work of Christ, and therefore in baptism, is stressed. Some might see this as advocating "cheap grace," though the reports make it clear that grace was bought at a great cost on the part of God, but which he freely gives. There is a concern to stress justification by faith through grace, in Christ, and offered in baptism. Any demand for prior faith as a necessary prerequisite is to be regarded as synergism.

(iv) The reports take the side of the "Calvin against the Calvinists" school. As in Karl Barth and subsequent writers such as J. B. Torrance, Holmes Rolston III, and M. Charles Bell, the development of Covenant Theology in the Heidelberg theologians and the later Federalists (Robert Rollock being a connecting link) was regarded not as a *development* of Calvin, but as a *distortion*. The emphases of Federalism were seen as ultimately undermining the grace which is offered prior to human commitment and response.[18]

[17] Karl Barth, *Church Dogmatics* IV/1; T. F. Torrance, "The Mind of Christ in Worship. The Problem of Apollinarianism in the Liturgy" in *Theology in Reconciliation;* "Athanasius: A Study in the Foundations of Classical Theology," in ibid.; *Space Time and Incarnation,* (London: Oxford University Press, 1969); *The Mediation of Christ; The Trinitarian Faith,* (Edinburgh: T & T Clark, 1988).

[18] Karl Barth, *Church Dogmatics* IV/1. T. F. Torrance, *Kingdom and Church* Oliver and Boyd, Edinburgh, 1956; J. B. Torrance, "Covenant or Contract? A Study of the Theological Background of Worship in Seventeenth Century Scotland," *Scottish Journal of Theology* 23 (1970) 51–64; Holmes Rolston III, *John Calvin Versus the Westminster Confession,* (Richmond: John Knox Press, 1972); M. Charles Bell, *Calvin and Scottish Theology,* (Edinburgh: The Handsel Press, 1985); John Von Rohr, *The Covenant of Grace in Puritan Thought,* (Atlanta: Scholars Press, 1986); D. A. Weir, *The Origins of the Federal Theology in Sixteenth-Century Reformation Thought,* (Oxford: Clarendon Press, 1990); Richard Muller, *Christ and the Decree,* (Grand Rapids: Baker Book House, 1988). See also Andrew A. Wolsey, "Unity and Continuity in Covenantal Thought: A Study in the Reformed Tradition to the Westminster Assembly," Ph.D. thesis, University of Glasgow, 1988.

This is a highly complex debate, including Aristotelian method in Beza, double versus single predestination, unilateral or bilateral covenant, and limited Atonement. The two extremes in the debate seem to be R. T. Kendall, *Calvin and English Calvinism to 1649,* (Oxford: Oxford University Press, 1969), and

It is not the intention of this essay to scrutinize the Special Commission's Biblical doctrine or whether the reports gave fair treatment to Federal Theology.[19] Some of the sharp contrasts drawn in the earlier reports were mitigated in the revised texts of 1961-62, though one might suggest that as regards the vicarious work of Christ and grace, the views of John Mcleod Campbell, deposed from the ministry of the Church of Scotland in 1831, find here considerable vindication![20] However, the suggestion made in the final report that the new Act adequately expressed the practical implications of the reports is difficult to substantiate. It is true that the final report stated that the Church may baptize only where the Gospel is proclaimed and believed, and only within the community where the mighty acts of God in Christ are effectively operative through the Word and Spirit. However, the whole thrust of the reports was that baptism is an expression of free grace, and is unconditional, though it calls forth a response. The new Act seemed little more than a reiteration of the earlier Acts. The question to be addressed here, however, is how the theology of the reports could be expressed liturgically; how could this stress on vertical divine grace be expressed in the horizontal human rite?

The 1959 report had identified both an objective and subjective element in the baptismal rite in the *Presbyterian Forms of Service* 1891 of the United Presbyterian tradition; in *A New Directory for Public Worship of God* 1898 and *Directory and Forms for Public Worship* 1909 of the Free Church the emphasis was not so much on the divine action in baptism as on the act of the parents in presenting the child, and the act of the congregation receiving the child into membership of the Church. The Church of Scotland's *Prayers for Divine Service*, authorized by the General Assembly in 1923, and the *Book of Common Order* 1928 of the United Free Church reflected the influence of the more superficial liberal theology of the post-

---

Paul Helm, *Calvin and the Calvinists*, (Edinburgh: Banner of Truth Trust, 1982), both of whom have been criticized for quoting out of context.

[19] See above for the literature and see Woolsey for a defence of Federalism.

[20] Christian D. Kettler, *The Vicarious Humanity of Christ and the Reality of Salvation*, (Lanham and London: University of America Press, 1991); J. B. Torrance, "The Contribution of McLeod Campbell to Scottish Theology," *Scottish Journal of Theology* 26 (1973) 295-311. It has been suggested that the views of Barth and McLeod Campbell have been read back into Calvin.

war period, and the emphasis in baptism is as "an act of dedication—an act of man towards God rather than upon God's seal of His own act of love and grace towards man." When turning to the current *Book of Common Order* 1940, the Special Commission noted:

"In the *Book of Common Order* (1940) we see a gathering together of the various strands of our Scottish tradition: the theological teaching of men like J. S. Candlish and H. R. Mackintosh from the Free Church side, the theological emphasis upon worship of men like H. J. Wotherspoon and J. M. Kirkpatrick from the Established Church, the Christological emphases of the Secessionist tradition, the missionary orientation of men in each part of the divided Church, and not least the Biblical theology of men like William Milligan , A. B. Davidson, James Denney, H.A.A. Kennedy, and William Manson."[21]

Although this statement might suggest that the Church already possessed a balanced baptismal rite, the 1961 report offered a series of revisions necessary in the light of the baptismal reports, including the title of the rite, rubrics, the "preamble" or exordium, and the confession of faith and parental vows.[22] The General Assembly of 1961 requested the Committee on Public Worship and Aids to Devotion (under the chairmanship of Stuart Louden) to revise the rites in the light of the reports. Draft forms of service were presented to the General Assembly in 1963, 1965, 1967 and 1968. The final texts were "received" in 1968 and published by the Oxford University Press. It provided four services: An Order of Divine Service with Holy Baptism; Confirmation and admission to the Lord's Supper; Holy Baptism, Confirmation, and Admission to the Lord's Supper; and Adult Baptism. Our concern here is with the first of these, infant baptism.

One most obvious difference between the 1940 rite for infant baptism and that of 1968 is the setting. Although Reformed theology stressed the importance of baptism during normal worship, this was not spelled out in 1940, whereas in 1968 this is made quite explicit. The rite of baptism follows the liturgy of the Word

[21] RGA 1959, 631.
[22] In fact it referred to the 1952 slightly revised edition of the 1940 text. Very little was altered in the baptismal rite.

and intercessions. Its opening exordium is similar in substance to 1940, including the citation of Matthew 28:18-20. However, 1940 had then given a definition of the sacrament:

"The Sacrament thus instituted is a sign and seal of our ingrafting into Christ; of forgiveness of sins by His blood, and regeneration by His Spirit; and of adoption, and resurrection unto everlasting life. By this Sacrament we are solemnly admitted into His Church, and are engaged to be the Lord's."

1968 omits this and continued by anchoring baptism in the historical work of Jesus, listing his baptism, his saving work on the cross and in the resurrection, and the events of Pentecost, and quotes Acts 2:38-9. Only then does it turn to the salvific effects of baptism:

"Holy Baptism is administered according to our Lord's institution and command. The pouring or sprinkling of water is a sign of cleansing from sin by the Blood of Christ, renewal by the Holy Spirit, adoption, and resurrection unto everlasting life. In this Sacrament believers and their children are received by name into the Church and sealed as members of the Body of Christ."

The promises of the parents then follow. In 1940 the parents alone were addressed, being asked whether they believed the Creed, and made promises regarding their duties to bring up the child. 1968 had slightly different promises, and the Creed follows the promises as the profession of faith of the whole assembled Church.

The prayer for the actual baptism is rather different from that of 1940. That prayer had asked God to ratify in heaven that which was being done on earth, and to sanctify the water to a spiritual use, asking that the child being baptized may be born again of water and the Holy Spirit, and remain among the faithful. 1968 began with a berakah of the Persons of the Trinity, and the Holy Spirit is asked to be sent to sanctify all and to bless the water, that the child who is "being born anew of water and the Holy Spirit" may receive the fullness of Grace, and be amongst the number of the elect. The 1940 rite, reflecting earlier Reformed theological debate, regarded baptism as only effectual for the elect. In the new prayer baptism is not empty, and it does something even if not all those baptized are ultimately among the elect. Here is Calvin's idea of the seed of faith, together with Barth's emphasis on the reality of God's power in reconciliation together with the actuality of refusal and rejection of Christ's universal victory and the "impossible possibility."[23] The declaration after the baptism is practically unchanged, as were also the prayers thanking God that the child was grafted in Christ and the Church, and for the home and for all the baptized.

In comparing the two rites, that of 1968 attempted to anchor baptism in the One Baptism of Christ simply by inserting new material in the exordium. It also stressed the objectivity of the sacrament. However, although the term covenant is not used, the parental duties, together with the revised Act of Assembly, could still be construed as suggestive of the bilateral covenant alleged of Federalism. The vast theological work had yielded little liturgical change. It was almost as though when it came to practical application in terms of pastoral discipline and liturgical rite, the Kirk suffered a loss of nerve. There remained a sharp divide between the *Lex credendi* of the reports and the *Lex orandi* of the revised liturgy.

(4) The Book of Common Order 1979

A new *Book of Common Order* was published in 1979, and the 1968 baptismal rite was incorporated into it. No Service of the Word was provided, though this was clearly envisaged by the opening rubric. The most notable difference was language; the "Thou" form of address had given way to "You." However, in the opening exordium the 1968 addition covering from Jordan to the

[23] See Bryan D. Spinks, "Calvin's Baptismal Theology and the Making of the Strasbourg and Genevan Baptismal Liturgies 1540 and 1542," *Scottish Journal of Theology* 48 (1995) 55-78; Joseph D. Bettis, "Is Karl Barth a Universalist?" *Scottish Journal of Theology* 20 (1967) 423-463. John Thompson, "Christology and Reconciliation in the Theology of Karl Barth," in (eds.) Trevor Hart and Daniel Thimell, *Christ in Our Place*, (Allison Park: Paternoster Press Exeter and Pickwick Publications, 1989); Karl Barth, *Church Dogmatics* II/1, 503-506. See also Horton Davies, *The Vigilant God. Providence in the Thought of Augustine, Aquinas, Calvin and Barth*, (New York and Bern: Peter Lang, 1992); John Colwell, "The Contemporaneity of the Divine Decision: Reflections on Barth's Denial of "Universalism," in (ed.) Nigel M. de S. Cameron, *Universalism and the Doctrine of Hell*, (Grand Rapids: Paternoster Press, Carlisle and Baker Book House, 1993).

Cross—an explicit textual addition inspired by the Christological basis for baptism emphasizes in the biblical reports—*was omitted*. The questions to the parents or other sponsors are the same. However, in the baptismal prayer, two versions were provided, both shorter than the 1968 prayer. The first version used the 1940 words "that this child may be born anew of water and the Holy Spirit," and the second used the 1968 words, suggesting that not all ministers in the Church of Scotland had been persuaded that sign and the thing signified were united in the sacramental rite. In some ways the 1979 rite could be considered as a retreat from the few textual gains made in 1968. There would seem to be a gulf between the Christocentrism and sheer grace of the reports of the Special Commission, and the more guarded rite of 1979 which, albeit loosely and anachronistically, might be termed semi-federalist.

II. 1980–1994

(1) The 1983 Report on Baptism

In spite of the fact that a new baptismal rite had been issued in 1979, the Panel on Doctrine had earlier been instructed to look again at the theology of baptism. In 1982 the "Lima Text," *Baptism, Eucharist and Ministry* was published, and the Panel was urged to take this into account. The Panel issued its report in 1983.

Although acknowledging certain developments since the work of the Special Commission, the Panel immediately endorsed a number of emphases from *The Doctrine of Baptism 1966*. Of particular significance was its endorsement of the Christocentric and vicarious natures of baptism:

"Thus there is one Lord, Jesus Christ, and there is one Baptism—his Baptism—in which, through the sacraments, we share, being made by him members of the Church which is his body. Christ's one Baptism includes both his whole life and ministry, in which he was baptized for us, and also his baptizing of us."[24]

Nevertheless, it also agreed that:

"The subjects of baptism are therefore children born of parents within the church, to whom the promise belongs, or else those who have responded to the offer of salvation in Christ and seek

[24] *RGA* 1983, 155.

baptismal incorporation into the people of God upon profession of faith.''[25]

Infant baptism is then defended on the grounds of the meaning of *oikos*—household—in the New Testament, which included children (cf. Jeremias and Cullmann) and on the traditional Reformed grounds of covenant in which baptism replaced circumcision and admits women and children. Yet the dangers perceived to lurk in unguarded Federalism are ruled out:

"Baptism does not arise out of any work of ours, but is baptism into the work of Christ on our behalf, and must be linked with the presence of the word which tells of that divine work. It is not offered to us as the authentication of anything we have done, or as an expression of anything we have done, or an approval of anything we have done or promised. None of these is the thing signified by the sign. What is signified is what God has done, does and will do. On this alone can human lives be grounded.''[26]

A considerable part of this report was concerned with the notion of re-baptism. It asserted that because Christ takes us, and is faithful to his Word, there can be no repetition of this sacrament. Behind this discussion lay the Boyd Case, 1976 and the Riach Case, 1981. Boyd, an elder, and Riach, a minister, had both been "re-baptised." The General Assembly had required Boyd to stand down from the Eldership, and Riach was admonished and rebuked, and required to uphold the Church of Scotland teaching on the baptism of infants. Riach subsequently demitted and joined the Baptists. However, by pronouncing judically in the Boyd Case, the Church of Scotland in effect declared its accepted doctrine and practice of baptism to be "of the substance of the faith.''[27]

This report also emphasized again the objectivity of baptism:

"God's word is effective and dependable. He does what he says, and he keeps what he promises. In Reformed language, baptism is a sign and a seal of the covenant of grace, not a badge of our decision or conversion, important as these are. Prior to and under-

[25] *RGA* 1983, ibid.
[26] *RGA* 1983, 156.
[27] My thanks to Rev. Colin Williamson, vice-president of the Church Service Society, for supplying me with this information.

lying anything that we do in baptism, or the vows we make (and this applies to baptism at *any* age), is the word of Christ addressed to us: his promise of forgiveness, and of our adoption through his Spirit as the sons and daughters of the Father. . . . After all, the efficacy of baptism depends on God's promises, not on ours."[28]

Since baptism is about the objectivity of God's grace, re-baptism is rendered unnecessary.

The report then turned to a number of pastoral issues—indeed the very issues which resulted in a Special Commission in 1953—that of infant baptism and "indiscriminate baptism." Here objectivity and pastoral care needed to be carefully balanced:

"Human nature being what it is, the possibility of pastoral errors cannot be avoided, whether infant baptism or believers' baptism is involved. Whether it concerns the sincerity and faith of the parents, or the genuineness of a "conversion," pastoral judgements always may be mistaken. But it does not follow that there is no baptism, for the reliable faithfulness of Jesus Christ rises above human error. On the other hand, the knowledge that this is so does not allow us to be casual or careless in our administration of the sacrament."[29]

With the various interpretations of the Acts of 1933, 1951, and 1963 in mind, the Panel commented: "Sadly, conditions rigidly insisted upon before baptism may seem to obscure or even deny the unconditional character of grace in the eyes of perhaps poorly informed parishioners."[30]

The report recommended that sponsors other than the natural parents should be permitted in certain circumstances, and it discouraged dedication in place of baptism.

(2) The 1986 Baptismal Rite

The tangible outcome of this report was a further revision of the baptismal rite. If on the one hand pastoral discipline would remind parents of their obligation and responsibility, in a liturgical context there was a determination that the very structure of the rite would clearly demonstrate the grace of God freely given.

[28] *RGA* 1983, 158.
[29] *RGA* 1983, 159.
[30] *RGA* 1983, 160.

Entitled *An Order for Holy Baptism* (OUP 1986), it was based upon the 1979 rite. However, both in revised phraseology *and structure*, this rite gave much fuller expression to the theology outlined by the 1953–1962 reports.

The setting of the rite was after the normal Liturgy of the Word. In the opening explication the connection between the baptism of Jesus in the Jordan and the baptism suffered on the cross was restored. The Christological nature of the rite was also emphasized with the addition of the words "for it is Jesus Christ himself who baptizes us by the Spirit of Pentecost into the one Church." Whereas in 1979 mention was made of the duty of parents presenting infants for baptism, in 1986 the intention of entering the Church and a Trinitarian affirmation followed immediately. Unlike 1979, no promise is requested at this point. What followed in 1986 was the prayer over the water, being the second prayer of 1979 with the words "being born again"; no alternative form was provided. Then came an address to the child taken from the rite of Baptism of the French Reformed Church:

"N . . ., It was for you that Jesus Christ came down into the world, struggled and suffered; for you he endured the agony of Gethsemane and the darkness of Calvary; for you he cried, "It is accomplished"; for you he died and for you he conquered death; yes, for you, little one, you who know nothing of it as yet. Thus the Apostles's words are confirmed: "We love God because he loved us first."

The baptism followed immediately, with a blessing, and a declaration that the child is now received into membership of the one, holy, catholic and apostolic Church. Only now came an address to the parents and a promise to teach the child the truths and duties of the Christian faith. The congregation then said the Apostle's Creed as a confession of faith of the one, holy, catholic and apostolic Church. Prayers for the child and its family followed.

Here in liturgical form is the unilateral covenant of grace argued for by the Special Commission of 1953—unilateral in origin, unilateral in fulfilment, and bilateral in fruition. The child is baptised *by Christ* without condition; God's grace depends only upon God himself. Only after the child has been born anew and received into the Church do the parents give their promise in terms of helping the child to make its own response of faith at some later time. The Federalism outlined in the 1953–1962 reports, whether or not a caricature, is finally rooted out of the very structure of the liturgical rite.

(3) Baptismal Debates, 1986–1992

Already when the draft of this rite had been introduced into the General Assembly in 1984, one leading evangelical had attacked the phrase of the prayer over the water "that this child being born again of water and the Holy Spirit," since it taught baptismal regeneration tied to the actual rite. However, since the phrase was in the 1968 rite which had been "Authorised" by the General Assembly, the objection that this was an innovation in the Church of Scotland could not be sustained.

The pastoral problems associated with baptism continued to be discussed. In *Ministers' Forum*, a monthly bulletin of news and views for Church of Scotland ministers, Jack Holt raised again in December 1989 the problem of diverse attitudes of ministers to those who requested baptism for their infants but who themselves had no real affiliation with the Church: either indiscriminate baptism or rejection. He advocated a service which celebrated new life as an alternative to baptism—the very reverse of the Panel's recommendations. In the same issue Quintin Blane argued for a change in the 1963 Act in the light of the 1983 report which urged that baptism is something which God does for us, and is not dependent on faith, works, preparation, or the visible faithfulness of a third party. In response (January 1990) some correspondents raised the issues of the relation to baptism of confirmation, and whether everything really centered upon a confession of faith; or if parents' motives for baptism, or "purity of intention," is an issue, then why not apply this to Holy Communion? Later correspondents (February, March, and April) continued to wrestle with the problem of practice at a pastoral level.

A weightier contribution to the baptismal debate was David Hamilton's *Through the Waters*, 1989. In this work Hamilton, Lecturer in Practical Theology at the University of Glasgow, examined the biblical images used for baptism. The preamble of the 1979 rite was criticized for referring only once to water, and Hamilton went on to examine the images of washing, deliverance, birth, belong-

ing and celebration. Commenting on the use of the French
Reformed rite in the 1986 rite, Hamilton wrote:

"Regrettably, the 'instruction' of the French Order is replaced
here by the introduction from *The Book of Common Order 1979*, very
slightly expanded but still lacking any reference to the overwhelming, destroying image of water, and even to the dying and rising
significance of baptism."[31]

However, Hamilton had no quarrel with the structure of 1986,
since he shared the Panel's dislike of the idea of baptism being
conditional:
   "Reformed churches have tended to stop short of a thorough-
going and distinctive infant baptism rite. Expressions like "this
promise is for believers *and also* for their children" or "little children do not understand these things *yet the promise is also to them*
(Jenson's "also" actually set in the liturgy!) betray a worrying
theological unsteadiness. The implication is that baptism is "also"
for children, not in their own right but because of their parents'
faith and membership—rather as they are included in the family
passport, able to travel only when and where their parents travel.
This is at bottom the argument for infant baptism from "covenant
theology." The claim is that a child qualifies for baptism through
the parents' membership of the covenant people. . . . at the heart
of baptism is the individual's relationship to God in Christ in her
or his own right, rather than in any sense derivatively. If that is
true for an adult, must it not also be true for a child, for is there
not but one baptism?"[32]
   However, in the final chapter under the heading "Celebration,"
Hamilton outlined the component elements necessary for a baptismal liturgy, and in an appendix provided a model for a rite which
combined infant and adult baptism with confirmation in one rite.
Although Hamilton had considered the image of birth, he argued
that that of dying and rising was more appropriate.

[31] David S. M. Hamilton, *Through the Waters*, (Edinburgh: T & T Clark, 1989)
118.
[32] Ibid., 80–81. The reference is to R. W. Jenson, *Visible Words*, (Philadelphia:
Fortress Press, 1978) 159ff.

(4) The Rite of Baptism in the Book of Common Order 1994

Under the secretaryship of Rev. Charles Robertson, the Panel on Worship had prepared a new *Book of Common Order,* due out in mid 1993, but finally appearing on Ascension Day (May 12) 1994.[33] The style of language is less austere than 1986. Much of the drafting of the rite was the work of Charles Robertson.

Originally it was intended that a single rite should be provided which would cover adult baptism and confirmation, and infant baptism. However, between proof stage and final publication this was revised, giving separate orders for infant and adult baptism.

In place of an opening exordium—criticized by Hamilton—the service commences with Words of Institution, or a series of small gobbets of scripture from which the minister can choose a few. As well as those found in the older exordium such as Matthew 28:18-20 and Acts 2:38-39, others include Isaiah 43:1-2a (cf. Hamilton), Ezekiel 36:25a, 26a, St. Luke 18:16-17, St. John 3:5-7; Romans 6:3-4; Ephesians 4:4-6a, Titus 3:4-7 and I Peter 2:9. A statement on baptism follows, which seems to be a response to Hamilton, since it freely uses dying/rising and washing terminology. However, the grace of baptism is clearly stated:

"In this Sacrament,
the love of God is offered to each one of us.
Though we cannot understand or explain it,
we are called to accept that love
with the openness and trust of a child.
In baptism,
N . . . is assured
of the love that God has for *her,*
and the sign and seal of the Holy Spirit
is placed upon *her.*"

This is followed by the Confession of Faith. In infant baptism the parents are asked if they receive the teaching of the Church which is confessed in the Apostles Creed. The question to an adult is different:

---

[33] I am deeply indebted to Rev. Charles Robertson who supplied me with xerox copies of the proofs so that this paper could be completed in 1993.

"In seeking baptism,
do you reject sin
and confess your need of God's forgiving grace;
and believing the Christian faith,
do you pledge yourself to glorify God
and to love your neighbour?"

A thorough-going anti-Federalist might question the use of the word "pledge" here, but in the overall context this is probably ultrasensitive.

This is followed by the Creed, which is now moved back to its 1979/1968 position. A new thanksgiving over the water is provided, recalling Old Testament types such as Noah and Moses. Again, echoing Hamilton's emphases, the language of dying and rising has been employed. The proof version read:

"Send your Holy Spirit
upon us and upon this water,
that all who are buried with Christ in baptism
may rise with him to newness of life;"

By oversight rather than design this has resulted in the removal of "new birth" imagery which had been promoted in the 1956 report. In response to my observations on this, the text was redrafted to read:

"Send your Holy Spirit
upon us and upon this water,
that N . . .,
buried with Christ in baptism
may rise with him to newness of life;
and being born anew of water and the Holy Spirit
may remain for ever
in the number of your faithful children;"[34]

There follows a re-worked version of the French Reformed address to the candidate which had been used in 1986:

[34] Again I am greatly indebted to Charles Robertson who quickly responded to my queries about the imagery, and who telephoned me to read out a proposed revision of the proof text to redress the unintentional oversight.

"N . . .,

for you Jesus Christ came into the world:
for you he lived and showed God's love;
for you he suffered the darkness of Calvary
and he cried at the last, "It is accomplished";
for you he triumphed over death
and rose in newness of life;
for you he ascended to reign at God's right hand.
All this he did for you, N . . .,
though you do not know it yet.
And so the word of Scripture is fulfilled:
'We love because God loved us first.' "

In the case of an adult the text reads "All this he did for you, before you knew anything of it." Here we have the vicarious work
of Christ, his *katabasis* and *anabasis*; the teaching of the 1955–1962
reports that grace is freely given through the vicarious work of
Christ is here in a nutshell.[35] The baptism follows with a blessing,
and then as in 1986, come the Promises—of the parents in the case
of infant baptism, or of the candidate in the case of an adult being
confirmed. After this the congregation is addressed, reminding it
that the ecclesia itself has a responsibility to all the baptised. Then
prayers for the candidate follow.

How far does this rite of 1994 do justice to the baptismal reports
which have appeared from 1955 to 1983? At first sight it may appear that the placing of the Creed before baptism has reintroduced
some condition for baptism. The 1955 report had pointed out that
in his ministry Jesus sometimes required prior faith in a person, or
a parent or master, but sometimes required no prior faith. However, as became apparent in the exchange in *Ministers Forum*,
some ministers of the Evangelical and Conservative Reformed wings
of the Church were not convinced that this applied to baptism,
and argued strongly for a confession of faith at this point, particularly in the case of adults. This demand is met by the recitation of
the Creed, but by the whole Church rather than the individual or
the parents alone. If this is to be regarded as a compromise or a
move back from the 1986 rite, it has been done in order to give

[35] It could also justly be described as Barthian election and covenant in a
nutshell, though not Barth's doctrine of Baptism.

the Church a rite which upholds the objectivity of God in the sacrament, and the objectivity of the Christian faith, but without alienating sections of the Church of Scotland. As far as possible the Panel on Worship has tried to compile a rite in which the *Lex orandi* expresses the *Lex credendi* of the reports on baptism; it has attempted to give the Church of Scotland a rite of baptism which "is to bear basic testimony to eternal, free and unchanging grace as the beginning of all the ways and works of God."[36]

[36] Karl Barth, *Church Dogmatics* II/2, 3.

Thomas H. Schattauer

12. The Reconstruction of Rite: The Liturgical Legacy of Wilhelm Löhe

When one visits the small, Franconian town of Neuendettelsau in the modern state of Bavaria, the legacy of Wilhelm Löhe looms large. From 1837 to 1872, Löhe was pastor of the Lutheran parish, in what was then a remote rural village. Today the parish church of St. Nikolai still stands at the center of town, although a turn-of-the-century Romanesque-revival building has replaced the extremely humble pre-Reformation structure of Löhe's day. Very near the church is the former parish house, where Löhe lived and received his parishioners and frequent visitors.[1] A short walk up the street one finds the *Missionswerk* of the Evangelical Lutheran Church in Bavaria, which furthers in a global way the heritage of Löhe's enterprising mission to German immigrants and native people in North America.[2] Not much further away lie the mother house and church of the order of deaconesses founded by Löhe and a cluster of social-welfare institutions, which today make up the Neuendettelsau *Diakoniewerk*, the offspring of Löhe's earlier efforts with the deaconesses "to serve the Lord in his poor and needy."[3] Parish

[1] For a drawing of the church and parish house in Löhe's day as well as exterior and interior photographs of the church, see Thomas H. Schattauer, *Communion Patterns and Practices: Announcement, Confession, and Lord's Supper in the Pastoral-Liturgical Work of Wilhelm Löhe* (New York: Peter Lang, forthcoming).

[2] For a history of the Neuendettelsau mission, see Georg Pilhofer, *Geschichte des Neuendettelsauer Missionshauses* (Neuendettelsau: Freimund, 1967); and James L. Schaaf, "Wilhelm Löhe's Relation to the American Church: A Study in the History of Lutheran Mission," (Dr. theol. diss., University of Heidelberg, 1961).

[3] From the deaconess vows; for a history of the Neuendettelsau deaconesses and their work, see Hans Lauerer, *Die Diakonissenanstalt Neuendettelsau, 1854–1954*

church, mission center, and diaconal foundation were the principal spheres of Löhe's activity, and the lively inheritance of each has exerted a perceptible influence upon church life not only in Germany but also in the United States, Brazil, Australia, and New Guinea.[4]

These visible, institutional monuments to Löhe's legacy reveal only a part of his churchly activity. Löhe lived and worked through an unsettling period of transition for the Lutheran territories newly incorporated into the Catholic kingdom of Bavaria, and he applied his considerable energies to both fundamental and practical questions about the nature and mission of the Church, its organization, order, and confessional identity. Against the historical backdrop of the religious rationalism and individualism promoted by the Enlightenment, the social turmoil caused by industrialization, and the political upheaval surrounding the revolutions of 1848, Löhe pressed for a renewal of church life at every level.[5] In relation to these ecclesial concerns, Löhe fostered a high view of the pastoral office and a comprehensive understanding of its

(Neuendettelsau: Diakonissenanstalt, 1954); also Löhe's own account, *Etwas aus der Geschichte des Diakonissenhauses Neuendettelsau* (1870), GW 4:259–341. Throughout this essay, GW is the abbreviation for Wilhelm Löhe, *Gesammelte Werke*, 7 vols., ed. Klaus Ganzert (Neuendettelsau: Freimund, 1951–1986).

[4] Adam Schuster, *Aus tausend Jahren Neuendettelsauer Geschichte* (Ansbach: Brügel, 1963), provides a chronological overview of Löhe's activity in Neuendettelsau and its result. For Löhe's biography see [Johannes Deinzer], *Wilhelm Löhes Leben. Aus seinem schriftlichen Nachlaß zusammengestellt*, 3 vols. (Gütersloh, 1901 [3rd ed.], 1880, 1892); and the extensive biographical introduction by Klaus Ganzert in GW 1:15–240. See also the essays in Friedrich Wilhelm Kantzenbach, ed., *Wilhelm Löhe—Anstösse für die Zeit* (Neuendettelsau: Freimund, 1972).

[5] See *Drei Bücher von der Kirche. Den Freunden der lutherischen Kirche zur Überlegung und Besprechung dargeboten* (1845), in GW 5/1:85–179; [ET: *Three Books about the Church*, trans. and ed. James L. Schaaf (Philadelphia: Fortress, 1969), with an excellent brief introduction to Löhe and his work]; *Vorschlag zu einem Lutherischen Verein für apostolische Leben samt Entwurf eines Katechismus des apostolischen Lebens* (1848), in GW 5/1:213–252; and *Unserer kirchliche Lage im protestantischen Bayern und die Bestrebungen einiger bayerisch-lutherischen Pfarrer in den Jahren 1848 und 1849* (1849/50), in GW 5/1:371–492. The most extensive work on Löhe's ecclesiology is Siegfried Hebart, *Wilhelm Löhes Lehre von der Kirche, ihrem Amt und Regiment: Ein Beitrag zur Geschichte der Theologie im 19. Jahrhundert* (Neuendettelsau: Freimund, 1939); see also Walter H. Conser, Jr., *Church and Confession: Conservative Theologians in Germany, England, and America, 1815–1866* ([Macon, GA]: Mercer UP, 1984) 57–72.

responsibilities in the areas of preaching, catechesis, liturgy, pastoral care, church discipline, and the education of the young.[6] Furthermore, he collected and prepared several volumes of devotional literature, which were widely disseminated and used.[7] Finally, Löhe was regularly occupied with matters of liturgical restoration and reform. Compelled by his churchly theology and commitments, and backed up by his study of historic—and especially Lutheran—liturgical sources, Löhe sustained a deep and abiding concern for liturgical forms and practice in the parish church and deaconess chapel at Neuendettelsau, a concern that further extended to the wider Bavarian Church and the German diaspora in North America.[8]

---

[6] See *Aphorismen über die neutestamentlichen Ämter und ihr Verhältnis zur Gemeinde. Zur Verfassungsfrage der Kirche* (1849), in *GW* 5/1:255–330. *Kirche und Amt. Neue Aphorismen* (1851), in *GW* 5/1:523–588; and *Der evangelische Geistliche. Dem nun folgenden Geschlechte evangelischer Geistlichen dargebracht* (1852/1858), in *GW* 3/2:7–317. For a presentation of Löhe's views on the pastoral office, see the previously mentioned study by Hebart, and also Todd Nichol, "Wilhelm Löhe, the Iowa Synod and the Ordained Ministry," *Lutheran Quarterly*, n.s., 4 (1990) 11–29; for an examination of specific themes in Löhe's legacy as a pastor, see Hans Kressel, *Wilhelm Löhe als Prediger* (Gütersloh: Bertelsmann, 1929), and *Wilhelm Löhe als Katechet und als Seelsorger* (Neuendettelsau: Freimund, 1955).

[7] See, for example, *Prüfungstafel und Gebete für Beicht- und Abendmahlstage. Beicht- und Kommunionbüchlein für evangelische Christen. Zum Gebrauch sowohl im als außerhalb des Gotteshauses* (1837/1858), in *GW* 7/2:232–317; *Samenkörner des Gebets. Ein Taschenbüchlein für evangelische Christen* (1840/1858), in *GW* 7/2:318–405 [ET: *Seed-Grains of Prayer: A Manual for Evangelical Christians*, trans. H. A. Weller (Chicago: Wartburg, 1912)]; and *Hausbedarf christlicher Gebete für Augsburgische Konfessionsverwandte* (1859/1864), in *GW* 7/2:9–164. For Löhe's relation to the tradition of Lutheran devotional literature, see Paul Althaus, *Forschungen zur evangelischen Gebetsliteratur* (Gütersloh: Bertelsmann, 1927).

[8] See *Sammlung liturgischer Formulare der evangelisch-lutherischen Kirche*, 3 vols. (Nördlingen, 1839–1842), of which the forewords to each volume have been reprinted in *GW* 7/2:690–702; *Agende für christliche Gemeinden des lutherischen Bekenntnisses* (1844/1853–1859), in *GW* 7/1 [ET of 3rd ed. (1884), abr.: *Liturgy for Christian Congregations of the Lutheran Faith*, trans. F. C. Longaker (Newport, Ky.: n.p., 1902)], initially prepared for immigrant pastors and congregations in North America; *Laienagende* (Nürnberg, 1852 [1st ed.] and 1853 [2nd ed.]), of which the foreword is reprinted in *GW* 7/2:702–704; and also *Haus-, Schul- und Kirchenbuch für Christen des lutherischen Bekenntnisses*, vol. 2 (Gütersloh, 1859), which Löhe hoped could begin to meet the need for a Lutheran *Book of Common Prayer*. The following parts of the latter work are reprinted in *GW*: the foreword, 3/1:726–729; the very substantial introductory

A comprehensive assessment of Löhe's contribution from a liturgical perspective faces at least two critical challenges. First, it must account for the wide range of Löhe's concerns and activities and ask what unifies his vision and various undertakings. Second, it must show how Löhe's liturgical work is integral to the whole of his work without either over- or underestimating its significance. The unfolding of Löhe's work does not warrant that we view his liturgical work as his chief concern, nor does it suggest that we can simply list liturgy as one among his many interests. It is here that some thoughts about rite from Aidan Kavanagh's rich and provocative work *On Liturgical Theology* offer a way to understand both the breadth of Löhe's efforts and its liturgical focus.[9]

In the midst of his reflections on liturgical theology, Kavanagh puts forth the following definition and description of rite:

"Rite can be called a whole style of Christian living found in the myriad particularities of worship, of laws called 'canonical,' of ascetical and monastic structures, of evangelical and catechetical endeavors, and in particular ways of doing secondary theological reflection. A liturgical act concretizes all these and in doing so makes them accessible to the community assembled in a given time and place before the living God for the life of the world."[10]

It is in this way that we speak of Eastern rite and Western rite Churches. Rite at once denotes the "whole style of Christian living" embodied in particular, historic Christian communities and the "myriad particularities of worship"—or rites—within a given tradition. The liturgical act of an assembly of Christians renders this way of living in ritual and symbol, making it a visible, audible, and palpable reality.

---

essay "Von den heiligen Personen, der heiligen Zeit, der heiligen Weise und dem heiligen Orte," 3/1:523–601, the lectionary for the church year, 7/2:714–719; and the essay "Die Privatbeichte und Absolution," 3/1:233–237. See also Löhe's *Abendmahlspredigten* (1866), in *GW*, Ergänzungsreihe, vol. 1, ed. Martin Wittenberg (Neuendettelsau: Freimund, 1991). For a survey of Löhe's liturgical work, see Hans Kressel, *Wilhelm Löhe als Liturg und Liturgiker* (Neuendettelsau: Freimund, 1952); on the preparation for and celebration of the Sunday Eucharist, see Schattauer, *Communion Patterns*, and an earlier article "Sunday Worship at Neuendettelsau under Wilhelm Löhe," *Worship* 59 (1985) 370–384.

[9] Aidan Kavanagh, *On Liturgical Theology* (New York: Pueblo, 1984) 100ff.
[10] Kavanagh, 100.

Kavanagh argues that this encompassing sense of rite, with its anchor in the liturgical act, began to break down among Western Christians in the fifteenth and sixteenth centuries due largely to two factors, which he terms "liturgical hypertrophy" and "textual absorption."[11] On the one hand, the excessive growth and unrestrained elaboration of liturgy in the late Middle Ages obscured and distorted the relation of the liturgical act to the structures of Christian life; and on the other, the advent of the printing press, which fueled the Renaissance and Reformation, enabled text to supersede rite and symbol as the preeminent form of theological transaction. Rite as a whole way of Christian living increasingly gave way to a Christianity of doctrines and theological concepts, and the liturgical act tended to dissolve into a didactic event.[12] While this analysis is surely subject to a number of qualifications, the thrust of the argument is persuasive. Modern Western Christianity lacks an encompassing sense of rite and shows little regard for the primacy of the liturgical act.

With this perspective on an earlier Christian sense of rite and its demise, we can interpret the variety of Löhe's churchly concerns and endeavors as a nineteenth-century, Lutheran effort toward the reconstruction of rite in its encompassing sense. Löhe's work was most immediately a reaction to the effects of the Enlightenment, which had furthered the dissolution of rite within the Churches by endorsing the exercise of human reason in the present over authoritative beliefs and practices inherited from the past and by elevating the autonomous individual over the community. According to Löhe, those were "the days of [the Church's] deepest disgrace, which is today coming to an end."[13] But Löhe also recognized a deficiency in the Reformation heritage to which he was otherwise a grateful and faithful heir. It was not a deficiency in doctrine *(Lehre)* but in churchly life *(Leben)*. In *Drei Bücher von der Kirche* (1845), he writes:

"Let us not be too narrow-minded in holding fast to certain forms and externals which have stood since the Reformation. Many a

[11] Kavanagh, 103ff.

[12] The dissolution of rite also made possible another, somewhat later development: a Christianity of religious experience or feeling, with worship as an expressive or therapeutic event.

[13] *Three Books,* 177; GW 5/1:177.

thesis has remained without an antithesis, many an antithesis without a thesis. Many a pious practice was also thrown out when the abuse connected with it was eliminated. Much was thrown out simply for polemical reasons, and after the controversy subsided no one bothered to restore it, to say nothing about church organization, church order, and the relation of church and state. In a word, our church has the doctrine which should be followed. If it is the pure church, why not the one church? If it is apostolic, why not catholic? If it is the simple and humble church, why should it not have everything in the world that is beautiful, glorious, and exalted? . . .

"Perhaps one could also put it this way: The reformation of doctrine has taken place, but the church does not rejoice as it should over the richness of pure doctrine and does not appreciate the importance which it has because of this doctrine. It still feels as if it lived by the tolerance and grace of men. It does not know that it has a charter from God to live openly and freely by his grace in faith and to make all the world happy with its riches. It does not recognize that when it became the true church it had priority over others as an heir of all divine promises. It is too conscious of dogma and too little conscious of its grace, its honor, and its power. In churchly consciousness, life, and work it is far from what the true church of the first centuries was. Here there are still things to reform. May the Lord and his Spirit reform us here! 'When he chastens us, he is making us great.' May he lead us in unchanging humility, but also lead us to the enjoyment of everything which belongs to the true church!'"[14]

Löhe took up his own challenge to complete the Reformation and dedicated his own work toward the reform of "churchly consciousness, life, and work" according to the model of the early Church. In doing so, Löhe directed his energies to the complex of ecclesial matters that make up "a whole style of Christian living," and thus furthered the reconstruction of rite in the modern Church.

The interpretation of the entirety of Löhe's efforts as an attempt at the reconstruction of rite also helps us to understand and ap-

[14] *Three Books*, 154–155; *GW* 5/1:161–162.

praise properly Löhe's pervasive concern for historic traditions of worship and concrete matters of liturgical practice in his parish church and the deaconess chapel as well as in the congregations of the *Landeskirche* and immigrant settlements in North America. If, as Kavanagh argues, the liturgical act concretizes the various structures and activities of churchly life by means of ritual and symbol, then we can see how it was that liturgical matters were neither Löhe's chief concern nor simply another item of his interest alongside many others. By intuition and conviction, Löhe recognized that the liturgical practice of gathered assemblies was foundational to churchly existence. Liturgy was not for him an antiquarian hobby or a piece of ritual decoration to the theological substance of Christianity. Löhe's liturgical work was integral to the reform of "churchly consciousness, life, and work" that he envisioned, and it could not be pursued apart from the matters of mission and service, church order and organization, confessional witness and integrity that occupied him.

My purpose here is to explore Löhe's liturgical legacy as a critical part of his efforts toward the reconstruction of rite in the modern Church. What follows will unfold under three headings: 1) "Sacramental Lutheranism," where we will reflect upon the thrust in Löhe's thinking toward an emphasis on the primacy of the liturgical act in relation to Christian life and doctrine; 2) "The Liturgical Act," where we will examine Löhe's statements about the liturgical *ordo* and the consequences for liturgical practice resulting from his high regard for the Lord's Supper; and 3) "The Liturgical Assembly," where we will look at how Löhe encouraged participation in the liturgy, and how he used structures of church discipline and penitence to constitute the community that gathered for Eucharistic worship.

SACRAMENTAL LUTHERANISM

Late in his life before a gathering of fellow pastors, Löhe characterized his theological position in this way:

"I am the same good Lutheran as earlier, but in a more profound way. Before, Lutheranism was for me little more than affirmation of the confessions from A to Z; now the whole of Lutheranism is for me hidden in the sacrament of the altar, in which, as can be shown, all the chief doctrines of Christianity, especially those of the Reformation, have their center and focus. The essential thing for me now is not so much the Lutheran doctrine of the Lord's Supper, but sacramental life and the experience of the blessing of the sacrament that is possible only through partaking of it abundantly. The words 'sacramental Lutheranism' signify my advance."[15]

In most respects, Löhe's "sacramental Lutheranism" shows substantial continuity with the whole course of his thought and work. The emphasis on ecclesial life over doctrine abstracted from its churchly context is characteristic of Löhe. As one who participated in the resurgence of confessionalism among Lutherans in the nineteenth century, Löhe had consistently focused his concern on the renewal of church life among Lutherans, not on the mere preservation of doctrinal formulations from the sixteenth century. We have already noted this ecclesial orientation in his *Drei Bücher von der Kirche*. There he argues for the churchly character of the Reformation and the need to restore the fullness of church life and practice among Lutheran Churches, precisely where the pure doctrine is most clearly taught.[16] Similarly, Löhe's proposal for the restoration of apostolic life in the Bavarian *Landeskirche* directed attention to the insufficiency of pure doctrine. Without vitality in worship and other forms of churchly life, the teachings of the confessions cannot preserve the Lutheran Church from the charge of "dead orthodoxy" or from being called a "professors' church."[17]

---

[15] October 3, 1865; quoted in Deinzer, 2:523. Cf. the statement from Löhe reported by a pastor in attendance at the same meeting: "I believe that I have made an advance, but whether you consider it such I do not know. I am speaking of the advance from doctrine to life. Not that doctrine ought to be done away with; however it is not the most important thing, but rather life. . . . When my friends and I entered into the struggle for the confession, it was not the time to distinguish between important and less important. But now that the struggle is won it is necessary to turn every energy to life. The holy Supper is the center of life. The first Christians celebrated it daily or certainly every Sunday" (J. G. Steinlein, "Erinnerungen an Pfarrer Löhe," ed. Adam Schuster, *Concordia* 42 [1954] 158). Kressel, in *Löhe als Prediger*, 178, pointed to this passage in what was then an unpublished manuscript from Steinlein.

Unless noted otherwise, the translations of Löhe are my own.

[16] *Three Books*, 149ff.; GW 5/1:158ff.

[17] *Vorschlag*, GW 5/1:219; see pp. 213ff.

Sacramental Lutheranism thus stands in continuity with Löhe's earlier concern for churchly reform and the call to apostolic life.

Nor does Löhe's sacramental Lutheranism present anything new in regard to the central place of the Lord's Supper in his thought and work. From the earliest days at Neuendettelsau, Löhe held up the regular and communally disciplined Eucharistic practice of the early Church as a model. "When one reads that the first Christian communities frequently partook of the Lord's Supper, it is a testimony of their love of the Lord and their life in the Holy Spirit,"[18] Löhe said in an 1837 paper to fellow pastors, a statement which, for him, stood in sharp contrast to the current state of church life. Löhe's liturgical works, principally his *Agende für christliche Gemeinden des lutherischen Bekenntnisses* (1844, 1853/1959) and the second volume of his *Haus-, Schul- und Kirchenbuch für Christen des lutherischen Bekenntnisses* (1859) demonstrate his attention to the restoration of the evangelical mass or *Communio* as the chief service of worship, as well as his elevation of the Lord's Supper over the sermon in his interpretation of the structures of Christian worship.[19] For Löhe, the Lord's Supper provided a comprehensive interpretation of Christian existence, as we see in this passage from an 1853 sermon for a Communion Sunday:

"For Christians, the whole time from the sacrifice at Golgotha until the return of the Lord is a true and unceasing Easter celebration, a time of the Paschal Lamb and the Lord's Supper *(Abendmahlszeit)*, not only in a figurative and symbolic way, but in the most perfect and holiest solemnity. New Testament congregations live from the preparation to the partaking of the Paschal Lamb, from partaking to preparation: between preparation and partaking time passes, until he comes. Ever anew they desire to partake of their eternal salvation in the Lamb of God who was slain and to be assured thereby full peace and joy in the Holy Spirit, full light and power for sanctification. There is no higher view of earthly life than this—and therefore also no more perfect blossom of earthly life, no time which more deserves the name 'high-time' *(Hochzeit)* than the time when one comes to the holy Supper and

---

[18] "Mitteilung der Windsbacher Predigerkonferenz (am 7. November 1837). Vom Abendmahlgenuß," in GW 5/1:47.

[19] For complete citations, see nt. 8.

partakes of the Paschal Lamb. To celebrate the Lord's Supper—indeed, that is the highest, most glorious work of a Christian congregation—or rather, not a work, but where it lays down every work, where it lives entirely by faith."[20]

The whole of Christian life was, in Löhe's view, a continual movement to and from the Lord's Supper, and the whole span of the Church's existence an *Abendmahlszeit*. These views about the centrality of the Lord's Supper were only strengthened and deepened by Löhe's struggle for a confessional Lutheran *Landeskirche*, in which he fought against open Communion at Lutheran altars for members of Reformed and Union Churches, and by his own pastoral work in the parish and in the deaconess community.

What then was the "advance" that Löhe wanted to underscore in the designation "sacramental Lutheranism"? It was in part, I think, a development in his understanding of the relation of doctrine and sacramental worship—of the *lex orandi* to the *lex credendi*, to use the terms of liturgical theology. Previously, Löhe had given primacy of place to doctrine; in his development toward sacramental Lutheranism, he came to recognize the primacy of the liturgical act. The earlier view is evident in *Drei Bücher von der Kirche*, where liturgy and the other matters of church life, are understood as "the consequences of doctrine."[21] There, he can write:

"The church remains what it is even without the liturgy. It remains a queen, even if dressed in beggar's rags. It would be better if everything else were lost and only the pure doctrine remained safe than for us to continue the ceremony and adornment of glorious services which lack light and life because the doctrine has become impure."[22]

Admittedly, pure doctrine, for Löhe, was never a matter of theological discourse abstracted from churchly life and worship; it had everything to do with the means of grace, with Word and sacrament, which lie at the heart of the liturgy. "Word and sacrament in a pure confession,"[23] to use Löhe's words, constitute the

[20] "Eine protestantische Missionspredigt innerhalb der Gemeinde" (1853), in *GW* 5/2:673; the text for the sermon was 1 Cor 5:6-8.

[21] *Three Books*, 152ff.; *GW* 5/1:160ff.

[22] *Three Books*, 178; *GW* 5/1:177–178.

[23] *Three Books*, 115, also p. 113; *GW* 5/1:135, 134.

Church in its faithfulness to the apostolic faith witnessed in the scriptures. Löhe's formula holds together the *lex orandi* and the *lex credendi* in the terms of a Lutheran confessional theology. His "advance," however embryonic in its theological formulation, was to see that Christian existence flows from Word and sacrament, and that the pure confession has its source precisely there, in the liturgical act. The sacramental life and the experience of its blessing were, as Löhe put it, the essential thing *(Hauptsache)*, in a way that the doctrinal formulations of the confessions were not, despite their continuing and critical significance for him.[24]

Some have charged that Löhe's sacramental Lutheranism placed too much emphasis on the Lord's Supper, particularly at the expense of the customary Lutheran emphasis on the Word of God

[24] Indeed, Löhe's opposition to Lutheran intercommunion with members of Reformed and Union Churches, based upon doctrinal differences (or indifference) concerning the real presence, did not diminish in the least; if anything the opposite is true, precisely because matters of practice had become foundational for him. Intercommunion with Roman Catholics was, of course, never at issue. See *Gutachten in Sachen der Abendmahlsgemeinschaft. Vor einigen Freunden gelesen* (1863), in GW 5/2:882–908; also *Abendmahlspredigten*, GW, Ergr. 1:142–145.

In this regard, it should be noted that a full account of what Löhe means by "sacramental Lutheranism" encompasses at least four separate, but interrelated themes:

1) The Lord's Supper is the beginning and end, the source and summit, of all churchly and spiritual life.

2) The Lord's Supper comprehends the most important Christian doctrines, notably the doctrines of justification and sanctification; it sums up the doctrinal formulations of the Lutheran confessions.

3) The Lord's Supper defines the Lutheran Church in such a way that intercommunion with members of other churches is not possible; consequently, the distinguishing mark of Lutheranism is sacramental.

4) The Lord's Supper grounds church life and doctrine in the liturgical act; the sacramental life has primacy over doctrinal formulations.

It is the last theme—Löhe's turn to the *lex orandi*, so to speak—that concerns us here.

On Löhe's sacramental Lutheranism, cf. Hebart, 280–292; Friedrich Wilhelm Kantzenbach, *Gestalten und Typen de Neuluthertums: Beiträge zur Erforschung des Neokonfessionalismus im 19. Jahrhundert* (Gütersloh: Mohn, 1968), 81–89, and "Wilhelm Löhe (1808–1872)," in *Klassiker der Theologie*, ed. Heinrich Fries and Georg Kretschmar (München: Beck, 1981–1983), 2:182, 188–189; and Ganzert, "Einleitung," GW 1:211–213.

in Scripture and proclamation.[25] There is, however, little evidence that Löhe desired to diminish the importance of the Scriptures or preaching or to set his sacramental perspective over and against a theology of the Word. On this controversial point, the interpretation of Löhe's work as an effort toward the reconstruction of rite in the modern Church may prove helpful to understanding his intent. With the dissolution of an encompassing sense of rite concretized in the liturgical act, the Reformation emphasis on God's Word often served to further the primacy of doctrine over church life and worship. Löhe's emphasis on the Lord's Supper represented a reassertion of the primacy of the liturgical act in the context of a broad reassertion of many elements of churchly life. This was not an attempt to displace God's Word in scripture and proclamation, but rather to situate it once again in the churchly context of rite and symbol. It is only in that context that the words of Scripture and preaching can be the Word of God bearing a life-giving relation to God, rather than a word about God teaching the propositions of a doctrinal faith. Far from overthrowing the place of God's Word, Löhe's sacramental Lutheranism restored the Word to its churchly and liturgical home.[26]

THE LITURGICAL ACT

While Löhe indeed gave preeminence to the Lord's Supper in his churchly thought and work, he by no means restricted his understanding of the liturgical act to the sacrament. The sacrament of the altar took its place within a liturgical order of prayer and praise, scripture reading and sermon that was the principal service (*Hauptgottesdienst*) of Christian worship on Sundays and feast days. Moreover, this service, called the *Communio* or Mass, took its place within a larger order or system of worship.

Löhe's most complete statement concerning the liturgical *ordo* as a whole is found in the introduction to the second volume of his *Haus-, Schul- und Kirchenbuch*. The title, "Von den heiligen Personen, der heiligen Zeit, der heiligen Weise und dem heiligen Orte" ("On Sacred Persons, Sacred Time, Sacred Practice, and Sacred

---

[25] In defending Löhe, Klaus Ganzert points to this charge in Hebart, 286f., and Kantzenbach, *Gestalten und Typen*, 26 ("Einleitung," *GW* 1:212–213, 234 [nt. 29]).

[26] See Kavanagh, 111–121.

Space"), itself points to a comprehensive understanding of the liturgical act as a holy action undertaken by people set apart for it and carried out in its own consecrated time and space.[27] In the section devoted to sacred action that immediately follows the discussion of sacred time, Löhe begins: "Our time is made holy by God's Word and prayer, and the use of this divine Word and prayer, together with everything connected with it, we call sacred practice *(heilige Weise)* or the holy way of life *(heilige Lebensweise)*."[28] What follows falls into six parts devoted to:

1. The Word of God (the liturgical reading of Scripture in Sunday and feast day lections as well as daily lections)
2. The Sermon
3. Churchly Prayer (the forms of liturgical prayer and principal orders of service)
4. Sacramental Actions (Baptism, Lord's Supper, and Absolution)
5. Blessings (concluding benedictions, ordination, confirmation, marriage, the churching of women, the consecration of the dying and the dead, and the blessing of church buildings, altars, vessels, etc.)
6. Sacred Practice or Churchly Ceremony[29]

For Löhe, the services of worship that the Church observes constitute not only a practice of worship but a whole way of life. "The church has put together according to holy orders . . . services of various kinds and esteems them to be understood by all the faithful as the highest harmony of earthly life and not only to be sung and spoken but to be lived."[30] In the liturgical *ordo* as a whole, the *Communio* or Mass liturgy has the highest place, and next to it stands the daily services at morning and evening, matins and vespers; all other services derive from these.[31] In his *Agende* and *Haus-, Schul- und Kirchenbuch*, we see Löhe's attempt to arrange the liturgical material that embodied this vision of the liturgical

[27] GW 3/1:523–601; cf. the section "Liturgisches," in *Evangelischer Geistliche*, GW 3/2:237–257.
[28] GW 3/1:560.
[29] GW 3/1:560–594.
[30] GW 3/1:570.
[31] GW 3/1:570.

ordo, which was, in his view, the very way of Christian life in the world.

When we look specifically at Löhe's understanding of the *ordo* for the principal liturgical act, we see that he looked to three loci of authority for the restoration of what could be regarded as a traditional *ordo* for the *Communio*.[32] In the first place Löhe gathered the textual material for his evangelical Mass and established its fundamental arrangement almost exclusively from Lutheran sources. Although he had explored broadly the historical riches of both Eastern and Western liturgical traditions, he depended for the most part on the Lutheran *Kirchenordnungen* of the sixteenth and seventeenth centuries for the rite for the *Communio* in his liturgical books.[33] For Löhe, this appeal to Lutheran liturgical tradition was not only a matter of his own theological and ecclesiastical commitment, but also a pragmatic pastoral strategy not "to expect more of the time than it can bear, enjoy and digest."[34] Secondly, using these materials, Löhe did not seek to set out a Lutheran liturgy, nor even less to invent something new, but rather to restore "the ancient liturgical *typus* of the West," purified and updated.[35] Consequently, his selection of material from Lutheran sources and their arrangement favors the elements and order of the Roman Mass.[36] Finally, Löhe appealed to something even more fundamental: the basic elements of worship from the primitive Christian community and their arrangement into a unified liturgical act in the early Church. In his interpretation, Acts 2:42 set forth "the great and fundamental liturgical ideas"[37] and "the chief parts of liturgical life"[38]: apostolic teaching (*Apostellehre*), fellowship (*Gemeinschaft*, a reference to the collection), the breaking of bread (*Brotbrechen*, a reference to the Lord's Supper), and prayers

[32] See Schattauer, *Communion Patterns*, chap. 4.

[33] See *Agende*, GW 7/1:10, 17–18. See also Deinzer, 2:132–133, and Theodor Schäfer, *Wilhelm Löhe: Vier Vorträge über ihn nebst Lichtstrahlen aus seinen Werken* (Gütersloh, 1909) 106.

[34] *Agende*, GW 7/1:18; cf. p. 12.

[35] *Agende*, GW 7/1:10.

[36] For his comments on the relation of Lutheran liturgical tradition to the Roman Catholic (particularly the Mass), see "Vorwort," *Sammlung*, vol. 3, GW 7/2:698–702; *Agende*, GW 7/1:10–12; and *Evangelischer Geistliche*, GW 3/2:251–253.

[37] "Brief vom 24. October 1848," GW 2:46.

[38] *Evangelischer Geistliche*, GW 3/2:250.

(Gebete). The *Communio* is the most complete liturgical act because it comprehends all four of these primitive elements, and, for Löhe, the evidence of the early Eastern liturgies displayed both the simplicity and the splendor of this arrangement.[39] What Löhe sought in his evangelical Mass was an *ordo* that mediated the Roman Mass through the restorative critique of Lutheran theology and liturgical practice and that was, furthermore, transparent to the fundamental elements and spirit of early Christian worship.

Löhe's published rite for the *Communio* in the second edition of his *Agende* shows the results of his effort to set out an *ordo* for the principal service of Christian worship (see Fig. 1). This is also the *ordo* that Löhe worked to establish in his own parish.[40]

Fig 1. The *Communio* in Löhe's *Agende* (1853)[41]

Note: The outline employs **bold face** to indicate a title provided in Löhe's text of the rite.

The Communio or Principal Service

Hymn
Confiteor

Introit or Hymn
Kyrie eleison together with Gloria in excelsis
    a. Kyrie
    b. Gloria together with Et in terra
Collects

---

[39] For Löhe's use of Acts 2:42, see "Vorwort," *Laienagende*, GW 7/2:702–703; *Evangelischer Geistliche*, GW 3/2:250–251; and also "Brief 10/24/1848," GW 2:46.

[40] The official parish reports *(Pfarrbücher)* from Löhe and his predecessor offer a remarkable view into the actual course of Löhe's liturgical work in his parish. I have used the exemplars of Löhe's 1843 and 1864 reports held in the Landeskirchliches Archiv Nürnberg and that of the 1833 report from Gottlob Weigel found in the Pfarrarchiv Neuendettelsau. For a fuller commentary on Löhe's *Communio* and the evidence of its relation to liturgical practice in the Neuendettelsau parish, see Schattauer, *Communion Patterns*, chap. 4. See also Kressel, *Löhe als Liturg*, 114–152.

[41] GW 7/1:47–76. Cf. *Agende für christliche Gemeinden des lutherischen Bekenntnisses* (Nördlingen, 1844), 3–34; *Laienagende*, 2nd ed., 1–25; and *Haus-, Schul- und Kirchenbuch*, 2:190–211.

Epistle
Alleluia
German Hymn
Gospel
Credo
Sermon, concluding with:
    Intercessions
    Announcements

Offertory, with:
    Offering
    Preparation of Bread/Wine and Pastor
General Prayer

Preface with Sanctus
Consecration (= Institution Narrative)
Agnus
Our Father
Pax
Distribution, with:
    Prayer
    Confessio corporis et sanguinis Christi
    Hymn or Psalm
Nunc dimittis or Song of Simeon Luke 2 or Hymn

Conclusion
    a. Collect
    b. Benedicamus
    c. Lord's Blessing

Apart from the obvious influence of the Roman Mass and Lutheran liturgical tradition, it is especially worth noting how the fundamental elements of Christian worship that Löhe gleaned from his reading of Acts 2:42 (and subsequent liturgical history) helped to shape his published rite and motivated much of his practical liturgical efforts. The three central structures of his *ordo* correspond to apostolic teaching (Epistle-Sermon), fellowship (Offertory-General Prayer), and the breaking of bread (Preface-

Nunc dimittis), and attention to the forms of prayer is evident throughout.

Together with the celebration of the Lord's Supper, the forms of churchly prayer were, according to Löhe, the most important means of liturgical formation. "Teach your congregation the prayers of the church," he writes; "a praying congregation is a truly liturgical congregation."[42] And consequently we see in the *ordo* for the *Communio,* as well as in the liturgical practice of his own congregation, the restoration of historic forms of public prayer: e.g., the collect, the Eucharistic preface, and a general prayer refashioned (under the influence of Eastern models) to include a congregational response to each of the petitions.[43]

The Word of God at the center of the Church's life was, for Löhe, the apostolic Word recorded in the New Testament Scriptures,[44] and his *ordo* for the *Communio* gave new emphasis to the place of this apostolic teaching in the liturgy. It provided for both epistle and gospel readings in contrast to the previous practice in his own parish, presumably not uncommon, which called for one or the other. Although the *Agende* itself does not include a lectionary, we know that Löhe was committed to the restoration of the traditional epistles and gospels of the Western Mass lectionary, which many Lutheran Churches had maintained at the time of the Reformation but the use of which had been disrupted during the Enlightenment.[45] Moreover, Löhe was concerned to protect the practice of a formal, liturgical reading of Scripture against ration-

[42] "Vorwort," *Laienagende,* GW 7/2:703; see also *Evangelischer Geistliche,* GW 3/1:253, and *Agende,* GW 7/1:20–21.

[43] For Löhe's comments on the collect, see *Agende,* GW 7/1:56, 125–128, "Von den heiligen Personen," GW 3/1:569, and "Vorwort," *Die Episteln und Evangelien des Kirchenjahres samt Kollekten und Verzeichnis passender Psalmen und Lieder für lutherische Gemeinden* (1861), in GW 6/3:830–831; on the preface, see "Vorwort," *Sammlung,* vol. 3, GW 7/2:700–701, *Agende,* GW 7/1:64–66, and *Abendmahlspredigten,* GW, Ergr. 1:58–59; on the general prayer, see *Agende,* GW 7/1:63, "Von den heiligen Personen," GW 3/1:569, and *Evangelischer Geistliche,* GW 3/1:253.

[44] See *Drei Bücher,* GW 5/1:97–118 [ET: *Three Books,* 61–91].

[45] The Brandenburg-Nürnburg *Kirchenordnung* of 1533, the most important Reformation church order in Franconia, did not commend the use of the historic lectionary, but favored the *lectio continua* reading of a chapter from an epistle followed by a chapter from a gospel or Acts; see Emil Sehling, ed. *Die*

alistic sentiment that questioned its necessity and completely failed to understand "that the common reading [of Scripture] has its own particular blessing, how splendid it is when the whole congregation stands and honors the Word of the Lord with solemn devotion and reverent attention to every syllable."[46]

Löhe's provision for an offertory song during which "the congregation offers its free will gifts for the poor, the sick, and for churchly purposes, especially mission"[47] was his attempt to reconstruct this portion of the liturgy through a recovery of the early Christian fellowship of goods *(Gemeinschaft)* rather than through the sacrificial notions that characterized the offertory in the Roman Mass and rejected by the Lutheran reformers. Löhe wanted to include in the offertory "the prayerful presentation of the elements," but he hesitated to give such an offering of the bread and wine formal liturgical expression because of the potential for misunderstanding and conflict.[48] Instead of an offertory prayer, Löhe encouraged his congregation to pray silently while the pastor solemnly brought the bread and wine to the altar.[49] To this evangelical offertory he joined the general prayer *(gemeines Gebet)*, modeled after one found in several Lutheran church orders. The prayer includes a series of petitions addressed to God for the Church and its ministers, for worldly authorities, for enemies, for

---

evangelischen Kirchenordnungen des XVI. Jahrhunderts, vol. 11 (Tübingen: Mohr, 1961) 194–195.

For Löhe's reflection on lectionary matters, see *Evangelischer Geistliche, GW* 3/2:242–243; "Vom Bibellesen," (1858), in *GW* 3/1:328–329; "Von den heiligen Personen," *GW* 3/1:561–565. For his work on the lectionary for Sundays and feast days, see especially *Die Episteln und Evangelien des Kirchenjahrs samt Kollekten und Verzeichnis passender Psalmen und Lieder für lutherische Gemeinden* (Nürnberg, 1861), of which only the foreword is reprinted in *GW* 6/3:828–832; see also the evidence in *GW* for the daily lectionaries that included the epistles and gospels for Sundays and feasts, *Lektionarium für das Kirchenjahr* (1850/1851), in *GW* 7/2:708–714, and "Lektionarium für das ganze Kirchenjahr," *Haus-, Schul- und Kirchenbuch*, vol. 2 (1859), in *GW* 7/2:714–719. Löhe was acquainted with the historical work on the Roman lectionary by Ernst Ranke, *Das kirchliche Perikopensystem aus den ältesten Urkunden der Römischen Liturgie dargelegt und erläutert* (Berlin, 1847) (Kressel, *Löhe als Liturg*, 123).

[46] "Von den heiligen Personen," *GW* 3/1:561.

[47] *Agende, GW* 7/1:60.

[48] *Agende, GW* 7/1:19.

[49] *Abendmahlspredigten, GW*, Ergr. 1:155–156.

all in need, for protection from physical and spiritual affliction, for the fruits of the earth and for human activity, and a final petition, composed by Löhe himself, for the elect and the consummation of God's purposes. In effect, the fellowship expressed in the offering continues in prayer. And Löhe wanted these actions of fellowship, the offering of gifts and the prayers for all, understood as sacrifice (Opfer), the "liturgical manifestation of the spiritual priesthood of all Christians."[50]

The bulk of Löhe's liturgical work on the *ordo* for the *Communio*, however, focused on the breaking of bread, the celebration of the Lord's Supper itself. Among his initiatives, three were most fundamental: 1) the structural integration of the Lord's Supper into the principal service, 2) a more frequent celebration of the Supper, and 3) the construction of a fuller Eucharistic action.

It was Löhe's conviction that without the Lord's Supper the principal service on a Sunday or feast day was sadly deformed; "it looked like a column in ruins, like a flower stem without its crown."[51] In contrast to the dominant conception of the principal service as a preaching service, Löhe stressed the unity of Word and table and the centrality of the sacrament in the ordering of the liturgical act. In the introduction to the first edition of his *Agende*, Löhe compared

"the train of thought in the liturgy of the principal service to a double-peaked mountain, one peak somewhat lower than the other, like at Horeb and Sinai. The first peak is the sermon, the second the sacrament of the altar, without which I cannot imagine a perfect service on earth. At the principal service, we are always engaged in climbing until we have reached the table of the Lord, where there is nothing higher above us but heaven. . . ."[52]

The sermon-dominated worship of the day presented two major obstacles to this vision of the place of the Lord's Supper. The

---

[50] *Agende*, GW 7/1:60; see also GW 7/1:19, and *Evangelischer Geistliche*, GW 3/2:253. For Löhe, discipline (*Zucht*), fellowship (*Gemeinschaft*), and sacrifice (*Opfer*) were the principal foundations for the common life of Christians (*Vorschlag*, GW 5/1:221–252).

[51] "Vorwort," *Sammlung*, vol. 3, GW 7/2:698; cf. *Agende*, GW 7/1:84.

[52] *Agende*, GW 7/1:13; cf. the even higher estimation of the sacrament in the second edition of the *Agende*, GW 7/1:18.

common practice of many Lutheran congregations limited the Lord's Supper to designated Communion Sundays in the spring and the fall, and, furthermore, most of the congregation was dismissed after the sermon so that only a smaller group of properly prepared communicants remained for the sacramental celebration. Although Löhe's *Agende* did make provision for Sunday and feast-day worship without the sacrament, it clearly presumed as the norm a celebration of Lord's Supper at a service for the entire congregation that joined sermon and sacrament.

In the practice of his own parish, we can see concretely how Löhe sought to accomplish his aims for a unified liturgical act and a more frequent observance of the Lord's Supper. Early in his ministry at Neuendettelsau, Löhe moved to bring an end to the celebration of the Lord's Supper as a separate service for communicants only, whenever the sacrament took place at the principal service. He stopped dismissing the congregation with the customary blessing after the sermon and vigorously encouraged everyone to stay and participate in the Lord's Supper even if they were not among those prepared to receive Communion. Although the physically infirm and some recalcitrant individuals continued to leave after the sermon, Löhe had established, in principle and in practice, a unified liturgical act joining Word and sacrament.[53]

A regular celebration of the Lord's Supper at the principal service on every Sunday and feast day was not so easily accomplished. When he arrived at the Neuendettelsau parish in 1837, Löhe inherited a pattern of seasonal communions: five or six consecutive Communion Sundays (*Abendmahlssonntage*) in the spring (*Frühlingscommunion*) and again in the fall (*Herbstcommunion*). The spring Communion was a kind of paschal Communion beginning with a celebration of the Lord's Supper on Palm Sunday (the day for confirmations) and then on Good Friday—not Easter—and continuing on into the Easter season; the fall Communion season began in October and always included Reformation Sunday (the first Sunday in November). This pattern of seasonal Communions had been established at the Neuendettelsau parish early in the century, and it reflected a common disruption of Lutheran liturgical tradi-

[53] The Neuendettelsau parish reports of 1833, 1843, and 1864 all provide evidence concerning this development; see Schattauer, *Communion Patterns*, chap. 4.

tion under the influence of the Enlightenment as churches moved away from the practice of observing the Lord's Supper on Sundays and feast days throughout the course of the church year.[54] Löhe's earliest effort to adjust the pattern to his own purposes involved shifting the spring Communion to the Lenten season and providing for the celebration of the Lord's Supper on major feast days—Christmas, Easter, Ascension, and Pentecost—as well as on Maundy Thursday. Then, in 1851, Löhe announced a return to the pattern of celebration that had preceded the spring and fall Communion seasons and posted a schedule that called for Communion Sundays every third week (including Easter, Pentecost, and Reformation Sunday) as well as celebrations of the Lord's Supper on Maundy Thursday, Ascension, and Christmas.[55] The full implementation of this schedule is not clearly evidenced until the mid-1850s, when the presence of mission students, deaconesses, and others related to the diaconal foundation may have helped to provide a sufficient number of communicants throughout the year.[56]

[54] The spring and fall Communions were perhaps a Lutheran adaptation of the seasonal observance of the Lord's Supper among Reformed Churches.

[55] See Hans Kressel, *Wilhelm Löhe als Katechet*, 158–160, where he quotes the entry from 5 Epiphany 1851 in Löhe's announcement book *(Abkündigungsbuch)*. Löhe also describes the change in his 1864 parish report. In addition to the celebrations of the Lord's Supper at the parish church, there were regular observances (eventually bi-annually) at churches in the two neighboring villages affiliated with the parish.

[56] The confession and Communion records *(Confitenten-Register* or *Beichtregister)* of the parish, mission school, and the deaconess house provide the most detailed information about the patterns of sacramental celebration and participation; see also *Abendmahlspredigten*, GW, Ergr. 1:134–140. For a more complete account of Löhe's efforts, see Schattauer, *Communion Patterns*, chapter 4.

Two further developments fill out the picture of the frequency of the Lord's Supper at Neuendettelsau during Löhe's pastorate and provide a context for understanding Löhe's comment in his *Abendmahlspredigten* that "the Neuendettelsau congregation now celebrates the Lord's Supper every Sunday" (GW, Ergr. 1:136). In 1864, Löhe instituted the practice of a small Communion *(kleine Communion)* on those Sundays when the sacrament was not celebrated at the principal service. It consisted of a brief order for the Lord's Supper proper preceded by a general confession and took place early on Sunday morning. In this way, Löhe established a regular Sunday celebration of the sacrament, though it was not always a great Communion *(große Communion)* at the principal service.

Finally, among Löhe's fundamental initiatives to restore and reshape the celebration of the Lord's Supper, we need to mention his attempts to provide an action of prayer to encompass the biblical words of institution. According to Löhe, the words of institution alone were not sufficient. Obedience to the Lord's command and example required a prayer of blessing or thanksgiving *(Segen, Danksagung,* also *Weihegebet)*, and such prayer was necessary for the consecration of bread and wine as Christ's body and blood.[57] Furthermore, Löhe sought to provide a formal liturgical anamnesis *(liturgisches Gedächtnis)* in accordance with the Lord's command to celebrate the Supper in remembrance of him as well as the Apostle Paul's understanding of the Supper as a proclamation of the Lord's death (1 Cor 11:26).[58]

In his *Agende,* Löhe constructed a simple Eucharistic action, recognizably Lutheran, but also informed by the broader liturgical tradition of Eucharistic prayer, both East and West. It moves from the thanksgiving of the Preface and *Sanctus* to the consecratory words of the institution narrative and then to what Löhe understood as an anamnetic proclamation of the Lord's death *(Todesver-kündigung)* in the German *Agnus,* all of which preceded the Lord's Prayer and *Pax* preparatory to the distribution (see Fig. 1). Löhe appeals to early Christian and Lutheran sources for this arrangement and points to the Roman Mass as well as to various Eastern liturgies published in the eighteenth-century collection by Eusebius

---

In 1860, the deaconess community gained permission to hold public worship in its chapel. The pattern of great Communions every third Sunday and on the second day of the feasts of Christmas, Easter, and Pentecost complimented the parish schedule. In 1868, regular small Communions began at the deaconess chapel and displaced the practice in the parish church.

Taking into consideration the patterns of small and great Communions at the four locations of worship in the Neuendettelsau parish—the parish church itself, the two neighboring village churches, and the deaconess chapel—we will understand Löhe's statement that "it can happen that among the various churches of our parish the holy Supper is celebrated twice, even three times, on a Sunday" *(Abendmahlspredigten, GW,* Ergr. 1:136). Still, there were Sundays when the Lord's Supper was not a part of the principal service at any of the locations.

[57] See *Abendmahlspredigten, GW,* Ergr. 1:57–59, 128–129.

[58] See *Abendmahlspredigten, GW,* Ergr. 1:64–68. For more on liturgical anamnesis, see *GW,* Ergr. 1:38–44.

Renaudot.[59] In an appendix to the rite, the *Agende* provides a summary of "the oldest Lutheran order for the second part of the Mass," based upon Luther's *Formula missae* (1523), and also reproduces a portion of the Egyptian anaphora of St. Basil.[60] These liturgical models served to demonstrate the antiquity of the sequence thanksgiving-institution narrative-anamnesis and its relation to Lutheran practice.[61]

Löhe continued to develop the Eucharistic action even after the 1853 edition of his *Agende,* and the latest evidence of its shape prior to Löhe's death can be found in the fifth edition (1871) of his *Beicht- und Kommunionbüchlein für evangelischen Christen.*[62] There we find the following elements:

Preface

Sanctus

Institution Narrative

Agnus

Prayer of the Breaking of the Bread *(Gebet des Brotbrechens)*

[59] *Agende,* GW 7/1:64-68; see also GW 7/1:77-78. Cf. "Vorwort," *Sammlung,* vol. 3, GW 7/2:609-701, and *Evangelischer Geistliche,* GW 3/2:251-253. The collection of texts by Renaudot had been recently published in a new edition; see *Liturgiarum orientalium collectio,* 2nd ed., 2 vols. (Frankfurt and London, 1847; Westmead, Farnsborough, Hants., Eng.: Gregg, 1970).

[60] *Agende,* GW 7/1:77-79, 71-83. Löhe's German translation of the latter is based upon Renaudot's Latin translation of the Coptic text, originally in Greek. Egyptian Basil is now regarded as one of the earliest Eucharistic prayers, perhaps as early as the late third century, and there is agreement that it lies behind the Byzantine anaphora of St. Basil (R.C.D. Jasper and G. J. Cuming, eds. *Prayers of the Eucharist: Early and Reformed,* 3rd ed. [New York: Pueblo, 1987], 67).

[61] On this liturgical structure in Löhe's Eucharistic action, see Schattauer, *Communion Patterns,* chap. 4.

[62] Frieder Schulz, "Der Beitrag Wilhelm Löhes zur Ausbildung eines evangelischen Eucharistiegebetes," in *Gratias Agamus: Studien zum eucharistischen Hochgebet,* ed. Andreas Heinz and Heinrich Rennings (Freiburg: Herder, 1992) 461-462. Schulz notes that the critical edition of *Beicht- und Kommunionbüchlein* in GW 7/2 has overlooked the 5th ed., which was the final edition during Löhe's lifetime (p. 466 [n. 31]). As Schulz shows, this edition provides the documentary evidence that allows us to firmly establish Löhe's hand in the most complete form of the Neuendettelsau order for the Lord's Supper, first published in *Gottesdienstordnung des evang.-luth. Diakonissenhauses Neuendettelsau,* 5th ed. (Neuendettelsau: Diakonissenanstalt, 1911). Cf. Kressel, *Löhe als Liturg,* 140-142.

Our Father

Pax

Proclamation of the Lord's Death *(Todesverkündigung)*

Distribution[63]

In the final form of the Eucharistic action that we have from Löhe, the Preface/*Sanctus*-Institution Narrative-*Agnus* structure remains intact, but two new elements enclose the Lord's Prayer and *Pax* before the distribution. The first is a prayer to be chosen from three options, all taken from the 1856 Bavarian *Agendenkern*. In the *Agendenkern*, it is called a Communion prayer *(Abendmahlsgebet)* and is placed before the Lord's Prayer and precedes the institution narrative.[64] Löhe preserves its relation to the Lord's Prayer, which in his rite places it after the institution narrative, and labels it a prayer of the breaking of the bread *(Gebet des Brotbrechens)* or *Oratio fractionis*.[65] Based upon his knowledge of the texts in Renaudot, it was Löhe's understanding that a fraction prayer had preceded the Lord's Prayer in the early Eastern liturgies,[66] and he found the new Communion prayers in the Bavarian *Agendenkern* suitable for this purpose as he continued to work on his own order. These prayers of preparation for Communion contain, in the observation of Frieder Schulz, a communion epiclesis *(Personen-Epiklese)* and other Eucharistic themes, such as the sacrifice of Christ, the kingdom of God, spiritual communion with Christ, and the fellowship

[63] Schulz, 462.

[64] *Agenden-Kern für die evangelisch-lutherische Kirche in Bayern. Mit vorangestellter Ordnung und Form des Hauptgottesdiensts an Sonn- und Festtage* (Nürnberg, 1856) 17, 84–85.

[65] The three Communion prayers from the Bavarian *Agendenkern* are first evidenced in the 4th ed. (1858) of Löhe's *Beicht- und Kommunionbüchlein, GW* 7/2:294, and subsequently in the 1859 *Haus-, Schul-, und Kirchenbuch*, 2:206-208; see also the 1st and 2nd ed. (1859, 1864) of *Hausbedarf, GW* 7/2:81–82. Although neither the sources noted here nor the *Agende* give any indication of a ritual breaking of the bread in the rite, Löhe undoubtedly intended that this prayer accompany an actual fraction. The elimination of the fraction had distinguished Lutheran practice from both Roman Catholic and Reformed. Löhe, however, considered the fraction an act of obedience to the Lord's institution of the Supper *(Abendmahlspredigten, GW*, Ergr. 1:59–63, 70–71, 128). Hans Kressel pointed to this evidence in his *Löhe als Liturg*, 137 (n. 61), where he cites his own summary of Löhe's *Abendmahlspredigten* in *Löhe als Prediger*, 176–179.

[66] *Agende, GW* 7/1:68.

of the Church.[67] The other new element is a second proclamation of the Lord's death *(Todesverkündigung)* in addition to the German Agnus, this time in the form of "a solemn liturgical anamnesis."[68] Here Löhe uses his rendering of the anamnesis in the Egyptian anaphora of St. Basil, which he had previously presented in the second edition of his *Agende*. There is further evidence from Löhe's *Abendmahlspredigten* that the modified version of this text found in the later *Gottesdienstordnung* of the deaconess house was already in use:

"Pastor: As often as you eat of this bread and drink of this cup, you shall proclaim the Lord's death until he comes.

Congregation: Your death we proclaim, O Lord, and your resurrection we confess.

Pastor: We celebrate the remembrance of your passion, your death, your resurrection from the dead, your ascension above all the heavens, your sitting at the right hand of majesty on high, and your fearful coming again to judge the living and the dead.

Congregation: Pray to the One who is to come, with fear and trembling."[69]

With this addition, Löhe completed his desire to amplify the element of remembrance in the Eucharistic action with a formal liturgical anamnesis, something he had probably contemplated at least as early as his 1853 *Agende*.[70]

---

[67] Schulz, 463.

[68] *Abendmahlspredigten*, GW, Ergr. 1:65–67.

[69] *Gottesdienstordnungen des evang. -luth. Diakonnissenhauses Neuendettelsau*, 6th ed. (Neuendettlesau: Diakonissenanstalt, 1925) 112–113; the text was first published in the 5th ed. (1911). Taken together, the quotations in the *Abendmahlspredigten*, GW, Ergr. 1:39, 66, 67, show clearly that Löhe himself modified the text as found in *Agende*, GW 7/1:83, and subsequently in the 5th ed. (1871) of the *Beicht- und Kommunionbüchlein*. The earlier version provided a literal translation of the source in Renaudot; the later version reflects Löhe's adaptation of the original for actual liturgical usage. Cf. the comments of Wittenberg, GW, Ergr. 1:39 (nt. 11), 67 (nt. 15) and Schulz, 461.

[70] See Löhe's discussion of the placement and form of the *Todesverkündigung* in *Agende*, GW 7/1:67–68, 77–78. The very presence of the Egyptian Basil text in the *Agende* suggests that he had already considered such an addition to his

All of this indicates the depth of Löhe's concern for the reconstruction and renewal of the liturgical act. This was not an antiquarian interest abstracted from his work as a parish pastor and his larger concerns for the Church of his day; these concerns came from his conviction that the services of the Church are acts to be lived, not merely observed. The liturgical act, as Löhe understood it, could not be reconstituted apart from the congregational assemblies of Christians gathered for worship.

THE LITURGICAL ASSEMBLY

"You have a liturgical people," observed one of the many visitors to Sunday worship at Löhe's parish in Neuendettelsau,[71] and that observation points directly to the fact that Löhe's concern went beyond the structure and ceremonial execution of the liturgical act to the liturgical assembly itself. His attention to the liturgical assembly was both theological and pastoral; he addressed ecclesiological matters in relation to the constitution of the assembly for Eucharistic worship and the participation of the entire assembly in the liturgical action, and he also worked out the practical means for constituting the assembly and for engaging its participation. It is to the issues of liturgical participation and the constitution of the assembly through the exercise of discipline and the practice of confession that we now turn.

Löhe's desire for a congregation that actively participated in the liturgy impelled him to confront the generally passive role of the congregation customary at the time. Hymn singing was the principal means of participation in a clerically dominated act of worship directed at the congregation. As Löhe observed, congregations which "only hear and are stimulated inwardly, do not want to be active themselves, and therefore do not want to pray."[72] The worship he envisioned called for a congregation actively engaged in the liturgy as its own act of prayer. If the people were to become "liturgically minded and liturgically formed,"[73] more was needed than encouraging certain practices identified as liturgical, like anti-

---

rite. His desire to be able to justify the thoroughly Lutheran character of his rite probably prevented him from including it earlier (GW 7/1:17–18).

[71] Deinzer, 2:130–131.

[72] *Evangelischer Geistliche*, GW 3/1:253.

[73] "Vorwort," *Laienagende*, GW 7/2:703.

phonal singing. It was a matter of shaping an ecclesial assembly that involved itself in the deepest movements of the liturgy. The essential means of such liturgical formation were, for Löhe, the celebration of the Lord's Supper, the use of various forms of liturgical prayer, and the offering of gifts for the needs of all.[74] These could shape an assembly in its communion with God in Christ and in a churchly fellowship directed prayerfully and sacrificially to the world and its needs.

In his own parish, there were indeed many evidences of the active participation of the congregation at worship. The congregational singing of the *Gloria in Excelsis Deo* and the *Sanctus* and the common recitation of the Nicene Creed impressed Sunday visitors to Neuendettelsau.[75] On Communion Sundays, all the members of the congregation remained for the Lord's Supper whether or not they were communicants, and many parishioners began to receive Communion more than the customary two times a year.[76] In contrast to common practice, the people learned to add their Amen to prayers and blessings.[77] Löhe's regular exhortations to prayer and sacrificial giving must have had some effect on the inward and spiritual levels of participation as well as on the visible and audible actions of the congregation.

The liturgy as a whole and in its parts was, for Löhe, a profoundly communal act, not the arena of clerical privilege and power. The notes in his *Agende* concerning the structure of the collect probably preserve for us something of what he taught his parishioners about this part of the liturgy as an act of common prayer. The salutation ("The Lord be with you"/"And with your spirit") confirms the unity of pastor and congregation and renews "the consciousness of churchly fellowship"; the *Oremus* ("Let us pray") is "the sign of communal prayer"; the collect itself, although spoken or sung by the pastor, is the "prayer of the assembled

[74] "Vorwort," *Laienagende*, GW 7/2:703, and *Evangelischer Geistliche*, GW 3/1:253.

[75] Deinzer, 2:131.

[76] For Löhe's instruction as to how often to receive Communion, see *Abendmahlspredigten*, GW, Ergr. 1:136–140.

[77] "Erklärung vom 31. Juli 1846" [= "Löhes Stellungnahme zur Beschwerde wegen Einführung einer neuen Kirchenordnung"], in GW 5/1:188–189; see also Deinzer, 2:130.

congregation"; and "the Amen belongs to the congregation," not the pastor.[78] Pastor and people join together in the assembly that conducts the liturgy's acts of prayer, praise, thanksgiving and offering. These actions of the assembly revolve around the pastoral acts of proclamation and sacramental consecration and distribution, where the pastor functions as the minister of God's Word, as that Word is directed to and received by the assembly in faith. It was Löhe's conviction, nonetheless, that the entire congregation, as the proper subject of the liturgy, bore responsibility for the whole act of worship, including its specifically ministerial actions.[79]

Löhe's efforts to structure the preparation for Eucharistic worship further clarify his understanding of the liturgical assembly, particularly as it gathered for the Lord's Supper. Löhe argued for and promoted two things: first, he sought to restore the effective exercise of church discipline through the practice of the announcement *(Anmeldung)*, whereby a person intending to be a communicant registered that intention with the pastor (the announcement also served to identify those who would prepare themselves for Communion by making confession); second, Löhe wanted to revitalize the practice of confession *(Beichte)* itself, in part through a restoration of private confession. The announcement and confession were both inherited practices that had functioned to assist the individual preparing for Communion, lest he or she partake in an unworthy manner (1 Cor 11:27-29). While Löhe's use of the announcement and confession clearly furthers the tradition of preparing individuals for a worthy participation, he seems equally concerned about how these practices constitute an assembly capable of celebrating the sacrament.

A statement from an early work promoting the announcement as a means of church discipline in relation to the Lord's Supper points to Löhe's ecclesiological concern:

"A person can eat and drink judgment against himself, and does eat and drink it against himself whenever he does not come as a Christian. Preaching and baptism are for the congregation in formation *(werdende [Gemeinde])*, the Lord's Supper for the perfected

---

[78] GW 7/1:55-56.
[79] *Abendmahlspredigten*, GW, Ergr. 1:171-178.

congregation *(gewordene Gemeinde)*. Whoever is not a Christian is not invited.''[80]

It was not only the individual Christian that concerned Löhe, but also the congregation that assembled for the Lord's Supper. The use of the announcement to warn a person deeply ignorant of the faith or to discipline the heretic or the unrepentant sinner was to prevent such individuals from profaning the sacrament and incurring God's judgment. It also served to define the boundaries of Eucharistic fellowship *(Abendmahlsgemeinschaft)* and thus to establish the Eucharistic assembly as the gathering of a visible community of faith, especially in the context of a state church, where baptism was tantamount to a privilege of birth and a nominal Christianity all too prevalent a factor in church life. For Löhe, it was critical that the relation of the assembly of genuine believers to the Church in its concrete historical, institutional, and liturgical life not be dissolved by a sharp distinction between the invisible and the visible Church; rather he likened that relation to the essential unity of soul and body in the human person.[81] In the context of a Church that was, in Löhe's view, all too neglectful of the standards of Christian faith and life, the exercise of church discipline at the announcement prior to the assembly for the Lord's Supper was a necessary and practical instrument for defining and safeguarding the visible, Eucharistic assembly as a genuine community of faith.

The distinctive features that emerge in the Neuendettelsau practice of the announcement reflect Löhe's deep concern to foster a disciplined community of faith and life in its assembly for the Lord's Supper.[82] From the start, Löhe insisted on a personal an-

---

[80] ''Vom Abendmahlsgenuß,'' *GW* 5/1:47.

[81] For Löhe's discussions of the visible and invisible Church, see *Drei Bücher, GW* 5/1:115–118 [ET: *Three Books,* 87–91]; *Kirche und Amt, GW* 5/1:527–529; and ''Von den heiligen Personen,'' *GW* 3/1:526–528; also Hebart, 55, 118–126, 243–249, 289–290, 297–298. On the general discussion of this issue at the time, see Holsten Fagerberg, *Bekenntnis, Kirche und Amt in der deutschen konfessionellen Theologie des 19. Jahrhunderts* (Uppsala: Almqvist, 1952) 127–131.

[82] The most important documentation of Löhe's conduct of the announcement is found in the following: the 1843 and 1864 *Pfarrbüchern;* ''Wie es mit der Übung der Kirchenzucht in der Pfarrei Neuendettelsau gehalten wird und gehaltern werden soll'' (1857), in *GW* 3/2:369–372; ''Erklärung vom 2. Februar

271

nouncement and criticized the custom that allowed a person to be registered by someone else (a wife, child, or servant) and thus avoid an encounter with the pastor. Because Löhe understood the congregation as the locus of the scriptural mandate for church discipline (cf. Matt 18), the announcement at his parish eventually took place publicly in the church (on the Friday morning before a Communion Sunday) rather than privately in the pastor's office. At Neuendettelsau, the pastoral responsibility to withhold absolution and the sacrament from unrepentant public sinners was taken with utmost seriousness by Löhe himself; moreover, it was exercised with the assistance of the congregation and particularly the members of the church council, who stood alongside their pastor in judgment of all who came to announce themselves for confession and Communion.

The application of church discipline at Neuendettelsau went far beyond the customary concern for sexual immorality, which often limited itself to the misconduct of women. The evidence of Löhe's conduct of the announcement and the reflections he shared with fellow pastors indicate that he sought to apply the Church's discipline to a wide range of behavior that he regarded as incompatible with Christian life: e.g., angry disputes between neighbors; the theft of property; dancing, drinking, gambling, swearing, and the running and frequenting of taverns, where such things often took place; as well as the sexual immorality of both men and women. In addition to these and other matters of moral behavior, Löhe believed that the Church's discipline ought to be applied to those who persisted in holding to false doctrine.

1859," in GW 5/2:741–743; Ernst Lotze, *Erinnerungen an Wilhelm Löhe: Aus dem Nachlaß vom D. Ernst Lotze, Geh. Oberkirchenrat in Gera*, ed. Diakonissenanstalt Neuendettelsau (Neuendettelsau: Diakonissenanstalt, 1956) 30; Friedrich Bauer, *Vater Löhes Ehrengedächtnis* (Nürnberg, 1872) 10; and Deinzer, 2:168. For Löhe's reflections on the practice of the announcement and the exercise of Eucharistic discipline, see "Vom Abendmahlsgenuß," GW 5/1:47–46; and "Von der Zucht," GW 5/1:503–505; "Von den heiligen Personen," GW 3/1:575–579; and *Der sakramentliche Teil des Konfirmandenunterrichts. Zur Repetition für Konfirmierte* (1860), in GW 3/1:512–513, 516–518. A more general statement of his views on church discipline is contained in *Vorschlag*, GW 5/1:226–244. See also Klaus Ganzert, *Zucht aus Liebe: Kirchenzucht bei Wilhelm Löhe*. Bekennende lutherische Kirche 2 (Neuendettelsau: Freimund, 1949); Kressel, *Löhe als Katechet*, 77–79, 137–138; and Schattauer, *Communion Patterns*, ch. 2.

Löhe applied two further restrictions to sacramental participation at Neuendettelsau. Profound ignorance of the basic Christian teaching about sin and grace, the benefits of the sacrament, and its worthy reception were cause for pastoral concern, especially, according to Löhe, among rural folk such as those he served in his parish. Löhe upheld the responsibility of the pastor to warn such people away, unless their lack of understanding could be mitigated before the requested participation in the sacrament. Furthermore, as a strict confessional Lutheran and against the common practice of his Church, Löhe also insisted on restricting the sacrament to confirmed Lutherans and not extending it to members of Reformed or Union Churches.[83] In Lutheran Neuendettelsau, this issue would have presented itself in the cases of farm and household workers from other locales as well as persons related to the mission school and deaconess community.

The exercise of church discipline at the announcement fostered a congregation capable of sacramental celebration and participation, and gathered a visible community of Christians out of a state Church that, in Löhe's estimation, lacked sufficient moral and doctrinal definition and catechetical formation. The practice of confession was the next step in the preparation of the Eucharistic assembly.[84] For a time, there were three kinds of confession avail-

---

[83] See, for example, "Kirchliche Briefe" (1860), in GW 5/2:847–849.

[84] For Löhe on confession in general, see Einfältiger Beichtunterricht für Christen evangelisch-lutherischen Bekenntnisses (1836), in GW 3/1:153–193 [ET, abr.: "Simple Instruction in Confession for Christians of the Evangelical Lutheran Communion," trans. Delvin E. Ressel, Una Sancta 10/2 (1951) 1–9, 10/3 (1951) 10–23]; "Vorwort," Sammlung 2, GW 7/2:692–698; Beicht- und Kommunionbüchlein, GW 7/2:237–283: "Von den heiligen Personen," GW 3/1:580–583; Konfirmandenunterrichts, GW 3/1:509–511; and Abendmahlspredigten, GW, Ergr. 1:164–170. For some contemporary descriptions of Neuendettelsau practice, see Lotze, 30–31; Bauer, 13–14; and Deinzer, 2:157–167. See also Kressel, Löhe als Katechet, 64–77, 134–137; Laurentius Klein, Evangelisch-Lutherische Beichte: Lehre und Praxis, Konfessionskundliche und Kontroverstheologische Studien 5 (Paderborn: Bonifacius, 1961) 212–216; Martin Wittenberg, "Die Beichte bei Wilhelm Löhe," Homiletisch-liturgisches Korrespondenzblatt, n.s., 17 (1987/1988) 5–43 [ET, abr. and rev.: "Wilhelm Löhe and Confession: A Contribution to the History of Seelsorge and the Office of the Ministry within Modern Lutheranism," trans. Gerald S. Krispin, in And Every Tongue Confess, ed. Gerald S. Krispin and Jon D. Vieker (Dearborn, Mich.: Nagel Festschrift Committee, 1990) 113–150]; and Schattauer, Communion Patterns, chap. 3.

able at Neuendettelsau. Löhe continued the customary general confession (allgemeine Beichte) for communicants following the penitential vespers (Beichtvesper), which took place the Saturday afternoon preceding a Communion Sunday.[85] In 1843, he restored the practice of private confession (Privatbeichte) and encouraged its use alongside the familiar general confession.[86] Private confession, which took place in the sacristy of the church before the penitential vespers, became the preferred place for pastoral care (Seelsorge) of the individual, and the announcement, which had until then served this purpose, was able to emerge as the locus for a more public and communal exercise of discipline. It was Löhe's conviction that those identified and disciplined as public sinners should be required to make a public confession (öffentliche Beichte), and so he established a practice of public confession in his parish and utilized it until around 1860, when pressure from the Landeskirche forced him to abandon it.[87] At a public confession, the members of the church council joined Löhe in hearing the confession, which

[85] On Löhe's conduct of and reflections on general confession, see the order provided in his Agende, GW 7/1:414–418; the 1843 and 1864 Pfarrbücher; and the sources and literature cited in nt. 79.
It should be noted that Löhe distinguished between general confession for the communicant preparing for the Lord's Supper and the form of confession proper to the beginning of the principal service (the Confiteor). This latter form was a common confession of pastor and the whole congregation in preparation for worship, and the absolution accompanying it was a general statement of God's mercy and forgiveness rather than a solemn pronouncement of the same as in general confession and private confession; see Beicht- und Kommunionbüchlein, GW 7/2:263–265; "Von den heilgen Personen," GW 3/1:581–582; and the formulas for the Confiteor in the Agende, GW 7/1:48–51.
[86] On Löhe's restoration of private confession and its conduct, see "Stellungnahme," GW 5/1:189–190; Evangelischer Geistliche, GW 3/2:275–280; "Neuendettelsauer Briefe" (1858), in GW 3/1:211–221; "Erklärung 2/2/1859," GW 5/2:739–740; and the 1843 and 1864 Pfarrbücher; see also the formulas for confession and absolution in Agende, GW 7/1:411–414. For Löhe's general reflections on private confession, which often provide insight as to how he instructed his parishioners and how he conducted confession, see Evangelischer Geistliche, GW 3/2:280–286; and "Privatbeichte," GW 3/1:233–237. See also the sources and literature cited in n. 79.
[87] On Löhe's conduct of public confession see "Erklärung 2/2/1859," GW 5/2:741–743, and the 1864 Pfarrbuch. See also Schattauer, Communion Patterns, chap. 2.

took place in the church before worship on the Sunday that the penitent was to be received back into the assembly as a communicant.[88]

Absolution was the high point of each form of confession, and for Löhe it had the character and solemnity of a sacrament. The clearest declaration and fullest expression of forgiveness was possible in response to a private confession or a public confession by the individual. Here the pastor spoke the formula of absolution directly to the penitent individual and accompanied it with a laying on of hands. In the case of general confession (which was an individual confession done in common), Löhe did not approve the use of an individual act of absolution as was customary in some places. Instead, the formula of absolution was addressed to the whole group of penitents, and there was no laying on of hands. Löhe also insisted on the use of a formula of retention at a general confession, whereby the proclamation of forgiveness was withheld for those lacking true penitence and faith.

Although confession and absolution were in themselves supremely individual matters, the penitential preparation of communicants for the reception of the sacrament as it was arranged and invigorated by Löhe realized a twofold significance for the Eucharistic assembly as a whole. In the first place, it signified that, despite a rigorous exercise of discipline in faith and morals, the holiness of the assembly that gathered for the Lord's Supper was founded upon God's mercy. The congregation forgiven and reconciled to God, and its members to one another, was prepared and set apart for its highest act of worship not by the pursuit of moral and spiritual perfection but by trust in the grace of God. Secondly, a renewed emphasis upon absolution as the individual reception of forgiveness in preparation for Communion, including a restoration of both private and public confession, allowed the Lord's Supper to emerge from purely penitential and individualistic associations. For Löhe, the principal service of Christian worship was primarily *communio* or fellowship *(Gemeinschaft)*, the assembly's communion with God in Christ and its members with one another in the body

---

[88] See the formulas for the announcement of excommunication and the announcement of reconciliation in Löhe's *Agende, GW* 7/1:418–424.

of Christ.[89] Lutheran sacramental theology and piety had tended to obscure this conception of the sacrament, stressing Luther's depiction of the Lord's Supper as a testament or promise of forgiveness.[90] Löhe's attention to the practice of confession and the bestowal of forgiveness in absolution assisted his retrieval of the *communio* concept and with it the role of the liturgical assembly at the Lord's Supper.

The efforts of Löhe that we have examined here—his efforts to gather a visible assembly of Christians disciplined in faith and life, to engage its participation in a pattern of worship focused on a celebration of the Lord's Supper reshaped according to historic models, and to move the Lutheran Church beyond satisfaction with the soundness of its doctrinal heritage and teaching into the practice and enjoyment of a vital liturgical and sacramental life—were all directed to his overarching concern for the identity of the Church as an apostolic community of witness, service, and worship in the modern world. If Kavanagh is correct in his observation that the modern Church suffers from the dissolution of rite, and thus the loss of an encompassing Christian way of life regularly made manifest and available in the liturgical act of particular assemblies of the faithful, then Löhe is one forbear who grasped the dimensions of the ecclesial problem and the critical role of the liturgy in addressing it. While Löhe's response will not in every instance be our own, the reconstruction of rite that he envisioned as a reform in "churchly consciousness, life, and work" stands as a legacy that continues to stimulate and challenge. He would no

---

[89] See *Abendmahlspredigten*, GW, Ergr. 1:69–77; for Löhe's understanding of the Church as *communio*, see Hebart, 48–50, 100–113.

[90] See Luther's *Treatise on the New Testament, that is, the Holy Mass* (1520), in *Luther's Works* (American Edition) [= LW], ed. Jaroslav Pelikan and Helmut T. Lehman, 55 vols. (St. Louis: Concordia, and Philadelphia: Fortress, 1955–1986) 35:82–92; *The Babylonian Captivity of the Church* (1520), in LW 36:37–44; and the *Small Catechism* and *Large Catechism*, in *The Book of Concord*, ed. and trans. Theodore G. Tappert (Philadelphia: Fortress, 1959) 351–352, and 447–450, respectively. The understanding of the Lord's Supper as a *communio* can also be found in Luther, especially in *The Blessed Sacrament of the Holy and True Body of Christ, and the Brotherhoods* (1519), in LW 35:50–67 (Yngve Brilioth, *Eucharistic Faith and Practice: Evangelical and Catholic*, trans. A. G. Hebert [London: SPCK, 1961], 95–98, 133–135). The Lutheran doctrine of the real presence is also implicitly related to the *communio* concept.

doubt have agreed that "the liturgy is not merely one ecclesiastical 'work' or one theological datum among others. It is simply the church living its 'bread and butter' life of faith under grace, a life in which God in Christ is encountered regularly and dependably as in no other way for the life of the world."[91]

[91] Kavanagh, 8.

Part II

Liturgical Studies

David N. Power, O.M.I.

13. Commendation of the Dying and the Reading of the Passion

The reading of the passion of Christ has disappeared from the *Ordo Commendationis Morientium*[1] of the revised Roman liturgy. All that remain are two brief excerpts, placed among a variety of biblical readings recommended for use during a person's final agony. These excerpts are from the Lucan passion narrative and illustrate Jesus' attitudes in face of his own death. One pericope gives the account of his prayer in the garden (Luke 22:39-46), while another is the commendation of his spirit to the Father upon the cross (Luke 23:42-43).[2] Jesus' acceptance of death and his commendation of himself to the Father in face of death serve as a model or example for the dying Christian, but there is no prolonged account of the passion.

Though the reading of the passion narrative is thus excluded from the present order, it belongs to the earlier strata of what we know to have been the rites of Commendation of the Dying in the Roman liturgy, and it remained among the possible aids in the final hours of dying (*"in agone exitus"*) in the *"Ordo Commendationis Animae"* of Title V, Chapter VII of the Roman Ritual of 1614, which was the one replaced by the order of 1975.

What is known of the history of this practice, and what can be said of the purpose and meaning of the tradition at the various

[1] It is promulgated as Chapter VI of the *Ordo Unctionis Infirmorum eorumque Pastoralis Curae* (Vatican City: Typis Polyglottis Vaticanis, 1975).

[2] The passion narratives are still mentioned among the biblical readings that could be used anytime in the course of visitation of the sick, but they are not put forward as appropriate to the hour of death.

stages of its development?[3] What is of interest is how within the immediate preparation for death, the passion is placed in different settings or contexts, which affect its meaning for the dying person. No doubt there is a measure of ritualism in liturgical history, some texts and actions being retained simply because they are in the sources put to use. There is, however, also evidence of deliberate decisions in the way in which usage is revised or augmented, and this reflects changing attitudes and spiritualities.

The aim of this essay is a better acquaintance with the vagaries of the practice. This may help us to understand how past ages helped the dying reflect on Christ's passion as they approached death, and thus may offer a starting point for reflection on current attitudes and ritual prescriptions.

HISTORY

The first liturgical indication of the reading of the passion is found in the earliest extant evidence for the Commendation of the Dying in the Roman liturgy, namely in *Ordo Romanus* XLIX,[4] where one finds a continuous rite for obsequies, starting with the final moments of the dying person and continuing through to the preparation, waking and burial of the body. In this order, the reading of the passion[5] begins after the giving of Viaticum and ceases only in the moment of death, accompanying the dying person in the passage from this life.

It is in the Gelasian Sacramentaries of the eighth century, and in monastic rituals of the eighth and ninth, that we see rites of

[3] The tradition is briefly outlined by Damien Sicard, *La Liturgie de la mort dans l'église latine des origines à la réforme carolingienne*, Liturgiegeschictliche Quellen und Forschungen 63 (Münster: Aschendorf, 1978) 39–43.

[4] M. Andrieu, *Les Ordines romani du haut moyen âge*, vol. IV, Spicilegium Sacrum Lovaniense 28 (Louvain: Université Catholique, 1965) 523–530. The Roman pattern and the Gallican emendations have been carefully studied by Sicard, op. cit.

[5] "legenda sunt passionis dominice" is how the text reads. Later texts refer to the "passiones domini," probably giving the proper meaning intended by the poor Latin of OR XLIX. Though the term is in the plural, this does not seem to mean all the passion narratives, for wherever a text is specified it is the reading from Matthew. Possibly all narratives were at one time intended, but the Latin could also be understood to refer to the "sufferings" of the Lord recounted in the Gospel, rather than to the literary units of the passion narratives.

Frankish origin dominate the Roman practice in the Commendation of the Dying.[6] The Rheinau Sacramentary[7] has departed considerably from the Roman practice. Communion goes with
penitential reconciliation and anointing is considered a separate
and preceding rite. The dying person is accompanied in the immediate preparation for death by litanies and the prayer
"Proficiscere." There is no reading of the passion. In this,
Frankish traditions prevailed over Roman. This affected many
other ritual books which followed this same pattern. Thus in
many books ritual separated Viaticum from immediate preparation
for death[8] and left out the reading of the passion.

Other books blend Roman and Frankish traditions, and allow for
some retention of the reading of the passion. The Sacramentary of
Autun[9] kept it, but reversed the order of the Roman rite and put
the reading of the passion before Viaticum, specifying that the text
to be used is that of John's Gospel. It is followed by the psalm,
"Quemadmodum" (Ps 41/42), used in the Roman liturgy after ex-
piration, and a litany. Viaticum is provided on the point of death.[10]

The Pontificale Romano-Germanicum of the tenth century[11] keeps
the giving of Communion ("communicandus de sancto sacrificio") at
the point of death, but does not mention a reading of the passion
during the death agony, nor indeed among its varied rites for the
visitation of the sick. On the other hand, a Beneventan Ritual of
the eleventh century[12] keeps the order of the Sacramentary of
Autun: the passion is read (passiones domini is the term used, but

---

[6] For a study of this influence and development, see F. Paxton, Christianizing Death. The Creation of a Ritual Process in Early Medieval Europe (Ithaca &
London: Cornell University Press, 1990).

[7] Sacramentarium Rhenaugiense, ed. Anton Hänggi and Alfons Schönherr,
Spicilegium Friburgense 15 (Fribourg: Universitätsverlag, 1971) 1325–1326.

[8] F. Paxton, Christianizing Death, 92–161.

[9] Liber Sacramentorum Augustudonensis, ed. Odilo Heiming, Corpus Christianorum Latinorum 159B (Turnhout: Brepols, 1984) 1914.

[10] n. 1914: "Inde vero antequam egrediatur a corpore communicet eum
sacerdos corpus et sanguinem illum praevidentes ut sine viaticum non exeat."

[11] Le pontifical romano-germanique du dixième siècle, ed. Cyrille Vogel and
Reinhard Elze, vol. 2, Studi e Testi 227 (Vatican City: Biblioteca Apostolica
Vaticana, 1963) CXLIX, 1–7.

[12] Ein Rituale im beneventanischer Schrift. Ende des XI Jhdts, ed. A. Odermatt,
Spicilegium Friburgense 26 (Fribourg: Universitätsverlag, 1980) XIV, 212.

this could mean not several narratives, but the "sufferings" of Christ), then Communion is given with this prayer:

"May our prayers rise up to you, Lord, and may eternal joys receive the soul of your servant. May you command that she/he whom you have made a child of adoption, became a participant of your eternal inheritance."[13]

The *Liber Tramitis*, or House Customary, of Abbot Odilo of Cluny[14] in the eleventh century kept the rite of the *Ordo Romanus*, with the Communion first and then the reading of the passion *(legendae sunt passiones)*. To this the text adds the directive that the dying monk be placed on the ground, on sackcloth and ashes, for this is the proper way for a Christian to depart from this world, as has been exemplified by the deaths of many saints.[15]

A twelfth-century codex for a clerical/lay confraternity, the Confraternity of Santa Maria di Montefusco, follows much the same procedure in its Commendation of the Dying.[16] Viaticum and the reading of the passion are followed by the placing of the dying person on sackcloth and ashes. The rite is more fully developed than in the Cluny customary, with blessing prayers for the sackcloth and ashes and a pleading of Christ's fleshly mysteries.

[13] "Ascendant ad te, domine, preces nostre et animam famuli tui gaudia aeterna suscipiant et quem fecisti adoptionis participem, iubeas hereditatis tuae esse consortem. Per." Ibid., 214.

[14] See *Liber Tramitis Aevi Odilonis Abbatis,* vol. X of the Corpus Consuetudinum Monasticarum, edited by Petrus Dinter (Siegburg: Apud Franciscum Schmitt Success, 1980) 272.

[15] loc. cit.: "quia filius christiani non debet migrare nisi in cinere et cilicio sicut iam in multis exemplis sanctorum experti sumus." A similar directive is found in the *Consuetudines Cluniacenses,* Liber III, Cap. XXIX, compiled by Uldaric, and published in Migne's Patrology. See PL 149, 772A.

[16] *Istituzioni Ecclesiastiche e Vita Religiosa dei Laici nel Mezzogiorno Medievale. Il Codice della Confraternità di S. Maria di Montefusco (Sec. XII),* ed. G. Vitolo (Rome, 1982), Title VII on Obsequies. The rubric reads: "Then let the passion of the Lord be read by a presbyter or deacon." Though still influenced by monastic custom, the codex provides for elements of the common life for diocesan clergy, with considerable attention to how they are to assist one another in dying and in death. It allows for some participation of lay persons, especially in the benefits of a communal approach to helping one another in sickness and in dying, and in the burial and commemoration of the dead.

Monastic rituals set the tone, as they do for all rites for sick, dying and burial. Thus a ritual from Biburg in the twelfth century[17] prescribes the reading of the passion narrative from Matthew, rather than John, (though the reading is referred to in the plural—*passiones*) at the final agony, Communion having been previously connected with confession and anointing. In the Ritual of St. Florian (twelfth century) published by Adolph Franz,[18] the order of Commendation is as follows: Communion, litany, seven penitential psalms, and the reading of the passion from Matthew *(passiones)* until the dying person expires, when the *"Subvenite"* is sung, followed by the *"Proficiscere"* prayer. Another twelfth-century monastic ritual, that of Saint Fleury,[19] like the Biburg ritual, has the reading of the *passiones*, but no Communion on point of death, Viaticum having preceded, followed by anointing. The passion accounts are to be read after the litany, and in conjunction with the singing of psalms, if the moribund is attentive and conscious *(si eger habuerit memoriam)* and the time of dying *(obitus)* is prolonged. As soon as the person has died, the *"Proficiscere"* is said.

Outside the monastic ambience, the twelfth-century Roman Pontifical[20] kept the order of OR XLIX, with Communion first and then the reading of the passion, the compiler having this order before his eyes, according to Andrieu's conjecture.[21] At this point of the Pontifical, he departed from his usual dependence on the PRG X. To the reading of the passion, however, he adds the reading of the Lazarus story from John 11 and the story of Jesus' visit to Mary, Martha, and Lazarus at Bethany, when he was anointed in preparation for his death (John 12).

Turning, however, to rites which greatly influenced later developments in the commendation of the dying and in burial rites in the

[17] *Das Klosterrituale von Biburg (12 Jh.)*, ed. Walter Von Arx, Spicilegium Friburgense 14 (Fribourg: Universitätsverlag, 1970) XXXVIII, 315-317.

[18] *Das Rituale von St. Florian aus dem Zwölften Jahrhundert*, ed. Adolph Franz (Fribourg: Herdersche Verlagshandlung, 1904) 86-88.

[19] *The Monastic Ritual of Fleury*, ed. Anselme Davril, Henry Bradshaw Society CV (London: Boydell Press, 1990) 225.

[20] M. Andrieu, *Le pontifical romain du XII siècle*, vol. 1 of *Le pontifical romain au moyen âge*, Studi e Testi 86 (Vatican City: Biblioteca Apostolica Vaticana, 1938) Lib, 1.

[21] *Ordines romani* IV, 524.

Roman liturgy, one notes the prevalence of the Frankish pattern. The thirteenth-century Pontifical of the Roman Curia,[22] and the Franciscan ritual,[23] do not provide for a reading of the passion. In the prescriptions of the Curial Pontifical, the dying person is to receive Communion and to be stretched out on blessed sackcloth and ashes, as has already been seen prescribed by Odilo and in the Montefusco codex. Litanies and the *"Proficiscere"* accompany the dying person's last moments. In the Franciscan ritual, there is neither a final Viaticum nor a reading of the passion during the death agony.

Despite the Roman and Franciscan influence, in some rituals or orders for the Commendation of the Dying, the reading of the passion remained even after the thirteenth century.[24] As late as the sixteenth century, it is found in the *Liber Sacerdotalis* of Castellani (1523), and in the 1584 ritual of Gregory XIII, from where it entered the 1614 edition of the Roman Ritual.[25] The *Liber Sacerdotalis* of Castellani allows for the reading of all four accounts, followed by the discourse of Christ at the Supper, in John 13–17. The Gregorian ritual, edited by Cardinal Sanctorius, gives preference to the Johannine account, which is to be preceded by the reading of the Supper discourse in John 13–17. If the dying person continues to survive and to remain conscious, the other three passion accounts may be read.

In the 1614 ritual,[26] it is the Johannine account that is given, and it is preceded by the so-called sacerdotal prayer of John 17. This is in fact the second of three sets of texts to be used in a person's final agony. First, there are the prayers of Frankish custom, the litany, the *"Proficiscere,"* with oration, and *"Commendo,"* followed by the *"Libera"* prayer. Several late medieval prayers follow as part of this unit, including one to Mary and one to Joseph.[27] The

[22] M. Andrieu, *Le pontifical de la curie romaine au XIII siècle*, vol. 2 of *Le pontifical romain au moyen âge*, Studi e Testi 87 (Vatican City: Biblioteca Apostolica Vaticana, 1940) L, 5–7.

[23] *Sources of the Modern Roman Liturgy*, vol. 2, ed. S. J. P. Van Dijk (Leiden: E. J. Brill, 1963) 390–392.

[24] See Sicard, op. cit. 41f.

[25] Information in Sicard, l. c.

[26] Title V, chapter VII, 5.

[27] Ibid., 4:
May the most clement Virgin Mary, Mother of God, most loving consolatrix

second unit provides for a prolonged death agony *(si diutius laboret anima)* and consists of the Johannine readings, already mentioned, with a prayer to follow, and the recitation of Psalms 117 and 118, which are in turn completed by three highly devotional and personal prayers, addressed to Christ. The third unit, given under the heading *"De Exspiratione"* (chapter VIII of the Title) is a set of short aspirations, addressed to Jesus, Mary, and Joseph.

Through this somewhat muddled progression, despite the prevalence over time of Frankish elements in the Commendation of the Dying, and despite the introduction of new devotional elements, the reading of the passion remained in the Roman liturgy, though without the prescriptive sense of the original *Ordo Romanus* XLIX, where the text reads *legenda*.

INTERPRETATION

Does context and setting allow an interpretation of this custom or of the changes which affected it?

Ordo Romanus XLIX

In this order, the passion follows the reception of Eucharistic Communion given for the passage through death to the next life, that is the Viaticum, and is itself followed, on the point of death, by the *"Subvenite"* antiphon with the psalm *"In exitu Israel"* (Psalm 113 in the Latin Psalter). There is clearly a sense in which the reading of the passion is taken as an expression of the transition from this life in communion with the Lord, and a participation in the mystery of which the Eucharist is guarantee and anticipation. It is specifically said that this participation in the holy sacrifice will be a help and a defense at the time of the resurrection of the body, which was the main eschatological focus of early

---

of the suffering, commend the spirit of this servant to her Son: so that through her maternal intervention she/he may not fear the terrors of death, but may go joyfully, in her company, to the hoped-for mansion of the heavenly homeland.

To you, Joseph, I fly, patron of the dying, and I commend the soul of this servant, labouring in her/his last agony, to you, at whose passage from this world Jesus and Mary kept vigil, double and sweet guarantee, so that he/she may be freed through your protection from the snares of the devil and from eternal death, and may merit to come to eternal joy.

All English translations in this article are the author's own.

Christian centuries.[28] Though the rite looks forward to the resurrection, the thought of liberation from sin through the saving sacrifice of Christ is not absent from these prescriptions and could be heightened by the reading of the passion. *Adiutor* and *defensor* are significant words, especially when conjoined with the designation of the Eucharist as sacrifice, suggesting the need for Christ's sacramental protection in the face of evil and sins at the time of death and in the hour of resurrection. This way of relating Eucharist to death and sin is not alien to the Roman liturgy and practice and gives a certain nuance to the reading of the passion in conjunction with Viaticum.

The understanding that the Eucharist is propitiatory is expressed, for example, in the prayers of the *Veronense* for the Masses to be said for those who have been reconciled before death, but without the opportunity to do appropriate penance. There are three Mass formulas for persons who have died without the opportunity to do canonical penance: XXXIII, 1138–1140; 1141–1143; 1144–1150.[29] In these prayers the language of propitiation is quite evident. The prayers over the oblations and the insertion, *Hanc igitur,* into the Roman Canon in particular ask that the sacrificial offering may please and placate God, and that as offerings of propitiation they may obtain God's mercy for the deceased.[30]

This is not as strong or extravagant as the practices of offering propitiation after death, as found in the *Dialogues* of Gregory the Great; but it shows that, in addition to it being a sharing in the mystery of Christ's Passover, the Eucharist did have the sense in Roman liturgy of appealing to the offering made in remembrance of Christ's death as a remedy against sin and its eternal consequences. Viewing the Eucharist as a defense and help that looks forward to the resurrection of the dead, the dying person could meditate on the passion of Christ and thereby find in it both the

---

[28] loc. cit.: "communicandus de sancto sacrificio, defensor et adiutor in resurrectione justorum."

[29] *Sacramentarium Veronense,* ed. L. Mohlberg (Rome: Herder, 1960) XXXIII. The Masses seem to date to around the time of Leo the Great.

[30] Thus we find such phrases as "piae placationis officia," "propitiatus accipias, et miserationum tuarum largitate concedas," or "mortis vinculis absolutis."

assurance of transition to eternal life and a protection to appeal to in contemplation of one's own sins.

Romano-Frankish Sacramentaries and Rituals

The purpose of reversing the sequence in the Sacramentary of Autun—that is, putting the reading of the passion before Viaticum—is to have the dying person pass over into the other world with Communion in the mouth, or, at least in the belly.[31] This is to put even greater emphasis on the need to have, as it were, the price of admission.

In the blending of Roman and Frankish custom, the reading of the passion is preceded by the prayer for liberation through Christ's mysteries and followed by the prayer which commends the dead to a joyful transition. This contextualizes the reading of the passion, so that it both comforts in face of the need for liberation and forgiveness, assured through Christ's sufferings, and allows the dying person to anticipate the joy of eternal life and resurrection.

Some rituals gave a heavier accent to penitential expression in the hour of death. As recorded by Sicard, an order from the Church of Sienna states that the reading of the passion should excite the dying person to compunction.[32] The placing on sackcloth and ashes, such as is recorded in the Cluny practice, the Codex of Montefusco and the Curial Pontifical, clearly highlights this need for compunction at the hour of death; thus one can see how the reading of the passion as a contemplation of Christ's sufferings could contribute to such sentiments. On the other hand, the Curial Pontifical adds the reading of the raising of Lazarus to that of the passion, and thus introduces the hope of resurrection. It also has the story of the Bethany anointing which allows the dying penitent, strengthened by the company of caring friends, to anticipate death in a self-giving and accepting way.

Roman Ritual

Two features of the Roman Ritual suggest the meaning given to the reading of the passion, and they are anticipated in the Castellani and Gregorian ordinals. These are the relation of the narrative

[31] See Sicard, loc. cit., where he refers to Life of Melania.
[32] Sicard, loc. cit., 41.

of the passion to John 17, and the prayers addressed to Christ either by, or in the name of, the dying person, during the final agony ("in agone"). While the Castellani and Sanctorius commendations allow for the reading of the entire supper discourse in John 13–17, the Roman Ritual of 1614 singles out that section of John 17 which is sometimes referred to as Jesus' sacerdotal prayer, or his prayer of self-offering on behalf of humankind. Putting this along with the passion narrative from John invites the hearer to see the passion itself as Jesus' sacerdotal act, its intention and meaning being expressed in the sacerdotal prayer. The reading is to be followed by this prayer:

"God, who for the redemption of the world wished to be born, to be circumcised, to be rejected by the Jews, to be betrayed by Judas with a kiss, to be bound in chains, as the innocent lamb led out to be a victim, and to be indecently held up as a spectacle before the eyes of Anna, Caiphas, Pilate and Herod, to be accused by false witnesses, to be inflicted with whips and opprobrium, to be spat upon, to be crowned with thorns, to be beaten with rods, to be struck with a reed, to have your face veiled and your garments torn off, to be affixed with nails to the cross, to be lifted up on the cross, to be placed between thieves, to be made to drink vinegar and gall, to be wounded with a lance: may you, Lord, through these most holy sufferings and punishments,[33] which I recall in my unworthiness, and through your holy cross and death, free me from the pains of hell and deign to lead me there where you led the thief crucified along with you. Who with the Father and the Holy Spirit lives and reigns for ever and ever."[34]

The prayer accentuates, listing them one by one, the sufferings and indignities of Christ's passion, but in so doing appeals to them as sufficient to release sinners from the pains or punishments of hell. Freed from this fear by recollection of Christ's

---

[33] I use these two words to try to render the fuller sense of the word "poenas."

[34] loc. cit.:

Deus, qui pro redemptione mundi voluisti nasci, circumcidi, a Judaeis reprobari, a Juda traditore osculo tradi, vinculis alligari, sicut agnus innocens ad victimam duci, atque conspectibus Annae, Caiphae, Pilati, et Herodis indecenter offerri, a falsis testibus accusari, flagellis et opprobriis vexari, sputis

sufferings, the dying person can hope to join him, as did the thief, in his passage to glory. No doubt, if fervor is wanting in the dying sinner's repentance this is inspired by the memory of Christ's afflictions. Thus both the hope for release from the punishment for sin by reason of the merits of Christ's passion, and confidence in a peaceful transition in communion with him from this world, are combined. The prayer in effect, by briefly summarizing the content of the passion account, interprets its reading through this double emphasis. It is noteworthy that, rather than bring out the need to make reparation for the sin for which Christ suffered, the prayer inspires confidence in forgiveness and beatitude through the recollection of these sufferings. Both the note of repentance and that of trust are brought out by the recitation of Psalms 117 and 118 after the prayer. The *Confitemini* psalm is a song of access to Jerusalem after victory, and is full of thanksgiving and confidence. Psalm 118 is a meditation on the Law of the Lord, and thus conducive to a movement of conscience that judges one's adherence and transgressions.

The final prayers to be said[35] in the hour of last agony, after the reading of the passion and the recitation of Psalms 117 and 118, show just as clearly this same hope and confidence that come from the recollection of Christ's agony. They bring out, however, more the idea that Christ suffered for sinners and because of sin. Christ's heavenly intercessory action consists of continuing to show his wounds to the Father on behalf of sinners:

---

conspui, spinis coronari, colaphis caedi, arundine percuti, facie velari, vestibus exui, cruci clavis affligi, in cruce levari, inter latrones deputari, felle et aceto potari, et lancea vulnerari: tu, Domine, per has sanctissimas poenas tuas, quas ego indignus recolo, et per sanctam crucem et mortem tuam, libera me a poenis inferni, et perducere digneris, quo perduxisti latronem tecum crucifixum: Qui cum Patre et Spiritu Sancto vivis et regnas in saecula saeculorum.

This prayer is already found at the same spot in the *Rituale Sacramentorum, Gregori XIII iussu edit, auctore J. A. Card. Sanctorio* (Paris: Bibl. Couvent S. Jacques, 127A3) 375. On microfiche in the Mullen Library, The Catholic University of America, Washington, D.C.

[35] Together with three Paters and three Aves. These prayers are also found, among many others of the same style, in the Ritual of Gregory XIII, loc. cit., 405. The second of the prayers is in the *Liber Sacerdotalis* of Castellani, whose rites for the dying are devotionally much more sober.

"Lord Jesus Christ, through your most holy agony and through the prayer which you prayed for us on the mont of Olives, when your sweat became as drops of blood flowing out on the earth; I beseech you, that against the multitude of the sins of your servant you may deign to show to the almighty Father the extent of your bloody sweat which constrained by fear you shed copiously for us; free her/him in this hour of death from all the pains and tribulations which he/she fears to have earned for sins. Who, etc.

"Lord Jesus Christ, who deigned to die for us on the cross, I beseech you, that you may offer and show to the Father almighty for the soul of this your servant, all the bitterness and pain of your passion which you sustained on the cross for our sins, most of all in that hour when your most holy soul left your most holy body; free her/him in this hour from all penalties and sufferings which she/he fears to have deserved for sins. Who, etc.

"Lord Jesus Christ, who said through the mouth of the prophet: In everlasting love I have loved you, therefore in mercy I have drawn you: I beseech you that you may offer and show to the Father almighty for the soul of this your servant, that same love which drew you from heaven to earth to endure the bitterness of your sufferings; thus free her/him from all penalties and sufferings which she/he fears to have deserved for sins. Save her/his soul in this hour of departure. Open to her/him the gate of life, make her/him rejoice with your saints in everlasting glory. And may you, most loving Lord Jesus Christ, who redeemed us by your most precious blood, have mercy on the soul of your servant and deign to bring it to the ever green and sweet pastures of paradise, so that it may live in undivided love for you, and may never be separated from you and your elect. . . ."

The Ars Moriendi

This approach to the recollection of Christ's passion did not spring from nowhere in 1614. It may well have been inspired by the spirituality and attitude to the passion and the Cross expressed in The Art of Dying, which had been so highly developed in the preceding centuries until it reached its climax in a fifteenth-century anonymous text, which was widely circulated in the original and in translations. How much this art, or "ars," as it was fostered by spiritual writers and pastors, centered on the passion of Christ as liberation from sin and punishment appears from the questions put to a dying person, which were in the fourteenth century attributed to Anselm of Canterbury[36] and are found, among other places, in the work of Jean Gerson. The text reads:

"Do you rejoice that you shall die in the Christian faith?

"Do you confess that you have lived so badly that you have earned eternal punishment? Do you repent this? Do you intend to emend your life, should you be given the space to do so? Do you believe that our Lord Jesus Christ died for you? Do you give him thanks? Do you believe that you could not be saved except through his death?

"Endeavour, therefore, as long as your soul remains in you, to place your whole confidence in that death, so that you put confidence in nothing else. Commend yourself totally to that death, hide yourself in it alone, involve your whole self in it.

"If the Lord God wishes to judge you, say: Lord, I place the death of our Lord Jesus Christ between myself and your judgment, otherwise I would not contend with you.

"And if he should say to you, that you are a sinner, say: Lord, I place the death of our Lord Jesus Christ between myself and my sins.

"If he should say to you, that you merited damnation, say: Lord, I place the death of our Lord Jesus Christ between myself and my

---

[36] Interrogation of a dying person, attributed to Anselm of Canterbury by Galvano of Levanto, c. 1350, and adapted in the counsels for accompanying the dying in Jean Gerson. See Alberto Tenenti, *Il Senso della Morte e l'Amore della Vita nel Rinascimento (Francia e Italia)* (Turin: Einaudi, 1957) 86. The text used here is taken from the article by Balthasar Fischer, "Ars Moriendi. Die Anselm von Canterbury zugeschriebene Dialog mot einen Sterbenden. Ein untergegangenes Element der Sterbliturgie des Mittelalters," in *Im Angesicht des Todes. Ein interdisziplinäres Kompendium*, ed. H. Becker, B. Einig and P. Ullrich (St. Ottilien: Patmos Verlag, 1987) 1365. A version of these interrogations is given in the ritual of Gregory XIII, loc. cit., 379–381, and a transposition into material for an exhortation is found in the 1614 *Rituale Romanum*, Title V, 5, 3.

evil merits, I offer his merit for the merit that I ought to have gained but did not.

"If he should say to you, that he is angry with you, say: Lord, I place the death of our Lord Jesus Christ between me and your anger.

"When this is finished, the dying person shall say three times: Into your hands I commend my spirit."[37]

In this dialogue with the dying person, the first objective is to excite her or him to repentance and compunction for sin. With the recollection of the death of Christ, however, the dying penitent is exhorted to trust and confidence, placing this death before God and, as it were, hiding behind it, so that God sees only the love and the suffering of Christ, and not the vileness or faults of the sinner. Thus inspired, the moribund person can die in complete peace, using the words of Christ in his own death agony: Into your hands I commend my spirit.

According to Tenenti, Gerson and others of his time believed that the sufferings of the sick could be offered up in communion with Christ's sufferings as compensation for sin and for release from the pains of purgatory. This provides an added motivation for the meditation on the passion. Gerson does indeed give such an assurance, when he has the patient addressed in these words: "If with a contrite heart you willingly endure your necessary suffering (poenam), God will remit all penalty (poena) and fault (culpa), and you will certainly enter paradise."[38]

---

[37] For the form that the interrogations take in Gerson, see *Opusculum Tripartitum*, Pars III, "De Scientia Mortis." In *Joannis Gersonis Opera Omnia* (Antwerp: Sumptibus Societatis, 1706) col. 447–450. In the edition of Gerson's works by Msgr. Glorieux, *Jean Gerson. Oeuvres Complètes*, vol. 1 (Paris: Desclée & Cie., 1960) 42, it is noted that the original text was in French. The proposal to print this text in vol. 7 of the collection was not realized. On the art of dying and relevant literature, see Tenenti, op. cit., 80–107, and Mary Catharine O'Connor, *The Art of Dying Well: The Development of the Ars Moriendi* (New York: Columbia University Press, 1942).

[38] Ibid. The Latin reads: "Quod si sic corde contrito patiens poenam necessariam tanquam voluntariam feres, et omnem poenam et culpam remittet Deus, certusque paradisum introibis."

In the prayer in which he invites the dying person to address Jesus, Gerson shows how much the person is to look for release to the Passion of Christ:

"O most sweet Jesus, through the honour and power of your most blessed Passion command me to be received among the number of your elect. O my Saviour and Redeemer, I surrender myself totally to you, do not reject me; I come to you, do not spurn me. Lord, I ask for your Paradise, not on account of the value of my own merits, but because of the power and efficacy of your most blessed Passion, through which you willed to redeem me, a miserable sinner, and deigned to purchase me Paradise through the price of your blood. Hasten to confer it upon me, for in doing so neither your riches nor your power are lessened, nor is Paradise itself made any narrower or any less."[39]

There is not the detail of Christ's suffering in this prayer which is found in the prayers of the Roman Ritual, but the same basic reliance on the passion and a similar affect are given voice.

In the anonymous text of the fifteenth century to which the title *Ars Moriendi*[40] was given, and which was translated and widely divulged in different languages, we see how in the remembrance of Christ's passion and death, devotional attitudes tended to emphasize not just the value of his suffering but his subjective agony and turmoil. In chapter VI of the work, we find this prayer addressed to Christ, intended to be said for persons caught up in their dying moments:

---

[39] loc. cit. Gerson follows this prayer with one to the Virgin, one to the angels, and one to the favorite saints of the dying person. The Latin text of the prayer reads:

Dulcissime Jesu, ob honorem et virtutem tuae benedictissimae Passionis jube me recipi intra numerum electorum tuorum. Salvator meus et Redemptor meus, reddo me totum tibi, non me renuas; ad te venio, non me repellas. Domine Paradisum tuum postulo, non ob valorem meorum meritorum; sed in virtute et efficacia tuae benedictissimae Passionis, per quam me miserum redimere voluisti, et mihi Paradisum pretio tui sanguinis emere dignatus es: ipsum mihi conferre festina, propter quem nec tuae divitiae aut potentiae minuetur, nec ipse Paradisus angustior aut minor invenietur.

[40] Information and references are given in O'Connor, op. cit. See also Nancy Lee Beaty, *The Craft of Dying. A Study in the Literary Tradition of the Ars Moriendi in England* (New Haven & London: Yale University Press, 1970).

"My most sweet redeemer, most merciful Jesus and most benign Lord, for the most sorrowful cry that thou didst give forth in thy manhood when thou shouldst die for us and were so consumed with sorrow and travail of thy great passion that thou didst cry out forsaken of thy Father, be not angry towards our sister/brother thy servant but forgive him/her through thy mercy in the hour of his/her death, and be mindful of the grievous affliction and pain of her/his soul, for in the last hours of passing from this world, and of the giving up of the spirit, he/she has no power to call on anyone for help; but by the victory of the cross and the power of thy holy passion and thy loving death, think not of affliction but of mercy and comfort and deliver her/him fully from all manner of anguish; with the same hands that thou didst suffer to be nailed to the cross for her/his sake with sharp nails, good Jesus, sweet father and lord, deliver her/him from the torments ordained for him/her, and bring her/him into everlasting rest with a cry of exultation and the knowledge of thy mercy. Amen."[41]

An accompanying prayer addressed to Mary shows the same purpose in appealing to Christ's passion, even though now it is asked that Mary intercede for the sinner with her Son:

"Ever spotless and blessed Virgin Mary, singular help and succour in every anguish and necessity, give us thy sweet help and show thy gracious visage to our sister/brother now at her/his last end, and chase all his/her enemies from her/him through the power of the Cross of thy dear beloved Son, our Lord Jesus Christ, and deliver him/her from all manner of disease of body and soul, that she/he may thank and worship God without end."[42]

Within the *Craft of Dying*, as the Latin *Ars Moriendi* is aptly rendered in English versions, and its antecedent texts, there is much emphasis on sin, on the fear of hell, and on the need to confess. All of this was intended to move to solid repentance. Too often, it seems, practice maintained this emphasis on sin and on fear up to

[41] "The boke of the craft of dying." In *Yorkshire Writers. Richard Rolle of Hampole and His Followers*, edited by C. Horstman, vol. II (London: Swan Sonnenschein & Co., and New York: Macmillan & Co., 1896) 419. I have modified the archaic English so as to make it more readily comprehensible.

[42] loc. cit. These are but two of the several prayers addressed to God, to Jesus, to Mary, and to St. Michael.

the point of death, and even thereafter in the devotions associated with purgatory. In the *Ars Moriendi* itself, however, as in Gerson and then later in the Roman Ritual, when the hour of death approached, the contemplation of Christ's passion was used to inspire faith and confidence in forgiveness and in the promise of paradise.

In the sixteenth century, indeed, the *Ars Moriendi* literature had largely become the *memoria mortis*[43] which a Christian was to keep in mind through life, literature designed to afflict those dying in sin and the unpurged. It also insisted greatly on the importance of confession and anointing with the approach of death. However, sin once confessed, and the sacraments received, the literature bears witness to the fact that foreboding was to be set aside and a quiet death provided, with confidence in Christ's sufferings and merits, sole guarantee of heavenly rest. Modern readers may find some of the texts sentimental, or the portrayal of Christ's suffering a trifle lugubrious, but it cannot be said that the works of spirituality and the liturgical practice of the time affirmed sin and fear rather than trust and hope.

It is interesting to note that in his early Reformation writings, Martin Luther was very much in tune with this approach. He exhorted the dying to confession of sin, Communion, and unction; but, this done, he wished them to lay aside worries caused by sin, and to look to the passion of Christ as the assurance of God's mercy which removes fear in face of death, hell, and sin. With this before one's mind, in the hour of death itself it is possible to "laud and love his grace rather than fearing death so greatly."[44] No doubt, Luther has some of the common practices of pastors and people in mind and wishes to suggest an alternative, but there are firm roots to his approach in the spirituality and customs of the literature on the craft of dying. In this, the Counter-Reformation ritual texts of 1583 and 1614 and the 1520 counsels of the great Reformer coincide readily enough,[45] though of course significant differences had developed on how to bury and com-

---

[43] See Tenenti, op. cit., 317–370.

[44] See, "A Sermon on Preparing to Die." In *Luther's Work*, vol. 42 (Philadelphia: Fortress, 1960) 99–115. The work dates from 1520.

[45] The one characteristic note of Luther's faith and piety is his view of the nature of Christ's inner sufferings, as he was himself "assailed by the images of death, sin and hell just as we are." P. 107 of the sermon as published.

memorate the dead, largely having to do with Eucharistic understanding and practices, and the doctrine of purgatory.

The devotional approach to the contemplation of Christ's passion and death which has been outlined here, with its characteristic accentuation of Christ's personal agony, with its appeal to the
compensatory value of this suffering, and with its desire to incite
to confidence in the hour of death, gives some idea of the milieu
that inspired the prayers of the Roman Ritual.[46] Within the context
of such devotion, one can see the coloring or tone that is given to
the reading of the passion narrative, completed as it is by the
reading of Christ's priestly prayer from John 17, expressing his
intent of consecrating and offering himself for the world.

The Passion and Contemporary Rites

The trajectory of the ritual practice of reading the passion for the
dying moved through several phases, corresponding to changing
devotional attitudes. From its more sober conjunction with Viaticum in the early Roman order, it came to stand by itself, separated from Eucharistic Communion. In this setting, it served to
inspire a more subjective recollection of Christ's suffering, destined
in the first place to inspire a stronger repentance, but ultimately
intended to inspire confidence and trust in the worth of Christ's
suffering to atone for sin and to obtain divine mercy. While in the
earliest evidence it is the hope of the resurrection of the just
which prevails, there is already some penitential aspect present in
the rites. In some texts, the penitential aspect and the hope for
the forgiveness of sins carry more weight. A more personal and
devotional reliance on Christ's passion emerges in the literature of
the art of dying, which carries over into the 1614 Roman Ritual.
But the sacerdotal and expiatory character of Christ's self-offering
is what is brought out in the preference for the Johannine account, especially when it is accompanied by the priestly prayer of
John 17. The 1614 ritual, with its precedents in the work of Castelli
as well as Sanctorius (in preparing the ritual of Gregory the XIII),
gives to those who use it in prayer a confidence in Christ's salva-

---

[46] While the Roman Ritual has the prayer *"Proficiscere"* before all these devotions, the *Ars Moriendi* text concludes the assistance to the person in death
agony with this prayer, thus remaining liturgically faithful to the Frankish
tradition.

tion. By then, its purpose had become more clearly that of freeing from the fear of punishment for sin and serving as the earnest of complete trust in the saving, atoning and redeeming merits of Christ. At the same time, the concern was no longer with the final resurrection, but with the beatitude to be enjoyed on departing this world.

This tradition of reading the passion at the Commendation of the Dying may still allow for appropriation into contemporary contexts. In face of death, human persons both encounter the fear of dying itself and are confronted with the recollection of their sins and failings. Now, as in earlier centuries, they can turn to the remembrance of Christ's passion and pasch, and gain faith and trust from it.

However, if there is any thought of reviving the reading of the passion, it would be good to attend first to restoring Viaticum at the hour of death, so that together the sacrament and the Word of the gospel may allow communion with the mystery of the pasch. With the possibility of lay Eucharistic ministers today, there is little reason why the Eucharist cannot be given to sick and dying persons, as long as they are conscious and able to swallow, and up to the final hours of their death throes. It is regrettable that both Communion and the reading of the passion are excluded from the official rites for the liturgical Commendation of the Dying.

The situation of dying persons is such that a rigorous observance of ritual prescriptions is never adequate to the situation. Devotional practices and prayers inevitably enter into the picture. An advantage of the section on the dying in the Roman Ritual of 1614 was that it was not highly ritualized. It offered a selection of readings, psalms and prayers, to be used according to discretion and in keeping with the state of the dying person. In that sense, it was a manual providing useful texts, without imposing an inflexible format or content, sharing in that the direction often given to the revision of services after the Second Vatican Council.

Oddly enough, the only devotional element left in the revised Roman Ritual is the saying or singing of the *Salve Regina*. Otherwise, the prayers are abbreviated forms of the Litany and the *Proficiscere* inherited from medieval ritual, together with a selection of psalms and biblical passages or verses. A contemporary spirituality would hardly look upon this world as the valley of tears in which we spend our time lamenting existence, as in the *Salve Regina*. Neither would it espouse the kind of prayer inherited from the Roman Ritual of 1614. However, that is not the only type of meditation upon the passion possible in face of death. What is called for is some renewal of euchology to accompany the reading of the passion, or some fresh devotional prototype.

In the 1614 Ritual, the prayers on the passion reflect a theology which sees the suffering of Christ largely as atonement for sin, or a vicarious endurance of *poena*—or sufferings required in satisfaction for humankind's sin. In this light, death itself is an inevitable consequence of sin, an affliction which human sin has earned; the dying person can endure it as such in communion with Christ, looking forward to being freed from the pains of this world.

In contemporary soteriologies, the death of Jesus is also seen as an affliction which he endured, but in an altered light. For Jesus, death was a struggle which went with the struggle of his life against evil and suffering, indeed against death itself. In the death of Jesus, God shows pity and compassion for the world and, in Jesus, becomes one in humanity's struggle to overcome evil and suffering. Jesus suffered death to overcome death and, in the expectation of God's final liberation of people from sin, suffering.

There are those who in facing death are troubled by the remembrance of sin, or of a despair older than any remembered hope.[47] Without appealing to the passion of Jesus as suffering endured in satisfaction for sin and therefore earning pardon, one looks to it as compelling testimony to God's compassionate, forgiving, and liberating love, since Jesus died in the course of his testimony against evil and to the loving mercy of God which instills itself into humanity's struggle against sin and affliction.

---

[47] From a poem on a life from which tenderness has been absent since childhood, by the Australian poet, James McAuley, "Because," in *Contemporary Australian Poetry. An Anthology*, edited by John Leonard (Ferntree Gully: Houghton Mifflin Australia, 1990). The last stanza reads:

It's my own judgment day that I draw near,
Descending in the past, without a clue,
Down to that central deadness: the despair
Older than any hope I ever knew.

Others face death at the end of a long and harsh illness, such as cancer or AIDS. Giving them the power to give themselves over to God in hope, not only for themselves but for others who suffer pain or loss, is an act of grace. This too can be communicated through a meditation on Christ's passion, when it is seen both as a giving over of himself in trust and as an act of hope in God's liberating power, full of promise for a communal future for humankind. Seeing how Jesus through the acts of his own suffering gave context and meaning to his death by his communication with others, by his words and by his silence, enables persons to turn dying into an active communion with others, into shared hope.

In many parts of the world today, the situation of many people is that they face death as a consequence of inhuman conditions or in a struggle against pain and injustice. In the Western world, where medical arts are far advanced, life can be sustained for a long time, but then patients are faced even in their sickness with ethical decisions about the medical aid which is offered to them. If reflection on the passion of Christ can enable them to make these decisions, not just as matters concerning themselves personally, but in light of how this affects others, or of how it affects the general practices of the medical professions in their treatment of the sick, so much the better. The encouragement of Christ's communion with them in their affliction motivates or inspires their decisions and attitudes.[48]

It is odd in fact how little attention the American adaptation of the rites for the dying gives to the actual situation of dying persons in this social environment. This is true also of the revision of liturgical books for the Lutheran, Methodist and Episcopal Churches. The Lutheran *Occasional Services* include a prayer to be said, not by the dying when faced with a decision to make, but by a minister when a life support system is withdrawn. Though it is singularly drab,[49] it is the only time that in the prayer books of all

---

[48] The use of the passion at an earlier stage in the visitation of the sick, as is suggested in the revised Order for the visitation of the sick, is from this point of view appropriate, since it comes at a time when medical decisions have to be made.

[49] When a life-support system is withdrawn, the minister may say:

God of compassion and love, you have breathed into us the breath of life and have given us the exercise of our minds and wills. In our frailty we surrender

these Churches one gets a glimpse of what might possibly face dying people today.

It is inherent to Christian faith to allow the dying a more active, decisive and social role in the actions and decisions leading up to their death, and to help them if possible to go consciously to death. Meditation and prayer on the passion of Christ fosters a faith and spirit of communion with him in his consent to die, in his desire to free humankind from evil and suffering, and indeed from death itself, this being within the hope that comes from looking to God as compassionate lover and Savior of the world. Liturgical rituals could well offer more in this line. Keeping the reading of the passion, and prayer centered on the passion, as part of Christian assistance to the dying, would be a solid and contemporary appropriation of the habit, which remained alive in one form or another across the centuries, of finding in the passion of Christ, especially when related to the Eucharist, our comfort, strength, solace and exemplar in facing death.

---

all life to you from whom it came, trusting in your gracious promises: through, etc.

From the Commendation of the Dying, in *Occasional Services. A Companion to Lutheran Book of Worship* (Minneapolis: Augsburg Publishing House, 1982) 106.

R. Kevin Seasoltz, O.S.B.

14. The Liturgical Assembly: Light from Some Recent Scholarship

In 1978 the United States Bishops' Committee on the Liturgy issued their highly respected document *Environment and Art in Catholic Worship*.[1] One of its basic assertions is that the liturgical assembly is really the most important symbol in the celebration of the liturgy:

"To speak of environmental and artistic requirements in Catholic worship, we have to begin with ourselves—we who are the Church, the baptized, the initiated. Among the symbols with which liturgy deals, none is more important than the assembly of believers. It is common to use the same name to speak of the building in which those persons worship, but that is misleading. In the words of ancient Christians, the building used for worship is called *domus ecclesiae*, the house of the Church."[2]

In spite of that clear assertion concerning the primacy of the assembly, church renovations and even the programs for the building of new churches have often attended almost exclusively to the sanctuary area and have neglected to address the kind of integration which should be manifested in the worship space as those who execute distinctive ministries and those who constitute the larger assembly are brought together into unity by their common worship but are not meant to be divided from one another. Furthermore, there has been a long-standing consensus among Protestant scholars and some contemporary Catholic scholars that

[1] (Washington: National Conference of Catholic Bishops, 1978).
[2] Nos. 27–28.

303

a hierarchically constituted Church and consequently a hierarchically constituted assembly are rooted in an erroneous tradition which departed from the teaching of Jesus in the late first century. Acceptance of that consensus has resulted in a reluctance on the part of some liturgical assemblies to use a presider's chair or to allow for any distinction between the lay and the ordained members of the assembly.

The Second Vatican Council's Constitution on the Church, *Lumen Gentium*, clearly affirmed that the Church is both hierarchical and charismatic.[3] Any implementation of that assertion, however, should not result in a divided liturgical assembly but should express both the basic unity of the community and clear distinctions of roles in the community, roles that are determined by the sacramental character of those who carry out the distinctive ministries. The purpose of this article is to present the conclusions of some recent scholarly works which, though not dealing explicitly with the nature of the liturgical assembly, have significant implications for our understanding of the nature of the assembly as a unified body within which there are members representing both the hierarchical and charismatic dimensions of the Church of Jesus Christ.

SCRIPTURAL BACKGROUND

Since the scholarly works we shall summarize presume a familiarity with the concept of assembly in the Bible, a brief overview of that data will first of all be set out. The results of modern research have shown quite clearly that the Church of the New Testament is to be understood as the development of what the Old Testament called the assembly of the Lord.[4] Studies have

[3] Art. 42.

[4] James Tunstead Burtchaell, *From Synagogue to Church: Public Services and Offices in the Earliest Christian Communities* (Cambridge: Cambridge University Press, 1992) 209–227. See also Nicolas Afanassieff, "Le sacrement de l'assemblée," *Internationale Kirchliche Zeitschrift* 46 (1956) 200–213, James Challancin, *The Assembly Celebrates: Gathering the Community for Worship* (Mahwah, New Jersey: Paulist Press, 1989); Henri Chirat, *L'Assemblée chrétienne à l'age apostolique* (Paris: Edition du Cerf, 1949); Yves Congar, "L'Écclesia ou communauté, sujet intégral de l'action liturgique," in *La Liturgie après Vatican II.*, ed. J.-P. Jossua and Y. Congar (Paris: Edition du Cerf, 1967) 242–282, idem, "Réflexions et recherches actuelles sur l'assemblée liturgique," *La Maison Dieu* 115 (1973) 21–25; R. Gantoy,

stressed the massive cultural continuity between Judaism and primitive Christianity and also between the Jewish synagogue in the Second Temple period and the early Church.[5]

As they officially described themselves, the Jews were an assembly. The political and cultic gatherings of the whole population were understood to be so important that the notion of assembly provided the popular term by which one referred to the Jews. The assembly (*'edah, synagoge*) was a common name for the people, especially in the Pentateuch and the Book of Joshua. In the literature of the monarchy, however, the term gave way to other terms such as "Israel," "Judah," and "House of Judah," but the term "assembly" returned in later postexilic literature. In fact even stronger terms such as *qahal* and *ekklesia* were used to designate the Jewish people. A plenary assembly was the proper context for all major events and for the bonding of the community. The word that characteristically designated such meetings—*qahal* in Hebrew, *ekklesia* in Greek—derives in both languages from the root word meaning "to call" or "to convene." Closely associated with those terms is the Greek word *synagoge*.[6]

In the Septuagint *ekklesia* was the word regularly used to translate the Hebrew *qahal*, which meant both a call to assemble and the very act of assembling. The term *qahal* gradually took on religious meaning as the Israelites came to understand themselves as people who had been called by God to assemble. It was God's

"L'assemblée dans l'economie du salut," *Assemblées du Seigneur* 1 (1965) 55–80, Lawrence Hoffman, "Assembling in Worship," *Worship* 56 (1982) 98–112; Robert Hovda, "It Begins with the Assembly," in *The Environment for Worship: A Reader* (Washington: United States Catholic Conference, 1980) 35–41; Joseph Lecuyer, "The Liturgical Assembly: Biblical and Patristic Foundations," in *The Church Worships*, = Concilium 12, ed. Johannes Wagner (New York: Paulist Press, 1966) 3–18; Thierry Maertens, *Assembly for Christ: From Biblical Theology to Pastoral Theology in the 20th Century* (London: Darton, Longman and Todd, 1970); A.-G., Martimort, "The Assembly," in *The Church at Prayer*, ed. I. Dalmais et al., vol. 1: *Principles of the Liturgy* (Collegeville: The Liturgical Press, 1987) 87–111; Catherine Vincie, "The Liturgical Assembly: Review and Reassessment," *Worship* 67 (March 1993) 123–144; A. Hamman, "Assembly," in *Encyclopedia of the Early Church*, ed. Angelo Di Berardino, trans. Adrian Walford (New York: Oxford University Press, 1992) 1:90.

[5] Burtchaell, 201–227.

[6] Louis Bouyer, "From the Jewish Qahal to the Christian Ecclesia," in *Liturgical Piety* (Notre Dame: University of Notre Dame Press, 1955) 23–37.

word that called the Jewish people into assembly; it was divine initiative that gave them their religious identity.[7]

There is plausible continuity between the hellenistic Jewish synagogue and the early Christian Church, for there are various similarities between the two social units. Both met in plenary assembly for prayer, for reading, expounding and discussing the scriptures, for sharing ritual meals, for determining community policies, for implementing disciplinary measures, and for choosing officers of the group.[8] Certainly the New Testament use of *ekklesia* to name the Christian assembly was influenced by its Old Testament background. The term *synagoge* was generally applied to Jewish religious gatherings.

In order to distinguish themselves more clearly from their Jewish contemporaries, the Christian communities preferred the term *ekklesia*. That term is used in the Acts of the Apostles (8:1) to refer to the local community in Jerusalem, considered to be the mother church of all Christians. It is also used in Acts 15 to refer to the universal Church, that is, to all of the faithful who profess belief in Jesus Christ. Paul used the term in various ways in his letters. In Philemon 2, he used it to refer to Christians gathered in a house, in 1 Corinthians 11:18, for Christians gathered for worship, and in 1 Thessalonians 2:14, for a number of house churches in one city. For Paul the Christian assembly was one called together by God in Christ (1 Thes 2:14). The basic understanding of Church in the New Testament is that it is an assembly called by God in Christ through the power of the Holy Spirit, a gathering called ''assembly.''[9]

Another term which designated those gathered in Christ is the Greek word *koinonia*.[10] The term applies to those who share a common meaning. When Paul used the word, as he did in 1 Corinthians 1:9, he implied all those who share in the life of God through Jesus Christ and who consequently share life with one another through the power of the Holy Spirit. *Koinonia* is estab-

[7] Ibid., 24–28.

[8] Burtchaell, 339–340.

[9] Ibid., 272–338.

[10] See the report of the Second Anglican/Roman Catholic International Commission, *Church as Communion: An Agreed Statement* (London: Catholic Truth Society, 1991).

lished through baptism and is intensified above all through the celebration of the Eucharist. The Church, then, is most clearly expressed and made visible when it gathers for the celebration of the liturgy. The Constitution on the Sacred Liturgy emphasizes that point: "The liturgy is thus the outstanding means by which the faithful can express in their lives, and manifest to others, the mystery of Christ and the real nature of the true Church."[11] The Constitution on the Church stresses the importance of the local Church when it states:

"This Church of Christ is really present in all legitimately organized local groups of the faithful, which, in so far as they are united to their pastors, are also quite appropriately called Churches in the New Testament. For these are in fact, in their own localities, the new people of God, in the power of the Holy Spirit and as the result of full conviction (cf. 1 Thes 1:5). In them the faithful are gathered together through the preaching of the gospel of Christ, and the mystery of the Lord's Supper is celebrated 'so that, by means of the flesh and blood of the Lord the whole brotherhood of the Body may be welded together.' In each altar community, under the sacred ministry of the bishop, a manifest symbol is to be seen of that charity and 'unity of the mystical body, without which there can be no salvation.' In these communities, though they may often be small and poor, or existing in the diaspora, Christ is present through whose power and influence the One, Holy, Catholic and Apostolic Church is constituted. For 'the sharing in the body and blood of Christ has no other effect than to accomplish our transformation into that which we receive.' "[12]

The Second Vatican Council's assertions that the Church is most clearly manifested as an assembly, as the Body of Christ, when it gathers for the celebration of the liturgy and that the local Church is in fact just as truly Church as the universal Church are very important recoveries of principles that were emphasized in the early life of the Church. After considerable discussion, the fathers of the Second Vatican Council clearly stated that the Church, both on the universal and local levels, is both hierarchical and charis-

[11] Art. 2.
[12] Art. 26.

matic.[13] The constitutive nature of the Church has been a subject of intense controversy both in the past and in the years since the council. At the root of the controversy is often a misunderstanding of what is meant by the hierarchical nature of the Church and consequently the hierarchical nature of the liturgical assembly.

JAMES BURTCHAELL: *FROM SYNAGOGUE TO CHURCH*

The ordered nature of the assembly and the legitimacy of structures and offices within the assembly have been the subject of recent scholarly work by James Turnstead Burtchaell presented in his book *From Synagogue to Church: Public Services and Offices in the Earliest Christian Communities.*[14] Until recently there has been a scholarly consensus among Protestant theologians,[15] one adopted by certain contemporary Roman Catholic scholars, including Hans Küng,[16] Edward Schillebeeckx,[17] and Elizabeth Schüssler Fiorenza,[18] that maintains that the closer we draw to the time of Jesus, the less evidence we encounter of structure or office among the followers of Jesus. The consensus has stressed that as the first century drew to a close there were signs of strain between the free charismatic forms of leadership in the New Testament and the more structured and official forms of leadership which emerged as the first century moved along. The consensus holds that these structures must have emerged later and that, to the detriment of Christianity, the office holders prevailed against the charismatic figures. Those holding the consensus view have emphasized that the founding era of Christian practice should be normative for all that follows, hence authentic Christianity "in every age is obliged to purge itself of residual, inauthentic notions of institutionalized church-craft that presumes to invest human rituals or offices with

[13] Arts. 12, 18–29.

[14] See note 4 above.

[15] Burtchaell, 136–167.

[16] *The Church*, trans. Ray and Rosaleen Ockenden (New York: Sheed and Ward, 1967) 416.

[17] *Ministry: Leadership in the Community of Jesus Christ*, trans. John Bowden (New York: Crossroad, 1981); *The Church with a Human Face: A New and Expanded Theology of Ministry*, trans. John Bowden (New York: Crossroad, 1985).

[18] *In Memory of Her: A Feminist Theological Reconstruction of Christian Origins* (New York: Crossroad, 1985).

the power of the Spirit."[19] Burtchaell notes that "There has been, beneath the surface of this discussion, a propensity to color the Judaism of Jesus' time with the qualities Protestants found most retrograde in the Catholic Church."[20]

Contrary to the consensus, Burtchaell contends that from the beginning the followers of Jesus, like other distinctive communities within Judaism, would inevitably have framed their fellowship according to the general structures of the synagogue which was probably the only organization to which most of them ever belonged. From the outset, then, he maintains that the Christian communities, like the synagogues, would have included a presiding officer, a college of elders, and assistants. In order to assert the distinctiveness of their communities, the Christians would have referred to these officers by titles other than those currently used in the synagogues. The adoption of a distinctive nomenclature was a common practice among Jewish sectarian groups.[21]

Although these officials would have presided in the Christian communities from the beginning, there is little reference to them in the historical records because at first they were not important. "The vitality, initiative, derring-do, heroism, and summons to sanctity were not in those earliest days, to be found in the officers of the Church."[22] They were found rather in the charismatic apostles, prophets, and teachers to whom the officials deferred. Burtchaell offers a credible modern comparison:

"Somewhere in Calcutta today there is a parish priest whose name no reader of this book will ever hear, who will make no remembered mark on the story of the church here or there. In his parish a frail Albanian woman in a sari is a worshipping member. From our point of view it is she who counts for most there, but Mother Theresa would say it is he who presides. That we never hear of him does not mean he does not exist. But that he does exist does not mean that he is the leader and she the follower. She may lead though he presides."[23]

[19] Burtchaell, 184.
[20] Ibid.
[21] Ibid., 344.
[22] Ibid., 366.
[23] Ibid., 351.

Burtchaell has assembled impressive evidence for continuity in community structure from the hellenistic Jewish synagogue to the early Christian Church. There are multiple similarities regarding both the programs and undertakings of the two units. Both the *synagoge* and the *ekklesia* met regularly in plenary sessions for prayer, for reading and discussing the scriptures, for enforcing disciplinary measures, and for selecting and installing officers. They both shared in ritual meals, supported widows, orphans and other indigent members of their communities through a welfare fund. Likewise they both provided hospitality for members of their sister communities who were on a journey and buried their dead and maintained cemeteries.[24] Burtchaell maintains that while the three offices of ministry—president, elders, and assistants— existed from the beginning of the Christian Church, those who held the offices during the first century were not the leaders of the communities, they were rather dominated by the charismatic figures of the first century just as the charismatic figures of the second century were dominated by the bishops.[25]

Burtchaell sees the evidence he has assembled as favoring the Roman Catholic/Orthodox/Anglican view that bishops and their predecessors have presided in the Christian Church from the beginning. At the same time he sides with the Protestants that in the formative era the Church deferred to the judgment of those who were charismatically inspired but who did not hold offices in the Church. For our purposes the conclusion to be drawn from his book is that, in accord with the teaching of *Lumen Gentium:* the universal Church and the local assembly are both hierarchical and charismatic. Burtchaell maintains that ordained office is a foundational element in the Christian Church, but he acknowledges that while the officers of the community would have presided over the community from the first, they did not in fact actually lead the communities. As he notes, while James, the brother of Jesus, presided as the designated minister over the mother Church in Jerusalem, it was in fact Peter, Jesus' special disciple, whose voice carried most authority in the Church.[26] Burtchaell has certainly challenged very learned scholars in setting forth his thesis, and

[24] Ibid., 284–288, 339.
[25] Ibid., 340–347.
[26] Ibid., 343.

they in turn undoubtedly will challenge him. His thesis, if accepted, does provide important underpinnings for the assertion that the liturgical assembly is meant to be a unified body made up of both hierarchical and charismatic members.

JOHN N. COLLINS: *DIAKONIA*

Another supporting argument for the structured character of the Church of Christ and consequently the structured nature of the liturgical assembly has been laid out by the Australian theologian John N. Collins in his book *Diakonia: Reinterpreting the Ancient Sources.*[27] His major concern is to give an accurate interpretation of the term *diakonia*. It is often said that the text in Mark 10:45, "The Son of Man came not to be served but to serve and to give his life as a ransom for many," encapsulates the authentic vision of what ministry should be in the Church. It should be humble service of one's neighbor. This understanding of ministry has been summed up in the word *diakonia,* a term which has been popular in theological writings and which is associated with the Greek words *diakonein* and *diakonos,* from which we derive the English word "deacon." It has been widely believed that *diakonia* was originally a secular term which meant "service at table," waiting upon others, just as Jesus served the disciples when he washed their feet. Certainly all disciples of Jesus are called to a life of humble service, but then the question has been raised whether there is really any sound foundation for the traditional distinction between ordained and nonordained ministers in the Church and consequently in the liturgical assembly. Is there a basis for any kind of hierarchical structure of authority in the Church on universal or local levels? It has been claimed, especially by the various authors cited in Burtchaell's book,[28] that the way the ordained priesthood has functioned in the Roman Catholic Church has not been so much an expression of service as the assertion of power, authority, and status on the part of an elite group and hence a

---

[27] (New York: Oxford University Press, 1990).

[28] Burtchaell discusses at length the work of the following twentieth-century Protestant scholars: Hans Freiherr von Campenhausen, Eduard Schweizer, Leonhard Goppelt, Gerd Theissen, John Gager, Bengt Holmberg, David Verner and Wayne Meeks.

clear contradiction of Jesus' understanding of ministry and discipleship. Certainly any justification for such a charge must be eliminated from the life of the Church of Jesus Christ.

Collins maintains that the modern theology of ministry has been based on a particular understanding of *diakonia* which he has called into question. In 1839 Pastor Theodore Fliedner preached at the inauguration of a new community of Lutheran deaconesses at Kaiserwerth in Germany. The women were to be missionaries who would take the mercy of Christ to the sick, poor, prisoners and neglected children throughout Germany. They were to bring the presence of the servant Christ to the marginalized people in a nation devastated by the Napoleonic wars and thrown into chaos by the industrial revolution, just as the recently founded Roman Catholic congregations of women religious did in nineteenth-century Germany. In fact, Fliedner was accused of introducing women religious into the Lutheran Church.[29]

Fliedner's community of deaconesses provided the inspiration for H. W. Berger in 1935 when he wrote a widely publicized article which defined the words *diakonos* and *diakonein* as implying humble service at table.[30] His article became the standard reference work for New Testament scholars down to the present time. It is that widely accepted consensus that Collins has challenged.

He surveys the evidence of the early secular sources and concludes that the words *diakonos* and *diakonein* designate ''action of an in-between kind of people who operate in an in-between capacity, especially people (or spirits) who implement the intentions or desires of another.''[31] These people are not necessarily unimportant servants. In fact ambassadors, couriers, heralds, and generals could be called *diakonoi* because they are all commissioned to speak in the name of another or to carry out tasks on another's behalf.

When Collins applies this meaning to the New Testament, it becomes clear that for Paul to be a *diakonos* of God is not simply to be God's servant or a lowly waiter but to be an authoritative

[29] Collins, 9–11.

[30] *Theological Dictionary of the New Testament*, ed. Gerhard Kittel, trans. and ed. Geoffrey W. Bromley (Grand Rapids: Eerdmans, 1964) 2:81–93.

[31] Collins reviews the evidence of non-Christian sources at length and comes to this conclusion. See 77–191.

mouthpiece of God, speaking for God, and carrying God's gospel to the gentiles. Paul uses the word *diakonos* of himself when he collects money from the wealthy gentile churches for the poor in Jerusalem because he is mediating between two local Churches of the one Church of Jesus Christ.[32] When Mark says that Jesus has come not to be served but to serve, he means that Jesus is a mediator between his Father and humankind.[33] In the Acts of the Apostles there are explicit references to what we would call a hierarchical structure, including officials who were called "deacons."[34] In light of Collins' interpretation, it may be said that they were not only appointed to look after the widows and the poor, they were commissioned to represent the officials of the community.

Implicitly the book substantiates the claim that the Church of Jesus Christ is in fact a hierarchically structured Church, both on the universal and local levels. But that does not mean that the hierarchy should be authoritarian. The hierarchical structures of the Church, both universal and local, and consequently the hierarchical structures of the liturgical assembly, exist so that members of the assembly might not view themselves as solitary monads who are meant to have an individualistic relationship with God; they are rather meant to be ordered to one another as members of the one Body of Christ. The presence of the ordained priesthood in the assembly is meant to bring to light the fact that in Christ and through the power of the Holy Spirit we are ordered both to Christ as head of the Body and to each other as members of the Body. The task of the hierarchy, represented in the assembly by the presider, is to orient individual persons to God and each other just as the muscles and ligaments of the body bind it together and communicate vitality.[35] When the hierarchy, represented by the presider, does just that, then it is truly serving the community; there is no inherent contradiction between being a hierarchical Church and a servant Church. When the hierarchy functions properly, it helps to free the assembly from liberal individualism

[32] Rom 15:25, 31, 2 Cor 8:4, 19:20, 9:1, 12, 13.
[33] Mark 10:45.
[34] Acts 1:12-26, 6:1-6.
[35] Timothy Radcliffe, "As One Who Serves," *The Tablet* (July 11, 1992) 865–866.

which leaves the community ultimately fragmented and isolated from other assemblies.[36]

What is clearly needed is a proper experience of the hierarchical structures of the Church and hence of the ordained presider, as not simply a class division within the Church but rather as an expression of the common life of the whole Church which is both ordered and unified. It has been suggested that, because of the common misunderstanding of the term "hierarchical," it might be better to speak simply of bishops, presbyters and deacons in the Church. When the authentic nature of the Church is expressed architecturally, the areas in the church building do not mark off those who have power from those who do not. The experience should be that of the generous open spaces of God's many-roomed house in which all play various roles and exercise different gifts but are united to one another and oriented toward God by the presiding ministry of the ordained.[37]

When the Corpus Christi processions made their way through medieval towns, everyone had a proper place and role—guilds and sodalities, oblates and fraternities, monks, friars and diocesan clergy. They all had their emblems and songs and their patron saints. But they all walked under the headship of Christ present in the Eucharist carried aloft by the bishop or his representative. The procession was an image of the Church and the local liturgical assembly in which all have something to offer and some service to perform, but their ministry is ordered by the one who presides.[38]

MICHAEL RICHARDS: "HIERARCHY AND PRIESTHOOD"

There is no doubt that especially in the centuries following the Council of Trent up to the time of the Second Vatican Council the Roman Catholic Church was characterized as a pyramid both on the universal and local levels. There were seven steps upward to priestly ordination. Clergymen spoke openly of their careers. There were ranks and grades in the Church; those at the top were regularly spoken of as belonging to the hierarchy of the Church.

[36] Ibid.
[37] Ibid.
[38] Ibid. See also Miri Rubin, *Corpus Christi: The Eucharist in Late Medieval Culture* (Cambridge: Cambridge University Press, 1991) 243–271.

In a recent provocative article,[39] Michael Richards has examined the meaning of the term "hierarchy" in the teaching of the Second Vatican Council and draws out important implications for the ordained ministry and its role in the liturgical assembly. He notes that when the council fathers sought to affirm that there is an essential difference between the common priesthood of all the baptized and the priesthood of those baptized persons who have been ordained presbyters, they described the latter as both hierarchical and ministerial. It is important, then, to understand properly what concept of hierarchy the Council had in mind, for on it depends both our theory and practice concerning the nature of the Church and the role of the ordained priesthood in the liturgical assembly as well as in other areas of the Church's life.

Lumen Gentium asserts that ordained ministry differs from the common priesthood of the faithful "essentially and not only in degree,"[40] but the Latin text makes clear in what sense the expression "essential difference" is to be understood. As Richards notes,

"it says that the *sacerdotium communale*, the common priesthood, differs from the *sacerdotium hierarchicum*, the hierarchical priesthood, 'essentia, non gradu tantum': 'in essence, not just in degree.' Now in saying 'non gradu tantum,' the Council deliberately avoided saying that there is a difference both in essence and in degree (although it has often been misinterpreted in this sense); it is affirming 'essence' and setting 'degree' aside. It is saying that if you want to understand what difference ordination makes, you must look for an essential difference, a difference in kind, not a mere difference of degree: degree simply does not enter into it. The Council could have said 'both . . . and' (et . . . et); it could have said 'not only . . . but also' (non tantum . . . sed etiam); and it could have said 'together with' (una cum; a favorite conjunction in the documents of Vatican II). But it did not. It chose to use a precise form of words which in Latin indicates that the given alternative is to be excluded as irrelevant."[41]

Richards concludes that by the Council's own statement as well as by its proper interpretation in the light of scripture, the use of

[39] "Hierarchy and Priesthood," *Priests and People* (June 1993) 228–232.
[40] Art. 10.
[41] Richards, 229.

the term "hierarchy" by the Council must not be taken to refer to ranks or grades of importance. He insists that the word must be taken back to its basic roots: *hieros* and *arche*.[42] Since the Council sets aside the traditional interpretation of the term hierarchical as implying degrees, the common associations of the term must also be set aside so we can come to a more accurate understanding of the term. Richards emphasizes that it has nothing to do with the possession of status or rank or with membership in an elite group. He insists that in the formal declaration of the Council, it can only be interpreted as an application of the teaching given by Christ to his apostles when they inquired, "Who is the greatest among us?" Jesus told them that whoever wanted to be first must be last and become the servant of all.[43] In other words, one must be a person without any rank, a non-hierarchical person, as that term would be customarily understood today. Certainly Jesus removed any sense the apostles might have of being people of privilege; he asserted that his disciples must be like little children.[44]

When the Second Vatican Council wanted to assert the distinctive character of the ordained priesthood by affirming that it differs from the common priesthood and chose to describe it by using the word "hierarchical," it did not thereby imply that the distinction lies in any superiority in rank. It did not declare that bishops, presbyters and deacons are superior to lay people in the Church or that superiority constitutes the essence of the ordained priesthood.

Richards notes that in the documents of the Second Vatican Council, and specifically in *Lumen Gentium*, the term "hierarchy" is not being used in the sense that it has acquired in secular usage and also in certain ecclesiastical texts as an ordered structure of grades with one set above the other. If and when the term is used in that sense, it does not provide a proper key to understanding the fundamental meaning of the ordained priesthood. In light of the Council's careful use of the term and above all in light of a sound biblical interpretation of authority in the Church, the use of the term "hierarchy" by the Second Vatican Council must not be

---

[42] Ibid., 231.
[43] Luke 22:24-27.
[44] Luke 9:46-48, 18:15-17; Mark 9:33-37; Matt 18:1-5.

taken to refer to ranks or grades, one superior and the others inferior. The word rather must be grounded again in its basic roots: *hieros* and *arche*, holy and principle.[45]

The hierarchical priesthood is one which is responsible for mediating God's holiness into the lives of God's people. The special service which ordained ministers render to God and to others in the Church is to proclaim the gospel and to make available the other means by which the members of Christ's Body are made holy by the very holiness of God in Jesus Christ and through the power of the Holy Spirit. Ordained ministers of course are not the only ones who mediate the holiness of God to others, a point which must be regularly emphasized. Married couples surely mediate God's holiness to one another, just as parents mediate that same holiness to their children. But *arche* implies a special point of departure for the ordained and a special responsibility on their part. Under Christ and through the power of the Holy Spirit in the Church, the ordained ministers are Christ's commissioned representatives who have the special responsibility of proclaiming the Christian gospel and celebrating the Eucharist and other sacraments with the rest of the faithful so that the whole assembly of God's people might be made holy. Although the ordained ministers share their responsibility with others, it is they in a special way who must guarantee the authenticity of what is proclaimed, celebrated and shared.[46]

Richards stresses that *arche* also conveys the sense of rule or standard. The members of the hierarchy are authorized to assess and evaluate the authenticity of doctrinal statements purported to express the gospel faithfully. And of course they themselves must express the gospel and be faithful to its demands in their own lives. Such service of the word of God was a responsibility that the apostles were well aware of, but they also knew that such a responsibility must not be carried out in an arrogant or domineering way. It implied a distinctive gift, given to some in the community but not to others. Without that special gift with its purpose of enabling the Church to be called together and unified in mind and heart, the integrity of the Church would be nullified because there

---

[45] Richards, 231.
[46] Ibid.

would be no special reference point by which the unity of the community could be established and assessed.[47]

The holiness which should characterize both the ordained and lay members of the Church must be understood in the biblical sense. It is the holiness which Christ came to give to all God's people, a holiness that would enable people to be remade in the image and according to the likeness of God. It is the holiness required by the law in the Old Testament, a holiness spoken of by the prophets and in the psalms, a holiness achieved not by means of substitute sacrifices or rituals but a holiness given freely by God so that people might live in harmony with God's own nature and life and become what they were called to be from all eternity: images of God in creation. That is the very holiness spoken of in the New Testament, a holiness promised and made possible for all members of the human race forgiven and restored by God in Jesus Christ.[48]

The ordained members of the community of God's people have the special responsibility of being a channel, a means of access whereby God's holiness is shared with the community. They are not the only channels, but they are distinctive channels indeed. With the laity and among the laity, ordained priests are called to render service to the community by handing on the gospel effectively, coordinating the other ministries in the assembly of the Church, and leading the people in their worship of God so they might be sanctified, not by the ordained priests themselves but by God alone. The New Testament uses the images of shepherd, steward and servant to describe the ministry of the apostles and those who have a special responsibility for building up and caring for the Church. All those images imply an outward thrust towards others rather than a preoccupation with oneself and one's status.[49]

Societies in general and life itself would be impossible without certain office holders executing the fundamental human tasks of organizing and directing the activities of the group. The Church of Jesus Christ is no different in this regard. In order for the Church to exist and grow, in order for the liturgical assembly to gather and function effectively, there must be people who care for the

[47] Ibid.
[48] Ibid., 232.
[49] Ibid., 231.

whole life of the community and who have responsibility for its direction.[50]

It is with good reason, then, that the Second Vatican Council's Decree on the Ministry and Life of Priests, *Presbyterorum Ordinis*, carefully relates the ministry of the ordained to the ministry of Christ and only in that context does it highlight the special responsibilities of the ordained:

"The purpose . . . for which priests are consecrated by God through the ministry of the bishop is that they should be made sharers in a special way in Christ's priesthood and, by carrying out sacred functions, act as his ministers who through his Spirit continually exercises his priestly function for our benefit in the liturgy. . . . In the name of the bishop they gather the family of God . . . endowed with the spirit of unity and they lead it in Christ through the Spirit to God the Father."[51]

There is no doubt that other ecclesiastical documents, especially the ordination rites, give the impression that ordained ministers are elevated to a status above the laity in the community.[52] It must be emphasized that such language simply perpetuates a false understanding of the New Testament and infidelity to the commands of Jesus.

If the term "hierarchy" continues to be used in the Church, as it probably will be used, it must be understood in the proper sense. Ordained ministers are in fact ordained for the sake of God's people, not for their own sake. They are to be mediators through whom Christ shares his own holiness. But the service of the ordained is not simply for the service of humankind; it is also for the service of God made incarnate in Jesus, who gave us his teaching and appointed his special teachers. As Richards notes,

"The part for the whole, the leaven in the lump, the seed in the ground, the light that fills with light: these images express the

[50] Ibid.

[51] Art. 2.

[52] See David N. Power, *Ministers of Christ and His Church: The Theology of the Priesthood* (London: Geoffrey Chapman, 1969) 202; Mary Collins, "The Public Language of Ministry," *Worship: Renewal to Practice* (Washington: The Pastoral Press, 1978) 137–173.

way in which Christ works: sharing and growth, not a forced take-over . . . That he should make some . . . into hierarchical priests, giving them a gift he does not give to all, does not imply a personal and private possession of exclusive privilege, but the burden of responsibility for breaking the bread by which all are nourished. To give rise to the ordered harmony of the common meal, of the choir, of the orchestra, of the team, of the family, of the body: in that sense, hierarchy is holiness, the holiness of the One who treated 'Who is the greatest?' as a non-question."[53]

REASSESSING THE TERM "FAITHFUL"

A reassessment of the term "hierarchy" must be accompanied by a rethinking of the term "faithful," for in the past the latter was often used in a rather patronizing sense to denote the simple laity in the Church. It is however a term which denotes all who have been initiated into the Church, both ordained and laity alike, and in no way is meant to be indicative of those who have a subordinate place in the Church.

It goes without saying that the ecclesiology of *Lumen Gentium* stands in marked contrast to the ecclesiology of the post-Tridentine theological manuals which tended to attribute the right to govern, teach, and sanctify to the hierarchy alone and to relegate passive and receptive roles to the laity. The symbols and rituals of the post-Tridentine liturgy as well as church architecture expressed an ecclesiology in which the laity were not fully incorporated into the Christian assembly with the rights and responsibilities that come from Christian initiation. That view was clearly expressed by Pope St. Pius X: "In the hierarchy alone reside the power and authority to move and direct all the members of society to its end. As for the many, they have no other right than to let themselves be guided and so follow their pastors in docility."[54]

At the heart of the liturgical movement, beginning in the last century and continuing up till the Second Vatican Council, was an effort to recover the liturgy as a celebration of the whole community and consequently of the faithful as constituting all the bap-

---

[53] Richards, 232.
[54] *Vehementer Nos* (February 11, 1906), ASS 39 (1906) 8–9.

tized as the subject of the liturgical celebration. But as John
Gurrieri has convincingly shown, all of God's people belong to
the faithful, clergy and laity alike.[55]

In the past the term "faithful" was regularly thought to refer to
the laity but not to the clergy. As already noted, the ecclesiology
enunciated in the decades before the Second Vatican Council
placed almost exclusive emphasis on the hierarchical dimension of
the Church. From the Middle Ages on, lay people were relegated
to a passive role in the Church, a position of docility which denied
them any active role in the liturgy and which consequently
promoted an individualistic piety. Their voices were no longer
heard in the liturgy, and their roles were taken over by the clergy
so that the hierarchical character of the Church dominated and
tended generally to suppress the charismatic role of those who
were not ordained. But an individualistic piety also characterized
the clergy. Architecturally these developments were expressed by
the placement of a barrier between the clergy and laity: what was
originally a ministerial distinction between the ordained and the
laity came to be experienced and expressed as an opposition between two classes in the Church.

At the center of the revision of the liturgical rites since the Second Vatican Council has been an effort to rediscover what it
means to be one of the "faithful" in the Church of Jesus Christ.
As Gurrieri has noted, the term "faithful" (in Latin, *fidelis*) is
rooted in the experience of Christian initiation.[56] To be one of the
faithful is to have received the gift of faith from God, a gift which
comes with Christian baptism. In the process of Christian initiation and its newly restored rites, the faithful are those who are
communicants, not simply those who are baptized, but those who
are in communion with the Lord Jesus and with other Christians
through the celebration of the Eucharist. Eucharistic Communion
is the greatest expression of Christian faith. Only the faithful may
participate in the Eucharist. The word "faithful," then, applies not

---

[55] "The Praising Assembly: Reassessing the Term 'Faithful' in Light of
Today's Eucharist," in *The Assembly: A People Gathered in Your Name*, Federa-
tion of Diocesan Liturgical Commissions Meeting October 19–22, 1981
(Milwaukee) 12–15.

[56] Ibid., 12.

merely to the laity, but rather to all those who are fully initiated into the Church.[57]

Hence proper understanding of the term "faithful" must be grounded in participation in the Eucharist rather than in status within the assembly determined by whether or not one is ordained. The Eucharist determines the basic status and fundamental role of all the faithful as participants in the priesthood of Jesus Christ. Before any distinctions are made in the Christian assembly between those who are ordained and those who are not, it is first of all and above all important to acknowledge the local Church as a united assembly of all those faithful people who have been initiated into the mystery of Jesus Christ through baptism and the Eucharist.[58]

According to the rubrics of the Missal of Pius V (1570), Mass was celebrated *for* the people rather than *by* the people. The absence of the laity's role made that quite clear and reflected an ecclesiology in which the laity were both subordinated and subject to the clergy. By contrast, according to the General Instruction of the Roman Missal of Paul VI, the Eucharist is celebrated by the whole assembly of the faithful. There are various roles to be carried out by both the ordained and lay members of the assembly, but those roles are not meant to separate the clergy from the laity; rather they are meant to foster the full, active participation of everyone in the community. Active participation also applies to those ordained ministers who are present for liturgy but not engaged in distinctive ministerial roles. In the past it was not at all uncommon for clergy to be present at a Eucharist, but instead of being involved in the celebration they engaged in private devotions such as saying the rosary or they recited their breviaries.

None of the faithful are meant to assist passively at liturgical celebrations. Not only is the ordained priest a celebrant; he is one of the celebrants in the midst of the celebrating assembly. At times he presides in the midst of the assembly, but he never celebrates for the assembly. While treating the architectural arrangements of the church building, the General Instruction of the Roman Missal gives a sound summary of both the unity of the

[57] Ibid. See also Catherine Vincie, *The Role of the Assembly in Christian Initiation*, Forum Essays 1 (Chicago: Liturgy Training Publications, 1993).

[58] Gurrieri, 12.

liturgical assembly and the distinctive roles which rightly should exist within it:

"The people of God possess an organic and hierarchical structure, expressed by the various ministries and actions for each part of the celebration. The general plan of the sacred edifice should be such that in some way it conveys the image of the gathered assembly. It should also allow the participants to take the places most appropriate to them and assist all to carry out their individual functions properly. The priest and his ministers have their place in the sanctuary, that is, in the part of the church that brings out their distinctive role, namely, to preside over the prayers, to proclaim the word of God, or to minister at the altar. Even though these elements must express a hierarchical arrangement and the diversity of offices, they should at the same time form a complete and organic unity, clearly expressive of the unity of the entire holy people."[59]

Certainly the retrieval and reinterpretation of important biblical and historical data by Burtchaell, Collins and Richards help us understand how easily the Christian heritage can be distorted and how that distortion affects our liturgical assumptions and practices. By rooting the Church firmly in God's call and God's gifts they remind us of the importance of maintaining firm faith in God's initiative and absolute power in sanctifying human persons and communities and in transforming the world. Their insights also serve as very useful correctives to any tendencies towards clericalism in the Church as well as inclinations towards creeping laicism which would reject the need for ordered structures in the assembly and hence the hierarchical nature of the Church. The call to unity along with an affirmation of diversity in the liturgical assembly will continue to raise complex problems in the Church. Hopefully assemblies will more and more come to see that diversity is not an obstacle to unity but is rather the ground out of which true Christian unity grows.[60]

[59] No. 257.
[60] Vincie, "The Liturgical Assembly: Review and Reassessment," 141–144.

James F. White

15. Thirty Years of the Doctoral Program in Liturgical Studies at the University of Notre Dame, 1965–1995

Certainly not the least, and quite likely the greatest, of Aidan Kavanagh's many contributions to North American Christianity was in developing the doctoral program in Liturgical Studies at the University of Notre Dame. This program, which Kavanagh began directing in 1966, has made enormous contributions to the teaching of liturgy in North American seminaries and colleges, and to reforming worship among the Churches at national, regional, and local levels. The Graduate Program in Liturgical Studies has helped establish Liturgical Studies as a respected theological discipline on the North American scene. And it also helped greatly in the establishment of Notre Dame as a major center of graduate studies in Theology.

We shall examine the development of the doctoral program in Liturgical Studies at Notre Dame as a significant fragment of North American liturgical history. It will allow some insights into the evolution of a new academic discipline on the North American scene. In a broader sense, it will provide some background on the shaping of North American liturgy. We shall look at the faculty involved in this process, the courses offered, and the final product, the students and the ministries they provide.

The prehistory of the doctoral program at Notre Dame goes back to 1947 when Michael Mathis, c.s.c., instituted a modest summer program for undergraduates. As advertised in *Orate Fratres*, it was

324

intended to combine classroom lectures and liturgical services.[1] Mathis recruited the faculty and students and raised the funds to sustain the summer program. By the following year, he was able to persuade the University to institute a M.A. program provided that he recruit faculty and raise funds. For faculty during those early years, he found it necessary to invite over a whole galaxy of European stars: Louis Bouyer, Jean Daniélou, Balthasar Fischer, Josef Goldbrunner, Pierre-Marie Gy, Josef Jungmann, and Herman Schmidt. A "Who's Who" of the American liturgical movement also took part: Martin Hellriegel, H. A. Reinhold, Godfrey Diekmann, Reynold Hillenbrand, and Gerald Ellis.[2] The emphasis on liturgical chant, led by Ermin Vitry, was one aspect that changing needs erased in time. From the start, Mathis set high standards for the M.A. program. Mathis himself is listed among the University faculty as Professor of Religion beginning in 1953. In the years after his death in 1960, the program continued to thrive as a summer program. Three European members made up the faculty list for the summer of 1964 (Louis Bouyer, Boniface Luykx, and Cornelius Bouman). But in 1965, the name of Aidan Kavanagh joins those of Cornelius Bouman, Josef Goldbrunner, and two other Americans, Earl Johnson, and John Quinn. The reliance on Europeans was easing. In addition, the University of Notre Dame Press published a nine-volume Liturgical Studies series, mostly lectures from the summer program, which greatly increased the program's impact.

Doctoral programs in Liturgical Studies had been instituted in Europe a decade before Notre Dame. These began with the Institut Supérieur de Liturgie in Paris. Bernard Botte, who led in founding it in 1956, tells of the early years and the feeling of being threatened by the founding of the Pontifical Liturgical Institute at Sant' Anselmo in Rome in the early 1960s.[3] Even more important for the American scene was the Liturgical Institute in Trier. A long list of

---

[1] *Orate Fratres*, XXI (1947), 278. Cf. Robert J. Kennedy, *Michael Mathis: American Liturgical Pioneer*. (Washington: Pastoral Press, 1987) 11–18. A full-length treatment of Mathis is greatly needed.

[2] Cf. Kathleen Hughes, *The Monk's Tale: A Biography of Godfrey Diekmann, O.S.B.* (Collegeville: The Liturgical Press, 1991) 138–139 for Godfrey Diekmann's assessment of those early years.

[3] *From Silence to Participation* (Washington: Pastoral Press, 1988) 93–106.

distinguished American educators were among the thirty-three whose doctorates Balthasar Fischer directed during his years of teaching there. It is quite possible that the importance of the Rite of Christian Initiation of Adults in North American Catholicism stems from Fischer's work on this rite and the enthusiasm for it he engendered among his students who returned as advocates. Among these was Aidan Kavanagh. His dissertation at Trier was an ecumenical topic: *The Concept of Eucharistic Memorial in the Canon Revisions of Thomas Cranmer,* reflecting his own Anglican heritage.[4]

The advent of doctoral studies in theology at Notre Dame was part of the excitement engendered by Vatican II. In 1965, there was in existence at Notre Dame only a M.A. program in Theology, although twenty years earlier St. Mary's College had pioneered a doctoral program for women in its School of Sacred Theology. A Second Vatican Council Conference held at Notre Dame in 1965 brought together a number of nationally known theologians and helped in the formulation of doctoral programs in theology. These were launched in 1965 in four areas: systematic theology, historical theology, biblical studies, and liturgical studies. The initial vision may have come from President Hesburgh but the actual father of the doctoral programs was Albert Schlitzer, c.s.c., chairman of the department beginning in 1962. He managed to organize the programs and to attract such figures as John McKenzie, s.j., in Hebrew Scriptures.

Until 1965, the theology faculty were almost all priests, most of them Congregation of Holy Cross priests; that year, Josephine Ford joined the department. Those were heady times: Vatican II ended in 1965, ecumenism had suddenly become a safe subject for Roman Catholics, and liturgical change was already becoming manifest, especially after the appearance of the (First) *Instruction on the Sacred Liturgy* on September 26, 1964.

The faculty in liturgy had its actual beginning in 1966 with the advent of Aidan Kavanagh and was firmly established with the coming in 1967 of William G. Storey. But the first student, Kevin Ranaghan, had already enrolled in 1965 in anticipation of the program, having completed the Master's program in 1964. Course lists

[4] St. Meinrad: St. Meinrad's Press, 1964.

from the fall semesters of 1966 and 1967 are not in the Department of Theology files but Aelred Tegels, o.s.b., is listed as teaching liturgy as is Earl Johnson, o.s.b. Tegels, a monk of St. John's, taught in the first three years of the program before returning to St. John's where he eventually edited *Worship*. Kavanagh, Tegels, and Johnson were all Benedictines; except for Nathan Mitchell, that order has not been represented on the faculty for the last two decades. John Quinn, who entered the program in 1966, was involved in teaching from 1968 through the 1970s. He was a graduate student until 1980 as well as teacher but left without completing the doctoral program to teach elsewhere. The fall of 1967 saw the admission of eight more doctoral students (besides Ranaghan and Quinn who were already there). By that time, the program was firmly launched. Since that time, the program (through 1995) has produced fifty-nine Ph.D.s in Liturgical Studies, nearly three a year, beginning with the first degree awarded (Ralph Keifer in 1972).

There was much excitement in the early years of the liturgy program, almost a euphoria, as the processes of liturgical reform went on in the various Churches. Each new rite was welcomed as it appeared and made the hopes of many years become realities. For Roman Catholics and Episcopalians, the years 1967–1973 were the most significant; for Lutherans they extended to 1978 and United Methodist reform was launched in 1970. Notre Dame faculty and students contributed significantly to the process. Some key documents came out of Notre Dame such as Lutheran baptism and United Methodist ordination rites. These Notre Dame contributions to North American liturgical history deserve special study.

THE LITURGICAL FACULTY

In the years since its founding, over thirty faculty members have taught in the doctoral program in Liturgical Studies. Many of them were one-time visitors, but they include a wide selection of North American and European liturgical scholars. We shall concentrate on those who remained for several years to help shape the program as it evolved, but the procession of visitors is illuminating. They include: Richard Rutherford, Louis Bouyer, John Gallen, John Barry Ryan, William Martin, Anna Marie Aagard and Christian Thodberg (both from Denmark), Nathan Mitchell, Kenneth Stevenson, Eugene Brand, Stephen Happell, Willard Jabusch, Sarhad Jammo, Walter Burghardt, John Baldovin, Theresa Koernke, Lawrence Hoffman, John Leonard, Paul Meyendorff, Joanne Pierce, David Tripp, Balthasar Fischer, James Dallen, and Gilbert Ostdiek. Several of these (Martin, Koernke, Leonard, Meyendorff, Pierce, and Mitchell) are graduates of the program. John Gallen, John Barry Ryan, John Leonard, and Nathan Mitchell were on the staff, at various times, of the Notre Dame Center for Pastoral Liturgy, formerly the Murphy Center for Liturgical Research. This institution, completely separate and distinct from the Theology Department, nevertheless provides practical and theoretical experience for many graduate students and was the locus of much of Mark Searle's sociological research.

The number of visiting faculty has been greatly swelled by those teaching in the summer program, which has continued to thrive for nearly fifty years. This program offers a wide selection of courses for M.A. and unclassified students. A much smaller M.A. program in Liturgical Studies continues throughout the academic year with the same faculty as the doctoral program.

Our present concern is with the permanent faculty members and how their respective academic interests have shaped the program. Aidan Kavanagh, o.s.b., who established the doctoral program, left his Texas background to become a monk of St. Meinrad's Archabbey in Indiana. He received a B.A. degree there in 1956, an S.T.L. from the University of Ottawa in 1958, and an S.T.D. at Trier in 1963, the same year the *Constitution on the Sacred Liturgy* revolutionized liturgical history. His title at Notre Dame was Director of Liturgical Studies and, later, Director of Graduate Studies. Kavanagh's time at Notre Dame ended in 1974 when he went to teach at Yale Divinity School. Most of his books have been published since he left Notre Dame but his interests and influences are apparent in his Notre Dame days. In the early seventies, he organized a conference at Notre Dame, the papers from which were published as *The Roots of Ritual*, edited by James Shaughnessy, a priest of the Peoria diocese, then director of the Center for Pastoral Liturgy. This was a pioneering work for North America in stressing the importance of the human sciences in understanding liturgy and, in Kavanagh's words, the need for liturgists to understand that "ritual behavior has its own grammar and syntax."[5] This has been a continuing theme in his work and has helped to introduce a major ingredient in modern liturgical studies in this country. Undaunted by the cold water Victor Turner threw on these efforts by disparaging the post-Vatican II reforms, Kavanagh has helped make Ritual Studies a permanent part of the discipline of Liturgical Studies. His *Elements of Rite* is a practical consequence of these concerns.

Another perduring theme is the concern with Christian initiation, foreshadowed in articles on "Tactics and Strategy" and on the R.C.I.A. in another Notre Dame collection, *Made, Not Born*. This set the stage for his best known book, *The Shape of Baptism*, which has influenced a whole generation of liturgists. *Confirmation* is a historical study of one of the problems in initiation.

Yet another thread appears in Kavanagh's interest in liturgical theology. This became most explicit in lectures at Seabury-Western Theological Seminary, published in 1984 as *Liturgical Theology*. So already in Kavanagh are foreshadowed the three chief areas of the Graduate Program in Liturgical Studies even today: Liturgical History, Liturgical Theology, and Ritual Studies. His departure from Notre Dame in 1974 precluded the direction of the dissertations of many of the students he had taught in those early years but he did see to completion those of Ralph Keifer, Kevin Ranaghan, and Jacob Vellian.

William Storey, the second permanent member of the liturgy faculty, came from a quite different background and brought different strengths. Storey was a Roman Catholic layman with a B.A. and M.A. from Assumption College and a M.M.S. and D.M.S. (Medieval Studies) from Notre Dame. After his student days at Notre Dame, he taught at Duquesne University and he and Ralph Keifer were two of the first to be touched by the Roman Catholic charismatic movement. Storey had been trained as a medievalist and his dissertation had been on a medieval manuscript. One of his most useful works was the publication (with Niels Rasmussen) of a translation and revision of Cyrille Vogel's *Medieval Liturgy: An Introduction to the Sources*.

The historical and practical were combined in his interest in the liturgy of the hours, especially after the disappointing post-Vatican

[5] Grand Rapids: Eerdmans, 1973, 8.

II reforms of these offices. This manifested itself concretely in a series of books for daily prayer, many published by Ave Maria Press at Notre Dame. These were adumbrated by *Morning Praise and Evensong* published while he was still at Duquesne and dedicated to his friend, H.A.R[einhold]. No doubt, his greatest contribution in this area was *Praise God in a Song* which he compiled and edited in collaboration with John Melloh. This, in its various editions, still provides one of the most sensible versions of an accessible daily office. It consists of Morning Praise, Evening Prayer, and Resurrection Vigil of the Lord's Day.

Storey taught in the program longer than anyone else has so far, taking early retirement in 1985 to manage his South Bend book store, Erasmus Books. He succeeded Kavanagh as Director of the Graduate Program in Liturgical Studies. During his long tenure, he directed eight dissertations: John Leonard, Stanislaus Campbell, Andrew Ciferni, George Minamiki, Nathan Mitchell, Joanne Pierce, William Wade, and David Wright.

An ecumenical dimension was added to the faculty in 1971 when Leonel Mitchell, an Episcopalian, joined the program. He had received a B.A. degree from Trinity College, a S.T.B. from Berkeley Divinity School, a S.T.M. and a Th.D. from General Theological Seminary where he had worked with Boone Porter. He has kept up a longtime interest in initiation, reflected in his teaching at Notre Dame and in his dissertation, published as *Baptismal Anointing*, in a chapter in *Made, Not Born,* and his most recent book summarizing current developments: *Worship: Initiation and the Churches.* A course he taught undergraduates at Notre Dame provided the impetus for *The Meaning of Ritual.* More directly Anglican concerns shape *Liturgical Change, How Much Do We Need?* and *Praying Shapes Believing.* Mitchell taught at Notre Dame through 1978, then left to teach at Seabury-Western Theological Seminary. While at Notre Dame, he directed dissertations by Emmanuel Cutrone, William Martin, Donald Martin, Frank Quinn, and Frank Senn.

A major addition to the faculty was Edward J. Kilmartin, S.J., who came in 1975. Kilmartin had a background in Chemistry before taking up Theology. He had a M.A. from Boston College, a M.S. from Holy Cross, a S.T.L. from Weston, and a S.T.D. from the Gregorian University. Kilmartin's liturgical interests were so diversified it is difficult to categorize them although there were specialities in Liturgical Theology as shown in *Christian Liturgy: Theology and Practice,* in early Christian worship, as evidenced in the *Eucharist in the Primitive Church,* and in ecumenism, expounded in *Toward Reunion: the Roman Church and the Orthodox Churches.* He also dealt with specific issues as in his commentary on a Roman document on the Eucharist in *Church, Eucharist, and Priesthood* or in *Culture and the Praying Church.*

Most significant is the enthusiasm Kilmartin aroused in his students for doing liturgical theology. He managed to have liturgical theology made a major for liturgy students. He also played a leading role in organizing the liturgical theology work group in the North American Academy of Liturgy. He is commemorated in the eight dissertations he directed while at Notre Dame: Michael Aune, Craig Erickson, Michael Gilligan, John Grabner, Theresa Koernke, John Laurance, Mary Alice Piil, and Mary Schaefer. Kilmartin left in 1984 to teach at the Pontifical Oriental Institute in Rome and at Boston College. He died in 1994.

A year before Kilmartin, Robert F. Taft, s.j., began a long relationship with the liturgy program, beginning in 1974. Taft's relationship has been intermittent, teaching the fall semesters throughout much of the 1970s, staying all year in 1978–1979, and returning biennially for most of the 1980s. As the pre-eminent scholar of Eastern liturgies, Taft has made an important contribution in balancing the Western predominance of the program. He is best known for his volumes on the history of the Byzantine rite including *The Great Entrance* and *The Diptychs.* A collection of his most distinguished articles appeared in *Beyond East and West.* And more recently, he has turned his attention to the *Liturgy of the Hours in East and West.* Much of his teaching at Notre Dame has focused on Eastern rites but he has frequently taught courses on the liturgical year. Because of his intermittent presence, he has had less contact with dissertation writers, but directed Paul Meyendorff, Joseph Weiss, and John Klentos.

John Allyn Melloh, s.m., began teaching in the 1977 summer program and then joined the staff of the Center for Pastoral Liturgy at Notre Dame in 1978. Much of his work has concentrated on working with M.Div. students. He teaches courses dealing with Homiletics, Church Music, and Liturgical Celebration. In addition, he has served as Director of the John S. Marten Program in Homiletics and Liturgics for many years. His academic pedigree includes a B.A. and a B.S. from the University of Dayton, a M.A. from Notre Dame, and a Ph.D. from St. Louis University. He is well known for the musical portions of the various editions of *Praise God in Song*. Other publications include the *Wake Service* and *The Order of Christian Funerals: A Commentary*. In recent years, his research and teaching have moved in the direction of Ritual Studies and he has taught courses formerly taught by Mark Searle. Melloh directed dissertations by Michael Kwatera and David Stosur.

Mark Searle began teaching in 1978 with a concurrent appointment in the Theology Department and the Notre Dame Center for Pastoral Liturgy. Born in England, he had been a Franciscan priest but was laicized in 1980. His degrees included a S.T.L. from the Antonionum in Rome and a Diploma and Doctor of Theology from the Theological Faculty at Trier. His interests focused especially on initiation and Ritual Studies. The former was evidenced in *Christening: The Making of Christians* and *The Church Speaks about Sacraments with Children*. But his real pioneering work was done in the area of Ritual Studies. Here he was deeply involved with the Notre Dame Study of Catholic parish life which resulted in the publication of a number of reports using sociological analysis.

Searle increasingly moved in the direction of the application of semiotics to Liturgical Studies. His presidential address to the North American Academy of Liturgy in 1983 was a landmark in the systematic development of Ritual Studies as a distinct discipline within Liturgical Studies. Unfortunately, the promise of much of this work was cut short by his early death in 1992. *Semiotics and Church Architecture* (written with Gerard Lukken) was published in 1993. Above all, Searle was a person of deep spirituality and personal humility. He directed dissertations by Thomas Fisch, Kathleen Hughes, Thomas Schattauer, David Stosur, and Frederick West.

Niels Rasmussen, O.P., who came to Notre Dame in 1979, also died an untimely and tragic death. Born in Denmark, he had studied at the University of Aarhaus and did a Doctor of Theology at the Institut Catholique in Paris. His dissertation was on the pontificals of the high middle ages and he was preparing a major work on this at the time of his death in 1987. Previously, he had taught in the sister program at The Catholic University of America and joined Notre Dame as the second medieval historian of liturgy. For six years, he and William Storey were teammates, sharing courses on this period. They also collaborated on the revised edition of Cyrille Vogel's *Medieval Liturgy: An Introduction to the Sources*. During his eight years at Notre Dame, Rasmussen directed dissertations by Edward Foley and Joanne Pierce.

The next addition to the permanent liturgy faculty was the present author. After preliminary semesters in the fall of 1980 and spring of 1982, I came on a permanent basis in 1983 after twenty-two years of teaching at Perkins School of Theology and two years at Ohio Wesleyan University (1959–1961). Liturgy was indeed a lonely field in 1959 and I would like to think I have helped shape the teaching of the subject through my textbook, *Introduction to Christian Worship*, my source book, *Documents of Christian Worship*, and my doctoral students. My degrees are a Harvard A.B., a Union Theological Seminary B.D., and a Duke Ph.D. In addition, I had the good fortune to spend a year studying with E. C. Ratcliff at Cambridge, a postdoctoral semester at Yale, and a year at the Pontifical Liturgical Institute in Rome.

My training as an architectural historian is reflected in *The Cambridge Movement, Protestant Worship and Church Architecture, Architecture at Southern Methodist University*, and *Church Architecture*. I consider the most important of my books to be *Protestant Worship: Traditions in Transition* and *Roman Catholic Worship: Trent to Today*. Other interests include sacramental theology, liturgical biography, and liturgy and justice. During the 1970s, I was intensely involved in revision of the United Methodist service books, especially the Eucharist. I have had the privilege of directing or co-directing the dissertations of many students: John Grabner, Stanley Hall, Robert Hawkins, Charles Hohenstein, Fred Holper, Richard Leggett, Mark Luttio, Michael Moriarty, Paul Nelson, Beverley Nitschke, Robert Peiffer, Marjorie Procter-Smith, John Riggs, Ralph Smith, Mark Torgerson, Robert Tuzik, William Wade, and Karen Westerfield Tucker.

In 1985, the program was fortunate to attract a leading British liturgical scholar, Paul F. Bradshaw. He came after teaching in Anglican theological colleges at Chichester and Cuddesdon. Bradshaw had studied at Cambridge (B.A. and M.A.), Westcott House, and the University of London (Ph.D.). His coming brought the possibility of specialized work in early Christian liturgy. This is reflected in his volumes, *Daily Prayer in the Early Church*, *The Canons of Hippolytus*, and *Ordination Rites of the Ancient Churches*. He has special interests in daily public prayer (reflected in *Two Ways of Praying*) and ordination rites. His Anglican heritage is apparent in *The Anglican Ordinal* (his dissertation topic) and *Companion to the Alternative Service Book*. Most would agree that his recent book, *The Search for the Origins of Christian Worship*, marks a major turning point in liturgical study in its rejection of any facile finding of homogeneity in the worship of the early Churches. Bradshaw has directed or codirected the dissertations of Martin Connell, Maxwell Johnson, John Klentos, Patrick Malloy, Ruth Meyers, Edward Phillips, Grant Sperry-White, and Joseph Weiss.

A recent addition to the liturgy staff was Regis A. Duffy, O.F.M. He came in 1989 after an initial visit in 1983, coming from a position in the Washington Theological Union. His advent balanced the Trier (Kavanagh, Searle) and Paris (Rasmussen) legacy since his S.T.D. degree was from the Institut Catholique in Paris with a B.S.M. from Manhattanville College, M.A from S.U.N.Y., and a S.T.L. from Catholic University. He combined a specialty in Liturgical Theology with much expertise in Ritual Studies. His background in the human sciences is reflected in *Real Presence: Worship, Sacraments and Commitment*, *A Roman Catholic Theology of Pastoral Care*, and *On Becoming a Catholic*. He left Notre Dame for reasons of health in 1994. In the relatively short time he was at Notre Dame, Duffy directed dissertations by Marie Conn and Jeffrey Kemper.

In 1994, Michael Driscoll, a diocesan priest from Montana, joined the faculty as a specialist in Medieval Liturgy. His doctorate is from the Institut Catholique in Paris and the Sorbonne with degrees from Carroll College, Gregorian University and Sant' Anselmo. The permanent faculty consists at present of Bradshaw, Driscoll, Melloh, and White. There are obvious gaps yet unfilled (1995). Visiting faculty can fill some slots but future permanent appointments are necessary.

Two things seem to stand out in a survey of the courses offered in the past quarter century and more. There seems to be an underlying core of courses, largely historical, that have endured. At the same time, new emphases have come and, in some cases, gone. It is obvious that some things are firmly lodged, but also that Liturgical Studies is still evolving as a discipline. It should be borne in mind that the liturgy faculty are usually teaching at four levels: undergraduate, Master of Divinity, Master of Arts, and Doctor of Philosophy. Each level brings different emphases although there is often overlapping of interests. Frequently, Ph.D. students take M.A. courses; occasionally, M.Div. students enroll in M.A. courses, and they are sometimes merged.

Other members of the Theology faculty have also offered courses on liturgical subjects. For a number of years, Joseph Blenkinsopp taught a course on the "Jewish Heritage" which dealt largely with worship. Adela Collins gave a course on sacraments in the New Testament, while Michael Himes several times taught sacramental theology courses on the doctoral level. One of the advantages of the University is that doctoral students can take courses in other departments such as the Medieval Institute, Art History, Music, and the School of Architecture. The usual problem is the frustration of restricting oneself to a small portion of what the University has to offer at the graduate level.

There have been some interesting offerings at the undergraduate level. For several years, Aidan Kavanagh taught "Sociology of the Religious Experience," now more likely to appear in the Sociology Department. Leonel Mitchell instituted a course at this level on the "Meaning of Ritual." Courses on the Eucharist continue on the undergraduate level. More recently, a doctoral candidate, Michael Moriarty, taught for three years a well-received undergraduate course on liturgy and Lester Ruth inaugurated a popular course, "Protestant Worship." William Storey's tripartite courses on Church History were popular among Theology majors for many years.

At the Master of Divinity level, only a limited number of liturgy courses can be crowded into an already congested schedule. These include "Eucharist" as a necessary perennial offering and a course that initially covered both "Initiation and Reconciliation." It is significant that interest in initiation continued to grow so that reconciliation was eventually pushed out of the course, although logically connected. Some of the practical concerns of reconciliation were covered in counseling courses. The liturgical aspects ended up in a M.A. course on "Pastoral Rites." Both the Eucharist and initiation courses were paralleled or sometimes taught in connection with similar courses for M.A. students. In recent years, both M.Div. students and M.A. students have been predominantly lay people.

Practical approaches at the M.Div. level were listed under such headings as "Liturgical Leadership" or "Liturgical Ministry and Celebration," usually taught in recent years by John Melloh. In addition to the three required courses in Homiletics, he has also taught an occasional course on "Parochial Music."

At the M.A. level, in addition to "Eucharist" and "Initiation," certain courses have survived for twenty years or more. These include "The Divine Office," begun in 1974, transmuted into the "Liturgy of the Hours," and more recently into "Liturgical Prayer." Storey, Taft, Rasmussen, Melloh, and Bradshaw have taken turns teaching it. "The Liturgical Year" was introduced in summer school by Thomas Talley, then into the regular school year, first under Leonel Mitchell, then by Taft, Eugene Brand, Searle, Rasmussen, Duffy, and Bradshaw. A variety of other courses have come and gone as electives at the M.A. level including "Word and Sacrament" (Kilmartin), "Celebration of Marriage" (Kenneth Stevenson), "Pastoral Liturgy" or "Ritual Studies" (Searle), and "Pastoral Rites," i.e. marriage, healing, burial, and reconciliation (White). Some of these elective courses have been taken by Ph.D. as well as M.A. students.

The Ph.D. courses show the most variety, especially reflecting the changing faculty and visitors. Yet there are some important constants. Aelred Tegels taught "Early Christian Worship" the very first year of the program and seminars in this area still abound. The second year, William Storey introduced a "Medieval Liturgy Seminar," which still remains. When Storey and Rasmussen were both teaching, this topic was a major strength of the program. Where else could one find two medieval liturgists? In the fourth year, Kavanagh offered a "Modern Liturgical Development" course and a "Modern Liturgy Seminar" became a permanent part of the program. It must be remembered that in the late 1960s and 1970s much liturgical development was current in many Churches. Not until the Spring of 1975 was "Reformation Liturgy" offered (by Leonel Mitchell) but as the program became more and more ecumenical, this became a basic part of it. These four histori-cal areas (early, medieval, reformation, and modern) still form the basis of the historical part of doctoral work with special topics being introduced from year to year (liturgical architecture, ordina-tion rites, liturgical biographies).

In 1974, Robert Taft began teaching "Eastern Liturgies Seminar" and this became soon a permanent feature of the academic year as it had already been in summers. Taft usually taught it but in his absence Sarhad Jammo and Paul Meyendorff have led students through these mysterious mazes. For a time, there was a parallel "Western Liturgies Seminar" on a wide variety of topics and periods such as medieval commentaries on the Mass (William Storey) or neo-Gallican rites (F. Ellen Weaver). This seminar lapsed in the mid-1980s.

These historical courses have provided the backbone of the lit-urgy program and the majority of dissertations have been written on historical subjects. From an early time, Liturgical Theology and Ritual Studies appeared under various guises. The third year of the program, Kavanagh taught "Theology of Symbolic Forms" and it is likely many of the early courses simply labeled "Liturgy Seminar" dealt with what would later be recognized as Liturgical Theology. During the Kavanagh years, an anthropological ap-proach to worship was a major concern of the program. With the advent of Edward Kilmartin, Liturgical Theology became a distinct ingredient, one which was continued by Regis Duffy.

The advent of Mark Searle gave Ritual Studies a new focus. Taught first as "Pastoral Liturgy," Searle was a pioneer in making Ritual Studies a recognized specialty within a theological program. It never achieved the status of a major but was accepted as a minor. Since Mark Searle's death, John Melloh has done much teaching in this area with Gilbert Ostdiek guest teaching once. The core of the program remains solidly historical but increasingly students are attracted to Liturgical Theology and Ritual Studies and several dissertations have been written or are underway in each area.

Visiting scholars have added much variety, including courses on "The Celebration of Marriage" (Kenneth Stevenson), "Ritual and Symbols in Systematic Context" (Anna Marie Aagaard), "The Preached Word" (Walter Burghardt), "History of Preaching" (O. C. Edwards), and a seminar on initiation (Balthasar Fischer). But there has been a rather extraordinary constancy in the historical courses offered and a gradual growth in Liturgical Theology (often taught historically) and Ritual Studies (whether taught by anthropological, psychological, sociological, or semiotic methods).

THE DOCTORAL STUDENTS

In many ways, the most interesting part of the program has been the students. Not only have they brought an immense variety of gifts from varied backgrounds but they have gone out to work in many diverse positions. For many, if not all, graduate work meant major sacrifices, both financial and in family time, often with a dim prospect of a job at the end. Many problems beset the graduate student and, for most, financial exigencies necessitate teaching or other forms of support during graduate study. Some students have remained far longer than expected, the record being fourteen years.

Admissions is always competitive. Several times the number apply as there is available financial aid to open slots for them. Almost all doctoral students receive free tuition and most a stipend. The other side of the picture is that in the thirty years of the doctoral program, a total of 124 students have been admitted and enrolled for an average of about four and a half per year. Five would seem to be the ideal; in recent years, because of financial reasons, the number has sometimes dropped as low as two or three. Another factor is the shortage of Roman Catholic priests and religious. From 1987 to 1992, neither was represented among entering students. The advent of more lay Roman Catholic future liturgists compensated somewhat for this loss.

The other question is that of retention. Of the 124 admitted, one must deduct, of course, the nineteen students currently in the program, leaving 105 previously enrolled. Of these, fifty-nine had completed their doctorates by the end of 1995 or almost sixty per cent. Dropouts occurred for a wide variety of reasons: financial, family, church demands, and inability to meet the standards of the program. Many of the dropouts completed a M.A. Of the forty-two students admitted in the 1980s, thirty have finished and another is expected to do so soon. That would indicate a gratifying three-quarters retention rate which may be the result of greater selectivity.

The length of graduate work of those who completed the Ph.D. varies from four years (one individual) to twelve (one individual) with seven being the greatest number (15), then six years (11), eight or nine (both 9), five years (6), ten years (5), and eleven years (1), for an average of 7.4 years. This is deceptive, for many, if not most, of these students were involved in teaching and quite a number were not in residence in their latter years.

By 1968, the program had become ecumenical with the arrival of a Lutheran pastor, Hans Boehringer. Three more Lutherans had enrolled by 1970 and William Martin, an Episcopalian, arrived in 1971. William Wade, a United Methodist, came in 1973. Nine Lutherans have finished, seven United Methodists, six Episcopalians, three Presbyterians, two United Church of Christ, and one each Orthodox Church of America, Greek Orthodox, and Evangelical Covenant. Another Evangelical Covenant student is about finished. Of the fifty-nine graduates, half are Roman Catholics (29); Protestants account for 28 and Orthodox for 2.

The ministries these graduates enter have all focused on Church and academy. Nearly half (29) have been employed in seminary teaching on the staff of about one eighth of the accredited seminaries in English-speaking North America. Eleven are teaching at the college or university level and one has retired from this. Seven are working at the parish level; five work with their religious order; four are liturgical bureaucrats or editors, and three are deceased. One would like to think that these graduates have had and will have an enormous influence on the North American Churches. Several have made contributions in the form of books published beyond the dissertation: Craig Erickson, Edward Foley, Kathleen Hughes, Nathan Mitchell, Marjorie Procter-Smith, Frank Senn, and Susan White spring to mind. Many others will do likewise in the course of time.

There are demographic gaps in the list of graduates. No American minorities are represented so far although some have entered the program. With the exception of two Asians, all are North

Americans. Unlike the European liturgical institutes, the program has not had much appeal overseas. That may be a consequence of finances, but may also be attributed to an unawareness of what the program offers. Only ten (17%) of the graduates are women although Kathleen Hughes (1981) well may be the first woman to gain a Ph.D. in Liturgical Studies from any institution.

It remains to look at the areas in which students did their doctoral dissertation research. This will tell us much about the future development of Liturgical Studies since many graduates will likely continue to do their research and teaching in related areas. It is not easy to categorize these topics, so some allowance must be made for topics that slide into several fields. One is immediately struck by the overwhelming preponderance of the historical approach: fifty-three out of fifty-nine dissertations. Even more striking is that of these historical topics, thirteen are modern and another nineteen more specifically North American. That leaves seven each for early Church, medieval, and the Reformation period. Three each have been completed in Liturgical Theology and in Ritual Studies.

We can only indicate approximate titles here, but it is worthwhile to indicate the names of these graduates and their topics. Remember, the categorization is admittedly arbitrary and the authors might feel more comfortable being classified elsewhere.

The early Church topics include Martin Cornell on the liturgical year, Emmanuel Cutrone on saving presence in Cyril of Jerusalem, Maxwell Johnson on the sacramentary of Sarapion, Ralph Keifer on oblation in early Italian and Egyptian canons, John Laurance on liturgical leadership in Cyprian, Edward Phillips on the ritual kiss, and Grant Sperry-White on *Testamentum Domini*. The medieval topics include John Leonard on Easter vespers, Marie Conn on the Dunstan and Brodie pontificals, Edward Foley on the Ordinary of St. Denis, John Klentos on monastic rites, Joanne Pierce on the prayerbook of Sigebert of Minden, Mary Schaefer on twelfth century Latin commentaries on the Mass, and David Wright on Innocent III on the Mass.

Interpreting the Reformation period fairly broadly, we find Robert Hawkins on the hymnic complement to the Lutheran symbols, Donald Martin on Ash Wednesday in Tudor England, Paul Meyendorff on the liturgical reforms of Patriach Nikon, John Riggs on the development of Calvin's baptismal theology, Frank Senn on Eucharistic restoration during the Swedish Reformation, Ralph Smith on sixteenth century German Lutheran ordination rites, and Jacob Vellian on the latinization of the Malabar liturgy.

We are flooded with post-Reformation topics: Stanislaus Campbell on reform of the Roman office, 1964–1971, Andrew Ciferni on recent discussion of the Praemonstratensian rite, Michael Gilligan on the offering Church in twentieth-century Roman Catholic theologians, Jeffrey Kemper on the work of I.C.E.L., Michael Kwatera on Prosper Guéranger's evaluation of neo-Gallican rites, Richard Leggett on Anglican ordination rites, 1970–1989, Mark Luttio on Japanese Lutheran Funeral Rites, Patrick Malloy on the post-Reformation English "Manual," William Martin on the validity of lay baptism in Church of England discussions, George Minamiki on the modern phase of the Chinese rites controversy, Frank Quinn on the revised rites of confirmation, Roman Catholic and Episcopal, Thomas Schattauer on liturgical renewal under Wilhelm Loehe, and Joseph Weiss on the Jesuits and the liturgy of the hours.

The largest number, almost a third, focus specifically on North American topics: Michael Aune on American Lutheran liturgical theology and practice, 1946–1976, Craig Erickson on sacramental theology among American Presbyterians, 1945–1979, John Grabner on the history of American Methodist ordination rites and the 1980 ordinal, Stanley Hall on American Presbyterian directories for public worship, Charles Hohenstein on the revisions of the rites of baptism in the Methodist Episcopal Church, 1784–1939, Fred Holper on office and ordination in American Presbyterianism, Ruth Meyers on renewed understanding of Christian initiation in the Episcopal Church, 1950–1979, Nathan Mitchell on liturgical reform at Mercersburg, 1843–1857, Michael Moriarty on the work of Associated Parishes in the Episcopal Church, Paul Nelson on the 1982 Lutheran ordination rite in North America, Beverley Nitschke on confession and forgiveness in the *Lutheran Book of Worship*, Robert Peiffer on the revision of the United Methodist liturgical texts, 1968–1988, Marjorie Procter-Smith on women in Shaker community and worship, Kevin Ranaghan on initiation rites in American Pentecostal Churches, 1901–1972, Mark Torgerson on the church architecture of Edward Sövik, Robert Tuzik on Reynold Hillen-

341

brand's contributions to the liturgical movement, William Wade on public worship in episcopal Methodism, 1784–1905, Karen Westerfield Tucker on the rites of marriage and burial in American Methodism, 1784–1968, and Susan White on the Liturgical Arts Society, 1927–1972.

Those dealing with Liturgical Theology, in some cases, overlap with those above but specifically include: Theresa Koernke on the pneumatological dimension of the Eucharist, Mary Alice Piil on offering Church in the post-conciliar period, and Frederick West on Anton Baumstark's comparative liturgy in its intellectual context. The three Ritual Studies dissertations completed so far have been Thomas Fisch on utilizing the thought of Gregory Bateson, Kathleen Hughes on the opening prayers of the sacramentary, and David Stosur on the *Book of Blessings*.

A considerable amount of liturgical scholarship has already been accomplished and will continue to develop as these students pursue their several ministries and mature as scholars. The Doctoral Program in Liturgical Studies at the University of Notre Dame has made notable contributions to the liturgical life of the Churches of North America.

Aidan Kavanagh, O.S.B.:
An Annotated Bibliography

Kavanagh, Aidan. *The Concept of Eucharistic Memorial in the Canon Revisions of Thomas Cranmer, Archbishop of Canterbury, 1533–1556* [S.T.D. Thesis, Trier, 1963]. St. Meinrad, Ind.: Abbey Press, 1964.

An examination of Cranmer's revisions of the Eucharistic anaphora in light of Reformation theologies of memorial and sacrifice.

_____. Review of *The Variety of Catholic Attitudes,* by T. L. Westow. New York: 1963. In *Worship* 38 (1964) 664–666.

_____. Review of *True Worship: An Anglo-French Symposium,* by L. C. Sheppard. Baltimore: 1963. In *Worship* 38 (1964) 440–441.

_____. "Liturgical Movement: Phase 3," *America* 111 (August 22, 1964) 183–185.

"Rubrics and ceremonies can be changed quickly, but the act of Christian *Worship* means far more than this."

_____. "Thoughts on the Roman Anaphora [The Relationship Between Jewish and Christian Berakoth]," *Worship* 39 (1965) 515–529, continued in 40 (1966) 2–16.

An analysis of the Roman Canon under the category of *berakah.* Part two examines the Canon, in Latin, in a section-by-section analysis.

_____. "Constitution on the Liturgy: Commentary [A 4-part series: 'The Liturgy as Service,' 5–11. 'Sacrament as an Act of Service,' 89–96. 'The Christian as Servant,' 131–138. 'The Minister as Servant,' 218–225]." *Worship* 39 (1965) 5–11, 89–96, 131–138, 218–225.

A systematic treatment of the Constitution on the Sacred Liturgy under the heading of "service." Liturgy as *diakonia.*

_____. "Thoughts on the Roman Anaphora," *Worship* 40 (1966) 2–16, continuation of 39 (1965) 515–529.

_____. "Liturgy and Unity in the Light of Vatican II," *Una Sancta* 23/1 (1966) 32–43.

Theological and liturgical concepts and expressions have a truly dynamic as opposed to a "static" and "eternal" character.

_____. "The Nature of Christian Penance: Metanoia and Reconciliation." *Resonance* 2/1 (1966) 8–14.

". . . We in the west have become too accustomed to regard penance only under the aspect of justice and the restoration of equilibrium." Penance must first be seen as *metanoia,* a turning toward God anew.

_____. "Cultural Diversity and Liturgical Language," *Una Sancta* 24/1 (1967) 69–71.

A short piece, the "prolegomena" to the development of a truly modern, liturgical language in English.

_____. "How Rite Develops: Some Laws Intrinsic to Liturgical Evolution," *Worship* 41 (1967) 334–347.

A paper delivered at a Consultation on Liturgical Development held at the University of Notre Dame, April 9–10, 1967. This paper marks Kavanagh's first use of sociological terms and categories to understand liturgical rites as such, though the treatment remains explicitly theological.

_____. "The Theology of Easter: Themes in Cultic Data," *Worship* 42 (1968) 194–204.

Keynote address delivered to the Valparaiso Liturgical Institute, Feb. 20, 1968, Valparaiso, IN. Asks the question "What is Easter?" "It is a cultic action accomplished through the concomitant media of myth and ritual."

_____. "Liturgical Needs for Today and Tomorrow," *Worship* 43 (1969) 488–495.

Describes seven prevalent assumptions regarding the nature of *Worship* which would virtually "assure its downfall." Cites Erik Erikson's, "Ontogeny of Ritualization in Man." "Surprise" and "spontaneity" are in themselves "no prescription for ritualization." Ritual, Aidan stated, is rather the "unexpected renewal of a recognized order in potential chaos."

_____. "Thoughts on the New Eucharistic Prayers," *Worship* 43 (1969) 2–12.

The new prayers "constitute a real step forward, so long as they do not come to be regarded as the last word or harbingers of the parousia."

_____. "Spirituality in the American Church: an Evaluative Essay." In *Contemporary Catholicism in the United States,* ed. P. Gleason and J. J. Coakley (Notre Dame: University of Notre Dame Press, 1969) 197–214.

Spirituality in general is defined as "that awareness any religious society has of itself . . . of its own living relationship with the continuum of faith objects in which it believes," p. 197. "Cultic patterns . . . are communication media that reach down into the depths of the psyche and thus make social intercourse possible, if richly ambiguous, precisely on matters of social concern," p. 213. Such cultic patterns seem threatened by certain negative qualities in American Catholic spirituality: notably its historical roots in a "defensive, subjective, individualistic, ideological and romantic" piety.

_____. "Religious Life and *Worship*," *Worship* 44 (1970) 194–204.

A talk presented to the Major Religious Superiors of Women. Also published in the Proceedings of that organization. Religious community "by definition must be a worshipping community." The Church, he stated, "is not a code-society, calibrated by ever-increasing religious professionalism." "Liturgical worship of religious communities should be clear, splendid, open and free with a latitude that goes beyond the scope permitted and possible in parishes."

_____. "Polycarp Sherwood: The Man," *Resonance* 5 (1970) 3–7.

A memorial essay for Fr. Polycarp Sherwood, o.s.b., a monk of St. Meinrad Archabbey.

_____. "Relevant Liturgy," *The Way Supplement* 11 (1970) 76–83.

Later expanded and republished in *Worship* 45 (1971) 58–72.

_____. "Relevance and Change in the Liturgy," *Worship* 45 (1971) 58–72.

A talk presented at the 1970 National Meeting of the National Federation of Diocesan Liturgical Commissions, Louisville, KY. Portions also appeared in *The Way* (1970) 76–83 and were presented at a diocesan liturgical convention of the Diocese of Windsor, Ontario, Oct. 4, 1970.

_____. "Initiation: Baptism and Confirmation; Phenomenology of Christian Initiation," *Worship* 46 (1972) 262–276.

Presents the argument from "initiatory sequence," baptism-confirmation-Eucharist. Attempts to explain the disintegration of the initiatory sequence in the West. Draws practical conclusions and suggestions for their reintegration.

_____. "Ministries in the Community and in the Liturgy," *Liturgy: Self-Expression of the Church*, [= Concilium 72]. Ed. H. Schmidt (New York: Herder and Herder, 1972) 55–67.

_____. "Liturgy is a Fallout of Prayer," *National Catholic Reporter* 8 (January 28, 1972) 5.

_____. "The Role of Ritual in Personal Development," *The Roots of Ritual*, ed. J. D. Shaugnessy (Grand Rapids: Eerdman's, 1973) 145–160.

Most of the contributions to this volume were first presented at a conference at the University of Notre Dame. Tradition is "not static, but an ongoing and thoroughly dynamic enterprise that never stops," p. 148.

_____. "The New Roman Rites of Adult Initiation," *Studia Liturgica* 10/1 (1974) 35–47.

_____. "The Norm of Baptism: The New Rite of Christian Initiation of Adults," *Worship* 48 (1974) 143–152.

_____. "Teaching Through the Liturgy," *Notre Dame Journal of Education* 5 (1974) 35–47.

Discusses the question, "How does a festive ritual celebration 'teach'?"

_____. "Liturgical Vesture in the Roman Catholic Tradition," *Raiment for the Lord's Service: A Thousand Years of Western Vestments*, ed. C. C. Mayer-Thurman (Chicago: Art Institute of Chicago, 1975) 13–15.

"The vestment is a garment, not a costume." Liturgical vesture serves a twofold function: 1) to designate the diversity of liturgical ministries and 2) to contribute to the dignity of the rite. Republished in *Modern Liturgy* 3 (May/June/July 1976) 12–13.

_____. "Christian Initiation of Adults: The Rites," *Made, Not Born* (Murphy Center for Liturgical Research, Notre Dame: University of Notre Dame Press, 1976) 118–137.

A commentary on the R.C.I.A. This essay also appears in *Worship* 48 (1974) 318–335.

_____. "Christian Initiation: Tactics and Strategy," *Made, Not Born* (Murphy Center for Liturgical Research. Notre Dame: University of Notre Dame Press, 1976) 1–6.

"Who does not know initiation does not know the Church. Who does not know the Church does not know the Lord. Who does not know the Lord does not know the world as God meant it to be from before always."

_____. "Draft Proposed Book of Common Prayer: A Roman Catholic's Appreciation," *Anglican Theological Review* 58 (1976) 360–368.

_____. "Liturgical Business: Unfinished and Unbegun," *Worship* 50 (1976) 354–364.

Kavanagh's response to the Berakah Award of the North American Academy of Liturgy, New Orleans, 1976. He described his life's works: liturgical language, liturgical music, initiation, ministry and the study of the distinction between *latria* and *dulia*. Liturgy, he claimed, "is possessed by, but does not possess the Church," it is something "which the Church must nonetheless obey in order to remain herself."

_____. "Christian Initiation for Those Baptized as Infants," *Living Light* 13/3 (1976) 387–396.

Adult baptism is presented as the paradigmatic model for all other Christian initiation.

346

_____. "Vesture—Not Vestments," *Modern Liturgy* 3 (May/June/July, 1976) 12–13.

Reprint of the introductory essay to *Raiment for the Lord's Service* (Chicago: Art Institute of Chicago, 1975).

_____. "Beyond Words and Concerts to the Survival of Mrs. Murphy," *Pastoral Music* 1 (April/May, 1977) 17–20.

1) Liturgical music is a service, a ministration. 2) "Music is an integral part of liturgical service." 3) Liturgical music is neither "secular" nor "sacred" but it is "liturgical."

_____. "Christian Initiation in Post-Conciliar Roman Catholicism: A Brief Report," *Studia Liturgica* 12/2–3 (1977) 107–115.

The Roman initiatory polity "is rightly perceived . . . to be explosive of the conventional patterns of church life," p. 111.

_____. "Prayer is the Choreography, the Poetry, the Symphony of Existence," *New Catholic World* 220 (Jan/Feb, 1977) 11.

_____. "Life-Cycle Events and Civil Ritual," *Initiation Theology: Ecumenical Insights*, ed. J. Schmeiser (Toronto: Anglican Book Centre, 1978) 9–22.

Presentation given at the 4th Symposium of the Canadian Liturgical Society, "Worship '77."

_____. *The Shape of Baptism: The Rite of Christian Initiation* [= Studies in the Reformed Rites of the Catholic Church, vol. 1]. New York: Pueblo, 1978.

_____. "The True Believer," *Sign* 57/7 (1978) 7–12.

"Baptism doesn't soften death—it destroys death. It doesn't confirm the status quo—it completely overturns it. And it doesn't insulate us against reality—it throws back the covers and kicks us out to dance naked with creation by the light of the moon."

_____. "Unfinished and Unbegun Revisited: The Rite of Christian Initiation of Adults," *Worship* 53 (1979) 327–340.

_____. "Life-Cycle Events, Civil Ritual and the Christian," *Liturgy and Human Passage* [= Concilium 112]. Eds. D. Power and L. Maldonado (New York: Seabury, 1979) 14–24.

A discussion of initiatory praxis in light of ritual studies.

_____. "Theology of Celebration," *Pastoral Music* 4 (1979) 16–17.

_____. "The Politics of Symbol and Art in Liturgical Expression," *Symbol and Art in Worship* [= Concilium 132]. Eds. L. Maldonado and D. Power (Edinburgh: T. & T. Clark, 1980) 28–39.

"It is idle to expect symbol and art to arise from a minimalist, a trivialized or a merely educative or therapeutic liturgy."

_____. "Christ, Dying and Living Still," *The Sacraments: Readings in Contemporary Sacramental Theology*, ed. M. J. Taylor (New York: Alba House, 1981) 265–274.

_____. "Initiation: Baptism and Confirmation," *The Sacraments: Readings in Contemporary Sacramental Theology*, ed. M. J. Taylor (New York: Alba House, 1981) 81–94.

_____. *Elements of Rite: A Handbook of Liturgical Style* (New York: Pueblo, 1982).

_____. "Christian Ministry and Ministries," *Church and Ministry: Chosen Race, Royal Priesthood, Holy Nation, God's Own People*, eds. B.L.H. Daniel C. Brockopp and David G. Truemper (Valparaiso: Institute of Liturgical Studies, 1982) 11–27.
Papers read at the thirty-third Annual Meeting of the Institute of Liturgical Studies at Valparaiso, IN, Feb. 8–10, 1981.

_____. "Unfinished and Unbegun Revisited: The Rite of Christian Initiation of Adults," *Studies in Formative Spirituality* 3 (1982) 363–376.
A paper presented at the NAAL, Christian Initiation Group, Princeton, NJ, 1979. "The RCIA presents such a vastly strategic overhaul of almost every way we look at the gospel in the Church that many are simply at a loss concerning when first to begin translating this vision into practice." The same title appears in *Worship* 53 (1979) 327–340.

_____. "Scripture and Worship in Synagogue and Church," *Michigan Quarterly Review* 22/3 (1983) 480–494.

_____. "Response: Primary Theology and Liturgical Act [Response to Geoffrey Wainwright's, "A Language in which We Speak to God,"] *Worship* 57 (1983) 321–324.
A talk presented to the NAAL, Annual Meeting, Jamaica, N.Y., 1983. Kavanagh defines liturgical theology as "the primary theological act of believing Christians." Secondary theology, the work of the academic theologian, is here firmly subordinated to the theology, however inchoate or inarticulate, of "Mrs. Murphy."

_____. "Liturgy and Ecclesial Consciousness: A Dialectic of Change," *Studia Liturgica* 15/1 (1983) 2–17.

_____. *On Liturgical Theology* (New York: Pueblo, 1984).
The Hale Memorial lectures of Seabury-Western Theological Seminary, 1981, revised and expanded.

_____. "Eastern Influences on the Rule of Saint Benedict," *Monasti-*

cism and the Arts, eds. T. G. Verdon with J. Dally. (Syracuse: Syracuse University Press, 1984) 53–62.

_____. "Christian Ministry and Ministries," *Anglican Theological Review* 66 / Suppl. ser. no. 9 (1984) 36–48.

Reprint of a speech given at Valparaiso Liturgical Institute, followed by a response by John H. Schütz on pp. 49–51.

_____. "Confirmation: A Suggestion from Structure," *Worship* 58 (1984) 386–395.

Confirmation, in the historical rites, can be said to "complete" baptism. This is a "structural" claim, not primarily a "theological" one. It is a "dismissal" into the Eucharist. The question "when" to have confirmation is thus "not a catechetical or an educational issue, but a baptismal one." Liturgical structure and the contemplation of its inherent logic must precede an explicitly theological reflection upon the "meaning" or discipline of the rite.

_____. "Spirituality, Really?" *Pastoral Music* 9 (1984) 17–22.

A talk given to a 1984 NPM Regional Convention, Providence, R.I. "To follow Christ is to be led away from little gods who ride like ticks in our hair, to stand shivering before the only and living God whose yoke is light, whose burden sweet."

_____. "Baptism: The Ecumenical Key," *Ecumenical Trends* 15 (1986) 146–149.

_____. "Theological Principles for Sacramental Catechesis," *Living Light* 23 (1987) 316–324.

A presentation given at the fifteenth Annual East Coast Conference for Religious Education, Washington, Feb. 1987.

_____. *Confirmation: Origin and Reform* (New York: Pueblo, 1988).

Historical study. Discusses how confirmation came to be disengaged from the initiatory process, followed by analysis of the Vatican II reform of the rite. Confirmation is a rite which the Church in the West developed to "transact the relationship" between baptism and Eucharist.

_____. "The Presentations: Creed and Lord's Prayer," (reprint), *Commentaries on the Rite of Christian Initiation of Adults,* ed. J. A. Wilde (Chicago: Liturgy Training Publications, 1988) 35–42.

Previously published in *Catechumenate: A Journal of Christian Initiation.*

_____. "Notes on Dismissals in the Divine Liturgy of Constantinople," *Traditio et Progressio: Studi Liturgici in Onore del Prof. Adrian Nocent, O.S.B.,* ed. G. Farnedi (Rome: Pontificio Ateneo S. Anselmo, 1988) 273–286.

_____. "Liturgical and Credal Studies." In *A Century of Church History: The Legacy of Phillip Schaff*, ed. H. W. Bowden (Carbondale: Southern Illinois University Press, 1988) 216–244.

An important and substantial essay on the history of the field of liturgical studies.

_____. "The Origins and Reform of Confirmation," *St. Vladimir's Theological Quarterly* 33/1 (1989) 5–20.

The Alexander Schmemann Memorial Lecture, St. Vladimir's Seminary, Jan. 30, 1988. Discusses how he arrived at the "confirmation-as-*missa*" hypothesis.

_____. "RCIA: Not a Peanut Butter Sandwich," *Pastoral Music* 13 (1989) 29–34.

What is the RCIA? It is first a rite, and not whatever else we may be apt to call it. 1) The RCIA must be perceived for what it is, 2) Its fundamental presupposed activities must be firmly grasped, and 3) It will succeed only in the midst of "a recovery of baptismal piety" and a literacy "centering on Easter."

_____. "Initiating Children: Historical Sketch and Contemporary Reflections," *Issues in the Christian Initiation of Children: Catechesis and Liturgy*, eds. K. Brown and F. C. Sokol (Chicago: Liturgy Training Publications, 1989) 33–46.

_____. "Catechesis: Formation in Stages," *The Baptismal Mystery and the Catechumenate*, ed. M. Merriman (New York: The Church Hymnal Corporation, 1990) 36–52.

_____. "Seeing Liturgically," *Time and Community: In Honor of Thomas J. Talley*, ed. J. N. Alexander (Washington: Pastoral Press, 1990) 255–278.

"Liturgy is never merely text. It is something people do; they see themselves doing it, and doing it causes them to see differently," p. 259. A major essay on the theme that Christian liturgy proposed a new "root metaphor" for Roman antiquity, and so transformed the culture, one person at a time.

_____. "Jewish Roots of Christian Worship," *The New Dictionary of Christian Worship*, ed. P. E. Fink (Collegeville: The Liturgical Press, 1990) 617–623.

_____. "Response to Paul Turner's, 'The Origins of Confirmation: An Analysis of Aidan Kavanagh's Hypothesis,'" *Worship* 65 (1991) 320–336, 337–338.

Turner's article was basically an extended book review of *Confirmation: Origin and Reform*. Kavanagh responded: "If it is anything, confirmation is a liturgical act with a liturgical grammar before it is a theological problem, a biblical allusion, or a catechetical opportunity."

_____. "Introduction," *Removing the Barriers: The Practice of Reconciliation,* ed. J. Dallen (Chicago: Liturgy Training Publications, 1991) 1–3.

_____. "Liturgy," *Modern Catholicism: Vatican II and After,* ed. A. Hastings (London, New York: S.P.C.K. and Oxford University Press, 1991) 68–73.

_____. "Reflections on the Study from the Viewpoint of Liturgical History [Study of Post-Vatican II Liturgy in 15 U.S. Parishes]," *The Awakening Church: 25 Years of Liturgical Renewal,* ed. L. J. Madden (Collegeville: The Liturgical Press, 1992) 83–97.

Papers presented at a colloquium held Dec. 3–5, 1988 at Georgetown University, to celebrate the 25th Anniversary of the Constitution on the Sacred Liturgy of Vatican Council II.

_____. Review of *The Monk's Tale: A Biography of Godfrey Diekmann,* by K. H. Hughes (Collegeville: The Liturgical Press, 1991). In *Catholic Historical Review* 78 (1992) 479.

_____. "Textuality and Deritualization: The Case of Western Liturgical Usage," *Studia Liturgica* 23/1 (1993) 70–77.

Text of a presentation to a conference on Ritual Studies hosted by the Center for Pastoral Liturgy, University of Notre Dame, Oct. 1992.

_____. Review of *Early Christian Baptism and the Catechumenate: Italy, North Africa and Egypt,* by T. M. Finn (Collegeville: The Liturgical Press, 1992). *Catholic Historical Review* 79 (1993) 311–312.

Contributors

The Rev. Canon **Paul F. Bradshaw,** Ph.D. (London), is Professor of Liturgy at the University of Notre Dame, Indiana. He is editor-in-chief of *Studia Liturgica* and the author of *The Search for the Origins of Christian Worship* (New York: Oxford University Press, 1992) as well as several other books and numerous articles on liturgy.

The Rev. **John Baldovin,** s.j., is Professor of Liturgy at Jesuit School of Theology in Berkeley, California. Among his recent publications is *Worship-City, Church and Renewal* (Washington, DC: The Pastoral Press, 1991).

The Rev. **Aelred Cody,** o.s.b., is a monk of the St. Meinrad Archabbey, Indiana. He has written *A History of Old Testament Priesthood* (Rome: Pont. Biblical Institute, 1969) and *Ezekiel, with an Excursus on Old Testament Priesthood* (Collegeville: The Liturgical Press, 1984). He is editor of the *Catholic Biblical Quarterly.*

The Rev. **Regis Duffy,** o.f.m., teaches at Saint Bonaventure University. He has authored *Real Presence* (New York: Harper & Row, 1982), *A Roman Catholic Theology of Pastoral Care* (Philadelphia: Fortress, 1983), and *On Becoming a Catholic* (SanFrancisco: Harper & Row, 1984).

Peter S. Hawkins is the editor of *Civitas: Religious Interpretations of the City* (Atlanta: Scholars Press, 1986) and, with Anne H. Schotter, of *Ineffability: Naming the Unnameable from Dante to Beckett* (New York: AMS Press, 1984).

Nathan D. Mitchell, Ph.D., is Associate Director for research at the Notre Dame Center for Pastoral Liturgy. His books include *Cult and Controversy* (NY: Pueblo, 1982) and *Eucharist as Sacrament of Initiation* (Chicago: LTP, 1994).

Dr. **Joanne M. Pierce** received her Ph.D. in Liturgical Studies from the University of Notre Dame; her specialty is Medieval Liturgy. She is Assistant Professor of Religious Studies at the College of the Holy Cross, Worcester, Massachusetts. Ms. Pierce is also a Roman Catholic member of the Anglican-Roman Catholic Commission of the U.S.A.

The Rev. **David N. Power,** O.M.I., is the Shakespeare Caldwell-Duval Distinguished Professor of Theology at The Catholic University of America in Washington, where he has taught since 1977. For the Studies in the Reformed Rites of the Catholic Church series, for which Fr. Kavanagh was consulting editor, Fr. Power wrote *Gifts that Differ: Lay Ministries Established or Unestablished* (New York: Pueblo Publishing Co., 2nd ed., 1985). His most recent book is *The Eucharistic Mystery: Revitalizing the Tradition* (New York: Crossroad, 1992).

The Rev. **R. Kevin Seasoltz,** O.S.B., is a monk of St. John's Abbey, Collegeville, Minnesota. He is a professor in the School of Theology at St. John's University and is the editor of the liturgical journal *Worship.*

The Rev. Dr. **Thomas H. Schattauer,** Ph.D., is Assistant Professor of Worship and Liturgy at Yale Divinity School and Institute of Sacred Music and a pastor in the Evangelical Lutheran Church in America.

The Rev. Dr. **Bryan Spinks,** is Chaplain of Churchill College in the University of Cambridge and Affiliated Lecturer in Liturgy in the Divinity Faculty of the University. He is the Dean and Lecturer in Doctrine at the Cambridge Religious Study Centre. An Anglican, in recognition of his work on Reformed liturgy he was elected President of the Church Service Society of the Church of Scotland. He is the author of *The Sanctus in the Eucharistic Prayer* (Cambridge: Cambridge University Press, 1991).

The Right Reverend Dr. **Kenneth Stevenson** is bishop of Portsmouth (England), and is the author of *Worship: Wonderful and Sacred Mystery* (Washington: Pastoral Press, 1992).

The Rev. **Robert F. Taft,** S.J., teaches at the Pontifical Oriental Institute, Rome. He is the author of numerous books and articles including *Beyond East and West,* (Washington: Pastoral Press, 1984), *The Liturgy of the Hours in East and West* (Collegeville: The Liturgical Press, 1986), and *The Diptychs* (Rome: Pontifical Oriental Institute, 1991).

The Rev. **Thomas J. Talley** is Professor Emeritus of the General Theological Seminary, Forest Hills, NY. He is the author of *The Origins of the Liturgical Year* (Collegeville: The Liturgical Press, 1991) and *Worship: Reforming Tradition* (Washington: Pastoral Press, 1990).

Jeffrey VanderWilt is completing work on his Ph.D. in Liturgical Studies from The University of Notre Dame. He is liturgy and music director at Benedict Center, Madison, Wisconsin.

Dr. **Louis Weil** is Professor of Liturgies of the Church Divinity School of the Pacific, Berkeley, California. He is the author of *Gathered to Pray: Understanding Liturgical Prayer* (Cambridge, Mass.: Cowley, 1986).

The Rev. **James F. White** is Professor of Liturgy at the University of Notre Dame, Indiana. Rev. White's recent works include *A Brief History of Christian Worship* (Nashville: Abingdon Press, 1993) and *Documents of Christian Worship: Descriptive and Interpretive Sources* (Louisville: Westminister/J. Knox Press, 1992).

Index